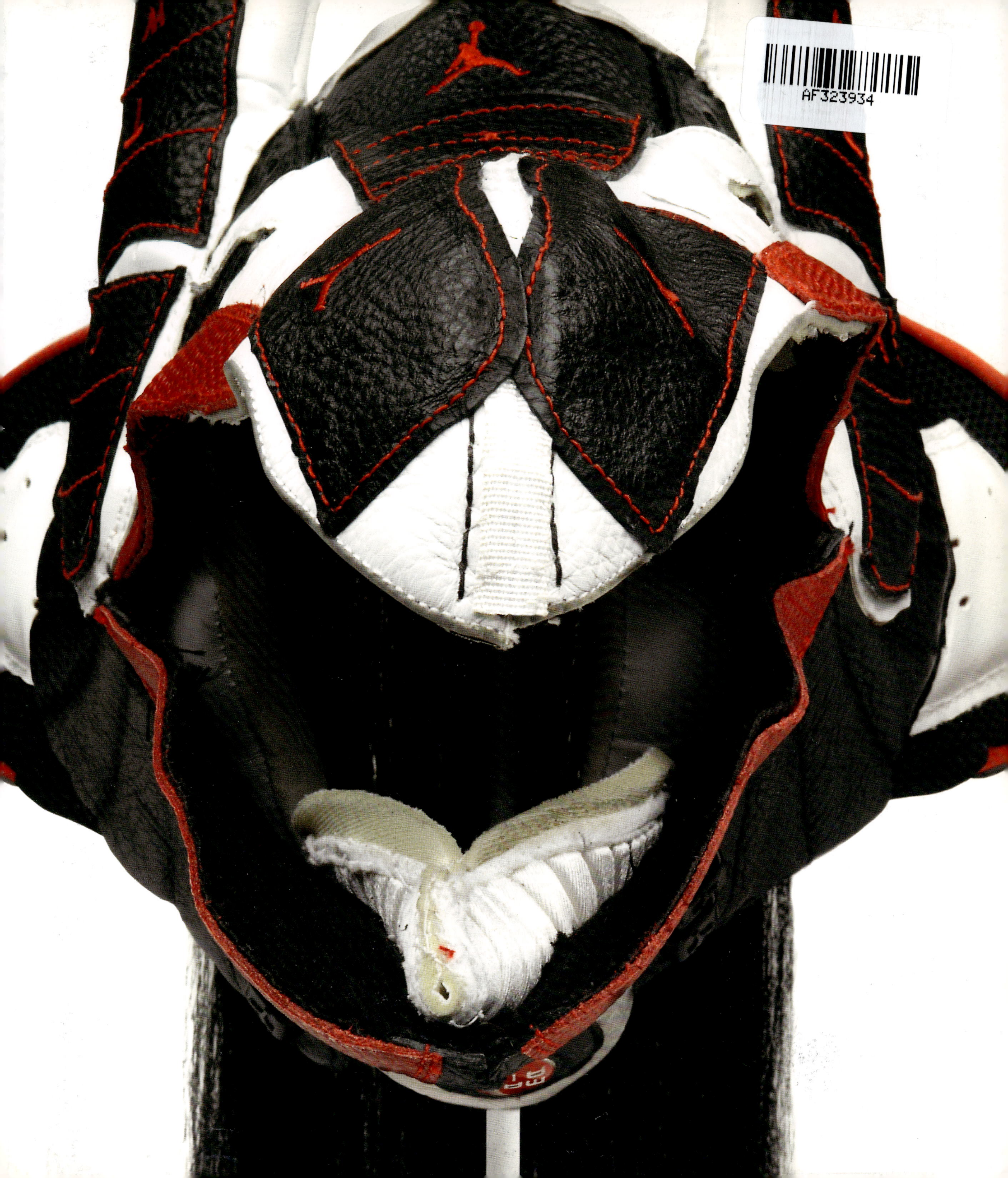

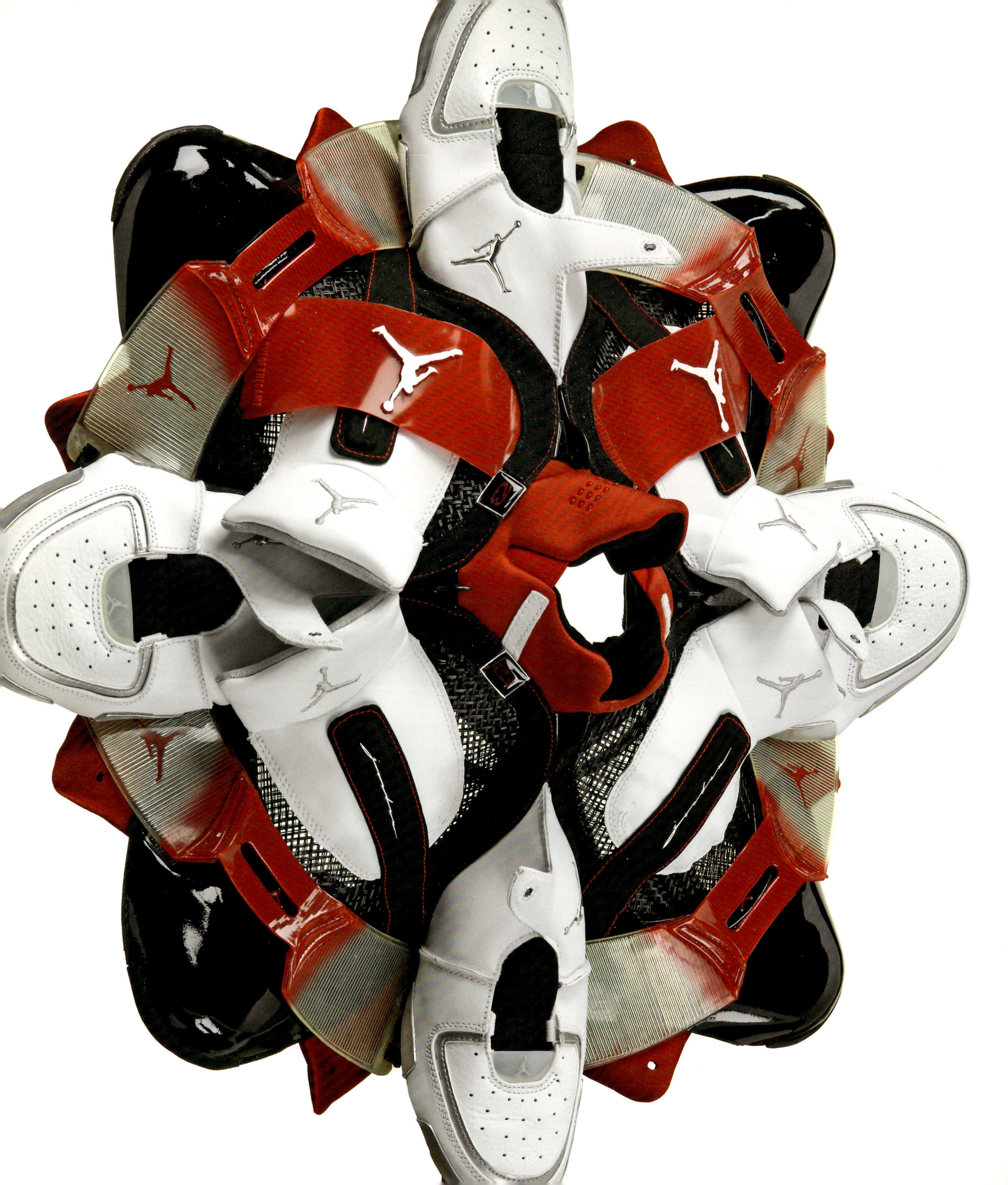

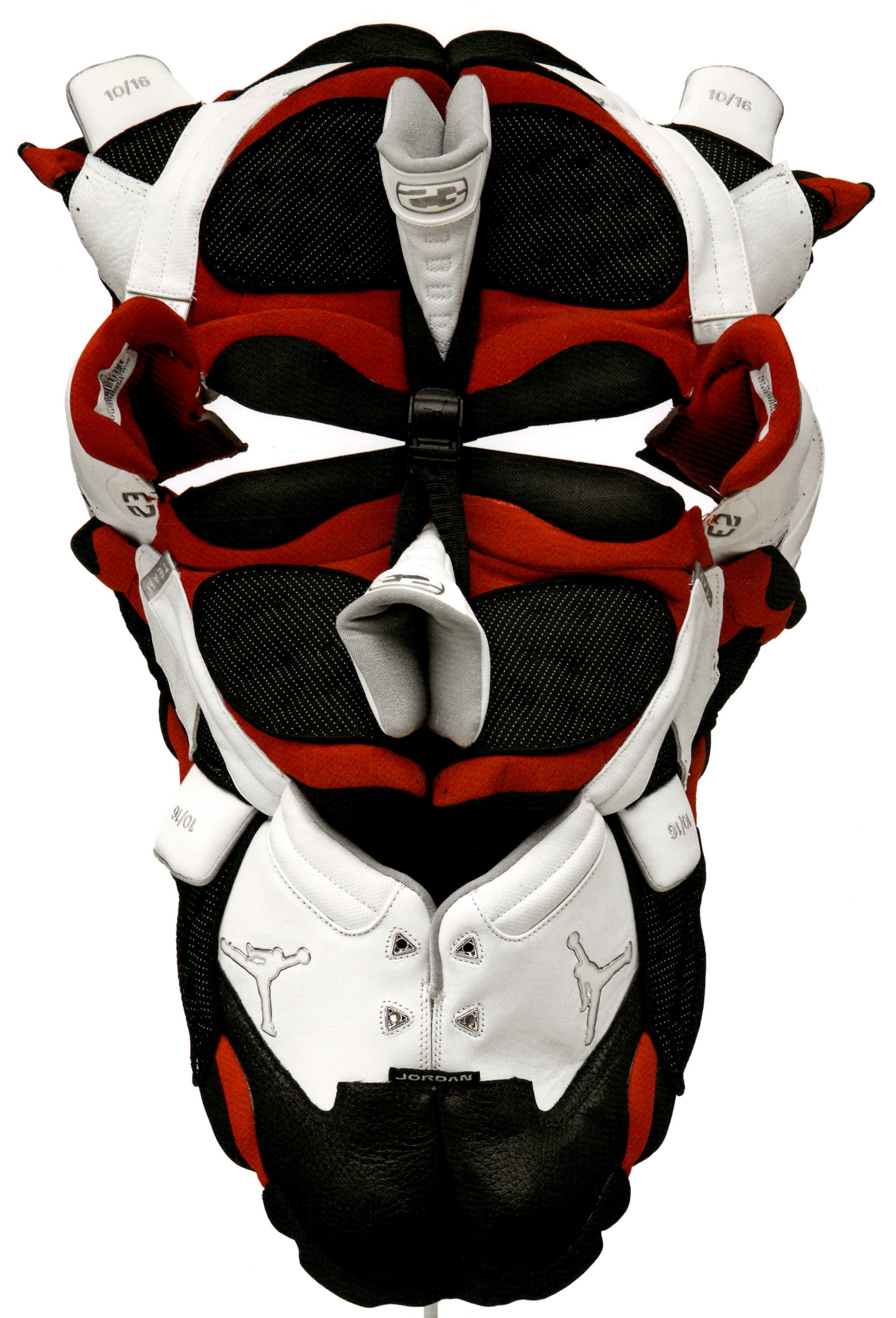

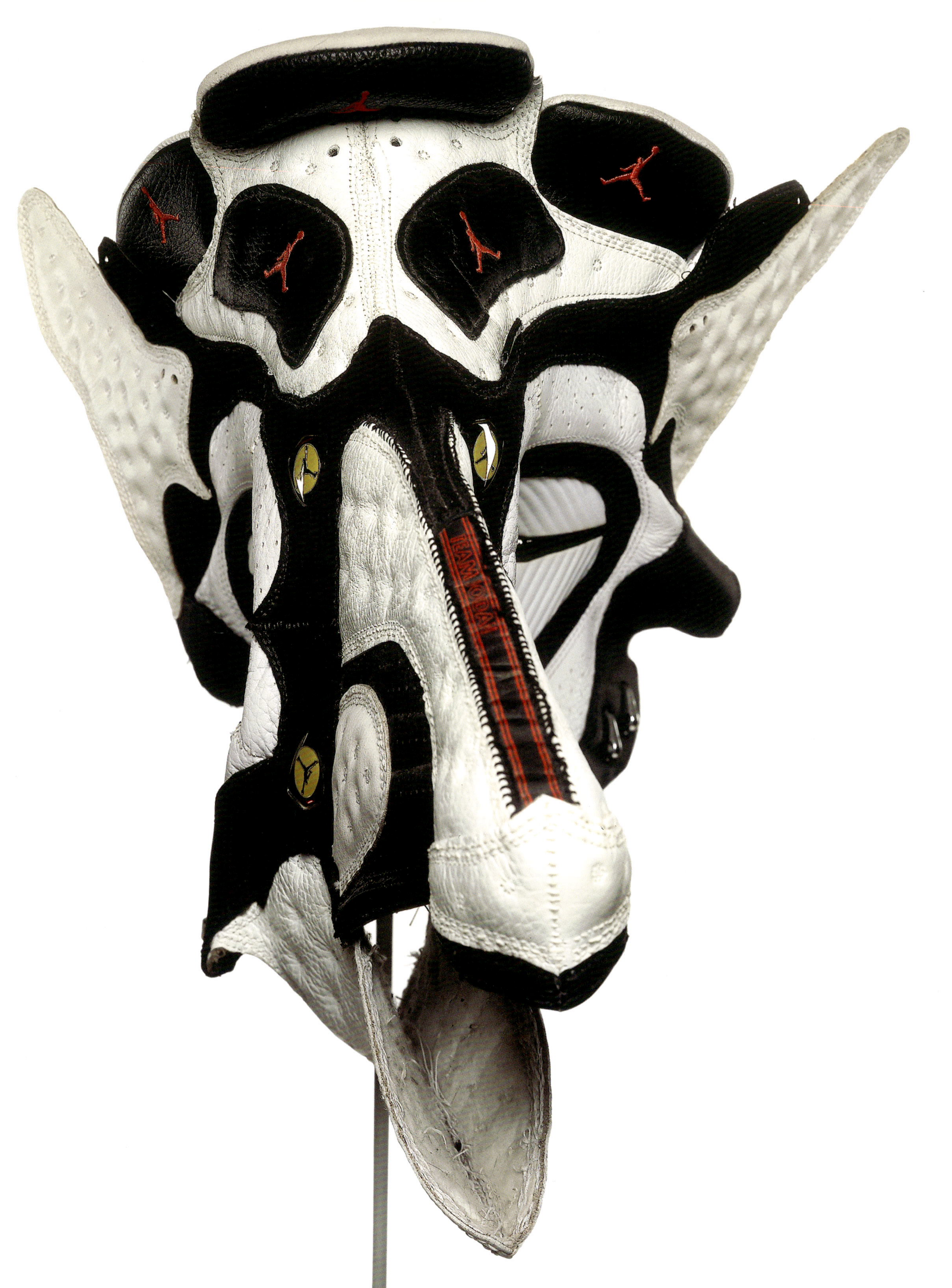

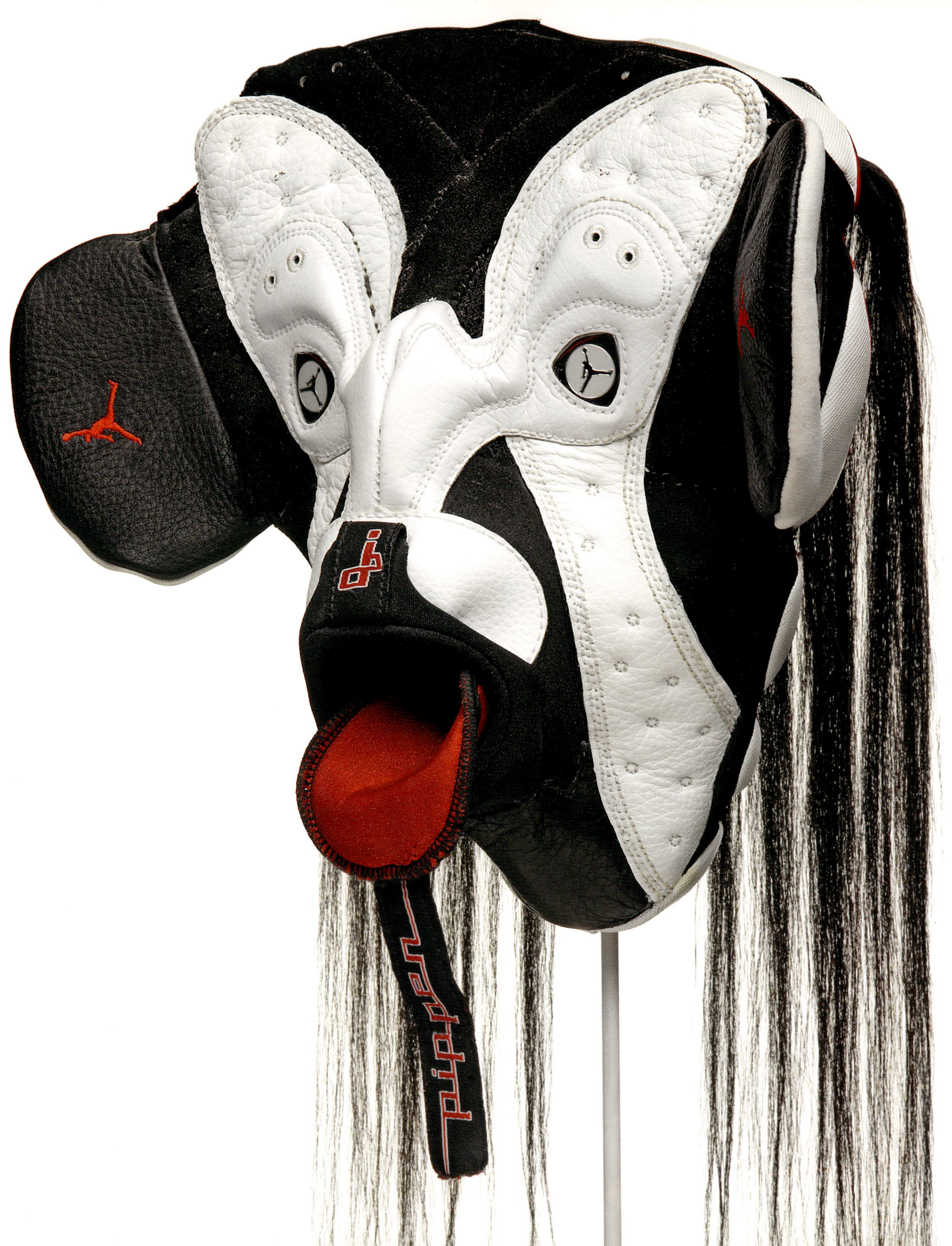

For Jake and Julie

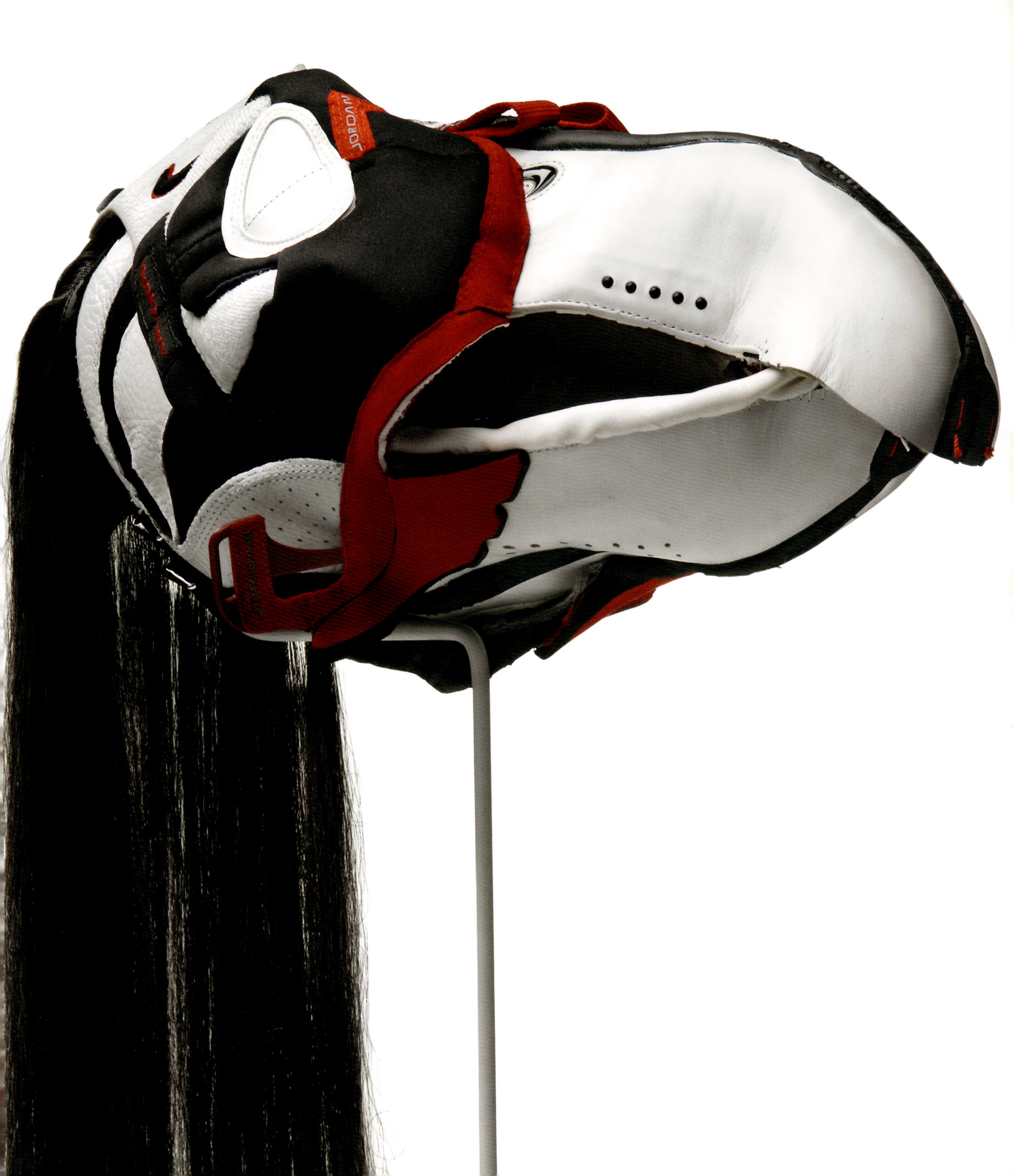

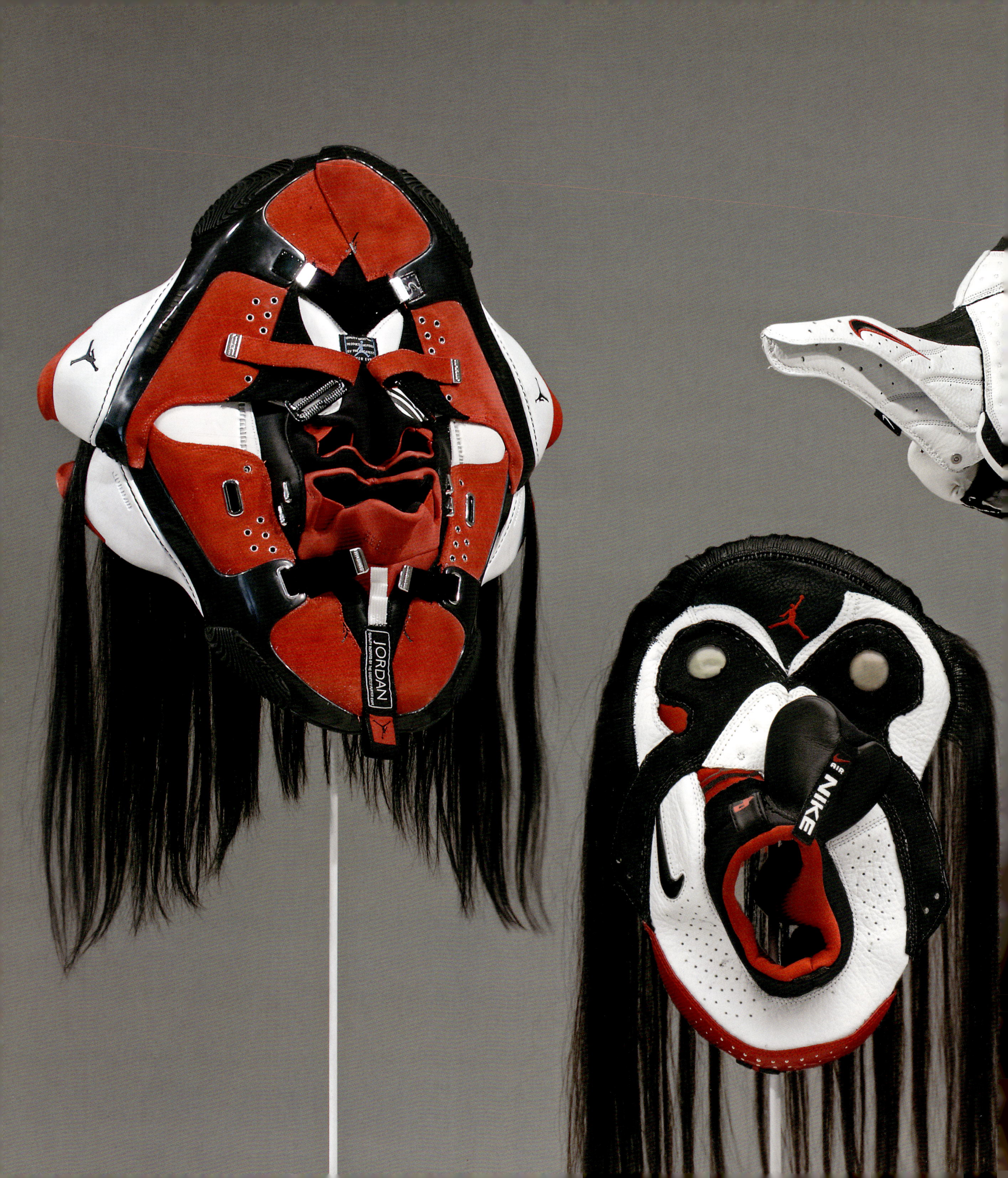

BRIAN JUNGEN

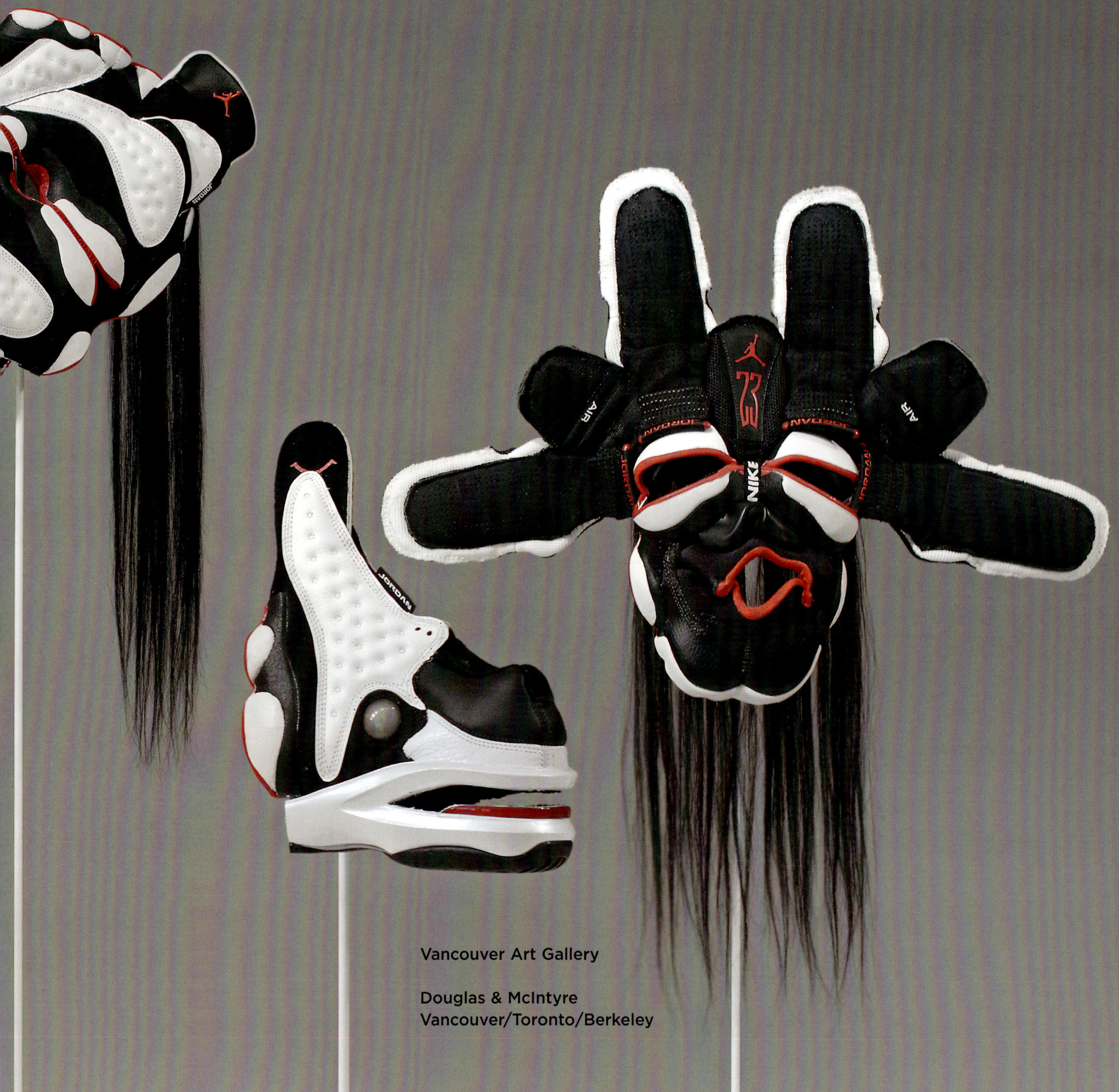

Vancouver Art Gallery

Douglas & McIntyre
Vancouver/Toronto/Berkeley

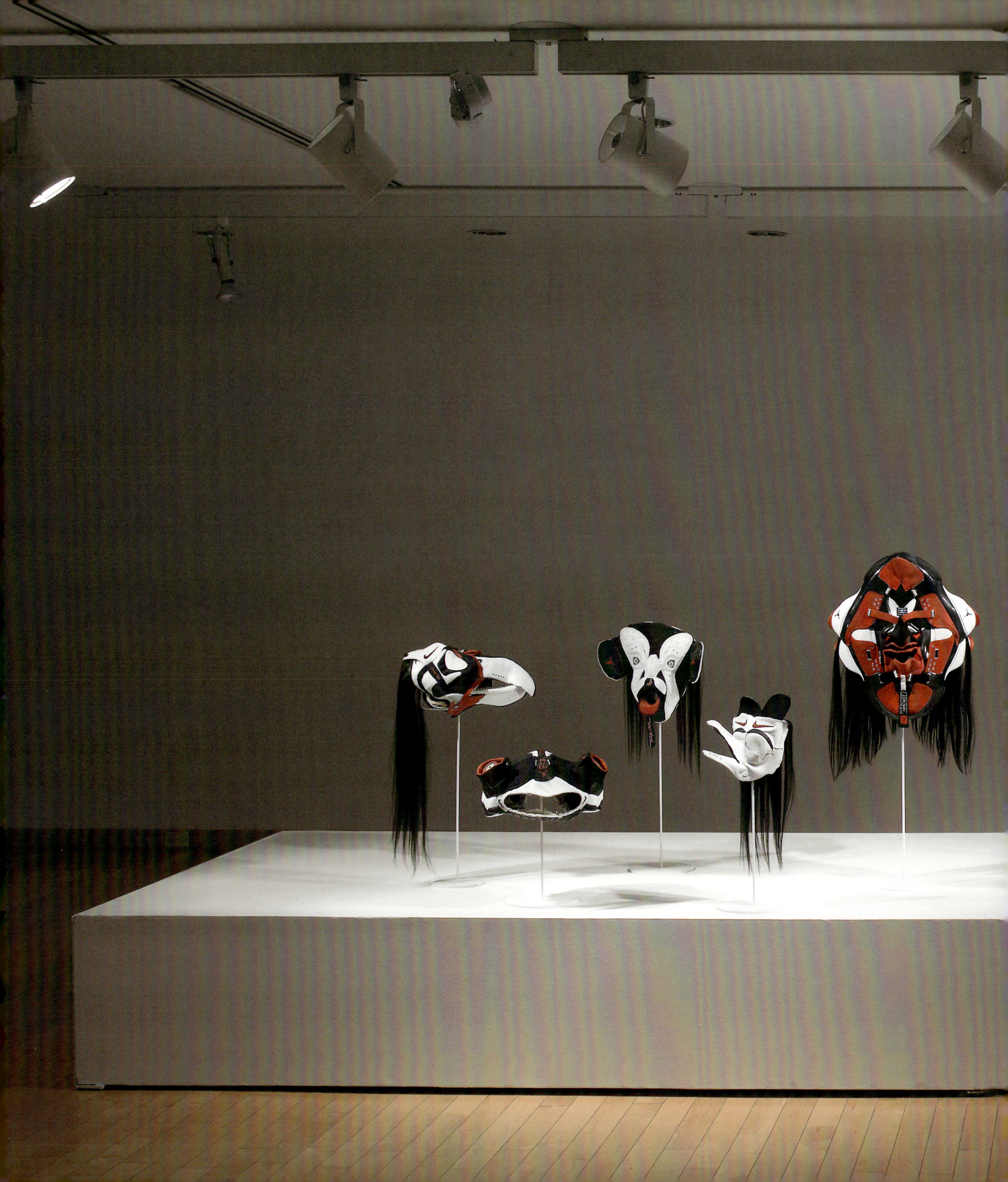

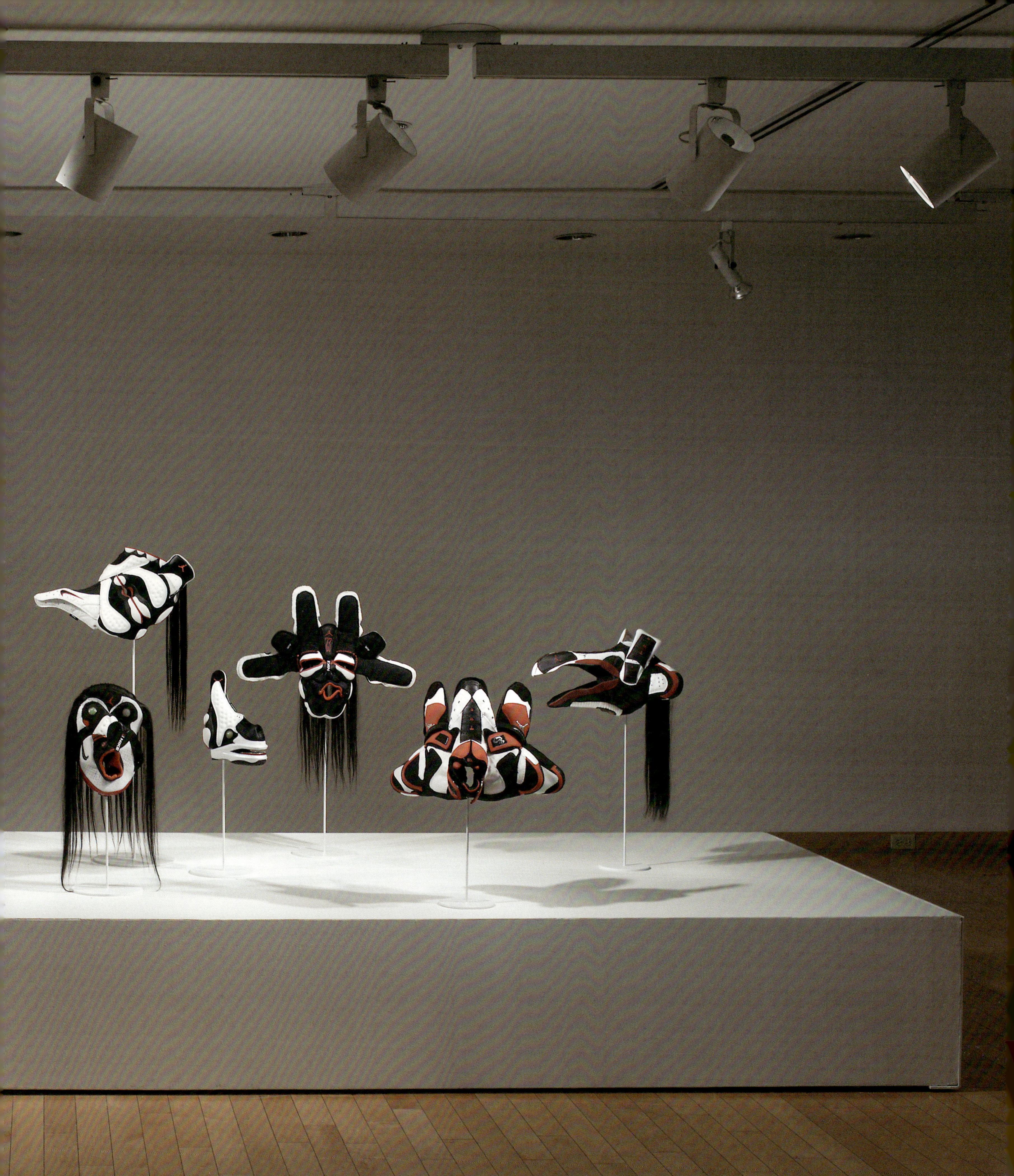

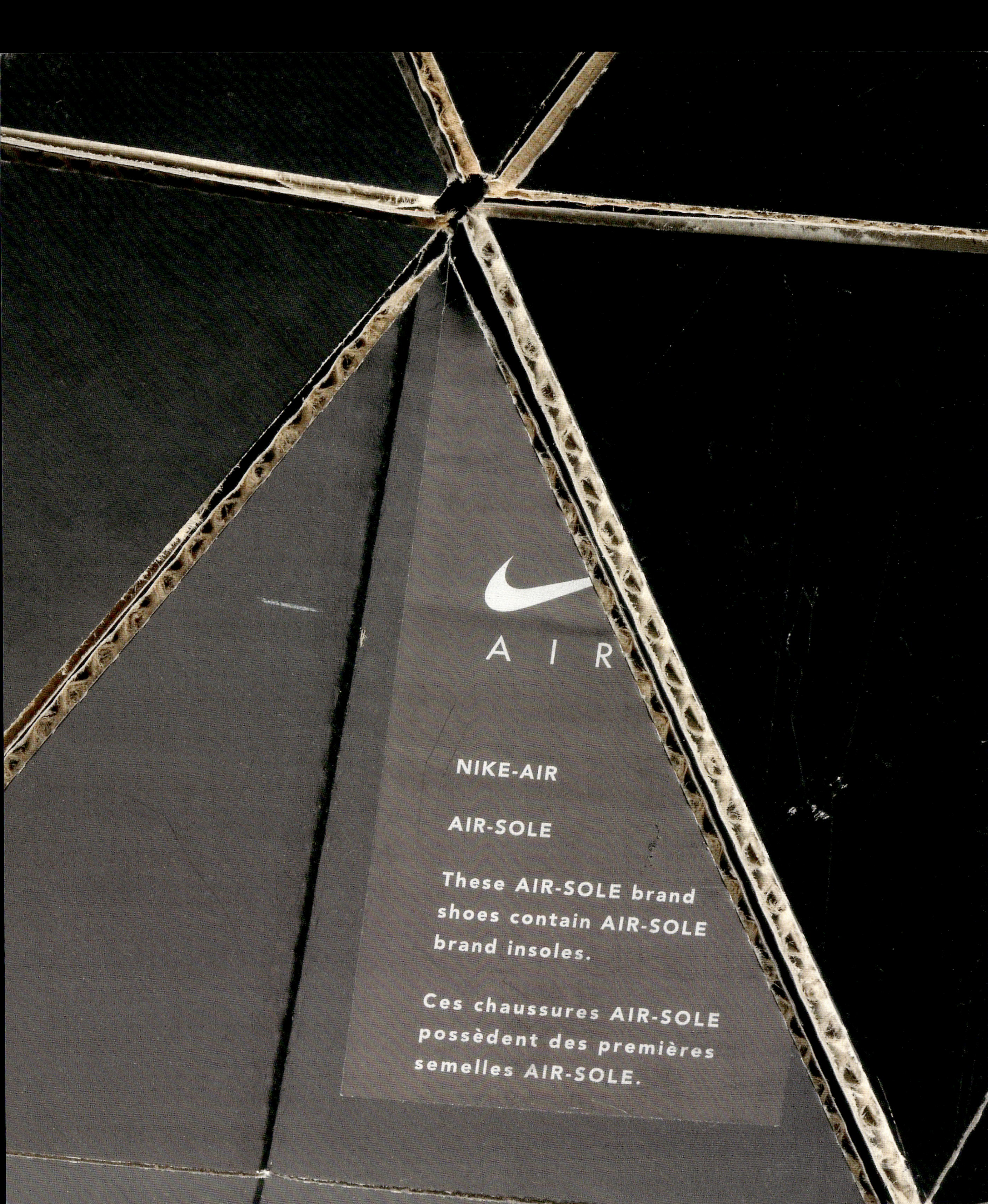

NIKE
AIR

NIKE-AIR

AIR-SOLE

These AIR-SOLE brand
shoes contain AIR-SOLE
brand insoles.

Ces chaussures AIR-SOLE
possèdent des premières
semelles AIR-SOLE.

Little Habitat II, 2004 (detail)
Nike Air Jordan boxes
65 x 65 x 30 cm (25 1/2" x 25 1/2" x 11 3/4")
Collection of Brett Shaheen, Cleveland
Photo: Trevor Mills, Vancouver Art Gallery

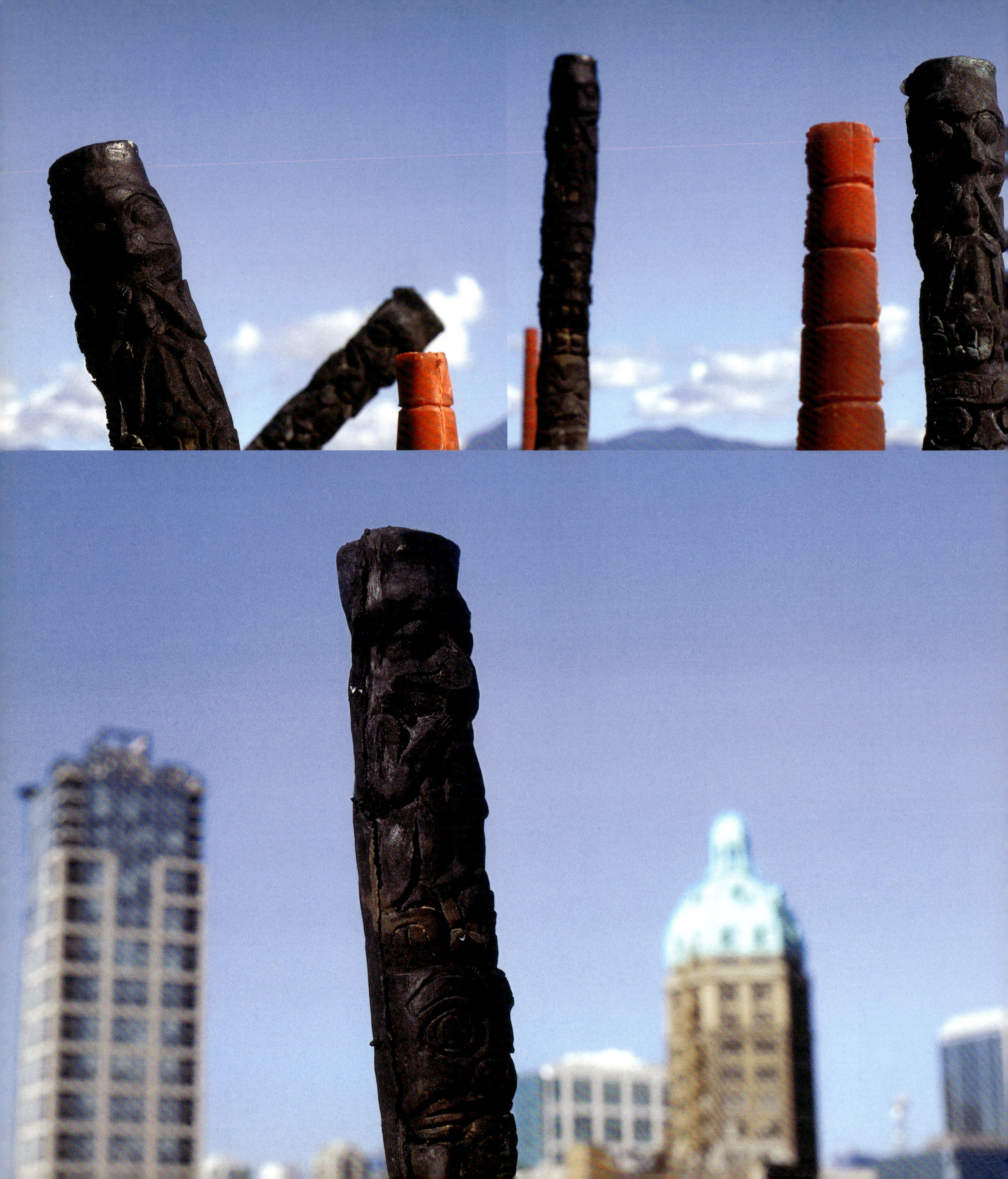

Director's Foreword

Brian Jungen is widely regarded as a leading member of a new generation of Vancouver artists whose rich insights into contemporary culture incorporate an innovative mixing of materials and media. Accompanied by this comprehensive publication, the exhibition *Brian Jungen* brings together Jungen's early drawings, his acclaimed works made from reconstructed Nike runners and cut-up patio chairs, his architecturally based installations, as well as new works made specifically for this exhibition. It marks the first opportunity to consider the full scope of Brian Jungen's remarkable oeuvre.

The Vancouver Art Gallery first exhibited the work of Brian Jungen in the 2001 group exhibition *Long Time: Selections from the Permanent Collection,* just after it acquired two of the earliest *Prototypes for New Understanding* (1998–2005), works constructed from Nike runners. Evocative of the ceremonial masks of Northwest Coast First Nations, Jungen's *Prototypes* forge powerful connections between his First Nations ancestry, Western art history and the global economy. Now, four years later, the Gallery presents all of these remarkable hybrid sculptures—a total of twenty-three, in reference to basketball star Michael Jordan's jersey number. Also assembled are the magnificent whale skeletons made from plastic patio chairs; one of these skeletons, *Cetology* (2002), is another addition to the Gallery's permanent collection. Other works in the exhibition point to an evolving dialogue with minimalism and utopian architecture. The presence of Jungen's transformative works within the Gallery invites the viewer to consider new ways of understanding the museum environment as being inextricably linked to broader cultural, social and economic concerns.

With group and solo exhibitions in leading institutions throughout Europe, North America and Korea, and with major projects recently completed in Montreal, New York and San Francisco, Brian Jungen's international prominence is growing rapidly. In 2002, he was awarded the inaugural $50,000 Sobey Art Award, the most lucrative Canadian award for emerging artists, in recognition of his outstanding achievement. In organizing Brian Jungen's first major survey exhibition, the Vancouver Art Gallery celebrates his significant accomplishments and looks forward to the further development of his unique practice.

This important exhibition would not have been possible without the enormous generosity of the Audain Foundation, which fosters visual arts in British Columbia, and New York's The Andy Warhol Foundation for the Visual Arts, which awarded the Vancouver Art Gallery its first major grant in support of this project. We are especially grateful for the cooperation of many individuals and institutions who lent works from their collections, enabling Brian Jungen's artistic vision to reach a wide international audience. Generous support for this publication has been provided by the Jack and Doris Shadbolt Endowment for Research and Publications at the Vancouver Art Gallery.

I thank the Board of Trustees of the Vancouver Art Gallery, particularly for the leadership provided by Chair George Killy, and the Gallery staff for their exceptional resourcefulness and commitment in seeing this project to fruition. Special thanks to Cuauhtémoc Medina, Ralph Rugoff, Kitty Scott, Trevor Smith and Simon Starling for their enriching contributions to the exhibition catalogue, and to Daina Augaitis, the Vancouver Art Gallery's Chief Curator/Associate Director, who organized the exhibition with extraordinary skill, vision and enthusiasm; we are grateful for her creative leadership on this project. Finally, on behalf of the Gallery, I extend our deepest appreciation to Brian Jungen for his generosity, creativity and truly inspiring contribution to art making.

Kathleen S. Bartels
Director

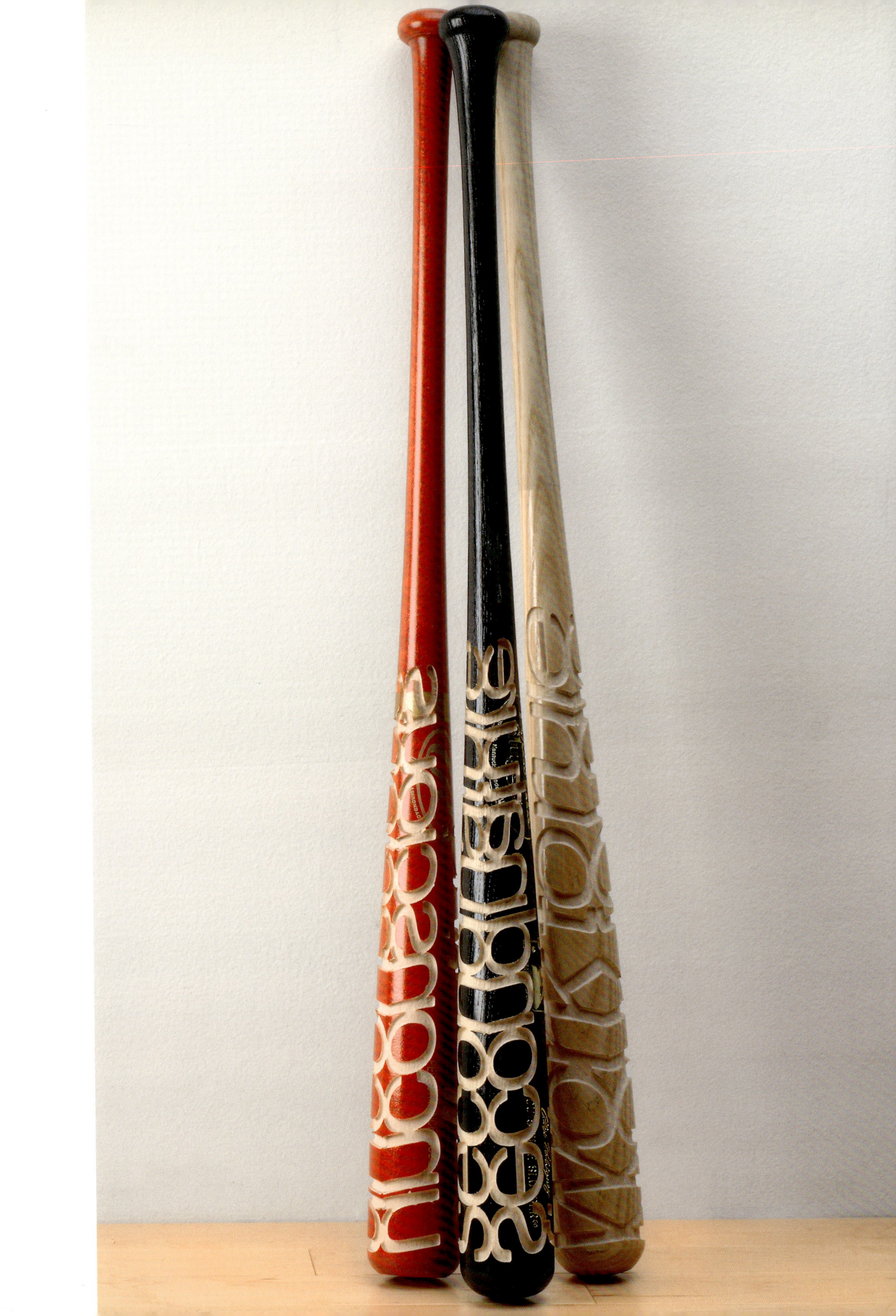

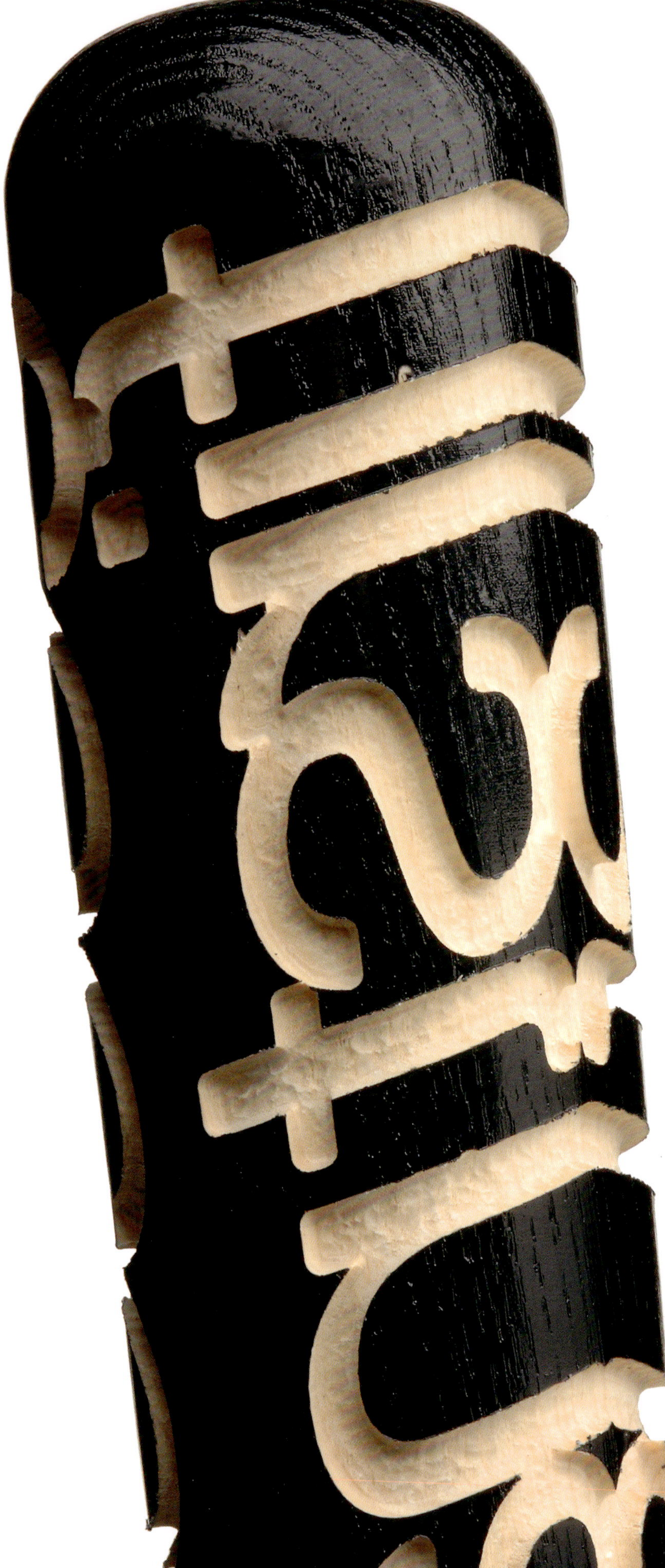

First Nation, Second Nature, 2005 (detail)
carved baseball bat, artist proof
83.8 cm x 7.6 cm (33″ x 3″)
Produced with support from the Province of British Columbia Spirit of BC Arts Fund
Photo: Trevor Mills, Vancouver Art Gallery

OPPOSITE (L TO R):
Collective Unconscious, 2005
carved baseball bat, artist proof
83.8 cm x 7.6 cm (33″ x 3″)
Produced with support from the Province of British Columbia Spirit of BC Arts Fund
Photo: Trevor Mills, Vancouver Art Gallery

First Nation, Second Nature, 2005
carved baseball bat, artist proof
83.8 cm x 7.6 cm (33″ x 3″)
Produced with support from the Province of British Columbia Spirit of BC Arts Fund
Photo: Trevor Mills, Vancouver Art Gallery

Work to Rule, 2005
carved baseball bat, artist proof
83.8 cm x 7.6 cm (33″ x 3″)
Produced with support from the Province of British Columbia Spirit of BC Arts Fund
Photo: Trevor Mills, Vancouver Art Gallery

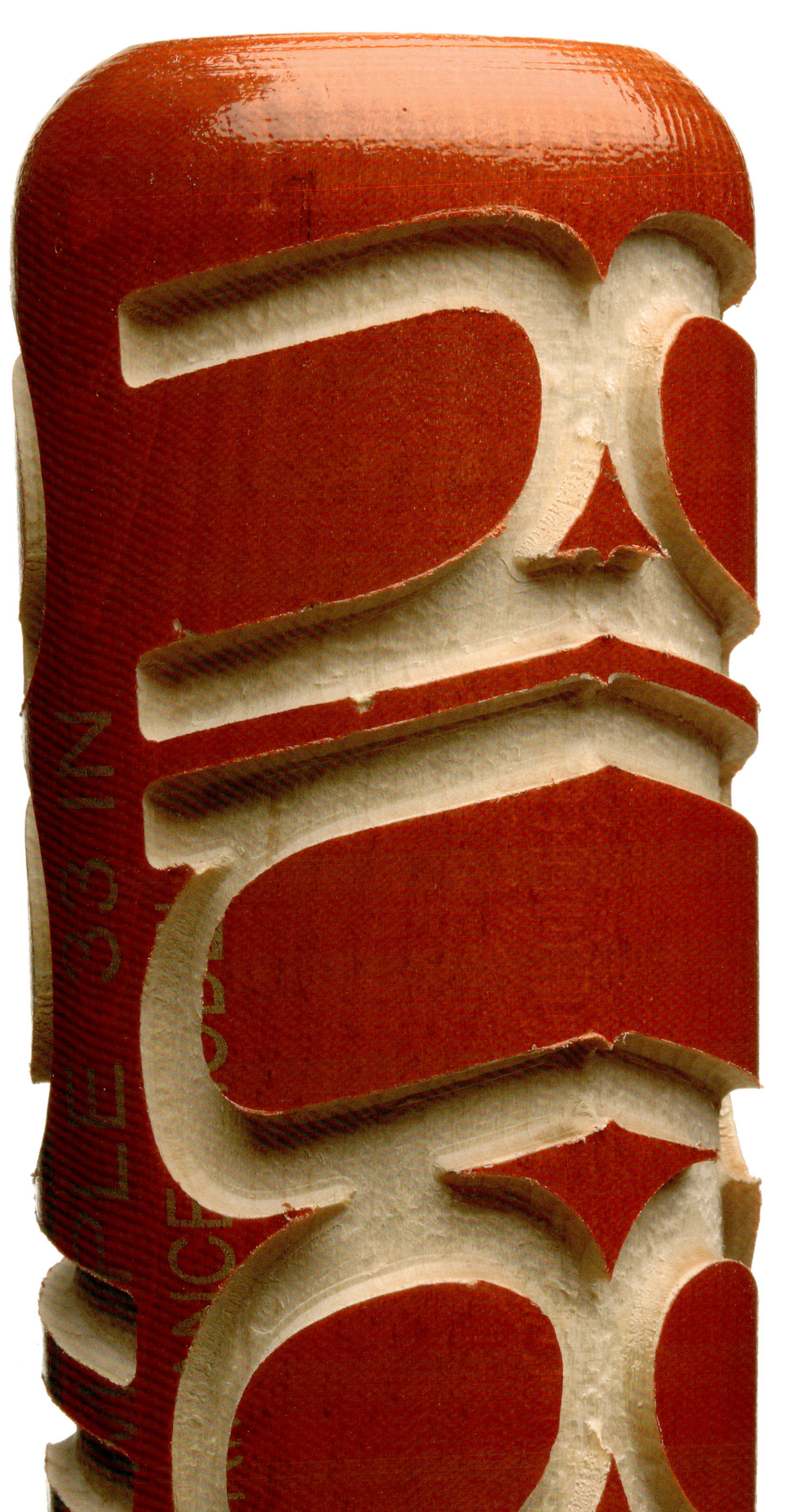

Prototypes for New Understandings
Daina Augaitis

In the past decade, Brian Jungen has emerged as a force in the contemporary art world because of the commentary his sculptures and installations bring to the conditions of globalization. Born and raised in the remote logging town of Fort St. John in the interior of northern British Columbia, Jungen was drawn to city life in the early 1990s and received his postsecondary education in Vancouver at a time when its thriving art community was heavily influenced by conceptual art. As a result of both his far-reaching experiences and his Aboriginal-Swiss identity, Jungen is a multifaceted individual epitomizing a new world hybridity: he is as well-versed in Dane-zaa family stories as he is in Western art history; as comfortable snowboarding through an old-growth forest as he is cruising through a hipster boutique, and, as an international artist, as adept at working in his Vancouver studio as he is at creating on-site pieces in San Francisco, Gwangju, London or Montreal.

It is this underlying complexity in Jungen's own life that may explain the artist's mistrust of things pure and simple. In a sense, his work begins to dismantle some rigid social conventions by breaking down existing stereotypes, embracing instability and opening up new spaces of engagement. He looks beyond the surface of everyday objects to extract more explicit meanings that begin to expose the roots of a social consciousness. This book and the exhibition it accompanies, which surveys Brian Jungen's work of the past decade, consider the ways in which he injects disorder into modernity's notions of order—by transforming materials and exposing interiors, and by rendering things impure and complex. As the title of his seminal "mask" series implies, he creates prototypes for new understandings of global culture.

OPPOSITE:
Collective Unconscious, 2005
(detail)
carved baseball bat, artist proof
83.8 x 7.6 cm diameter
(33" x 3")
Produced with support from the Province of British Columbia Spirit of BC Arts Fund
Photo: Trevor Mills, Vancouver Art Gallery

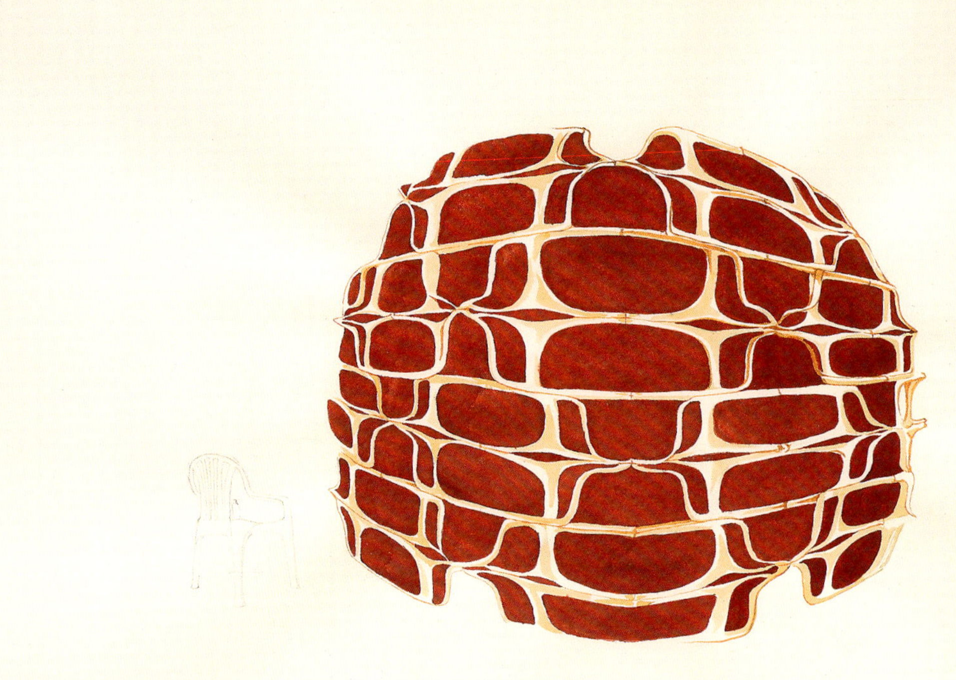

INTERIORITY

Brian Jungen grew up in the central region of British Columbia, an area commonly known as "the Interior." Hearing this word "interior" over and over again reinforced his innate interest in building interiorized spaces, possibly as a defence against a harsh climate and dramatic natural elements. This predilection has led to an interest in architecture and in making idealized domestic structures for birds, cats and other small animals. Paradoxically, this constant iteration of "interior" also pushed him to reveal the inner structure of things by taking them apart, making visible their core or their spine and showing how they might work from the inside. As Jungen's practice has evolved, this strategy of exposing physical interiors to comment on social and cultural issues has become increasingly resolute.

One trademark consumer good that Jungen disassembles is the Nike Air Jordan trainer, named for the basketball all-star Michael Jordan and proclaimed to be one of the most sought-after shoes ever made. According to the Air Jordan shoe index, there are 123 different styles of Air Jordans, selling for as much as $9,000 for the original 1985 model. Representing the conflation of high style and high performance, these shoes are the great equalizer, donned by wannabe hipsters as part of the sporty dress-down American fashion made popular by

Bush Capsule Study, 2000
graphite and ink on paper
101.6 x 132.1 cm (40" x 52")
Collection of John Cook, Ottawa
Photo: Courtesy of Walter Phillips Gallery,
Banff, Alberta

1980s rappers and also by aspiring athletes, including teens on Aboriginal reserves, where basketball has become the activity of choice for youth. Jungen's gesture of cutting up and taking apart such symbolic footwear, then, is a dramatic one—a rather violent act that dismantles a highly priced collectible and literally rips apart an icon of trendy consumerism, lancing the seemingly impenetrable hold of commodity culture.

In his *Prototypes* (1998–2005) and *Variant I* (2002), where cut-up Nikes are reassembled into simulations of Northwest Coast Aboriginal artifacts, the effect calls into question stereotypical representations of Aboriginal cultures. The style of shoe readily lends itself to references in Northwest Coast art; particularly important are the shoes' colours—black, red and white, a classic combination prevalent in many Aboriginal motifs. There is also the Nike "swoosh," a stylized V (for victory), which in Jungen's strategic placement becomes a reference to the classic U-form and ovoid shapes that are dominant components of Northwest Coast formline design. Jungen's appropriated use of the corporate logo casts doubt on the true meaning of victory as he collides two seemingly different commodities—a globally desirable piece of footwear and the First Nations mask, which has long been made expressly as an item of trade rather than only for ceremonial purposes.

Taking apart and reconfiguring ready-made objects is a strategy further explored in the installation *Court* (2004), where a basketball court is evoked by assembling a grid of 224 industrial sewing tables, the type used in garment factories to fill the orders of the fashion trade. In this installation, the tables are partially dismantled and where sewing machines, bobbin winders and sergers were once housed there are now large, gaping holes, suggesting how tenuous the foothold is for migrant labourers as they toil in sweatshops and play out a

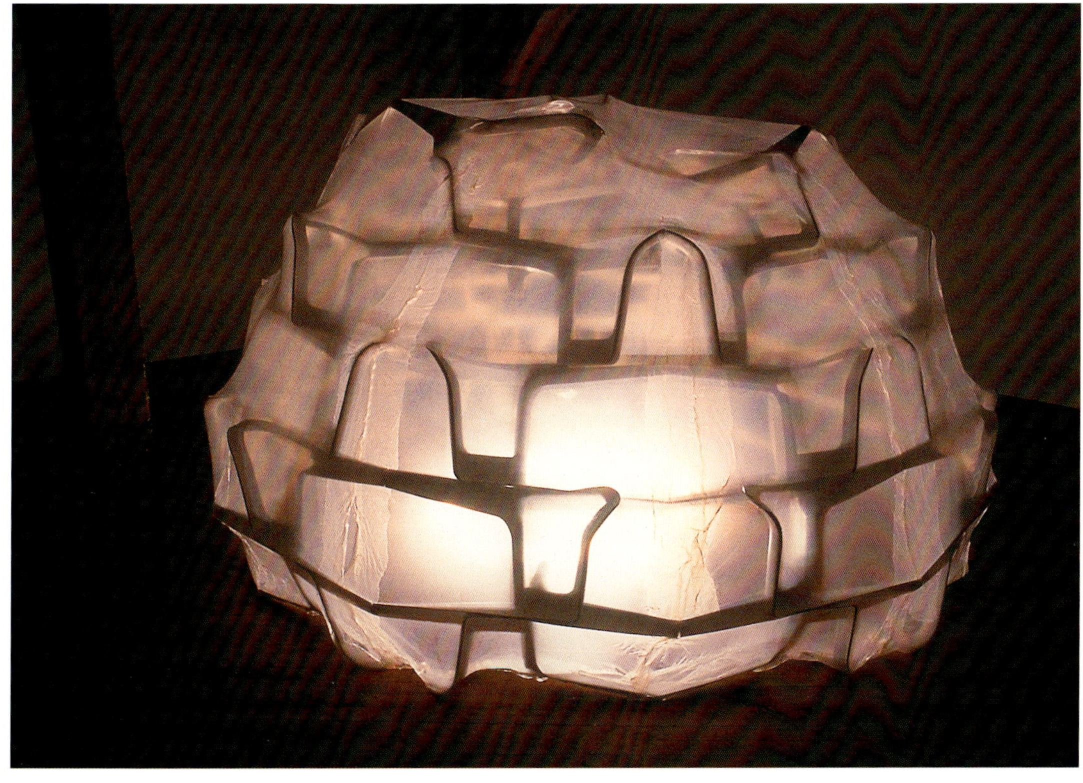

Bush Capsule, 2000
plastic chairs, polyethylene,
fluorescent lights
dimensions variable
Photo: Courtesy of Brian Jungen

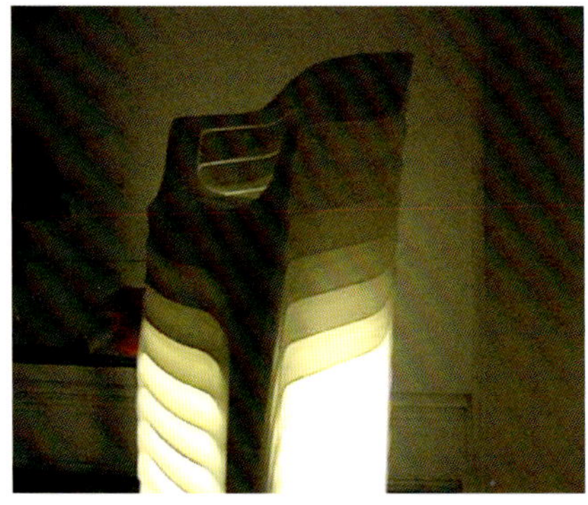

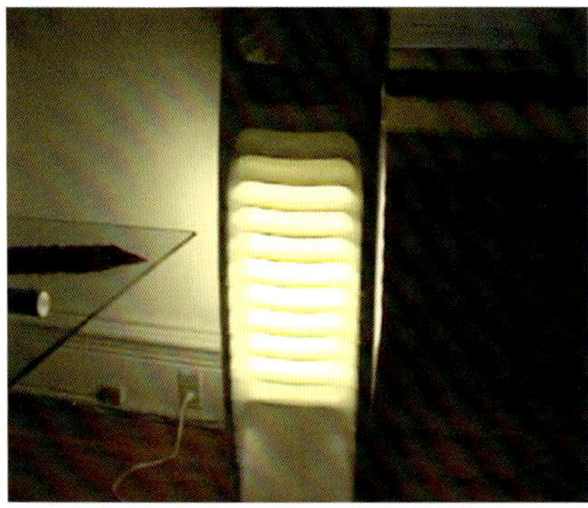

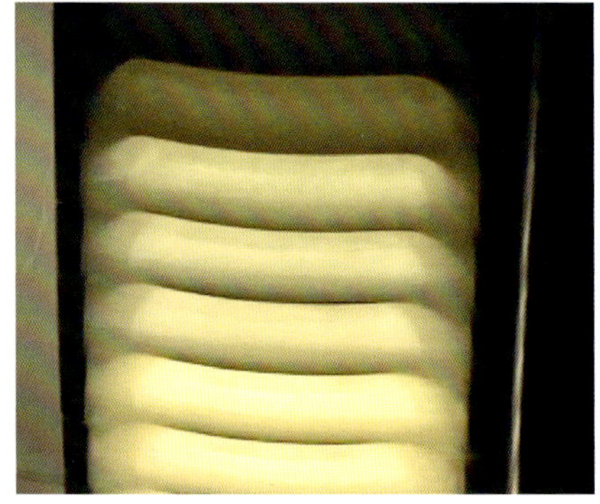

precarious game of survival. The exposed spaces in this constructed playing field reveal dark, unknown holes that might question the depth of the American dream.

Another work that makes explicit use of a clandestine interior space as a place to reflect on strategies of survival is *Isolated Depiction of the Passage of Time* (2001). It is made from nine waist-high stacks of coloured cafeteria food trays pushed tightly together to create one seemingly solid geometric cube. Emanating from the inside are the flickering glow and hushed dialogue of daytime television, suggesting that some hidden secrets lie inside this orderly mass of common objects. In fact, each tray colour represents a specific length of prison term served by Aboriginal males at Kingston Penitentiary, and the overall structure of the work references an actual "escape pod" built in 1980. This work cleverly memorializes the desperate aspirations of prisoners who carved hiding spaces and surreptitious passages into mundane materials in the hope that they might provide a means of escape. With social awareness and historical exactitude, Jungen's ingenious work yields a complex understanding of historical events and points to how perceptions and value systems become fixed within visual codes of representation.

THE SOCIAL SPACE OF MINIMALISM

Like many artists of his generation, Jungen references recent art history in his work. In particular, his sculptures and installations critique modernity's overarching move towards a pure abstraction devoid of contextual references. For example, in an early work entitled *Mise en scène* (2000), Jungen assembled a stockpile of white plastic patio chairs and wrapped them crudely in Cellophane, substituting refined industrial metal that is characteristic of Donald Judd's minimalist "stacks" with a low-grade consumer product. In doing so, Jungen seems to hitch a do-it-yourself tagline to the slick ethos of finely made minimalist sculpture.

In a later work, *Michael* (2003), Jungen again takes on the industrial manufacture of a poststudio practice inaugurated by minimalism and orders up a stack of commercially fabricated metal Nike shoe boxes. However, instead of the blank "what-you-see-is-what-you-see" surface of minimalist cubes, Jungen's geometric facsimiles are suffused with the silk-screened face of Michael Jordan, the corporate icon of the Nike brand. Rather than making a stack of actual Nike cardboard boxes emptied of their valuable goods, in a glib gesture reminiscent of Andy Warhol, Jungen has remade the boxes into permanent monuments that exaggerate the marketing apparatus surrounding the consumption of commodities.

Jungen's tussle with minimalism's legacy is apparent in yet another "stack," *Untitled* (2001), a set of ubiquitous wooden pallets that is displayed in a seemingly random pile, the way pallets might be found at the edge of a loading bay or in the corner of a derelict lot. This time, the work has been painstakingly handcrafted by the artist from red cedar (the wood most commonly used by Northwest Coast Aboriginal carvers). Jungen's abstractions are not just elegant geometric sculptures mimicking all too closely the mute monumentality of industrial form; his pallets are meticulously hand-cut, mitred, glued and sanded,

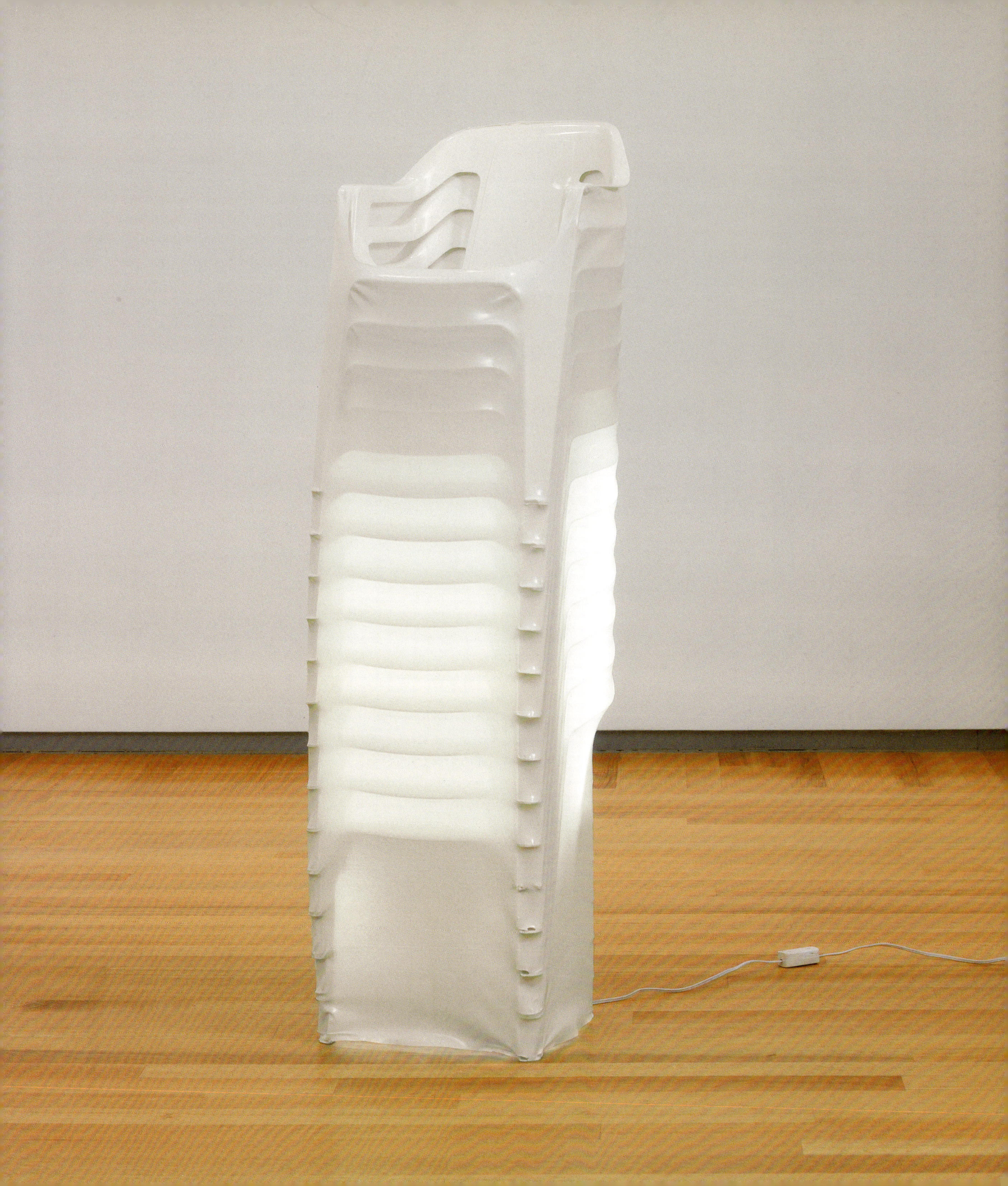

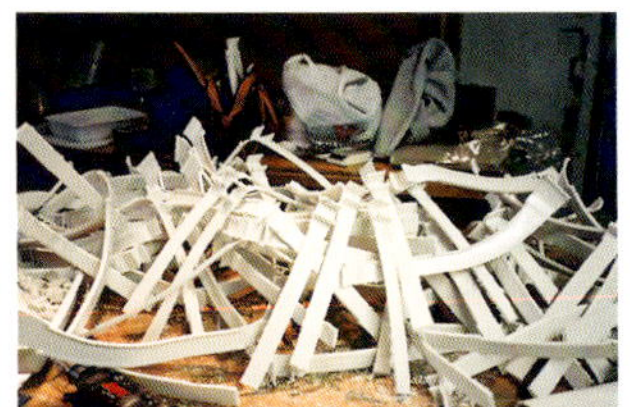
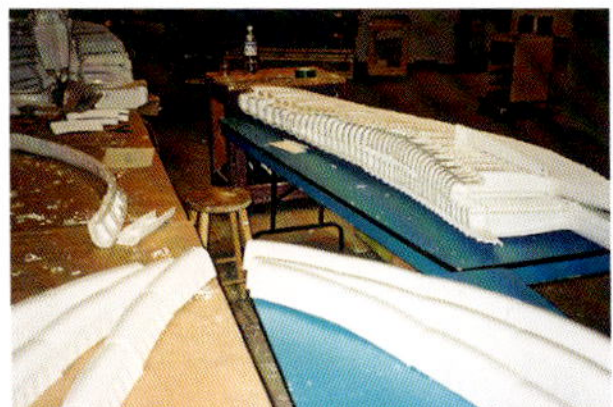
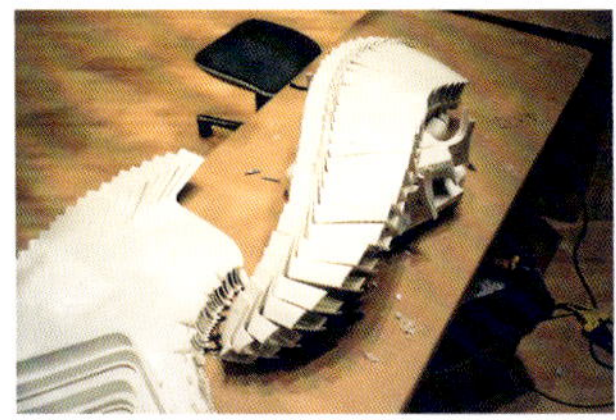
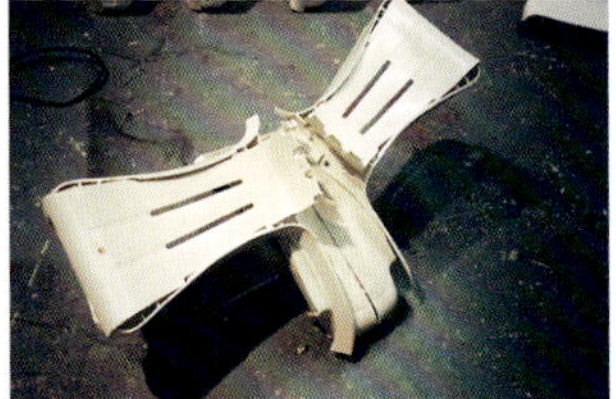
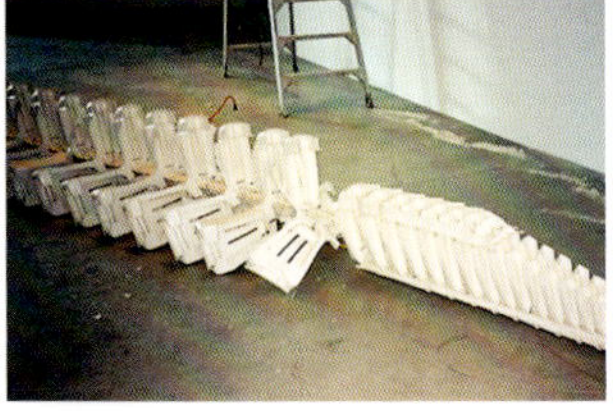
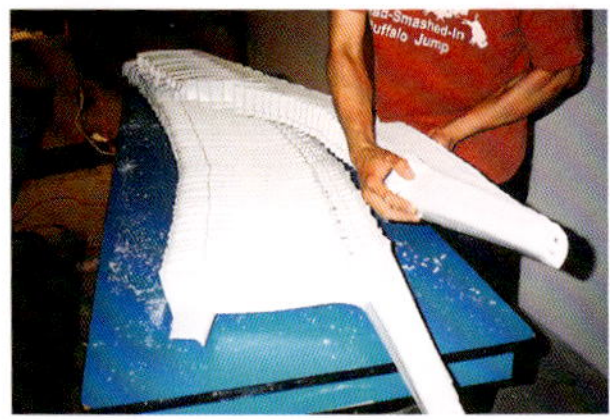
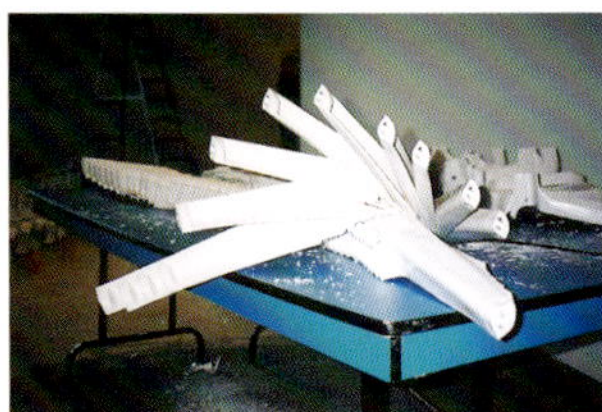

Production of *Cetology* in the
artist's studio
Photos: Courtesy of Brian Jungen

like fine pieces of furniture, and bestowed with a status that acknowledges their primacy as portable platforms supporting the international movement of goods.

Untitled draws attention to the physical foundation on which a global economy rests, its importance writ large in the work through the intense labour and fine craftsmanship behind its making, a rather old-fashioned method of working that cuts against the grain of minimalism's critique of traditional modes of production and questions the mimicking of industrial manufacture in art. In today's overly speculative art market, one is tempted by Jungen's well-made object to wonder if minimalism's slick look and its engagement with industrial production has itself fallen prey to the mechanisms of the international art market and been reduced to a recognizable consumer brand. Jungen's skill lies in inserting social content into minimalism's all too empty and austere forms and in making refined and seductive works that actively participate in a critique of consumer society.

HYBRIDIZATION AT WORK

Jungen is interested in the physicality of objects, especially those circulating as commodities, and his art emerges from an act of dramatic physical transformation that turns common, often prefabricated materials into highly symbolic sculptures and installations. This transformation of physical objects plays with the viewer's expectations, producing a startling effect when one comprehends not only the visual evocation of the piece but also the miraculous shift inherent in its making— as a "mask" returns to being a running shoe, a "birdhouse" is revealed as a set of file boxes, or a "totemic form" is exposed as a baseball bat. The believability of this transformation lies in the high quality of its execution, where clarity of vision is coupled with a deft use of tools, and carefully chosen materials are skillfully fused into the final aggregate form. Nowhere is this metamorphosis more evident than in Jungen's most monumental of sculptures, a series made from garden-variety plastic chairs that suggests a "pod" of whale skeletons. Once the sawed-up pieces of low-tech furniture are reassembled, the curves of the white chairs simulate the arc of whalebones and the result is fully transformative.

Such works as *Shapeshifter* (2000), *Cetology* (2002) and *Vienna* (2003), because they are made from recognizable source materials, are instantly imbued with the residue of everyday life while simultaneously pointing to the cultures of display found in natural history museums or public aquariums where these mammals are typically captured, contained and ultimately rendered lifeless. In the space of an art gallery, Jungen brings to life these inventively crafted objects as they hover between sculpture, natural history specimens and critiques of museum culture and even of certain whaling practices. He opens up a panoply of interpretations that suggest a reconfigured set of relations between the rarefied and fixed space of the museum and everyday political matters. He intentionally mixes references, recasts materials and disrupts influences from a variety of cultural sources as a strategy to question existing categories used to define societal norms.

Not only does he successfully complicate the meaning of both quotidian items as well as the products of high culture, but more importantly, Jungen's hybrid sculptures also confound the cultural specificity of objects, countering the belief that certain forms or styles associated with particular cultures exist in a predetermined order of privilege and status. Whatever hierarchies exist and are perpetuated through social codes and institutions are thrown into question by Jungen's rampant flagrancy in disregarding fixed and rigid orders of meaning. In his world, the Aboriginal is brought together with the colonizer, the rural with the urban, the natural with the artificial, the useful with the useless, into a space where art, identity and cultural traditions can transgress preset and inflexible versions of history.

SITE AS SOURCE

By the time Brian Jungen left art school, the legacies of a critical art practice had imprinted in him a strong sense of the importance of physical space and local context, and he was motivated to consider the specific circumstances of site in how he made and presented his work. In early drawings, for example, he began by considering the construction of his own identity and addressing, among other things, the assimilation of Aboriginal cultures into the larger fabric of Western urban society. In several installations across Canada in the mid-1990s, Jungen's work was the product of a socio-political exploration of the city at hand. Using the exhibition context as a research opportunity, this artist-as-ethnographer organized community surveys that asked people in the street to make their own quick sketches of Aboriginal art. The resulting images—many of which featured clichéd or debased Aboriginal stereotypes such as totem poles, dream catchers and Indians with headdresses—were enlarged and replicated as huge wall drawings and used to physically inhabit the exhibition space. As much as they marked the beginning of Jungen's extended engagement with the architectural

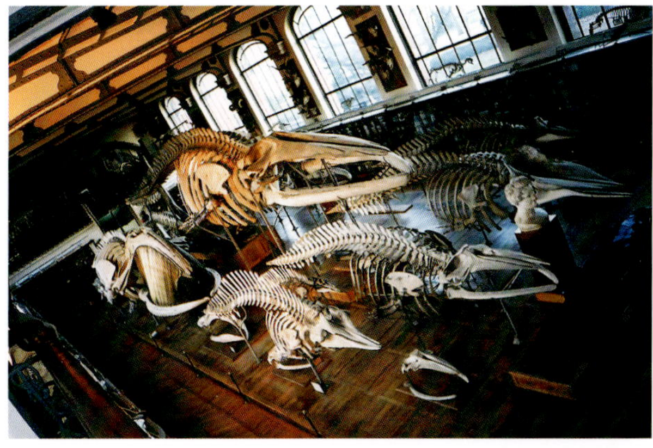

Whale skeletons at the Muséum national d'Histoire naturelle, Paris
Photo: Jacqueline Gijssen, with permission of Muséum national d'Histoire naturelle, Paris

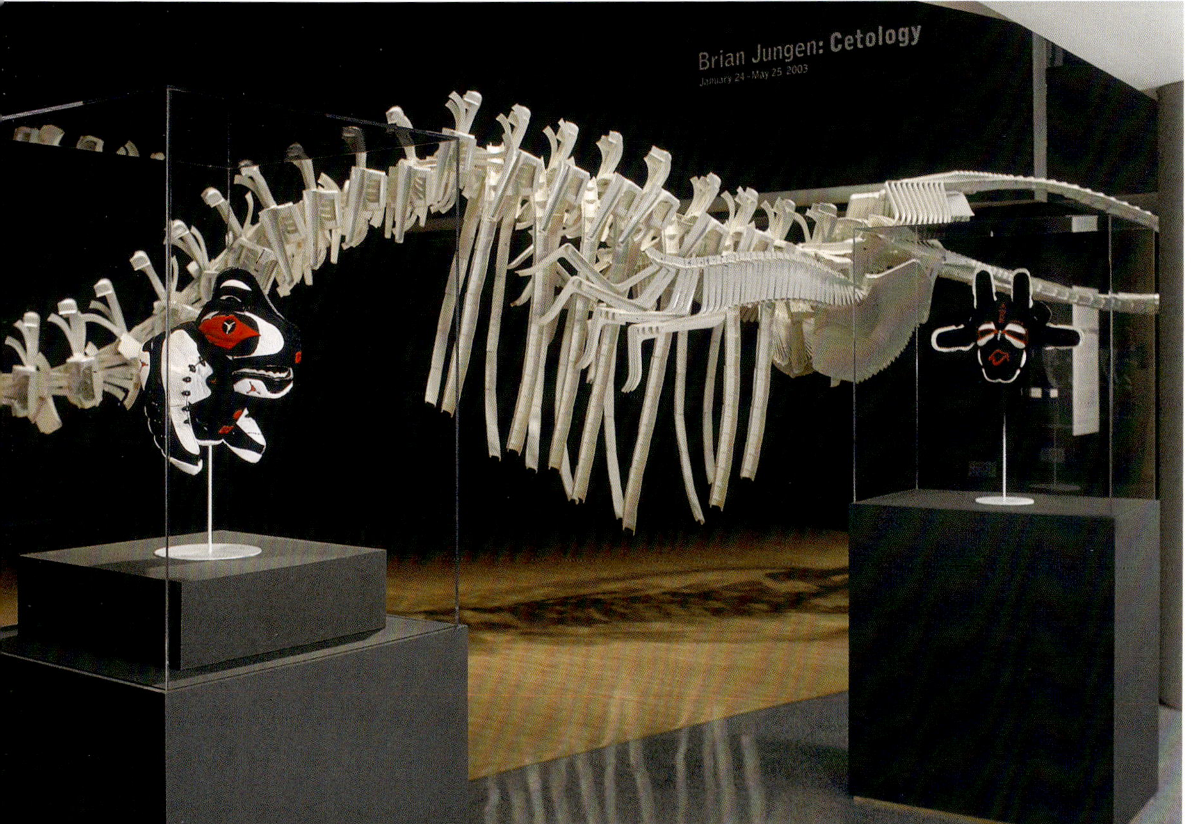

Cetology, 2002
Installation view at Henry Art Gallery, Seattle, 2003
plastic chairs
403.9 x 421.6 x 1491 cm (159" x 166" x 587")
Collection of the Vancouver Art Gallery
Purchased with the financial support of the Canada Council for the Arts Acquisition Assistance Program and the Vancouver Art Gallery Acquisition Fund, 2003
Photo: Brian Jungen

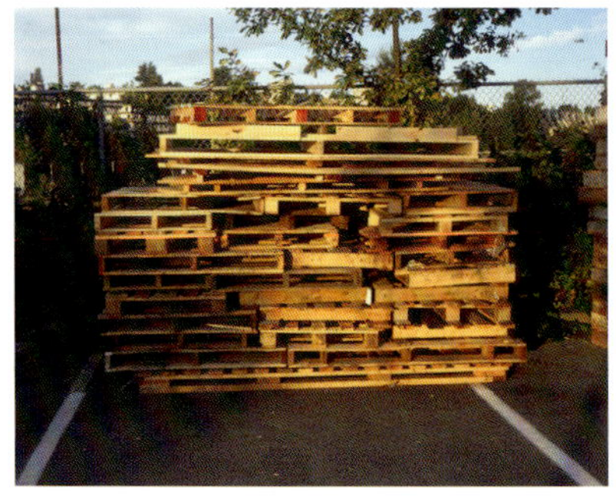

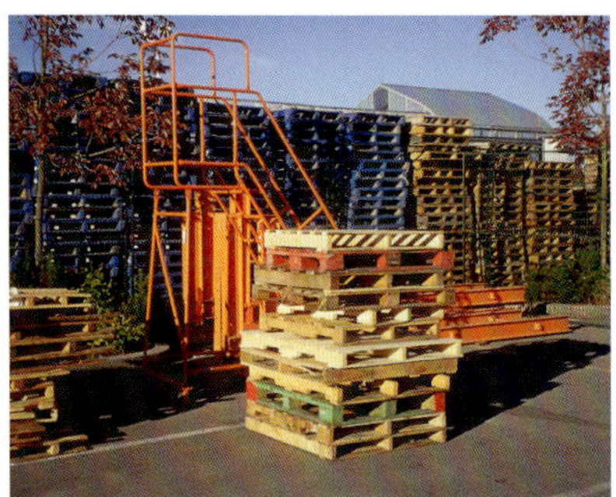

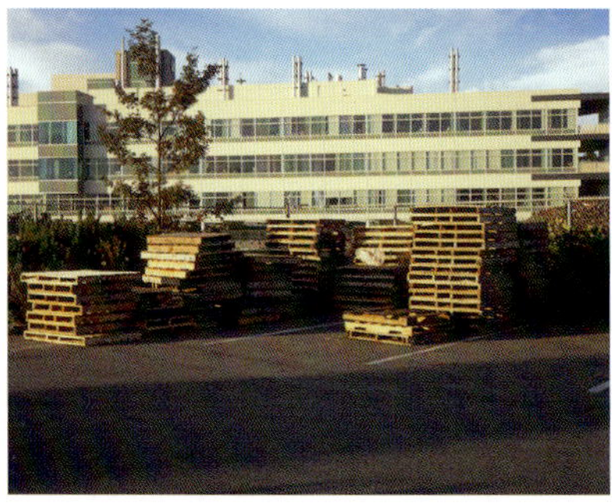

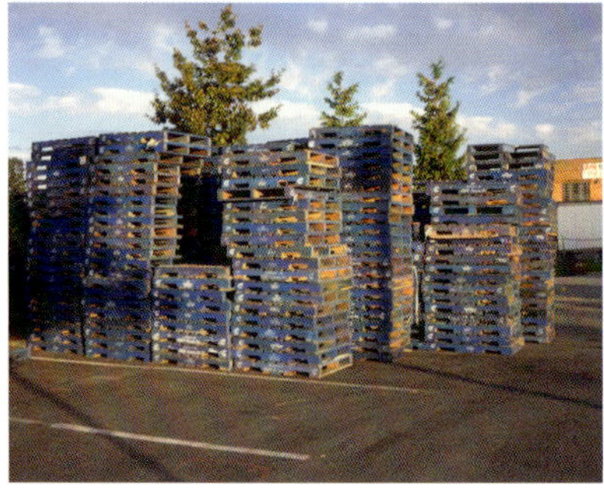

From the artist's ongoing
documentation of pallets
Photos: Courtesy of Brian Jungen

space of the art gallery, these works made visible various localized racial imperatives at play in defining identity.

Jungen's exploration of identity has not been limited to specific questions of race and its exoticization but has opened up to engage the larger and more complicated issues around globalization. As he noted in an interview with curator Matthew Higgs: "Certainly as a child the tension between being aware of my surroundings but also being exposed to the larger world via television informed my primary motivation to step outside of the world that was most familiar. So even as a child, I was exposed and conditioned by a rudimentary form of globalism."[1] Although Jungen's critical engagement with the world was born from these early experiences, it has been reinforced by the escalating assault of mass media, which more aggressively than ever instills consumer desire and dissolves the particularities of place under the veneer of globalization. Recent invitations to create new commissions in various international locations have heightened Jungen's interest in exploring the effects of a global economy. In particular, he has been drawn to architectural form as a foundation of human organization and interaction, architectural structures being the one relatively stable condition in an ever-moving, ever-changing world. Being particularly engaged with the legacies of modernist architecture (perhaps because of his familiarity with Vancouver as a city built largely in the mid-twentieth century), he has created a number of major works that are the result of carefully considering iconic buildings that are emblems of localized histories and social developments.

One such project is the *Arts and Crafts Book Depository/Capp Street Project 2004* (2004), in which he built a one-fifth–scale plywood architectural model of a famous California Arts and Crafts house that he then quartered in a gesture that references the splitting of buildings undertaken by 1970s conceptual artist Gordon Matta-Clark. The result exposes an interior that is fashioned as a resource area full of books and periodicals for the study of architecture and craft. Although the work specifically critiques deteriorating local conditions for studying craft at the California College of the Arts in San Francisco (which was, until recently, the California College of Arts *and Crafts*), more importantly it transforms the exhibition space into a depository of increasingly marginalized histories and a vehicle for expanded social interaction.

Jungen's Montreal installation *Habitat 04: Cité radieuse des chats/Cats Radiant City* (2004), a temporary encampment for homeless cats in the custody of the Society for the Prevention of Cruelty to Animals (SPCA), further extends and builds on specific local architectural references. Based on Moshe Safdie's famous Expo 67 building, Habitat, which was designed for economic apartment living, Jungen's installation unfolds Safdie's geometric shapes into a giant carpet-covered sculpture inhabited by cats and inhibited by video gear. The surveillance technology initially provides viewers with closer access to the cats' activities, but it also changes an idealistic habitat into a regulated zone of observation. This flamboyant shelter for the adoption of felines is both a conduit for deeper terms of engagement within an art institution (especially for those who actively participate by adopting a homeless cat) and an unsettling reflection on the failed egalitarian ideals of modernist architecture. If Jungen's early practice was predicated on the construction of hybrid objects as agents for a new understanding of global commodity flows, and for rethinking institutionalized identities within the frame of localized histories, his more recent architecturally grounded works may serve as prototypes for understanding anew the visionary moments of human organization and for uncovering ways in which more reflexive interactions between people may alleviate some of our social ailments.

Jungen's combined interest in architecture and nature has resulted in other enclosures for animals. *Little Habitat I* (2003) and *Little Habitat II* (2004) are the products of leftover Nike shoe boxes recycled into miniature versions of Buckminster Fuller's utopian architecture; exhibited casually in the corner of a gallery, these domes could conceivably serve as a refuge for a small mammal. In Jungen's world, no animal is too small or insignificant to warrant our consideration.

In his most recent project, *Inside Today's Home* (2005), Jungen worked exclusively with ready-made products from the local IKEA home furnishings store in Edmonton, Alberta, to create an indoor aviary for six domesticated zebra finches. This deluxe accommodation for birds is constructed from sleek wooden file boxes and features adornments made from prefabricated baskets, napkin holders and other IKEA home accessories as well as from shelving brackets that double as perches. So as not to disturb the chirping and mating birds delighted with their new, spacious habitat, visitors view the room-size aviary through peepholes and on closed-circuit television monitors. Rather like the implied voyeurism of reality TV, viewers witness delicate private lives being played out in the indifferent space of the public sphere. In a swift inversion of references, Jungen's architectural source is no longer the local, rarefied monument lying in the heart of the city. Instead, it is the ubiquitous suburban big-box store that has long replaced locally inspired consumer products and now caters to fulfilling worldwide desires to own a semblance of contemporary design. *Inside Today's Home* mines the ideals of Scandinavian modern design that are now made universally available through the massive international flow of IKEA products that carry with them the hefty price tag of subverting local specificity and individual expression.

To consider the full trajectory of Brian Jungen's work over the past decade is to encounter his persistent recontextualization of approaches and histories, and to come upon many of the same objects (patio chairs, Nike shoes, pallets) reused and reconsidered, transformed and exposed, continually accruing fresh potential. Jungen presents the material world, from an ever-shifting perspective and at various scales—from ubiquitous objects to utopian structures— as a model for the social imagination. The emphatically material quality of his historical insight, critical awareness and cultural inventiveness continuously asserts the social potential of making art.

NOTES

1. Matthew Higgs, "Brian Jungen in conversation with Matthew Higgs" in *Brian Jungen* (Vienna: Secession, 2004), 29.

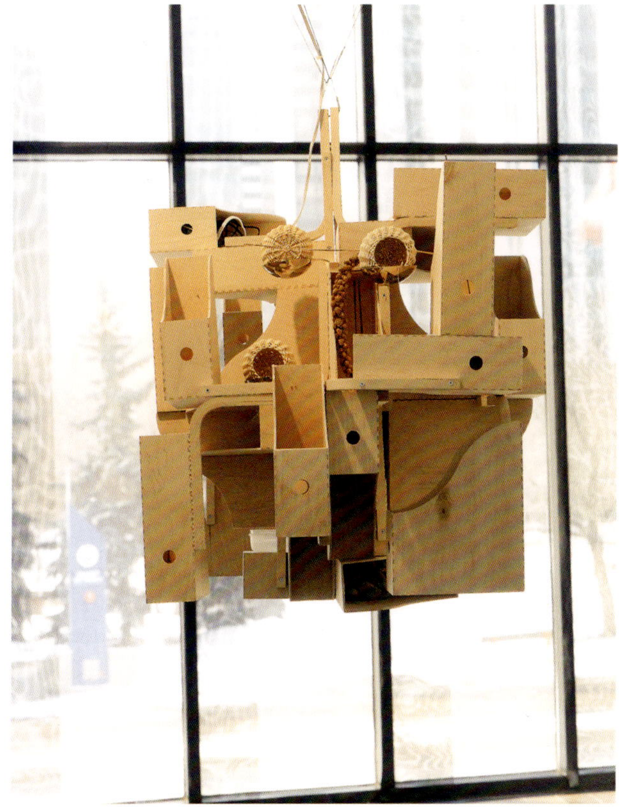

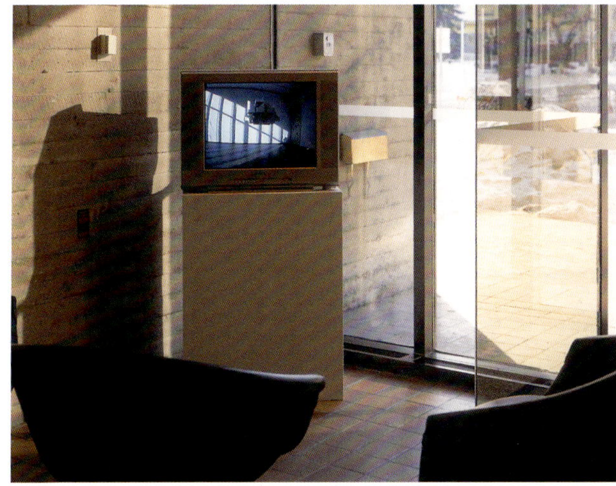

Inside Today's Home, 2005 (details)
Installation views at The Edmonton Art Gallery, Edmonton, Alberta, 2005
IKEA products, video camera, birds
106.7 x 134.6 x 340.4 cm (42" x 53" x 32")
sculpture only
4.27 x 7.62 x 7.0 m (14' x 25' x 23') room enclosure
Photos: Hutch Hutchinson, Courtesy of The Edmonton Art Gallery

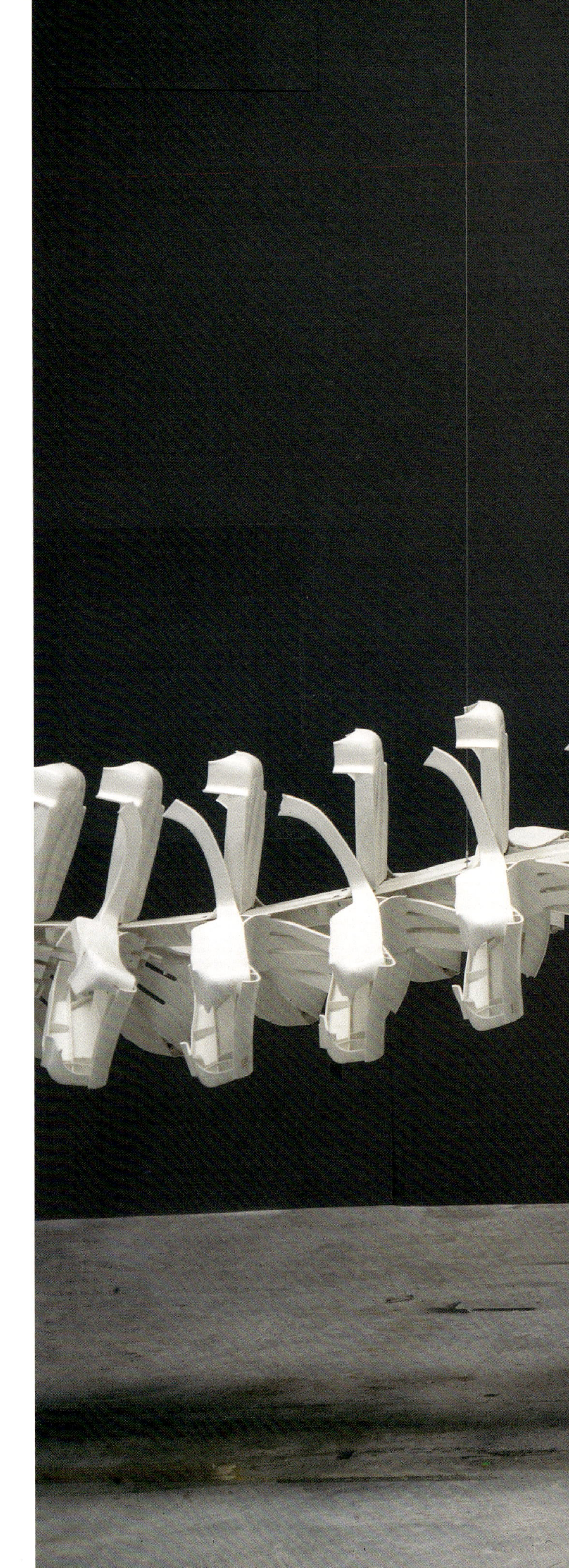

Cetology, 2002
plastic chairs
403.9 x 421.6 x 1491 cm (159" x 166" x 587")
Collection of the Vancouver Art Gallery
Purchased with the financial support of the Canada Council for the Arts Acquisition
Assistance Program and the Vancouver Art Gallery Acquisition Fund, 2003
Photo: Trevor Mills, Vancouver Art Gallery

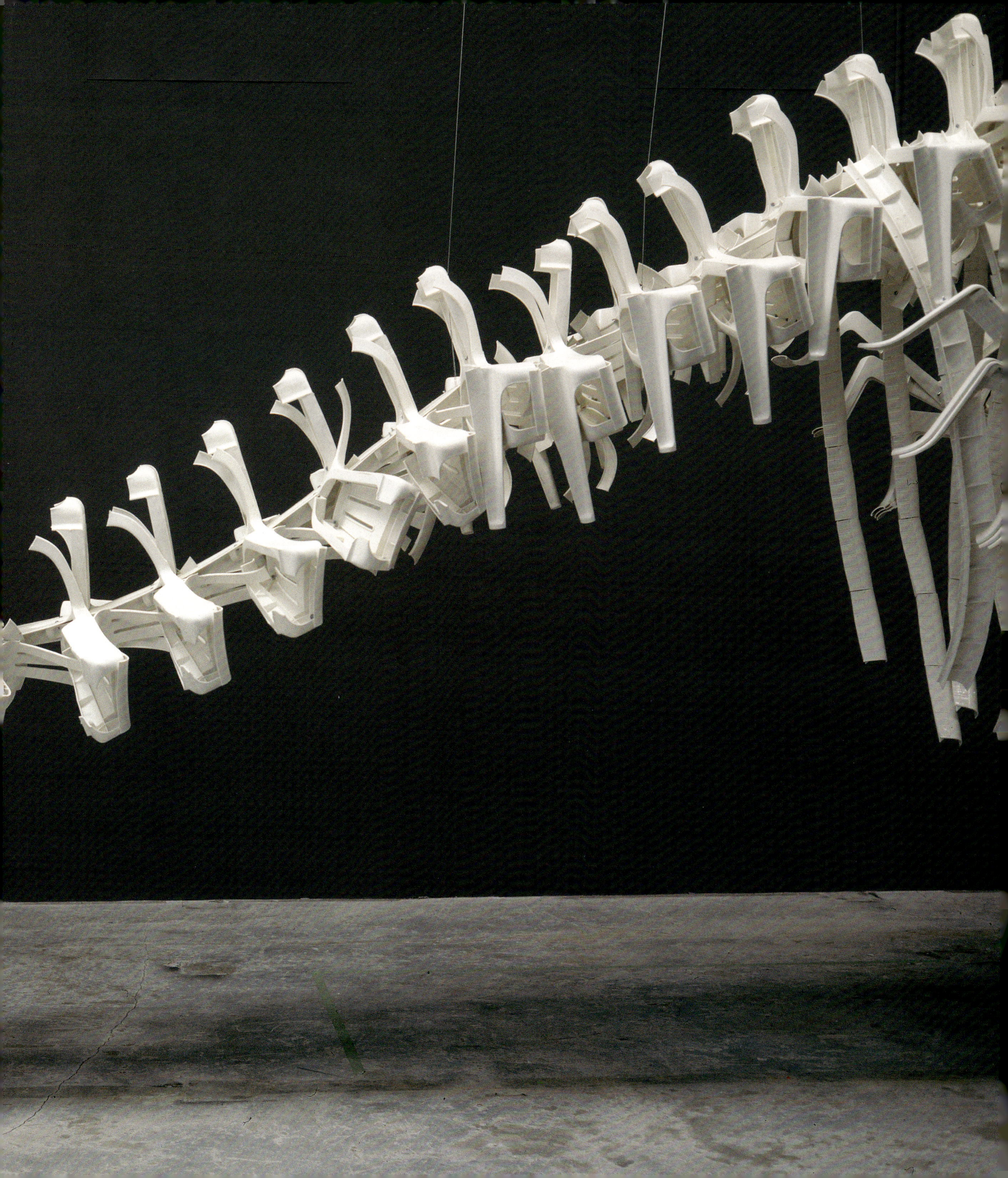

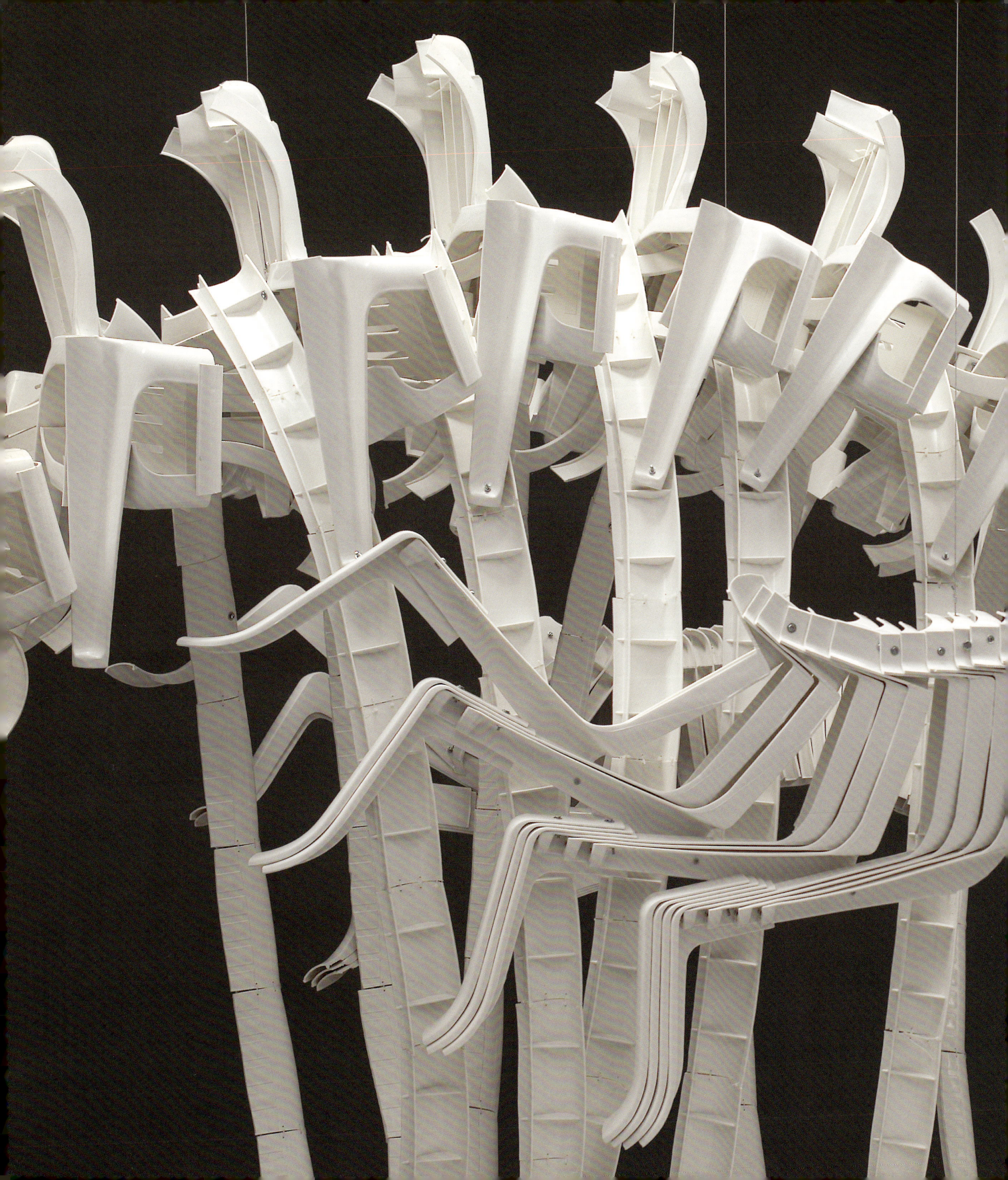

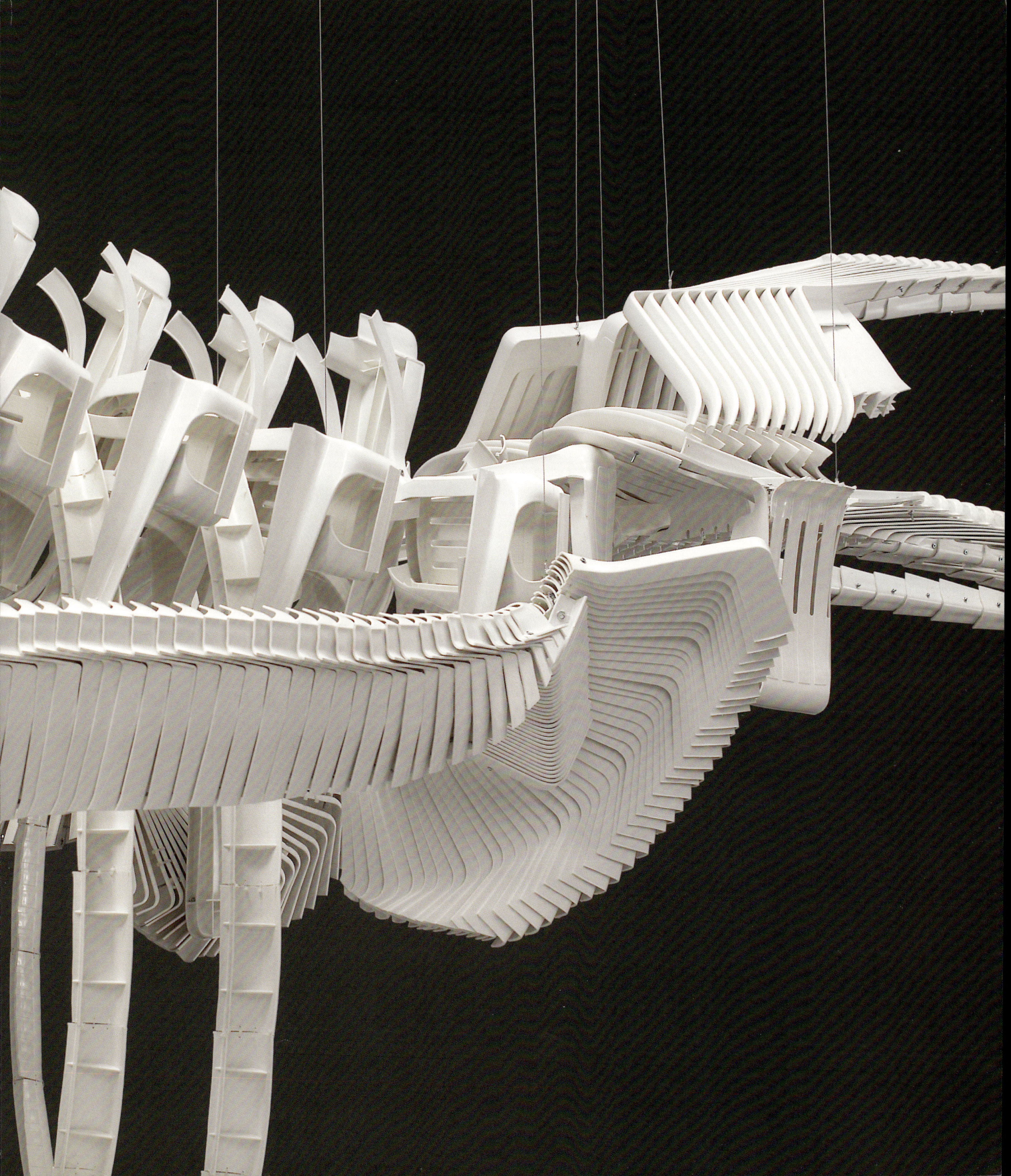

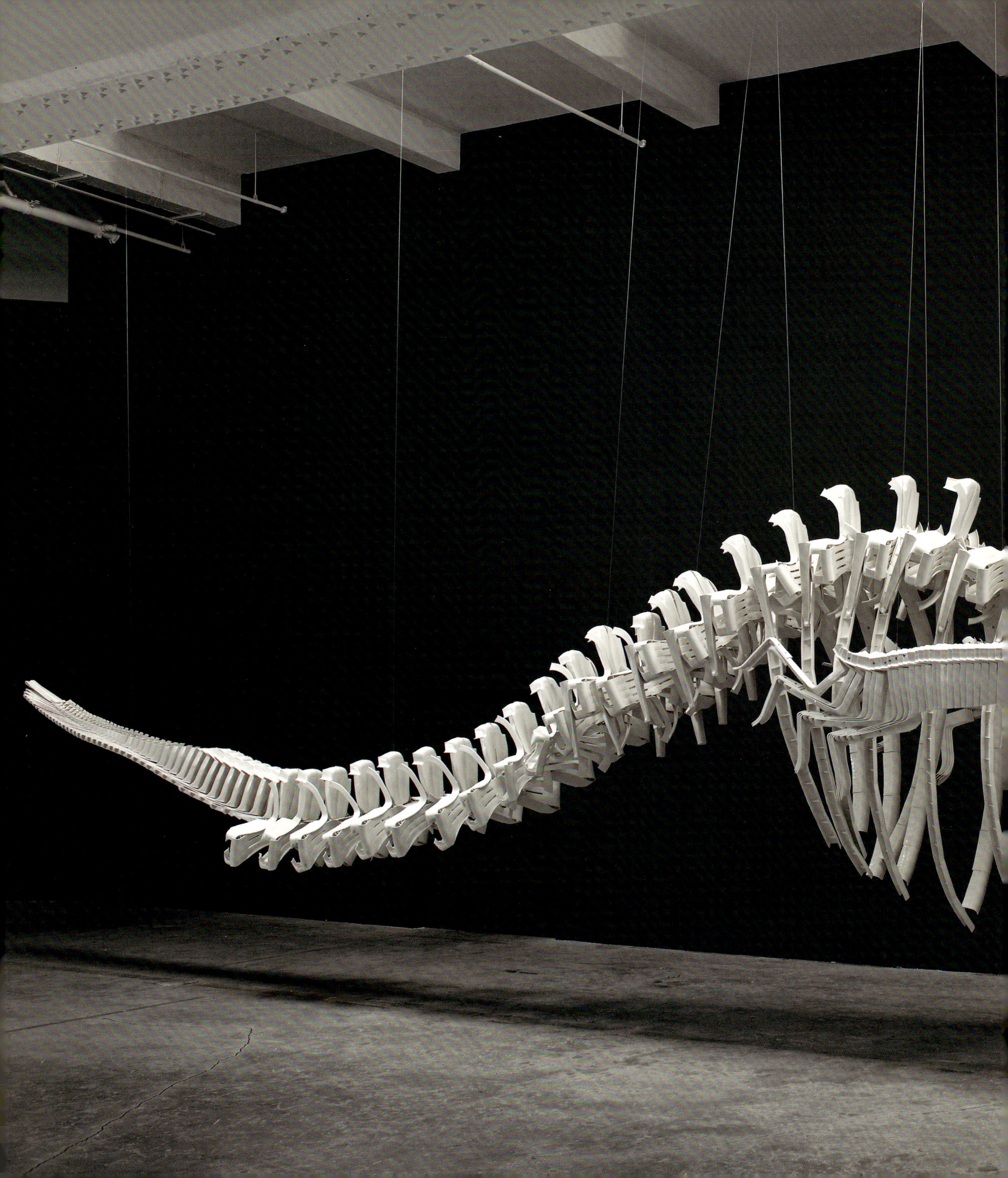

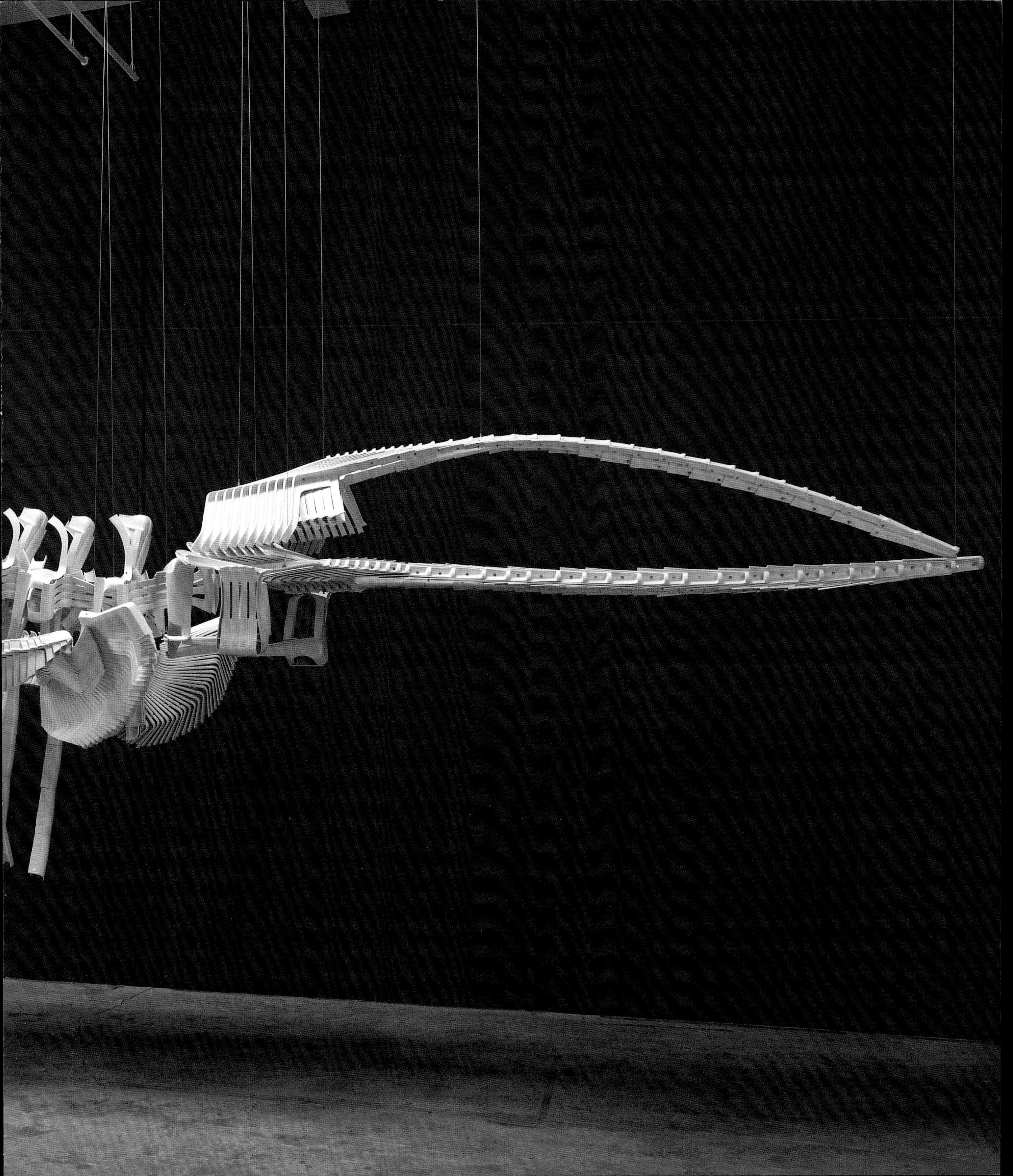

OPPOSITE:
Cetology, 2002 (detail)
plastic chairs
403.9 x 421.6 x 1491 cm (159" x 166" x 587")
Collection of the Vancouver Art Gallery
Purchased with the financial support of the Canada Council for the Arts Acquisition
Assistance Program and the Vancouver Art Gallery Acquisition Fund, 2003
Photo: Trevor Mills, Vancouver Art Gallery

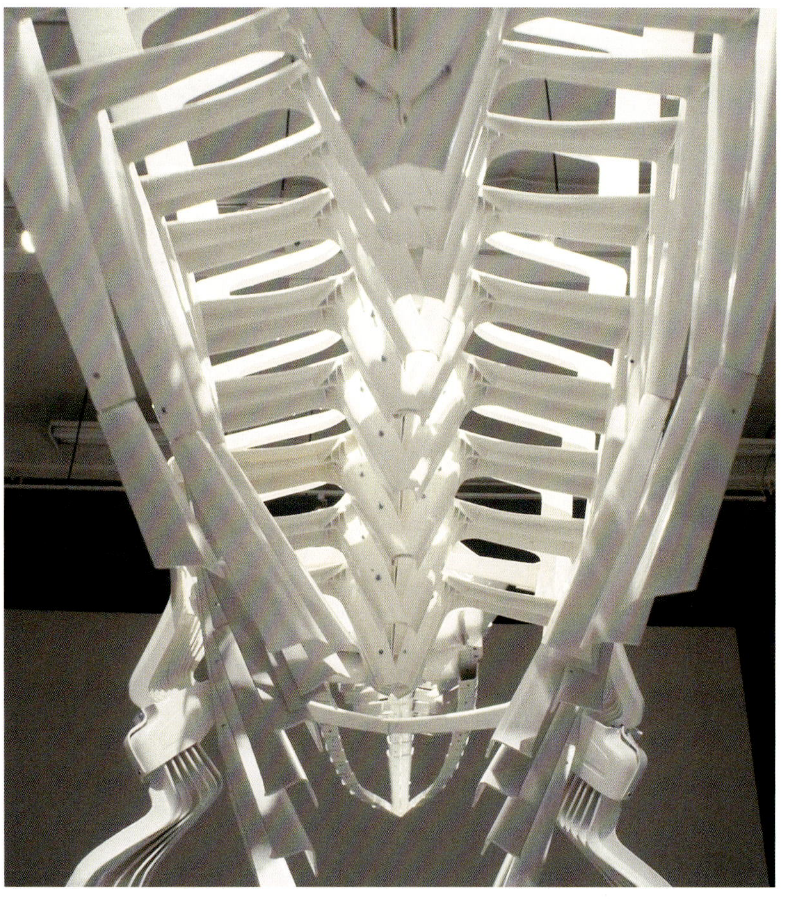

Shapeshifter, 2000 (detail)
plastic chairs
144.8 x 152.4 x 660.4 cm (57" x 60" x 260")
Collection of the National Gallery of Canada, Ottawa, purchased 2001
Photo: Linda Chinfen

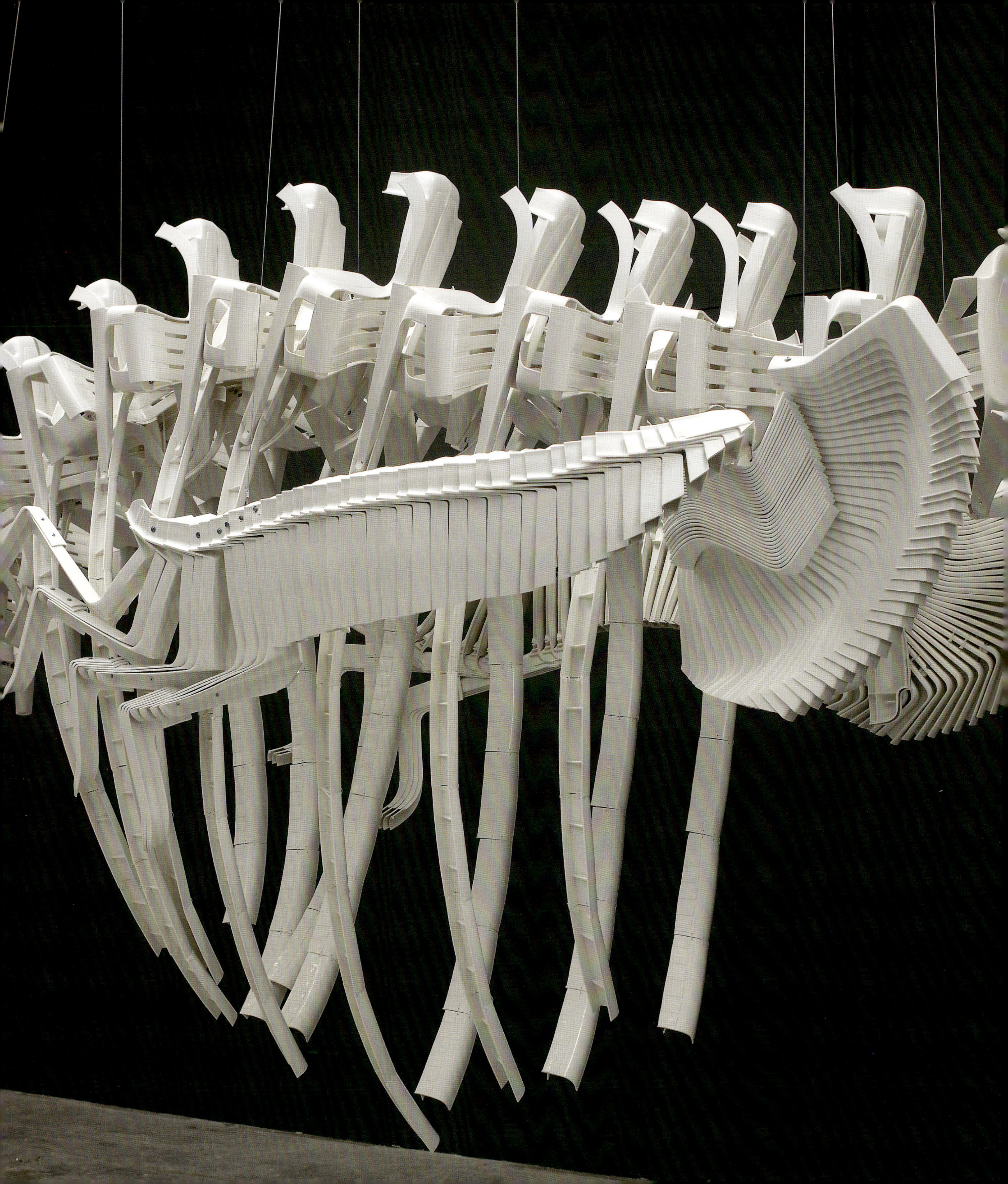

Shapeshifter, 2000
Installation view at Or Gallery, Vancouver, 2000
plastic chairs
144.8 x 152.4 x 660.4 cm (57" x 60" x 260")
Collection of the National Gallery of Canada, Ottawa, purchased 2001
Photo: Linda Chinfen

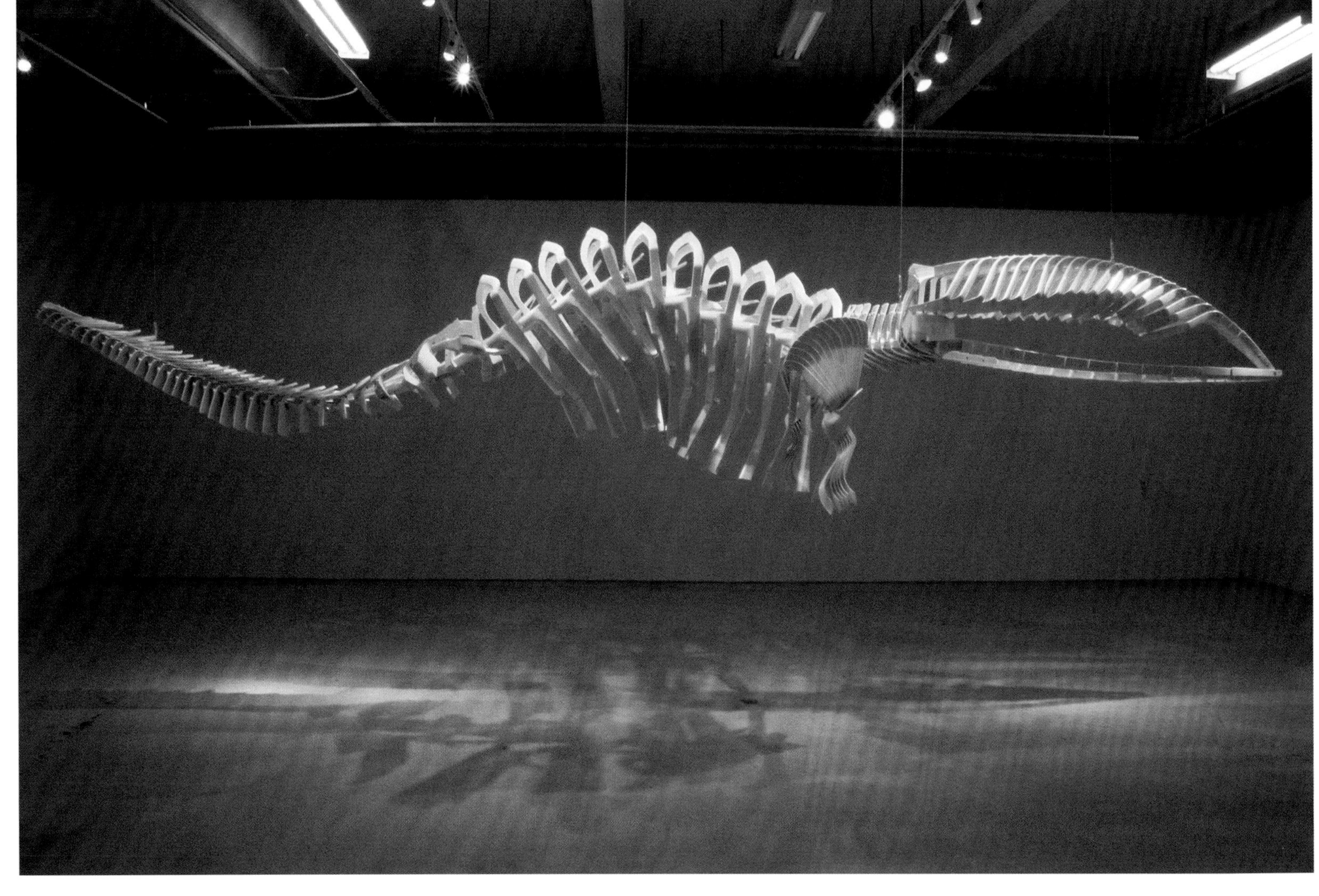

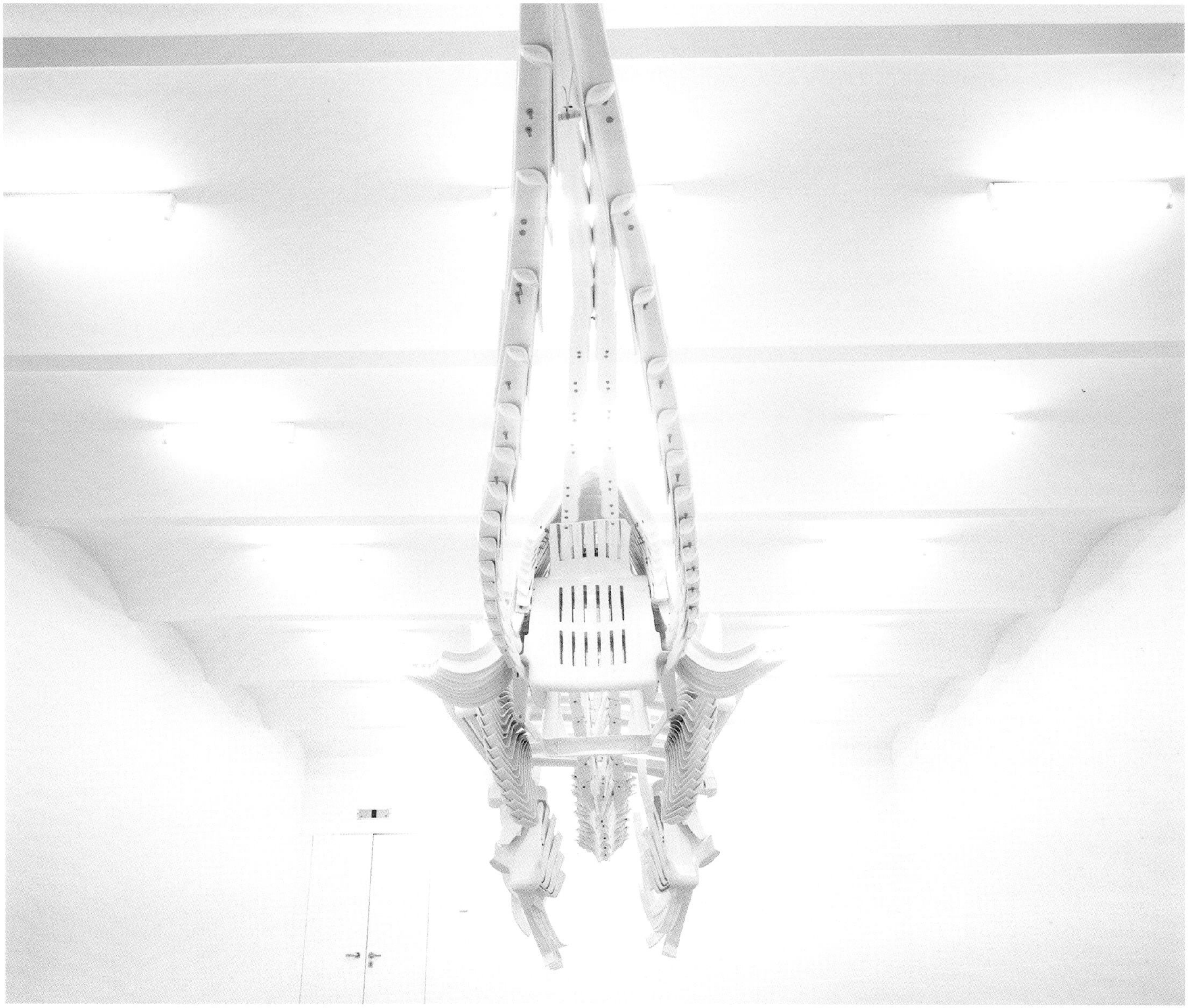

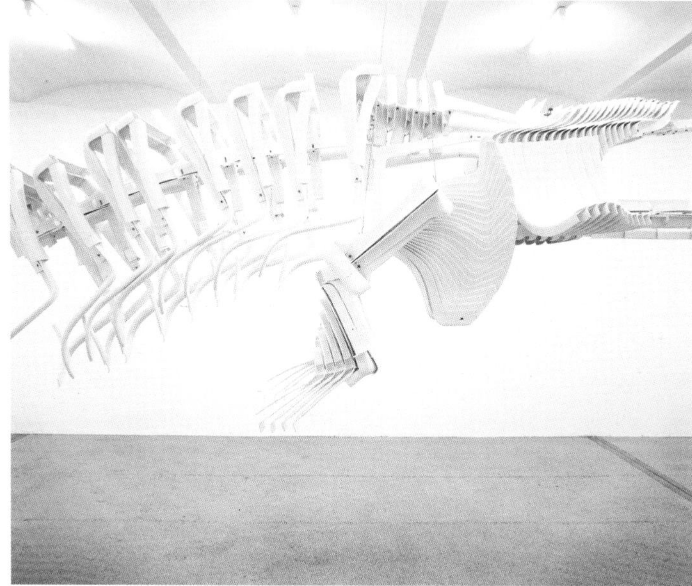

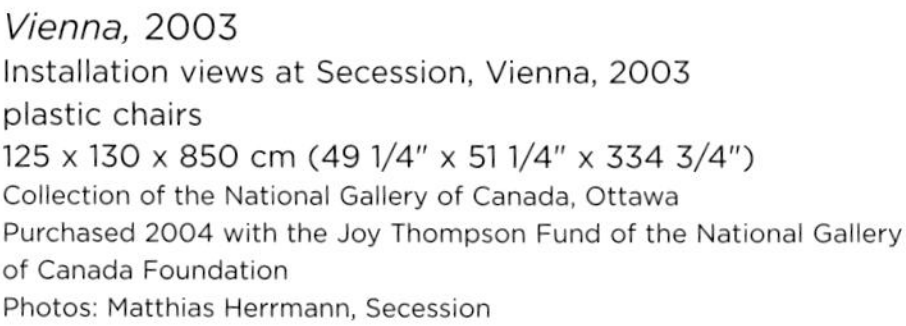

Vienna, 2003
Installation views at Secession, Vienna, 2003
plastic chairs
125 x 130 x 850 cm (49 1/4" x 51 1/4" x 334 3/4")
Collection of the National Gallery of Canada, Ottawa
Purchased 2004 with the Joy Thompson Fund of the National Gallery
of Canada Foundation
Photos: Matthias Herrmann, Secession

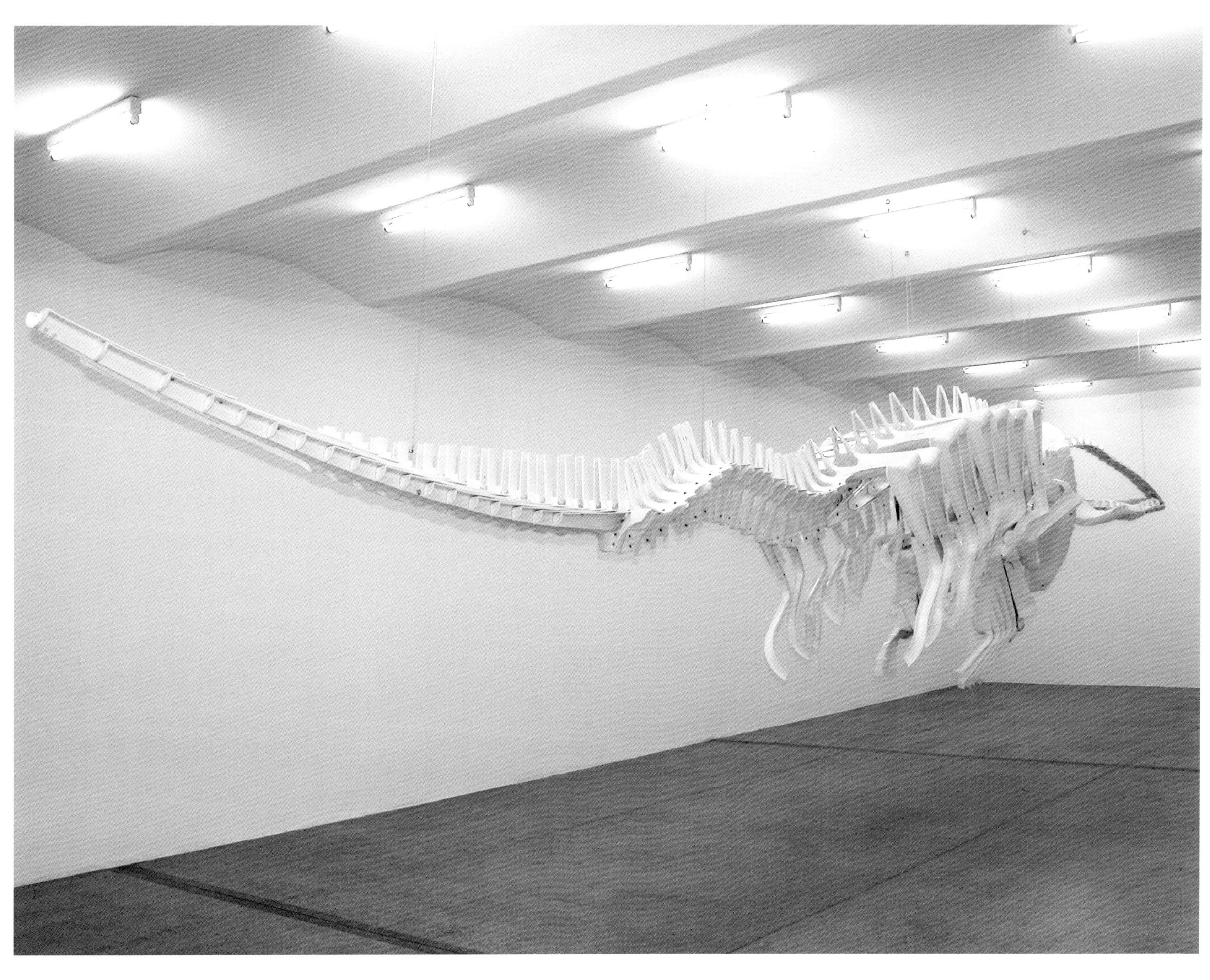

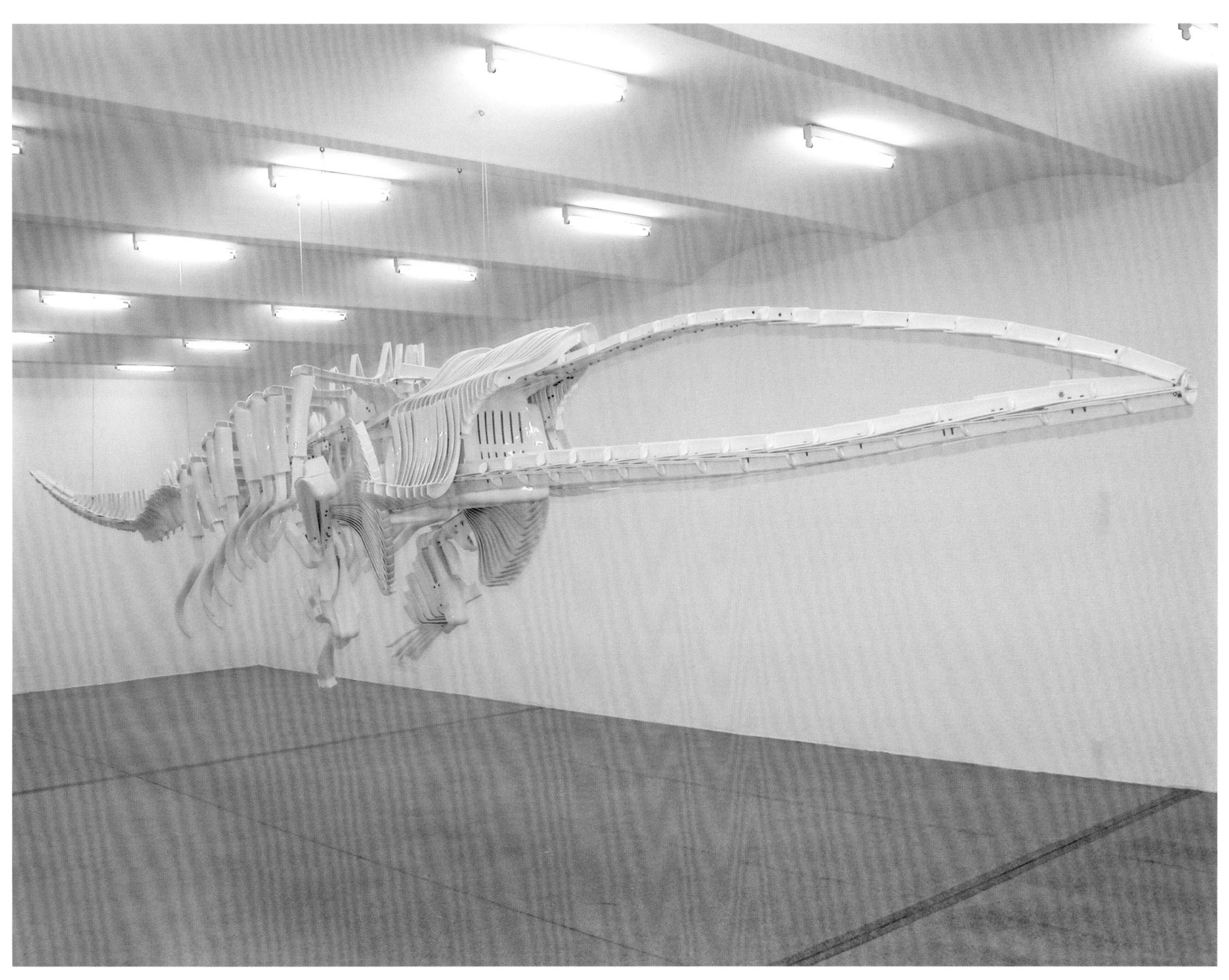

Vienna, 2003
Installation views at Secession, Vienna, 2003
plastic chairs
125 x 130 x 850 cm (49 1/4" x 51 1/4" x 334 3/4")
Collection of the National Gallery of Canada, Ottawa
Purchased 2004 with the Joy Thompson Fund of the National Gallery
of Canada Foundation
Photos: Matthias Herrmann, Secession

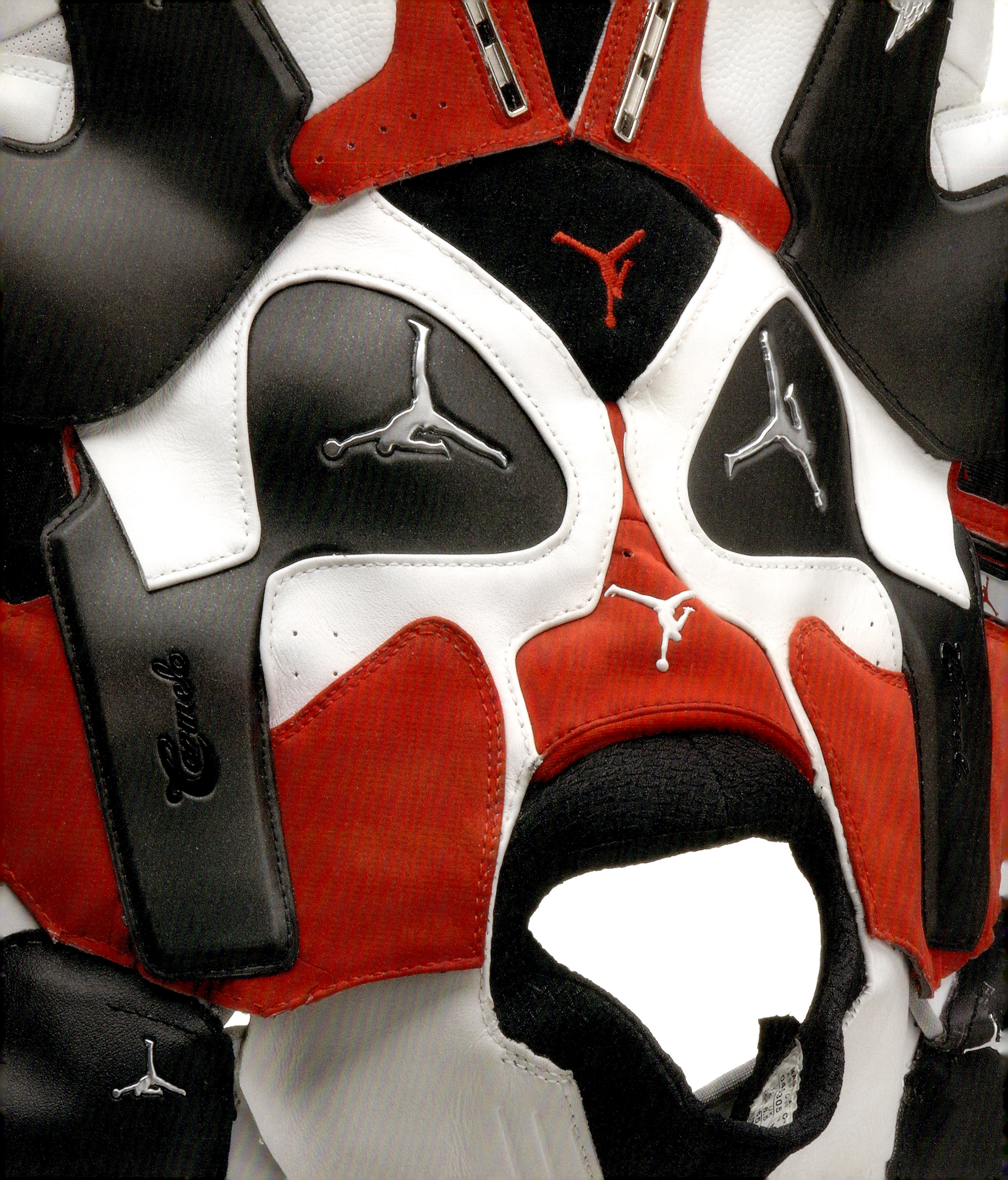

High Curios
Cuauhtémoc Medina

1. OFFER AND DEMAND

At the end of the 1530s, the Spanish conquerors' effort to enforce Christianity and extirpate the "idolatry of the Indians" in central Mexico reached a feverish state. In their effort to "rescue" the "Indians" from their "satanic" worshipping, Franciscan friars—the new civil authorities and, at times, overzealous colonizers—went through hundreds of towns to uncover and burn all kinds of "idols" and "demonic" books that were hidden in small domestic altars, or buried under the town squares or in remote mountain caves. Although chronicles from the time attest to the Spaniards' apparent success in turning the Aboriginal towns to Christianity—a conversion fuelled by the fear left by the conquest and the epidemics that had recently decimated the Aboriginal populations—they also obsessively describe the hundred and one ways in which the "Indians" refused to abandon their cult objects. To the outrage of the Catholic priests, the Aboriginals paid lip service to the new faith and at the same time dared to conceal their "devils," even under the carved stone crosses and churches being erected all through the friars' new kingdom.

Western iconoclasm created an unequal but nonetheless complex space of violence and negotiation revolving around the value (and lack of value) of the so-called idol. The zeal of the Spaniards had a dual effect, for instead of merely desacralizing the "Indian" objects and turning them into meaningless materials, the targeting of them as "demonic things" frequently reinforced their reputation as powerful objects.[1] At times, in fact, the Spaniards contributed to the perpetuation of idol making in the most paradoxical ways. According to Friar Toribio de Benavente Motolinia, around 1539 and 1540 some Spaniards, "thinking they were

OPPOSITE:
Prototype for New Understanding #23, 2005
(detail)
Nike Air Jordans
47 x 52 x 15 cm (18 1/2" x 20 1/2" x 5 7/8")
Collection of Debra and Dennis Scholl, Miami Beach, Florida
Courtesy of the artist and Casey Kaplan
Photo: Trevor Mills, Vancouver Art Gallery

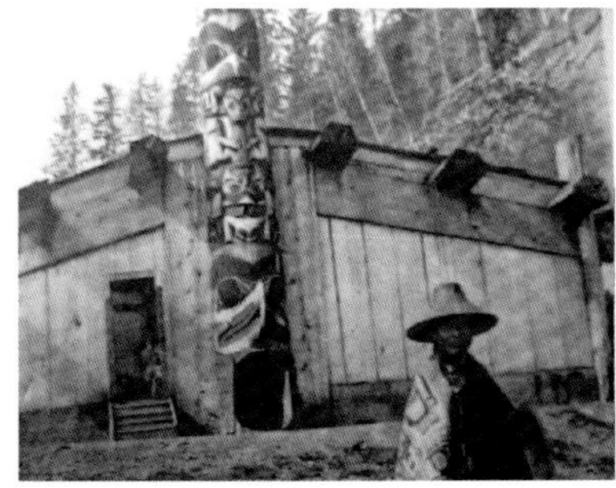

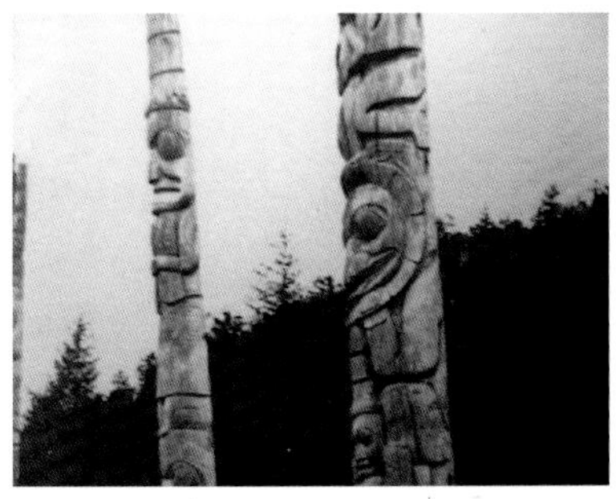

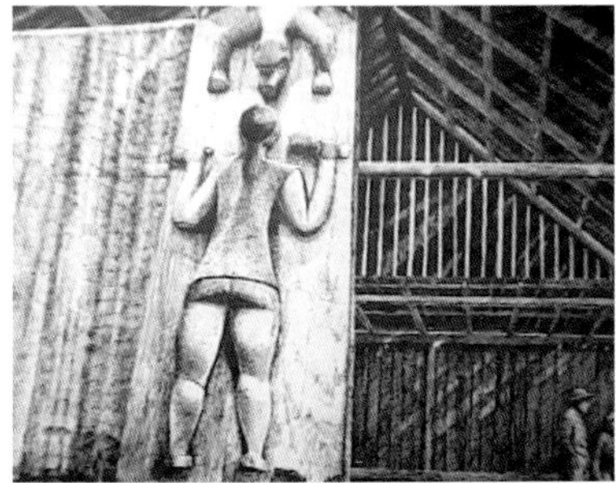

Video stills from artist's documentation
of First Nations carving
Photos: Brian Jungen

doing something," went beyond unearthing corpses and statues to "offer a reward to those that would hand them idols." Some Natives decided to comply and again started producing images of their deities, not for worshipping but to provide them to the new rulers, who enjoyed smashing them:

> And in some places the Indians were rewarded and pestered
> this way, so they searched all the idols that were forgotten
> or rotting under the earth to surrender them. And some of the
> Indians were so molested that in fact they made idols again,
> and gave them so that they [Spanish priests and soldiers]
> would stop bothering them.[2]

In the same way that art today may go straight from the artist's studio into the museum collection, the Natives of central Mexico created objects that went directly from the workshop of their maker into the bonfire of the inquisitor despite not having been involved in any religious or magical ceremony. Their only function was to fulfill a paranoid colonial expectation, and they were, in fact, among the first Amerindian objects produced solely for European consumption.

In hindsight, those makers of "idols"—by all appearances of Nahua[3] descent—invented a new strategy of colonial resistance. By effectively producing counterfeits of their ritual objects (the first "pre-Columbian fakes"), they reflected to the priests and soldiers exactly what the colonizers expected to see. In this strategy of over-representation, if the metropolitan subject expects the colonials to attest to his culture's preconceptions, trying to theorize an ambiguous position towards the predicament of westernization will not necessarily build a platform of understanding. In other words, sometimes it is better to use mis-understanding in one's favour by projecting towards the other the myth of the "authentic" First Nations artist, to enact their nightmare and accept the role of the idolatrous anthropophagic monster. If they want masks, why not sell them their own reflection?

Let me add in passing that this anecdote ought to be seen as detailing the true origins of art in the Americas: the production of objective mirages that mediate the interethnic imaginary of both individuals and communities on the North and South American continents. As skewed and convoluted as this "tradition" is by distrust, violent conflict and social struggle, the colonial process turned the making of symbolically charged images and artifacts into a field of negotiation of ethnic imaginaries. From the substitute sacralization of Christian saints in the native tailoring of cults like the Virgin of Guadalupe to the "shamanism" of Jackson Pollock's painting, from Wilfredo Lam's Afrocuban recapturing of cubism's primitivism to the vindication of *antropofagia* by Brazilian *modernismo,* not to mention Emily Carr's fauvist "communion" with the First Nations of the Pacific Northwest Coast, art in the Americas is traversed by the predicament of objects mediating colonial subjects. Sometimes, in fact, their efficacy seems to correlate to their inauthenticity. It may be that instead of representing indigenous history and lived experience, artists in the Americas have

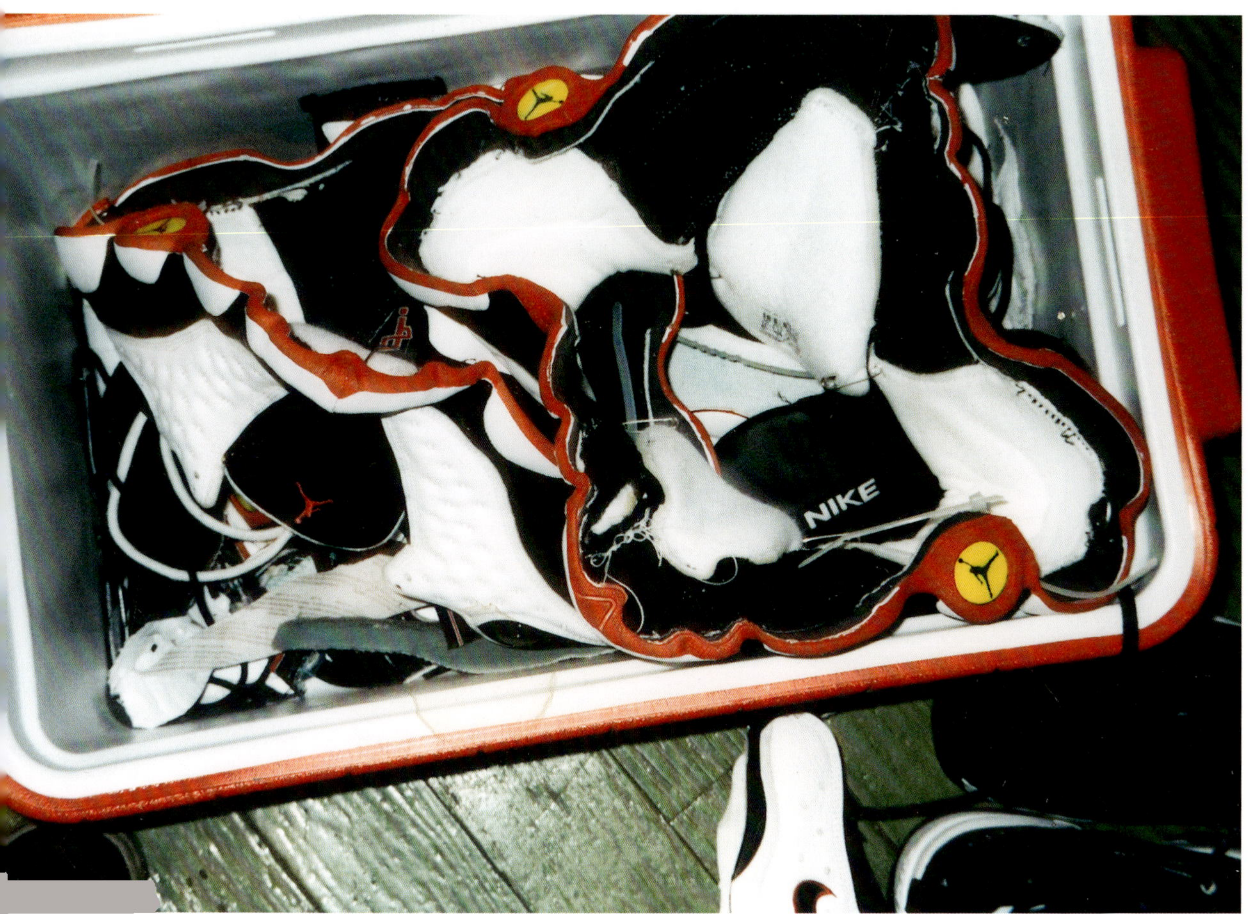

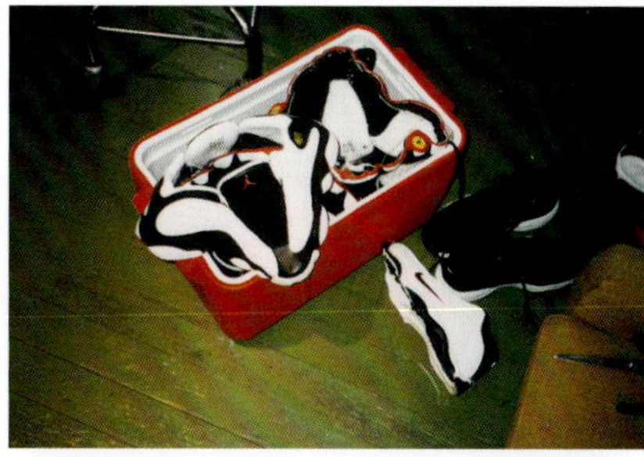

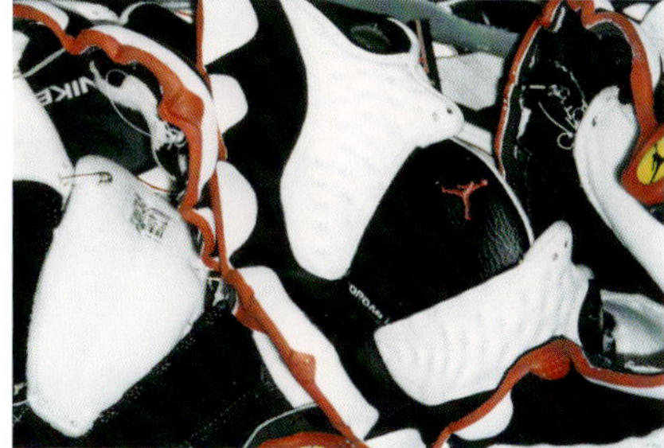

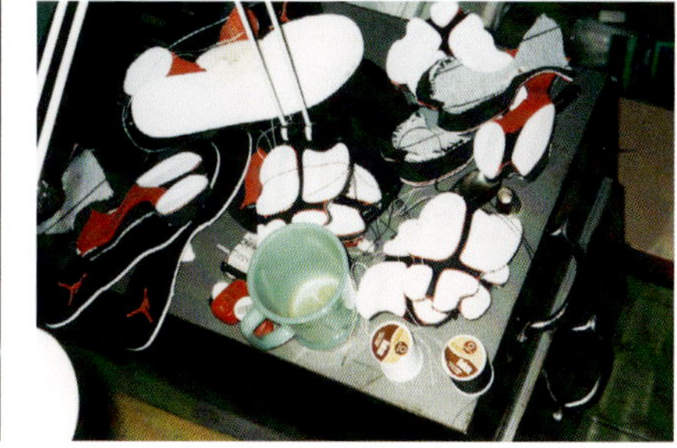

been particularly cunning at performing cultural distortions, for these are better able to play a mediating role between communities. Framed by a history of violence and betrayal, these images are more significant for their capacity to activate fear and distrust than as means of reconciliation.

My purpose in beginning this discussion of Brian Jungen's *Prototypes* (1998–2005) with this anecdote is to show that his art unfolds against a global context of colonial stereotyping. Jungen's work registers the art of his Northwest Coast First Nations ancestors as exoticized and commercialized, and also attends to the argument that this perception may have helped First Nations artists to circumvent the brutal prohibition of the potlatch in Canada from 1884 to 1951 and actually allowed Aboriginal art to survive.[4] I introduce this comparison with the Mexican context to consider his work as an allegory for an entire series of historical transactions between ethnic groups in which colonial categories such as "idolatry," "fetish," "Indian art" or "mask" can be effectively redirected to the colonizer, who, after all, is their original instigator. Brian Jungen's art can be seen as an example of how to use cultural stereotypes as a means of critical engagement. His works are games that mobilize aesthetic and cultural misunderstandings to explore ways to politicize cultural stereotypes in the age of global capitalism.

Production of *Prototypes for New Understanding* in artist's studio
Photo: Brian Jungen

29

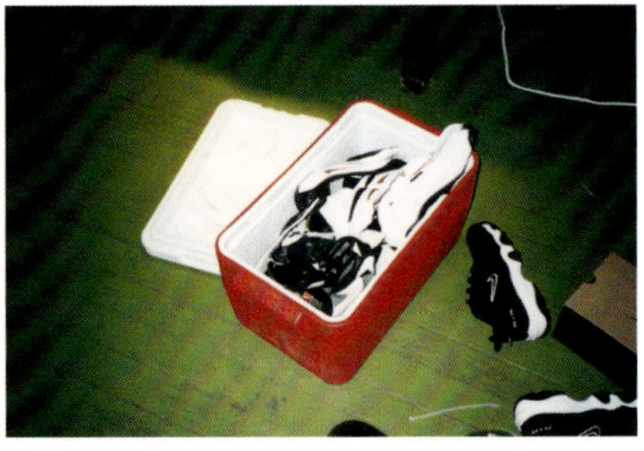

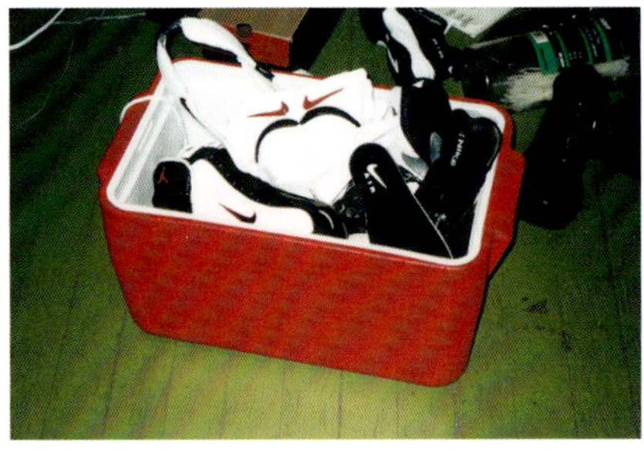

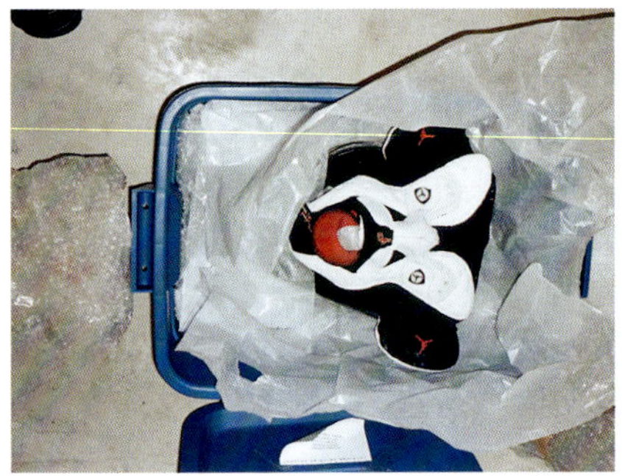

Production of Prototypes
for New Understanding
in artist's studio
Photos: Brian Jungen

2. AT THE CROSSROADS OF PREJUDICE AND MISUNDERSTANDING

When they were first shown at the Emily Carr Institute of Art + Design in Vancouver in 1999, Brian Jungen's *Prototypes for New Understanding* were deliberately inscribed in a structure of cultural *refraction,* that is, a structure in which an image is distorted by viewing it through an artistic medium.[5] Jungen offered the viewer an extraordinary example of contemporary bricolage: a set of what were purported to be Northwest Coast Indian masks[6] that, instead of being carved and painted, had been produced by slicing and reassembling red, black and white leather from Nike Air Jordan trainers. A *tour de force* of hybridization, these masks were bound to become Jungen's signature work. By displaying his pieces inside vitrines like reputed "masterworks" in museums of anthropology, Jungen subjected the masks to a certain neutralization[7] and suggested the emergence of a new kind of critique (but, as Jungen has emphasized, not "a censorious critique" that would naively assume a utopian pre-capitalist stage of purity[8]).

Not by chance, those reassembled trainers caught the audience's critical attention: they seemed to epitomize a contemporary practice that would use non-Western cultural tactics to focus as much on the powers of the commodity as on the way globalization has enticed non-Western subjects to commodify their cultural identities. These were works located at the crossroads of two kinds of distorted gaze, the first involving the racial preconceptions about "traditional cults," the second dealing with the extreme pleasure of acquiring goods, a psychological state related to the identification of the subject that Sigmund Freud described as the attempt to conform to an "ideal ego."[9] Jungen's strategy was to fuse these two fields to show their internal bond. As curator Reid Shier pointed out, this transformation of fanciful trainers into Aboriginal curios suggested a peculiar form of potlatch, in which fashion would be sacrificed for "the illicit satisfaction of witnessing the evisceration of a bunch of two-hundred-dollar trainers."[10]

Jungen's own discussion of his work underlines how a consumer icon such as Nike Air Jordan trainers, which are based on the exploitation of sweatshop workers all the way from Mexico to Thailand, becomes a fetish item at the same time that it comments on how banal and market-driven cultural traditions have become in the contemporary world:

> I was interested in the ubiquitousness of native motifs, especially in Vancouver, and how they have been corrupted and applied and assimilated commercially, e.g., in the tourist industry. It was interesting to see how by simply manipulating the Air Jordan shoes you could evoke specific cultural traditions whilst simultaneously amplifying the process of cultural corruption and assimilation. The Nike "mask" sculptures seemed to articulate a paradoxical relationship between a consumerist artifact and an "authentic" native artifact.[11]

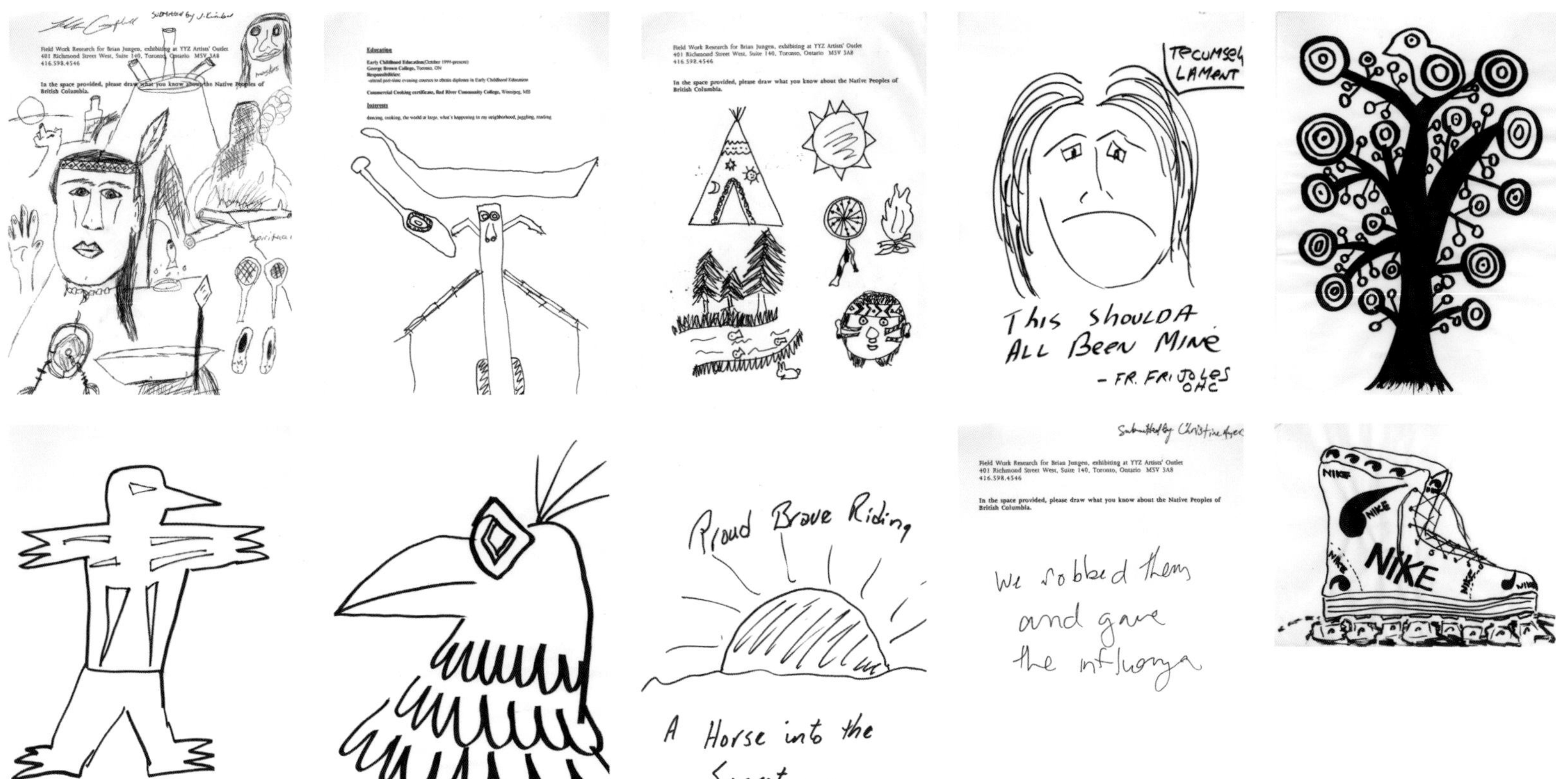

By comparing Western material fantasies and First Nations mythic characters, Jungen's trainers seem to debunk any pretence of Western superiority. No longer the (ephemeral) signifier of "cool," Nike trainers become, as one reviewer wrote, "ceremonial gear for the tribe of urban hipsters."[12] In avant-garde fashion, the montage-based beauty of Jungen's masks seems to signal the possibility that the allure of commodities can be defeated with a superior form of visual practice, a "sacrilegious" dissection of the "iconic" object.[13] They project back onto Western society all the suggestions of primitive delusion formerly attributed to so-called "totemic" societies, picturing capitalism as a variant of idolatry. In doing so, they symbolically retaliate against the way Aboriginal identities have been transformed into some sort of commercial lifestyle. Jungen's works position "ethnic" as a category of the service economy at a time when the market is booming with "exotic" therapeutic or spiritual practices that are ready-made to cater to postmodern anxieties, from ecological nostalgia and the preference for "natural remedies" to the search for metaphysical energies.

These masks and their associated meanings were nonetheless only one part of the original exhibition. On the walls of the Charles H. Scott Gallery, where *Prototypes for New Understanding* was first shown in Vancouver, Jungen also exhibited a handful of colourful vinyl mural drawings, which despite their cheerful appearance were in fact a concentration of ethnic prejudices. At a certain moment, Jungen had been practising a peculiar form of visual

Sketches solicited for wall drawings at Truck, Calgary, 1997, and at Charles H. Scott Gallery, Vancouver, 1999

Photos: Courtesy of Brian Jungen

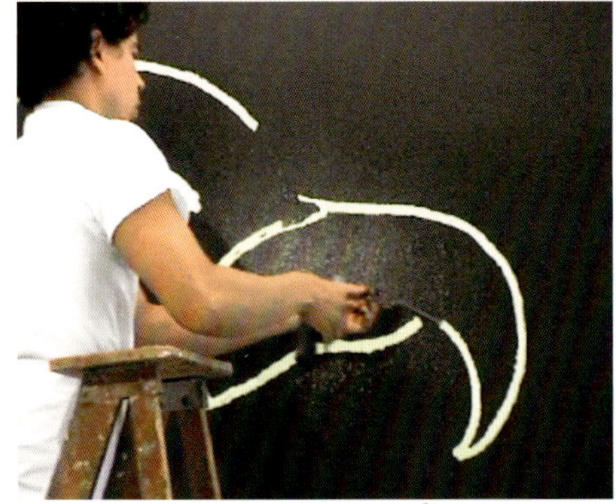

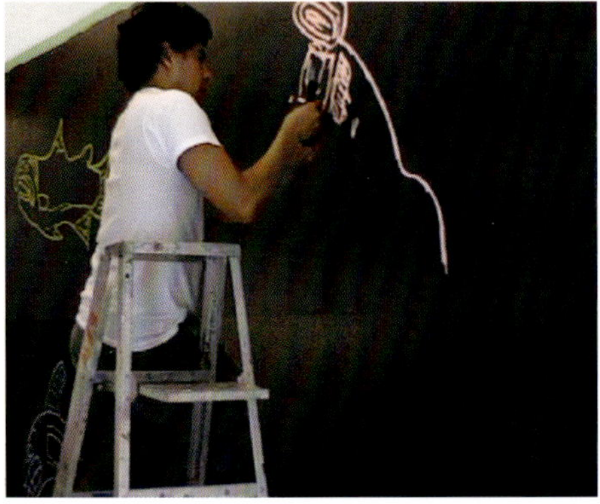

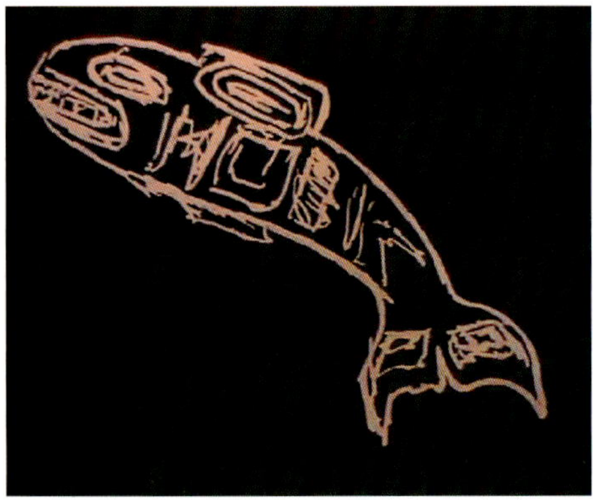

Brian Jungen installing wall drawings at Charles H. Scott Gallery, Vancouver, 1999
Photos: Courtesy of Brian Jungen

ethnography: soliciting passersby to draw for him images of their idea of "Indian art." The result was a collection of rather schematic and at times childish depictions of the usual clichés, "Indian" reduced to an almost cartoon-like simplicity: a smiling sun, a series of decorative whales, Aboriginal totem poles made of ridiculous primitive faces—which Jungen later transferred into "cheerful colour-fields." As the artist said in an interview, "it wasn't polite Indian art."[14] In fact, this was a collection derived to a great extent from images of Canadian ethnic stereotypes, ideologically driven and hammered down by advertising. With characteristic irony (the tool of choice of postcolonial critique at the end of the twentieth century[15]), Jungen focussed on "Indianness" as a social construction.[16]

Notwithstanding the relative control First Nations have claimed over their art and images and how they are circulated, Jungen shows that an Indian stereotype still exists. He also suggests that alongside the politics of self-representation, Aboriginal identity is always a cross-cultural construct and that it is used to market Canadian identity, which has absorbed First Nations mythology in creating its national ethos.[17] The imaginary of "Indian art," as recorded by Jungen's research, remains firmly defined by abjection and parody because the image of "the primitive" or Aboriginal continues to be part of the self-definition of modern national cultures.

Jungen addressed a visual culture that was traversed by political struggles for the recognition of Aboriginal treaties and rights during the 1990s in Canada. At the same time that First Nations struggles became increasingly politicized, "Indian" imagery was being used in airports and tourist shops, and there were even attempts to print First Nations designs on disposable napkins and cups.[18] The topic of Jungen's wall drawings, as curator Scott Watson has rightly argued, then, was "the identity of the viewer as much as that identity is perceived to be not 'Indian.'"[19] In effect, these drawings summarize the stereotyping of First Nations subjects as "the other" of mainstream Canadian society, and they show how consumer demand for Aboriginal objects and images constantly confirms and validates a clear-cut definition of ethnicity that is always infused with parody, mimicry and fear.

In that context, Jungen's wall drawings provide a frame of reference for his *Prototypes* very much as quaint museum murals do with archaeological and ethnographic evidence.[20] Although Jungen's masks are, by definition, movable artifacts that can migrate to a number of different locations and contexts,[21] murals can provide them with a critical context, ensuring that they are considered both as part of, and as a response to, the stereotyping of "Indian" art and culture as it happens in contemporary market society. If Jungen's *Prototypes* effectively suggest a new intercultural understanding, it is precisely because they are located at the crossroads of a number of racial and cultural mirages in what art history professor Charlotte Townsend-Gault has described as the "wallpapering" of habitus: the incorporation of "native" imagery into "the vast heaving mass of ephemeral and disposable forms" of the society of spectacle.[22] Rather than merely repudiating that process, Jungen amplifies the marketing and stereotyping of Indian culture that allows First Nations peoples to participate in the current economy and symbolic landscape and to transform their heritage into a form of capital.

If Jungen's masks are effectively *prototypes,*[23] it is because they project a futuristic product: a utopia in which street kids around the world will daydream about becoming Aboriginal dancers with the same gravitas with which they now "become" Michael Jordan when wearing Nike Air Jordan trainers. That is, Jungen's masks confront his mural drawings almost as if they were a market analysis of the very consumers who have been dutifully surveyed in the street to define their interests and desires. Essentially, after decoding what "people expect from Indian art," Jungen set out to design a new commodity that would capture these stereotypical expectations of Aboriginality. His *Prototypes* are a market fantasy like any other fashion product, a mixture of well-tested formulas (Nike trainers + Aboriginal curios) and the pretence of "the new." In other words, they are clearly recognizable as merchandise kept safely within the boundaries of the "Aboriginal culture" brand but with an inbuilt semblance of radicalism that is essential to capture the desires of the street-fashion victim. Instead of opposing the stereotype, Jungen fulfills and *exceeds* the expectations of the neo-ethnic market in a single go. The extraordinary success of the *Prototypes*[24] attests to the feasibility of the entire operation—consumers badly want their fetishes.

3. SHOE ME YOUR FETISH

> I defy any lover of modern art to adore a painting as a
> fetishist adores a shoe.
> —Georges Bataille, 1930[25]

Quite consistently, when speaking about making his *Prototypes,* Brian Jungen suggests that he considered them to be like bodies or corpses subjected to the sacrilegious intervention of the pathologist and/or taxidermist: "I went to a sports store and purchased a number of pairs of Air Jordan sneakers and began to dissect them, which in itself was interesting—in that it was almost a sacrilegious act: cutting up and 'destroying' these iconic, collectible (and expensive) shoes."[26] This new Dr. Frankenstein *dissects* those corpses to give life to new beings: this sole vocabulary suggests to what extent Jungen understood that he was working with objects whose importance for the contemporary consumer lies precisely in the fact that they are not perceived as inert matter but as quasi-living power objects.

There must be powerful reasons why modernity invested feet and shoes with an extraordinary sexual and aesthetic meaning. From the very moment nineteenth-century French psychiatry defined sexual deviation—the claim that the goal of normal desire and procreation could be "fixated" by the "erotomania" of a dangerous substitute[27]—feet and shoes have been central in our representation of modern fetishism. In the first renditions of psychoanalytic theory, Sigmund Freud gave them a particularly significant role in his discussion of the substitutes of the sexual object, claiming that feet are an archaic sexual symbol whereas shoes

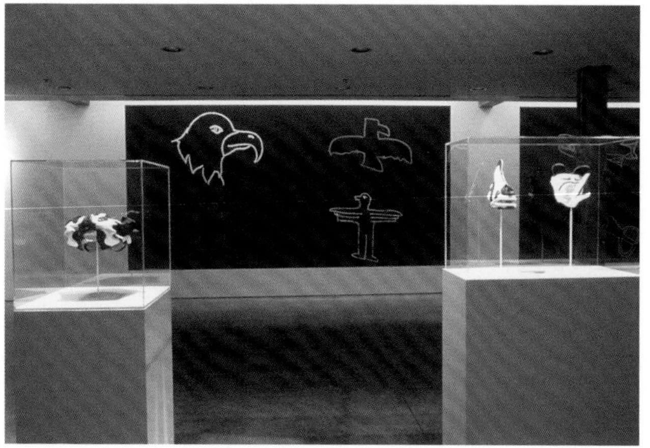

Installation at Charles H. Scott
Gallery, Vancouver, 1999
Photo: Brian Jungen

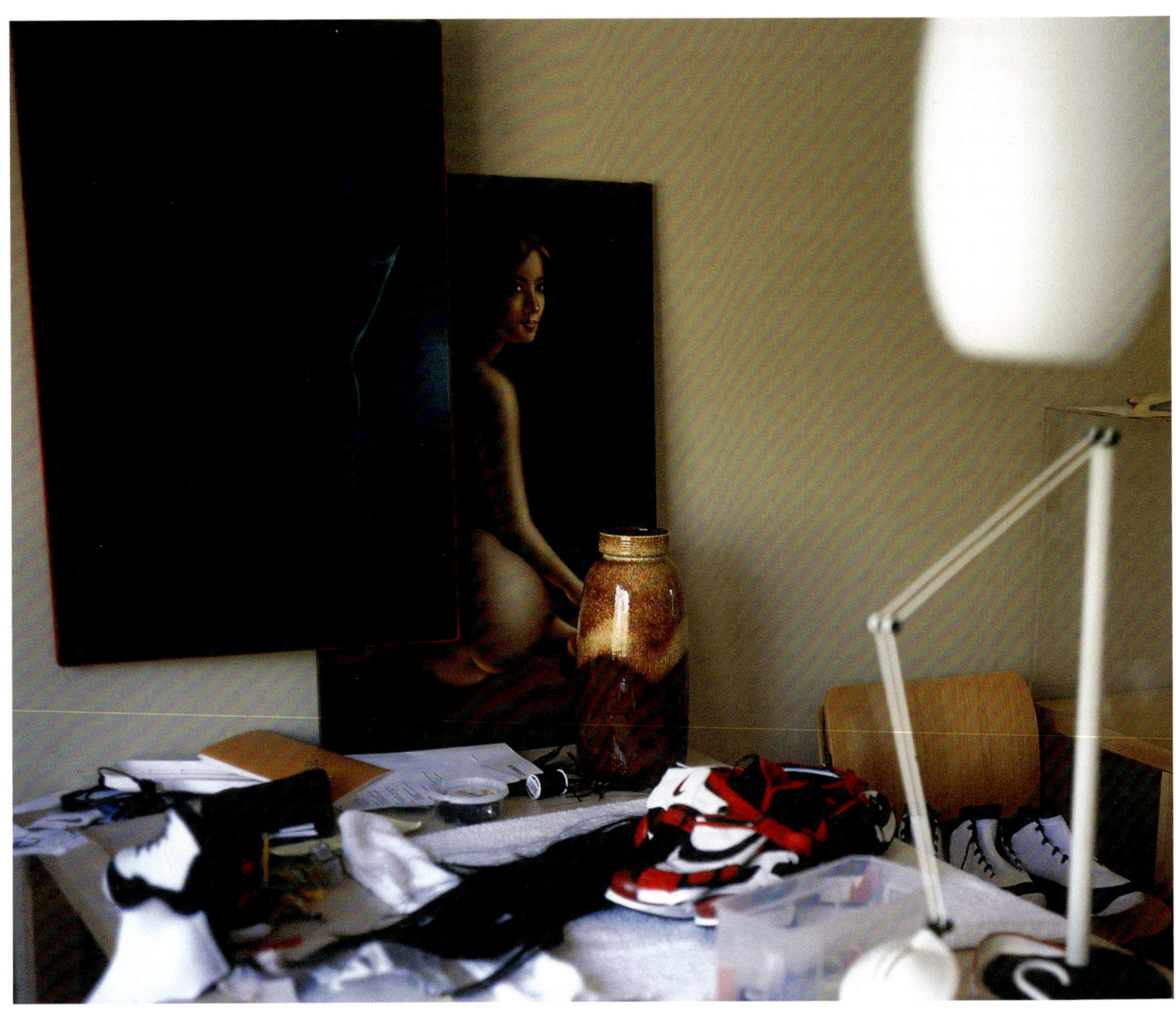

usually stand in for female genitalia,[28] a symbolism frequently mirrored in surrealist objects from Salvador Dali to Meret Oppenheim and in the early writings of Georges Bataille, who claims that the seductiveness of feet goes hand in hand with their "ignoble life," their relation with dirt and debasement.[29]

Aside from this theoretical genealogy, Jungen chose trainers for very specific historical reasons. Implicit in his *Prototypes* is a crucial sociological observation: shoes (and particularly designer trainers) are the contemporary consumer's mask, a tool for the Western ritual of impersonation that—as Jungen says in passing—involves "functional or ceremonial purposes."[30] That shoes are a shamanic tool of sorts can be easily attested to by advertisements, which usually portray them as quasi-magically transforming their user, fusing the phantasm of the sport's idol with the consumer. When we buy trainers, we are sold the idea that they transmogrify (us) nerds into suburban superheroes, bridging the divide between our pathetic daily lives and television mythology. Some years after Jungen produced his *Prototypes,* artist Carlos Amorales reached a similar conclusion about his own *Flames Maquiladora* (2002):

Production of *Prototypes for New Understanding* in artist's studio
Photo: Brian Jungen

34

Leading brands like Nike, Reebok or Puma specialise in designing shoes for the practice of different mainstream sports such as Baseball, Football or Basketball. These are the brands used by top-class multimillionaire athletes and, simultaneously, by the underdog, amateur and wannabe sportsmen. In a sort of Cinderella effect, wearing such brands provides the wider young population with the illusion of coming closer to stardom, in order to achieve the high-score democratic dream of economic mobility and success.[31]

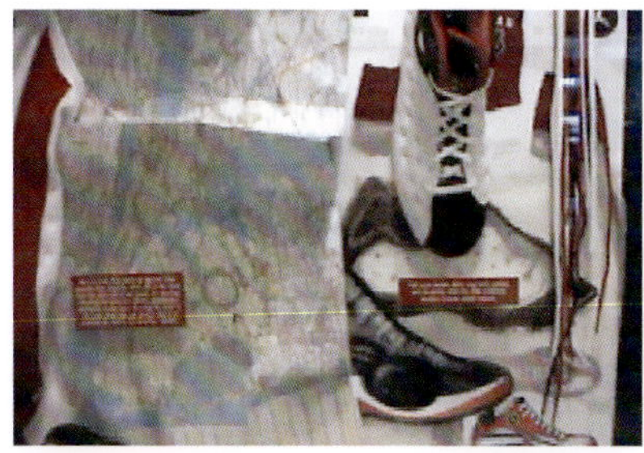

Like jewels and watches, shoes are meant to be objects of contemplation as much for their wearers as for others. They are, in fact, vessels of desire and fantasy: objects that seem to have a life of their own at the same time that they operate as mirrors of our identity. It is this role of Nike shoes as mediators between the individual and an ideal ego that Jungen disturbs by turning the mirror into an Aboriginal artifact: Michael Jordan is replaced by an undefined "totemic" deity. Now we can see why Jungen's willingness to play with stereotypes of "Indianhood" is so productive. In dissecting expensive shoes to produce pseudo-Aboriginal masks, in assembling plastic lawn chairs to emulate the skeleton of a whale (*Shapeshifter,* 2000) and in overtly devoting an excessive amount of artistry to the production of a pile of ten industrial-style pallets (*Untitled,* 2001), the artist aims to confuse economic and cultural values and to subject the viewer to the alienating experience of being unable to assess the status of objects. It is this disorientation that, seen in perspective, has had a major role in the critical thinking of capitalism.

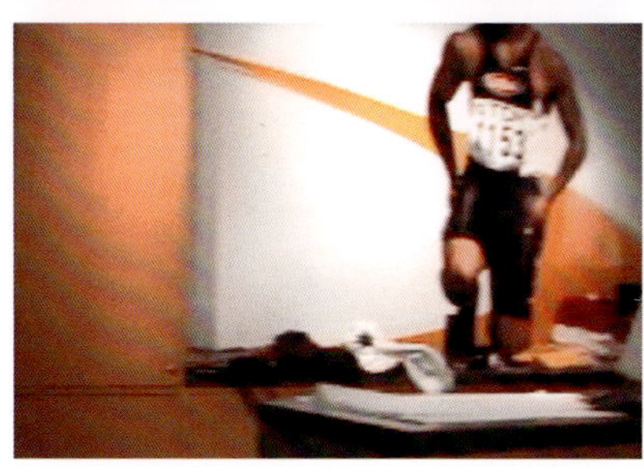

4. THE SAVAGE'S VIEWPOINT

As writer and scholar William Pietz has shown, "fetish" is a word deeply rooted in the history of complex transcultural transactions provoked by colonialism. Born out of the cross-cultural interaction on the West African coast in the seventeenth and eighteenth centuries, the *fetisso*—a neologism probably derived from *feitiço,* a mediaeval Portuguese word that meant "witchcraft" or "magical practice," which came from the Latin *facticius,* or "manufactured,"[32]—served European merchants and colonizers by describing those religions that did not exactly match their classical notion of idolatry but were believed to contribute to the Africans' different economic valuation of material objects.[33] Beginning with the Enlightenment, "fetish" became the category of choice for discussing the way individuals or cultures attributed social or personal values to material objects beyond their "natural" value as instruments,[34] either because an object was eroticized to the point of obstructing "normal" sexual behaviour or because utility and rationality did not seem to rule economic exchanges.

Jungen's transformation of an object of mystical identification—the Nike Air Jordan shoe—to the simulation of a "primitive" religious object—a First Nations mask—is, uncanny as it might seem, similar to the development of Karl Marx's theory of "commodity fetishism." According to Marx, in capitalist societies

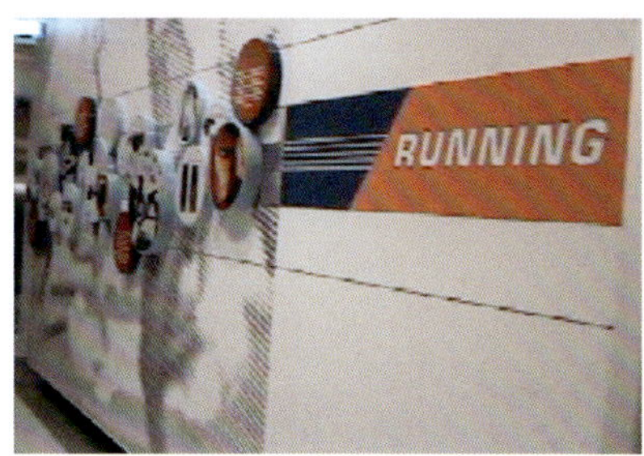

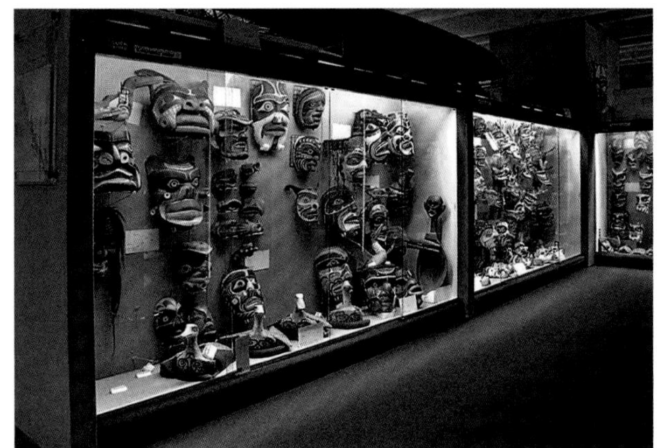

commodities take on an apparently magical quality that has consumers
attributing to them an inherent value that is independent of their origin in human
labour and entirely based on what they can receive in exchange. In the first
edition of *Das Kapital* (1867), Marx spoke mostly of the "mystic character" of the
commodity to explain the way in which social relationships were made manifest in
the modern subject by attaching a price (an abstract rate of exchange) to objects.
However, by the second edition (1872) Marx decided to present merchandise as a
modern "fetish," where the products of labour were construed as things that were
simultaneously "perceptible and imperceptible by the senses," sensuous and
supersensuous.[35] In doing so, Marx firmly rooted our critiques of the commodity
in questions of how the exchange of money and objects mediates our social
relations. By aligning modern economic behaviour with a primitivist stereotype,
Marx showed that the commodity works as an effective object of power, as a
material *and* as a supernatural agent that can be treated as if it has sacred
qualities and magical powers worthy of daily worship. In presenting economics as
a religion of everyday life, Marx wanted to suggest that our devotion to capital
cannot be simply exorcised by thought, for it constitutes both the materiality and
spectrality[36] of our social practice, traversed by the continuous impression that
we deal with superior and invisible powers.

In any event, for Karl Marx, Sigmund Freud or the surrealists who
once displayed French Catholic images as "fétiches européens,"[37] the best way
to expose the workings of modern subjects was to apply to them their own
representation of savages and primitives. As William Pietz has eloquently argued,
this process produces an effect akin to an anamorphism, that is, a distorted
spatial projection appears normal when viewed from a particular angle or through
a suitable mirror. In Marx's writings, it is only from a "savage" point of view that
it is possible to feign a new understanding of our own culture. If the notion of
fetishism is pregnant with all kinds of Western misconceptions about the
"primitive mentality," when projected onto modernity this mentality in turn lifts
the veil of rationality that covers standard practices:

> In Marx's writing… the bourgeois capitalist is perceived as
> himself a fetishist, one whose fetish, capital, is believed by its
> deluded cultists to embody *(super)natural causal powers of*
> *value formation,* but which is recognized by the savage… and
> worker… as having no real power outside its *social power to*
> *command* the labor activity of real individuals… Marx evoked
> the "savage" subject of religious fetishism as a (potentially
> theoretical) viewpoint *outside* capitalism…[38]

Thus, if the notion of the fetish was somehow ethnographic delirium coined by
European colonizers to describe West African societies, it became an accurate
social category once it was redirected to study the "civilized man" who devised it.
Similarly, by deciding to reshape cultural *stereotypes* into the prototypes of a new
understanding, Brian Jungen has reinvested his materials with the sacred quality

Northwest Coast First Nations
masks displayed in Visible
Storage at the Museum of
Anthropology, Vancouver
Photo: Monika Szewczyk, Courtesy of
Museum of Anthropology, Vancouver

of ceremonial objects, thereby repoliticizing a primitivist icon, the First Nations
mask, and making it more than a mere curio that can be bought and sold.

Jungen's *Prototypes* may be seen as an attempt to rescue these objects
from becoming commodities. If capitalism needs to capture non-Western power
objects, it is in part because they remain dangerous to the extent that they bear
witness to the prior existence of other forms of social agency, that is, other ways
of understanding motivations, causes, affects and effects—all of which we dismis-
sively call sorcery. Brian Jungen reactivates these alternative social modalities
through a continual process of transformation rendered, as the title *Shapeshifter*
suggests, by sculptures "in a kind of flux,"[39] by objects that swing between inertia
and fantasy, banality and metaphysics. This ambivalence constitutes their power:
rather than attempting to fuse different cultural traditions, they suggest an
unstable world in which the complexity of economic cycles and the dilemmas of
the postcolonial condition prevent ontological stability.

Variant I (2002), a square conflux of several Nike sneakers sewn together
to produce a crystal-like surface, is an example of this flux. Itself a variation on
the *Prototypes, Variant I* may reference the overall pictorial field of a work by
Jackson Pollock or the accumulative logic of neo-Dada assemblages, but above
all it is a mandala of the global economy opening to the four corners of the earth.
It also epitomizes the way Jungen's works keep viewers off balance, subjecting
objects and concepts to an anamorphic process. *Variant I* oscillates from artifact
to sculpture to consumer object, showing the viewer a glimpse of a different
material world. This, to be sure, is not the world as seen from an Aboriginal
viewpoint, nor a synthesis of the views of the West and the rest. No possible
perspective, no rational order, is able to accommodate those viewpoints. However,
because it is always shifting as if driven by some sort of cultural cubism, because
it is more than a view of the commodity world, *Variant I* compels viewers to
consider how their world view passes through a hallucinatory filter that yields
multifarious, almost paranoid views, as if they were seeing through the very "eyes"
of the commodity.

I would like to specially thank Monika Szewczyk for the many ways she helped me during
the writing of this article, by providing me with reading materials, feedback and references
without which I would not have been able to complete this text.

NOTES

1. See Serge Gruzinski, *La guerra de las imágenes: De Cristobal Colón a "Blade Runner" (1492–2019)* (México: Fondo de Cultura Economica, 1994), 51–53.

2. Fray Toribio de Benavente Motolinia, *Memoriales,* ed. Nancy Joe Dyer (México: El Colegio de México, 1996), 228. See also Gruzinski, 67.

3. Motolinia does not indicate the location of these events, but it is likely that they pertain to the Nahua Indians who made up most of the population in the central highlands of today's Mexico.

4. In this respect, see the testimony of Robert Joseph, "Behind the mask" in Peter Macnair, Robert Joseph and Bruce Grenville, *Down from the Shimmering Sky: Masks of the Northwest Coast* (Vancouver: Douglas & McIntyre and Seattle: University of Washington Press, 1998), 26.

5. See definition in *Merriam-Webster's Collegiate Dictionary,* 11th ed. (Springfield, MA: Merriam-Webster, 2004), also available online at www.m-w.com/cgi-bin/dictionary?book=Dictionary&va=refraction&x=15&y=15.

6. "I do not call them masks, because they have never been used for ceremonial purposes (Native or basketball)." Jens Hoffmann, "Brian Jungen," *Flash Art* 36, no. 231 (July–September 2003): 86.

7. "The vitrines reference the hermetic displays of traditional masks in anthropologic collections. I wanted the 'prototypes' to have the same institutional 'authenticity.' When I first exhibited the series in Vancouver, there were a few iconoclastic accusations, but most people understood my secular position." (Hoffmann, 86.)

8. "I am both dismayed and impressed by how the information technology arm of globalization has opened up possibilities for remote native reserves like mine. My band has discovered the marketability of its location and cultural heritage. Such ventures might confuse autonomy and community pride with profit margins but puts the individual behind the wheel of his or her own cultural exploitation. I think this kind of relationship is preferable to developing positive identities, especially considering the disparaging alternative: welfare." (Hoffmann, 88.)

9. See Sigmund Freud, "Group Psychology and the Analysis of the Ego" in *Civilization, Society and Religion* (London: Penguin, 1985), 134–40.

10. Reid Shier, "Cheap" in *Brian Jungen* (Vancouver: Charles H. Scott Gallery, 2000), 3.

11. Matthew Higgs, "Brian Jungen in conversation with Matthew Higgs" in *Brian Jungen* (Vienna: Secession, 2003), 25.

12. Beverly Cramp, "Contemporary Mask-Makers Carve a New Niche," *Georgia Straight,* June 17–24, 1999: 102.

13. Higgs, 24.

14. Ibid., 22–23.

15. In this respect, see Jungen's candid statement to writer Michael Turner: "The wall drawings developed after I began to exhaust the rounds of abject stereotypes I was creating in a period of drawing I did a few years ago. These drawings could represent an ironic strategy adopted by many artists working with identity politics in the late eighties to the mid-nineties." Michael Turner, "Prototypes + Petroglyphs + Pop," *Mix* 26, no. 3 (Winter 2001): 31.

16. Higgs, 24.

17. Daniel Francis, *The Imaginary Indian: The Image of the Indian in Canadian Culture* (Vancouver: Arsenal Pulp Press, 1992), 186–88.

18. For a remarkable analysis of the current situation of First Nations imagery in Canada at the Museum of Anthropology, University of British Columbia, see Charlotte Townsend-Gault, "Circulating Aboriginality," *Journal of Material Culture* 9 (2): 183–211.

19. Scott Watson, "Shapeshifter" in *Brian Jungen* (Vancouver: Contemporary Art Gallery, 2001), 16.

20. The ethnographic methodology of Jungen's research was entirely self-conscious: "I wanted to try to extract those images (abject or earnest) out of the imagination of the public consciousness and reproduce them as colour compositions arranged within the framework of classical ethnographic research." (Turner, 31.)

21. As a matter of fact, this writer saw them first in Helsinki as part of the *ARS 01* exhibition at the Kiasma Museum in 2001.

22. Townsend-Gault, 192–97.

23. The artist, in fact, insists that because they "don't function as masks, only mimic them," he prefers to call them "prototypes." (Hoffmann, 86.)

24. Michael Turner's statement in his interview with Jungen is in this sense symptomatic.

25. Georges Bataille, "L'Esprit moderne et le jeu des transpositions," *Documents,* 2nd year, no. 8, (1930): 49. Reproduced in [Georges Bataille] *Documents. Doctrines. Archéologie. Beaux-Arts. Ethnographie.* Préface de Denis Hollier, 2 vols. (Paris: Jean Michel Place, 1991). Quoted by Dawn Ades, "Surrealism: Fetishism's Job" in Anthony Shelton, ed., *Fetishism: Visualising Power and Desire* (London: The South Bank Centre–Lund Humphries, 1995), 68.

26. Higgs, 24.

27. Robert A. Nye, "The Medical Origins of Sexual Fetishism" in Emily Apter and William Pietz, eds., *Fetishism as Cultural Discourse* (Ithaca and London: Cornell University Press, 1993), 18.

28. Sigmund Freud, *Tres ensayos de teoría sexual* (1905), vol. VII, *Obras completas* (Buenos Aires: Amorrortu, 1978), 141.

29. See Georges Bataille, "The Big Toe" in Georges Bataille, *Visions of Excess: Selected Writings, 1927–1939,* ed. and trans. Allan Stoekl (Minneapolis: University of Minnesota Press, 1985), 20–23.

30. Higgs, 25.

31. See Amorales's statement in *SLG* 5 (London: South London Gallery, 2002), a newspaper produced for the exhibition *20 million Mexicans can't be wrong*. Amorales's *Flames Maquiladora* transformed the gallery into a sweatshop where the audience provided free labour for the production of red-leather wrestling trainers, which were to be sold for the economic benefit of the artist. It is interesting how different the operations of these two artists were, considering the similarity of their premises.

32. William Pietz, "The problem of the fetish, I" *Res. Anthropology and Aesthetics* 9 (Spring 1985): 5.

33. William Pietz, "The problem of the fetish, II," *Res. Anthropology and Aesthetics* 13 (Spring 1987): 39–41.

34. Ibid., 45.

35. In developing this argument, I have referred to a Spanish edition of *Das Kapital* that includes the different versions of Marx's chapter on the commodity: Karl Marx, *El capital: Crítica de la Economía Política,* ed. Pedro Scaron (México: Siglo XXI editores, 1975), vol. I-1, 87–102, and vol. I-3, 1006–16. I have also used an online English edition, based on the translation of Samuel Moore and Edward Aveling and published by Progress Publishers, Moscow, which is available at: www.marxists.org/archive/marx/works/1867-c1/.

36. On this issue, see Jacques Derrida, *The Spectres of Marx: The State of the Debt, the Work of Mourning, & the New International,* trans. Peggy Kamuf (London: Routledge, 1994).

37. See Dawn Ades's discussion of the exhibition the surrealists organized to counter the Colonial Exhibition in Paris in 1931. (Ades, 68.)

38. William Pietz, "Fetishism and Materialism: The Limits of Theory in Marx," in Apter and Pietz, *Fetishism as Cultural Discourse,* 141, 143 (italics in original text).

39. Higgs, 28.

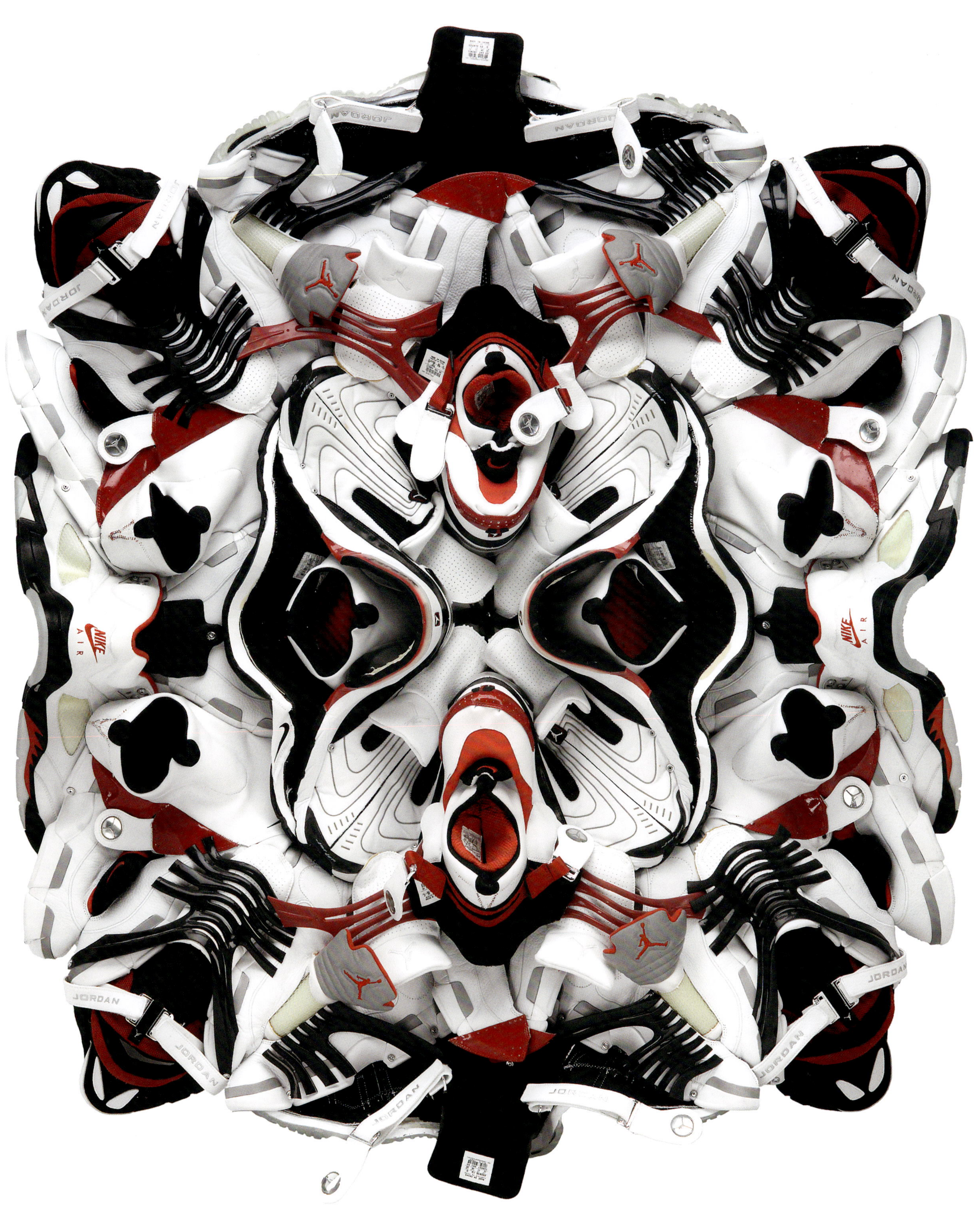

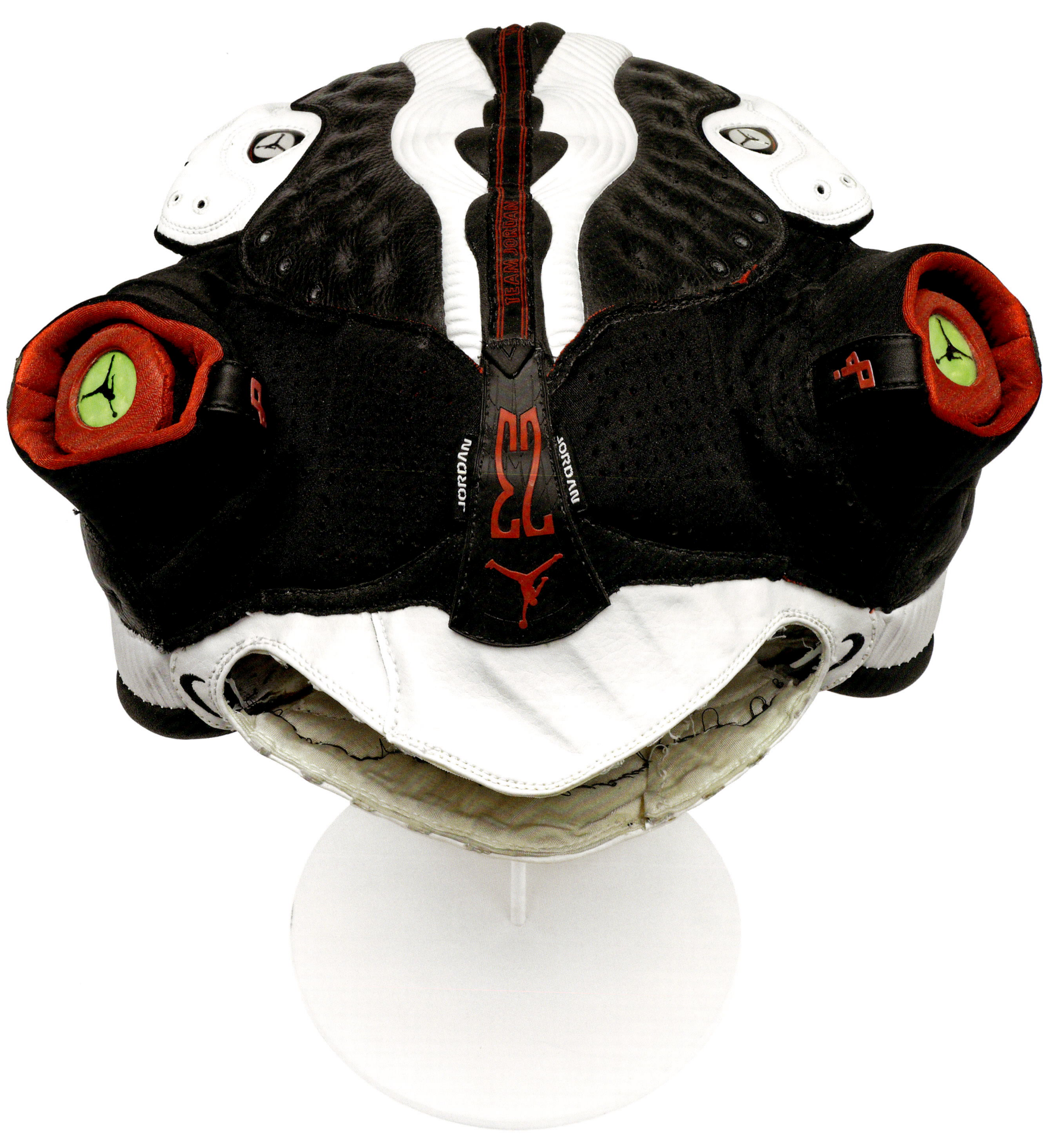

Prototype for New Understanding #1, 1998
Nike Air Jordans
17.3 x 37.4 x 34.5 cm (6 3/4" x 14 3/4" x 13 3/8")
Collection of the artist
Photos: Trevor Mills, Vancouver Art Gallery

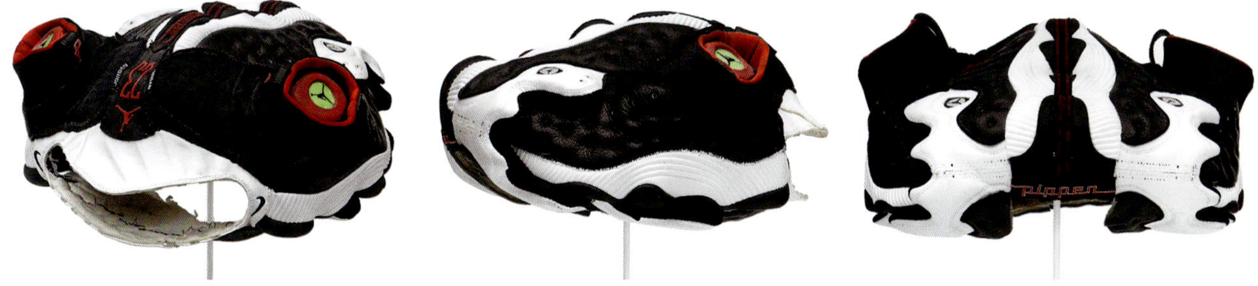

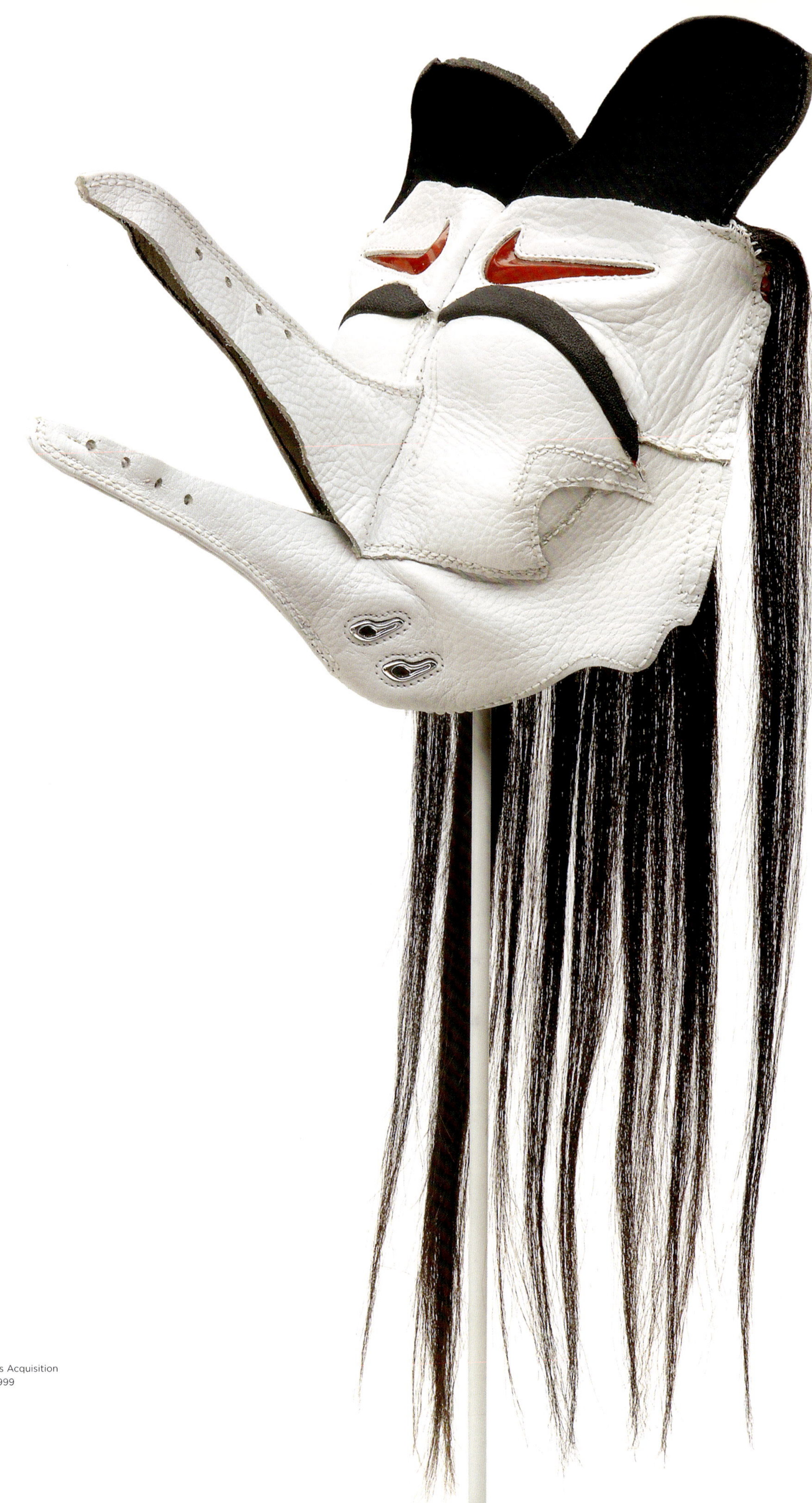

Prototype for New Understanding #2, 1998
Nike Air Jordans, human hair
48.9 x 21 x 25.5 cm (19 1/4" x 8 1/4" x 10")
Collection of the Vancouver Art Gallery
Purchased with the financial support of the Canada Council for the Arts Acquisition
Assistance Program and the Vancouver Art Gallery Acquisition Fund, 1999
Photo: Trevor Mills, Vancouver Art Gallery

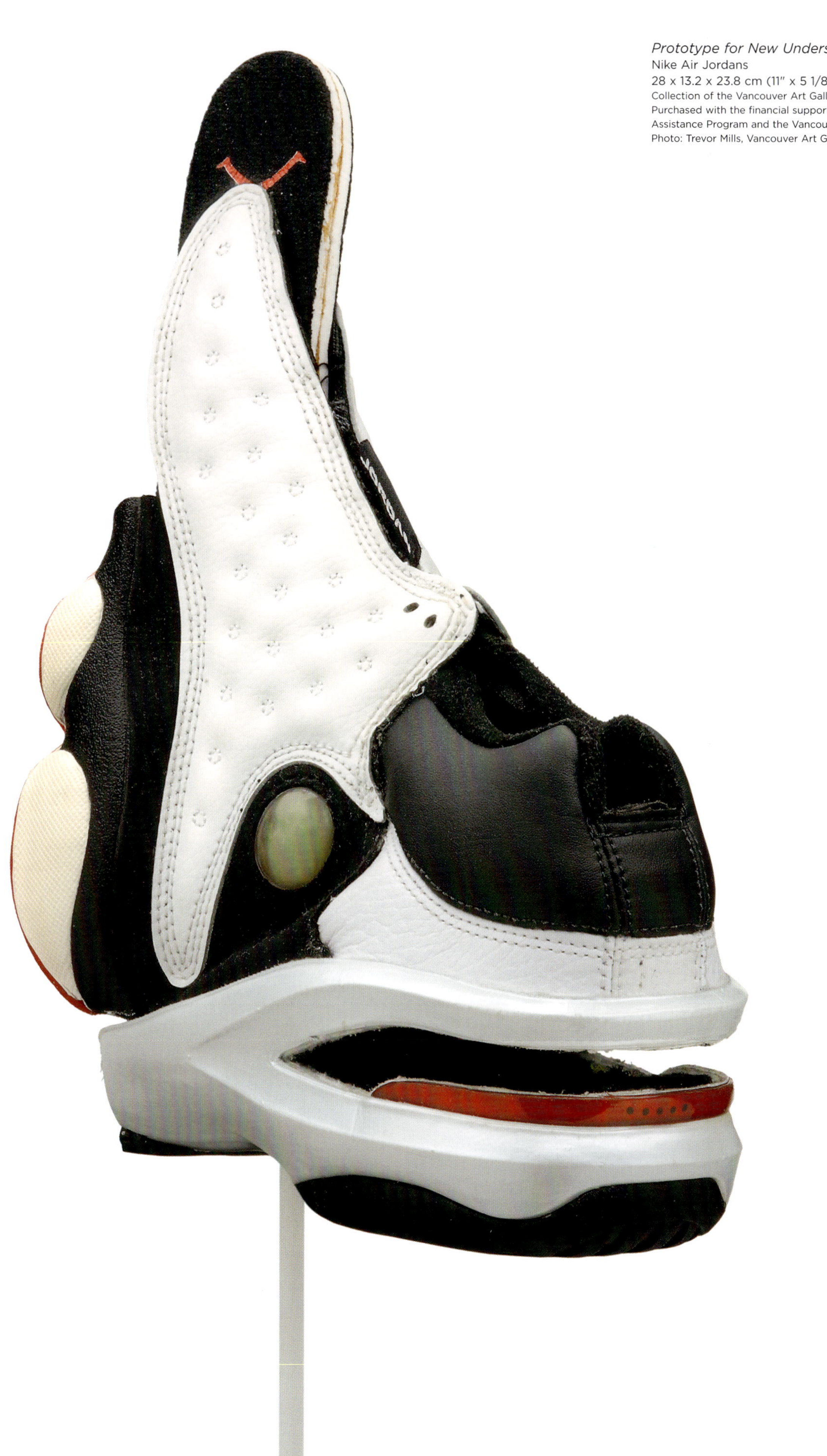

Prototype for New Understanding #3, 1999
Nike Air Jordans
28 x 13.2 x 23.8 cm (11" x 5 1/8" x 9 3/8")
Collection of the Vancouver Art Gallery
Purchased with the financial support of the Canada Council for the Arts Acquisition
Assistance Program and the Vancouver Art Gallery Acquisition Fund, 1999
Photo: Trevor Mills, Vancouver Art Gallery

Prototype for New Understanding #4, 1998
Nike Air Jordans, human hair
45.7 x 34 x 17.8 cm (18" x 13 5/8" x 7")
Collection of Claudia Beck and Andrew Gruft, Vancouver
Photos: Trevor Mills, Vancouver Art Gallery

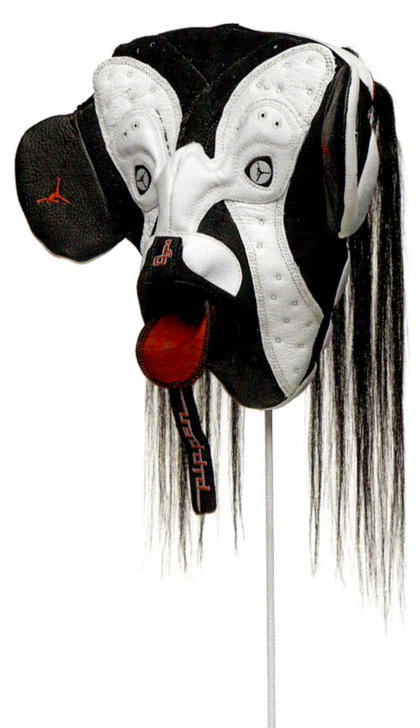
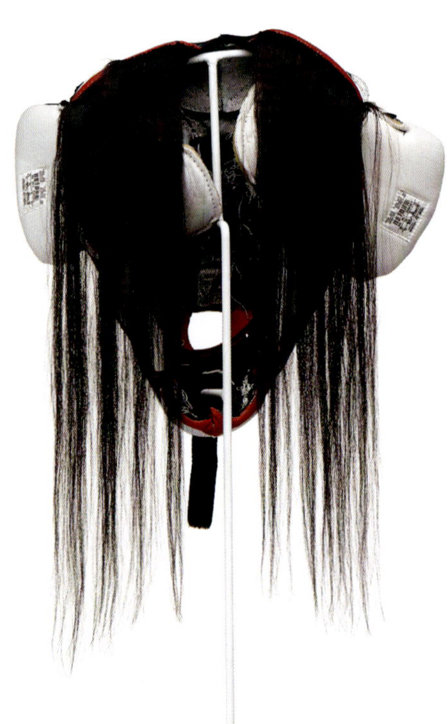
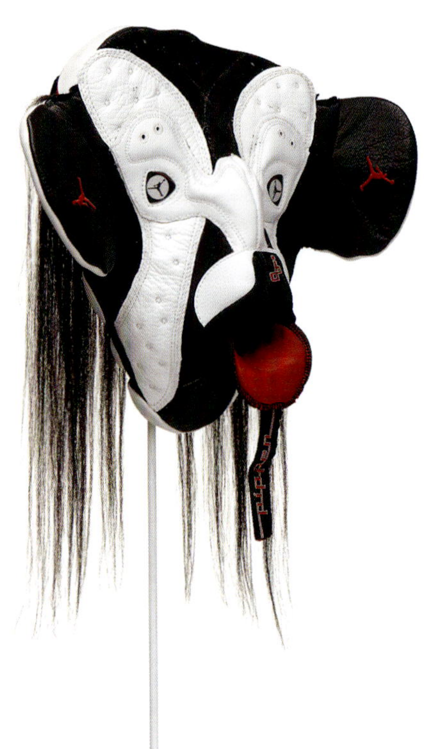

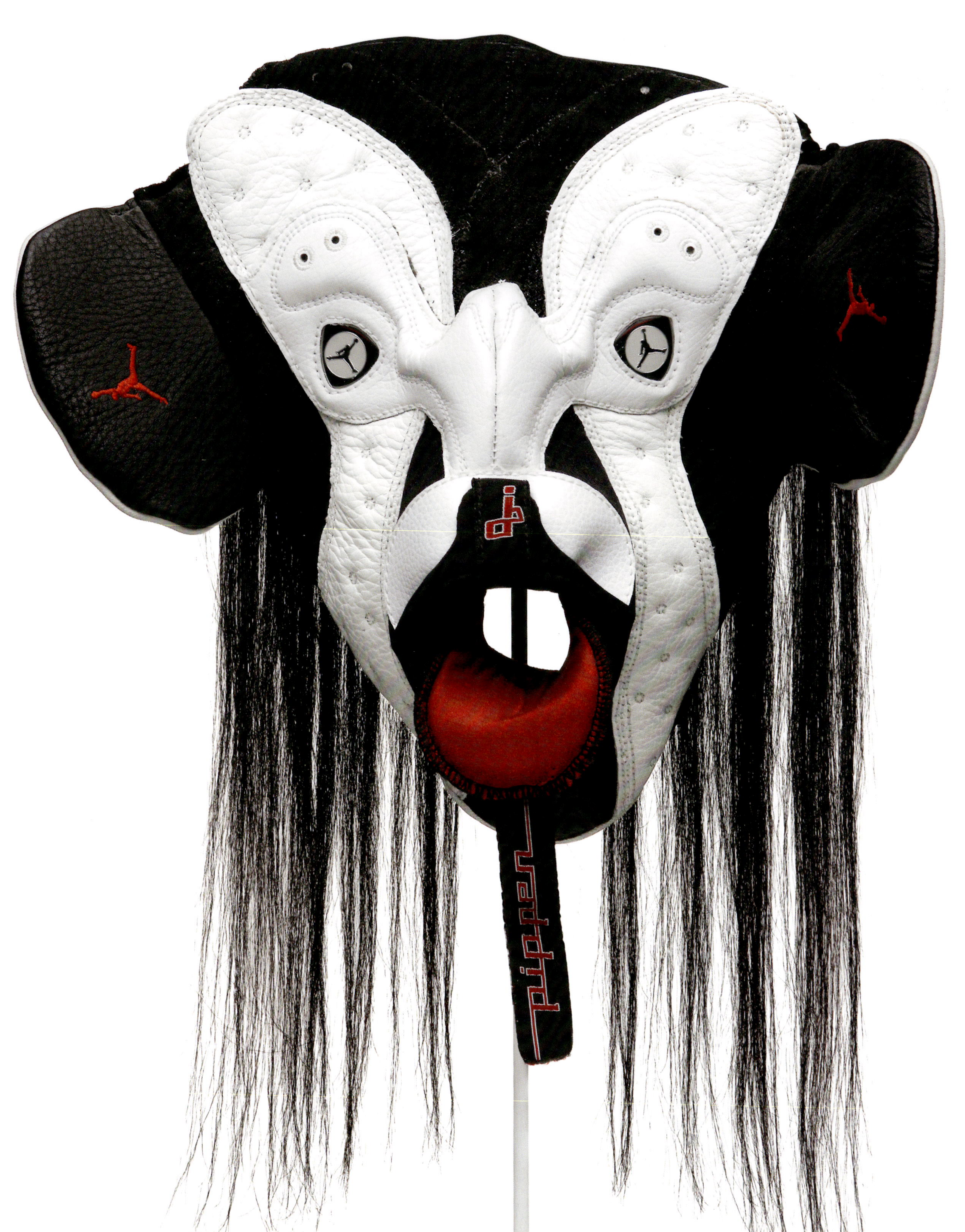
jd
pippen

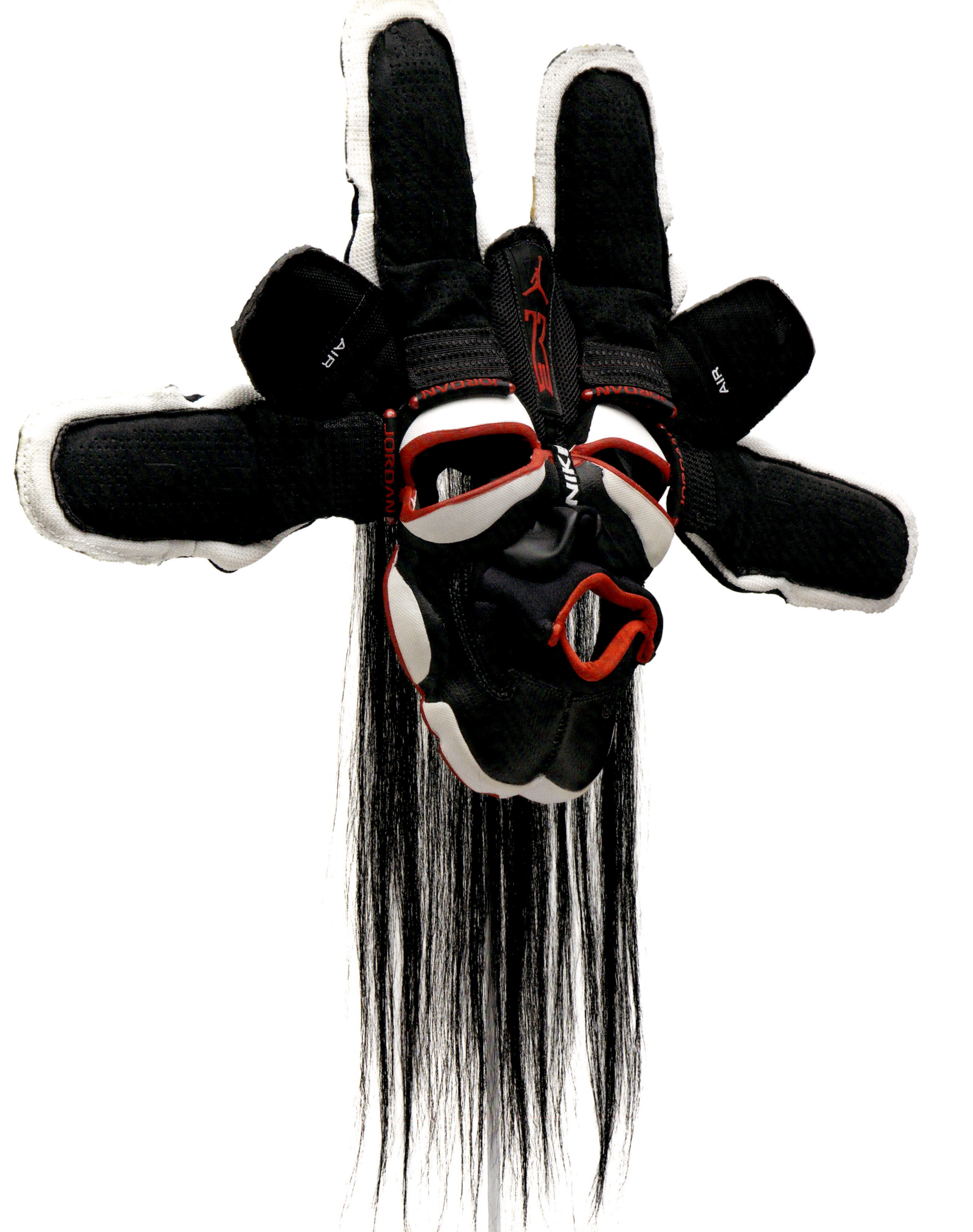

OPPOSITE:
Prototype for New Understanding #5, 1999
Nike Air Jordans, human hair
55.8 x 68.6 x 12.7 cm (22" x 27" x 5")
Collection of Douglas Coupland, Vancouver
Photo: Trevor Mills, Vancouver Art Gallery

Prototype for New Understanding #6, 1999
Nike Air Jordans
43.2 x 30.5 x 15.2 cm (17" x 12" x 6")
Collection of the Art Gallery of Ontario, Toronto
Purchased with financial support of the Canada Council for the Arts Acquisition
Assistance Program and with the assistance of the E. Wallace Fund, 2001
Photos: Sean Weaver, Art Gallery of Ontario

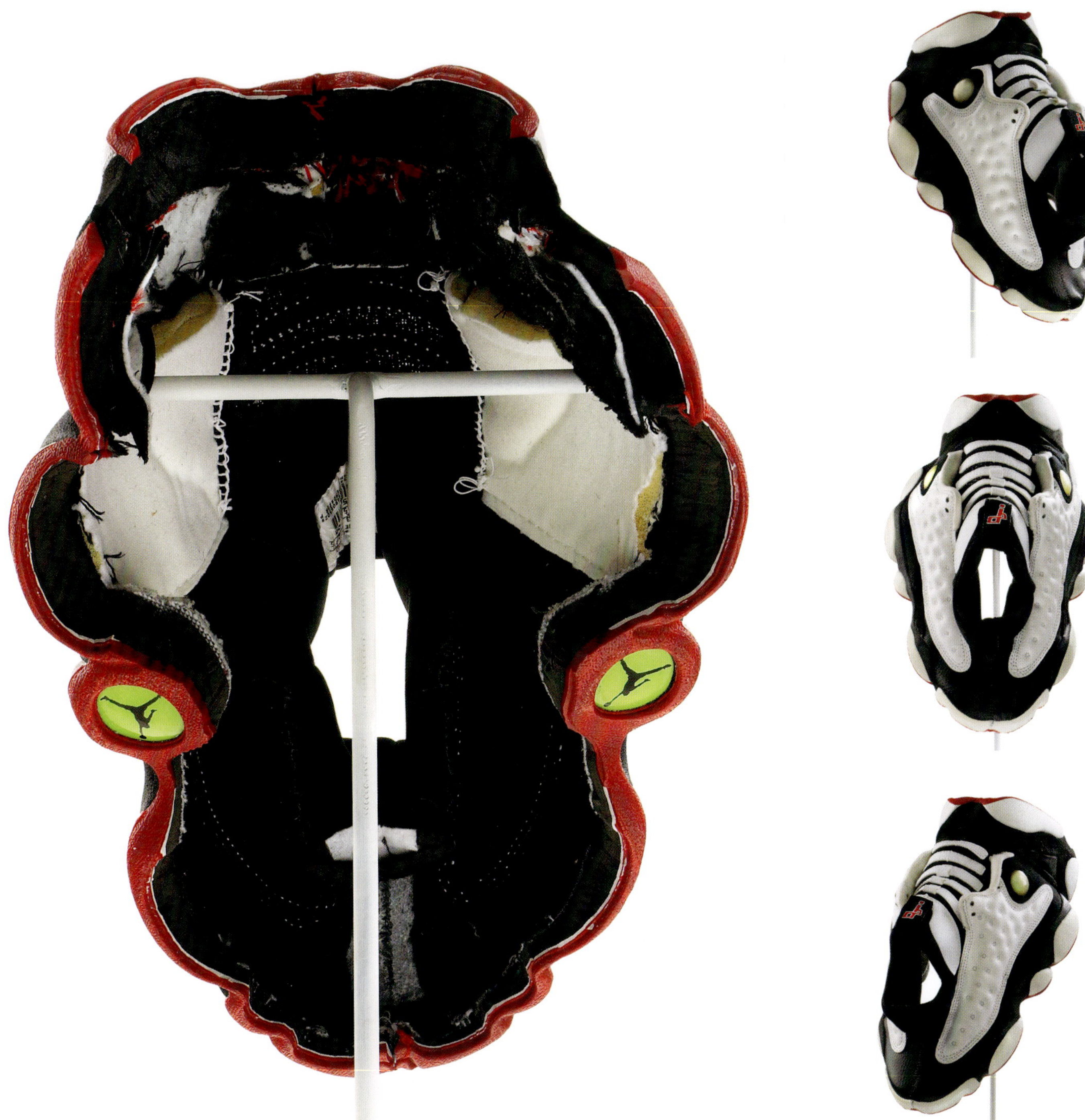

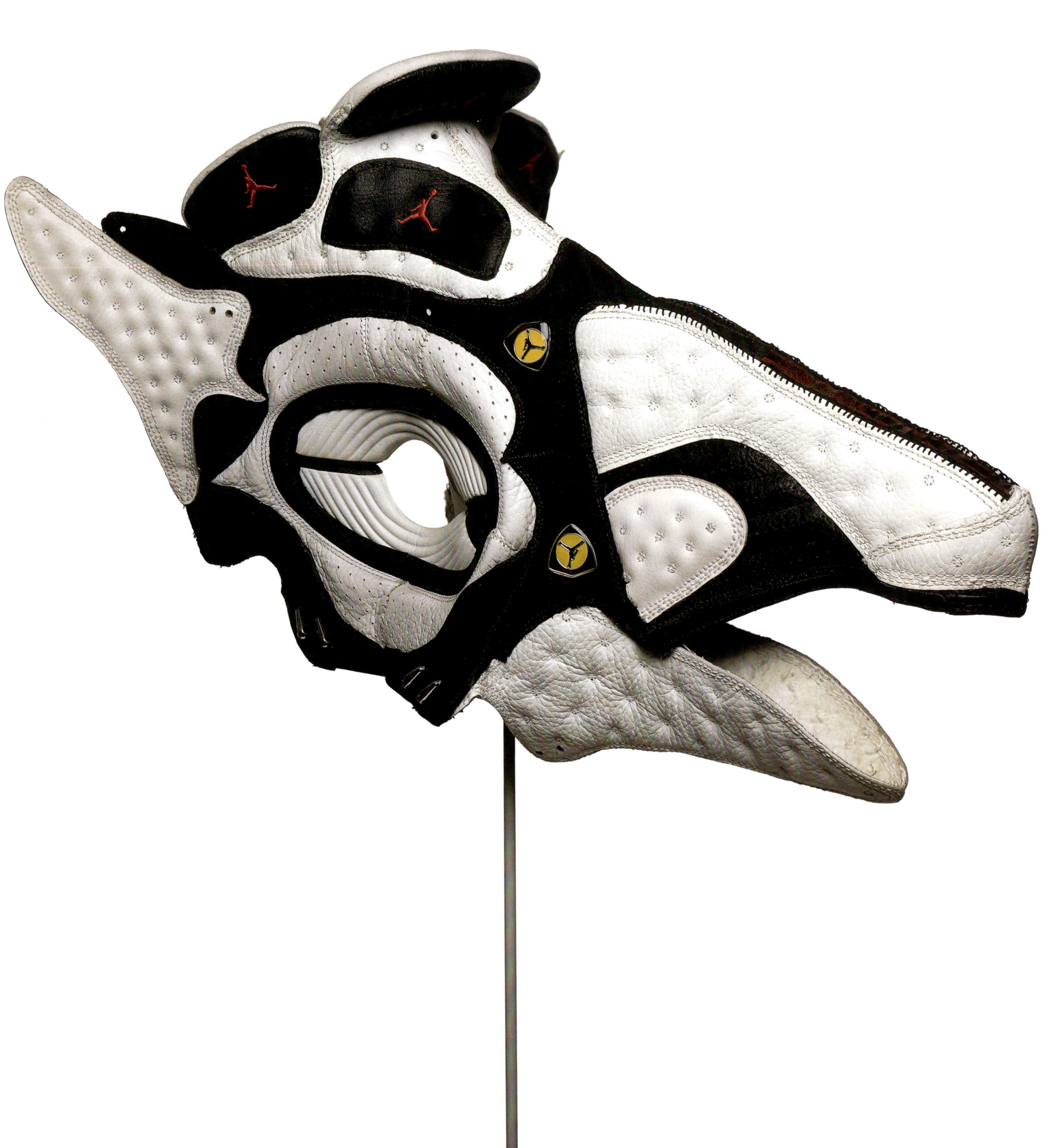

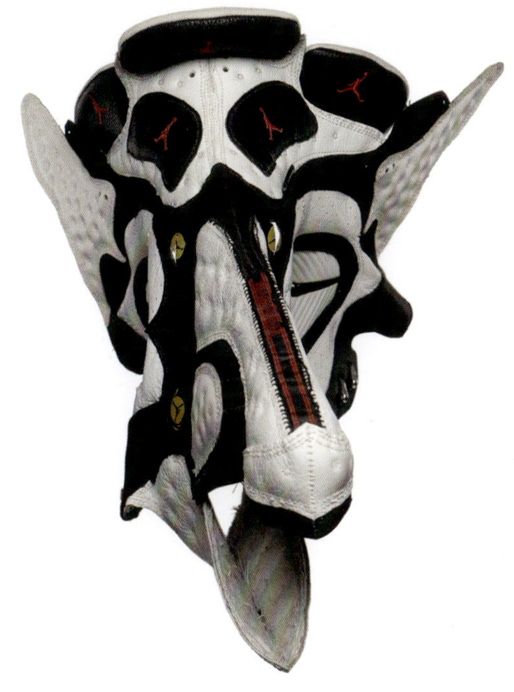

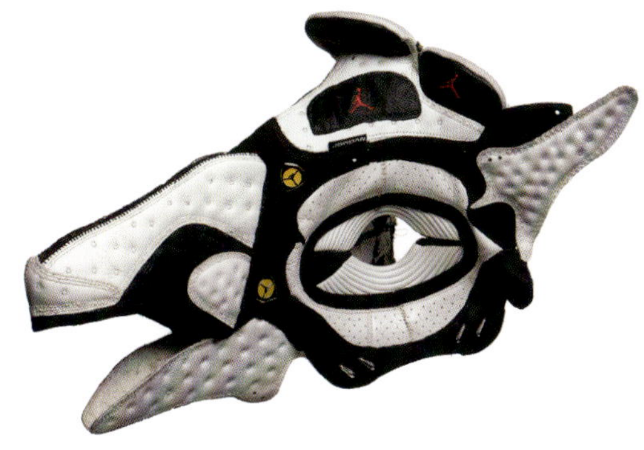

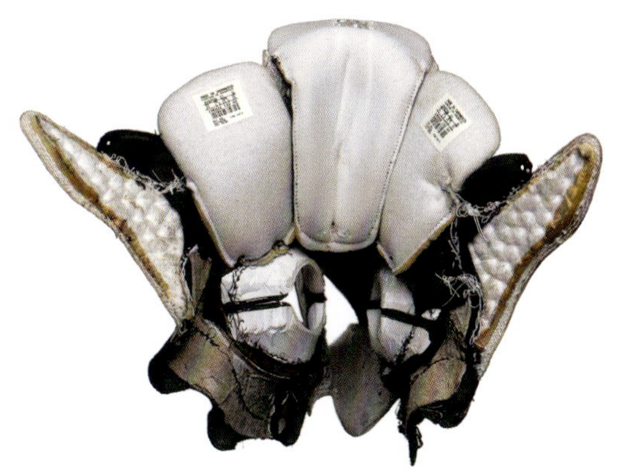

Prototype for New Understanding #7, 1999
Nike Air Jordans
27.9 x 35.6 x 55.9 cm (11" x 14" x 22")
Collection of Joe Friday, Ottawa
Photos: David Barbour, Courtesy of Carleton University Art Gallery

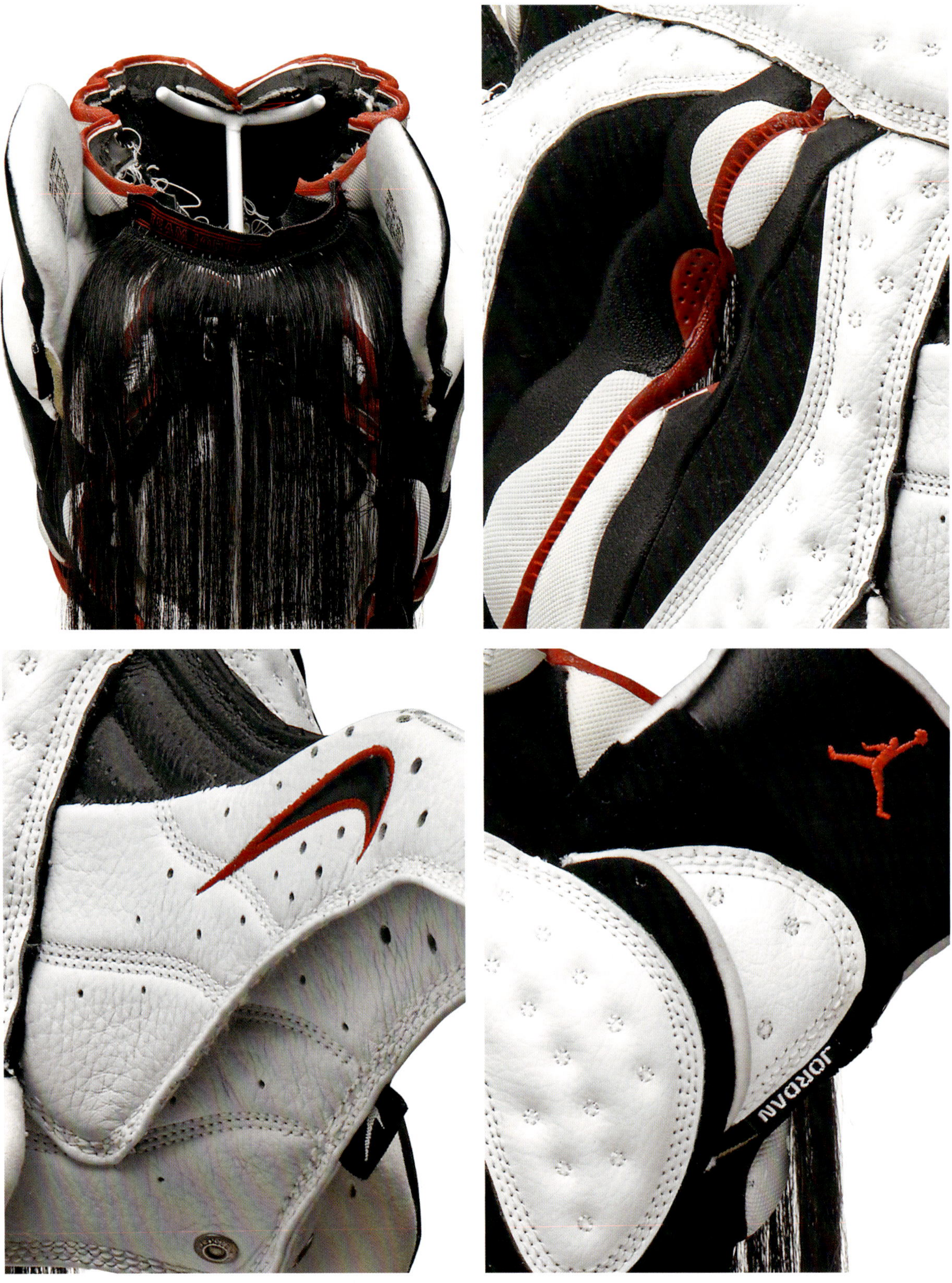

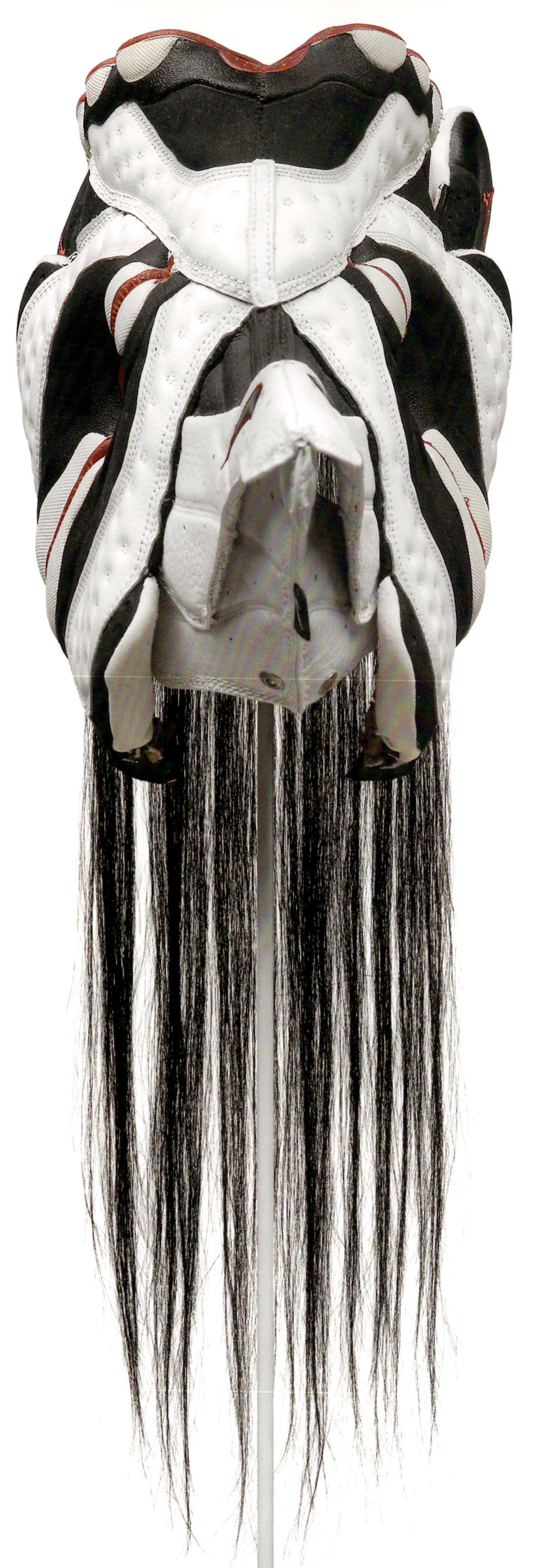

Prototype for New Understanding #9, 1999
Nike Air Jordans, human hair
60.5 x 25.4 x 12.7 cm (23 3/4" x 10" x 5")
Collection of Greg and Lisa Kerfoot, West Vancouver/Whistler
Photos: Trevor Mills, Vancouver Art Gallery

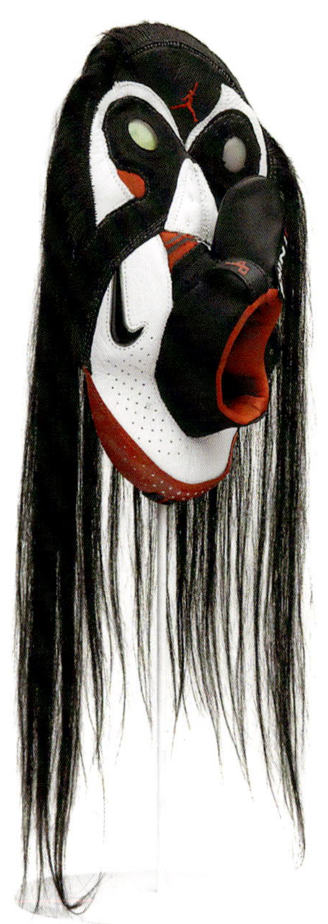
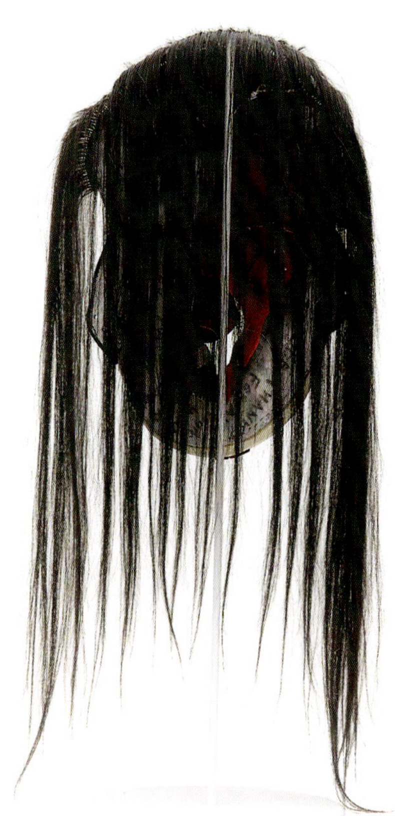
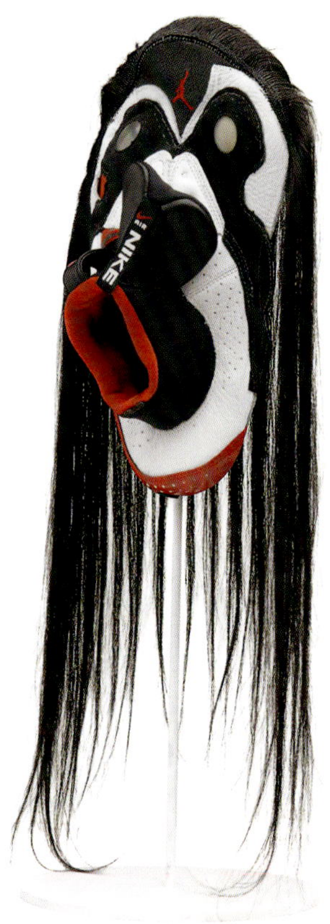

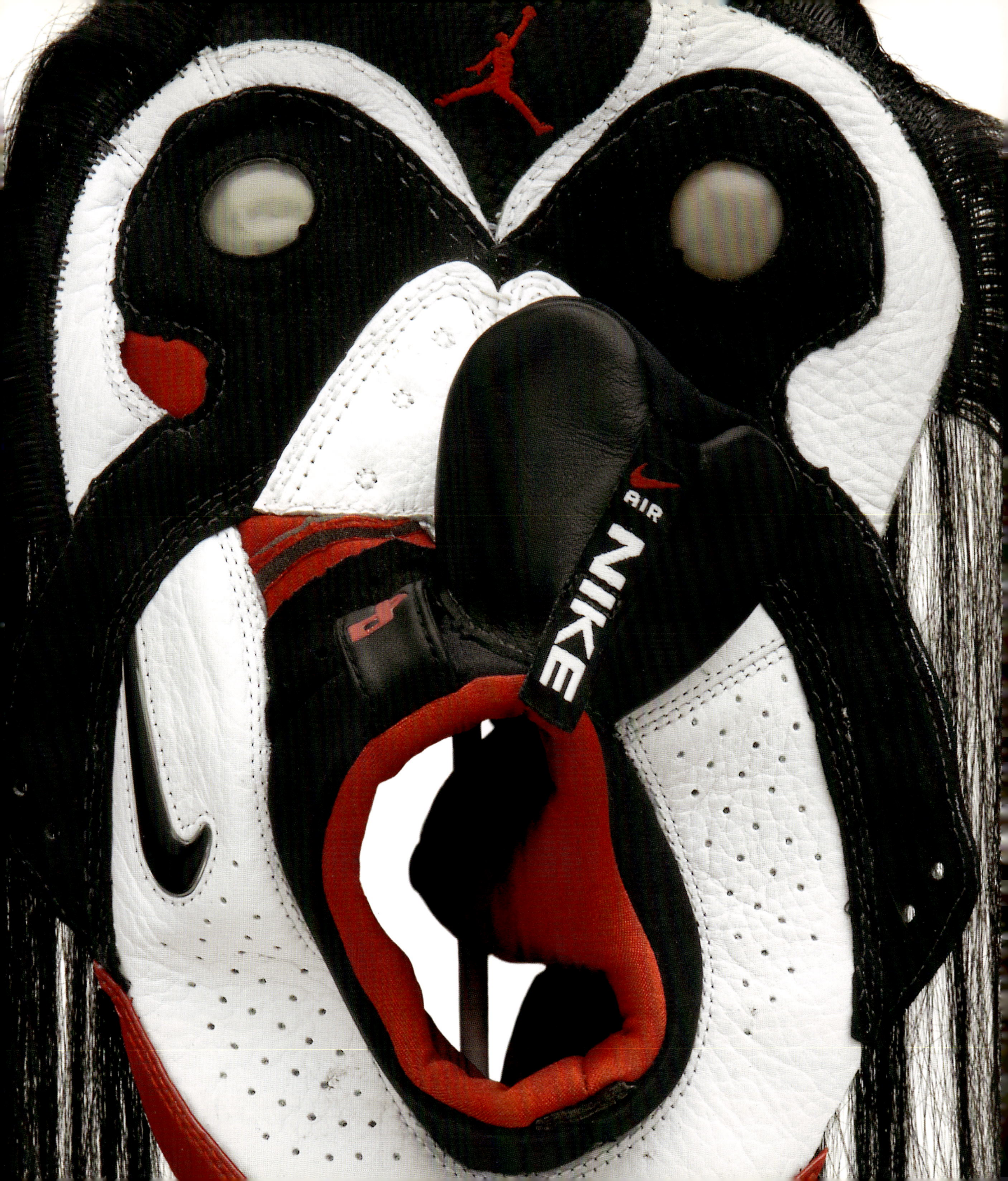

NIKE
AIR
NIKE

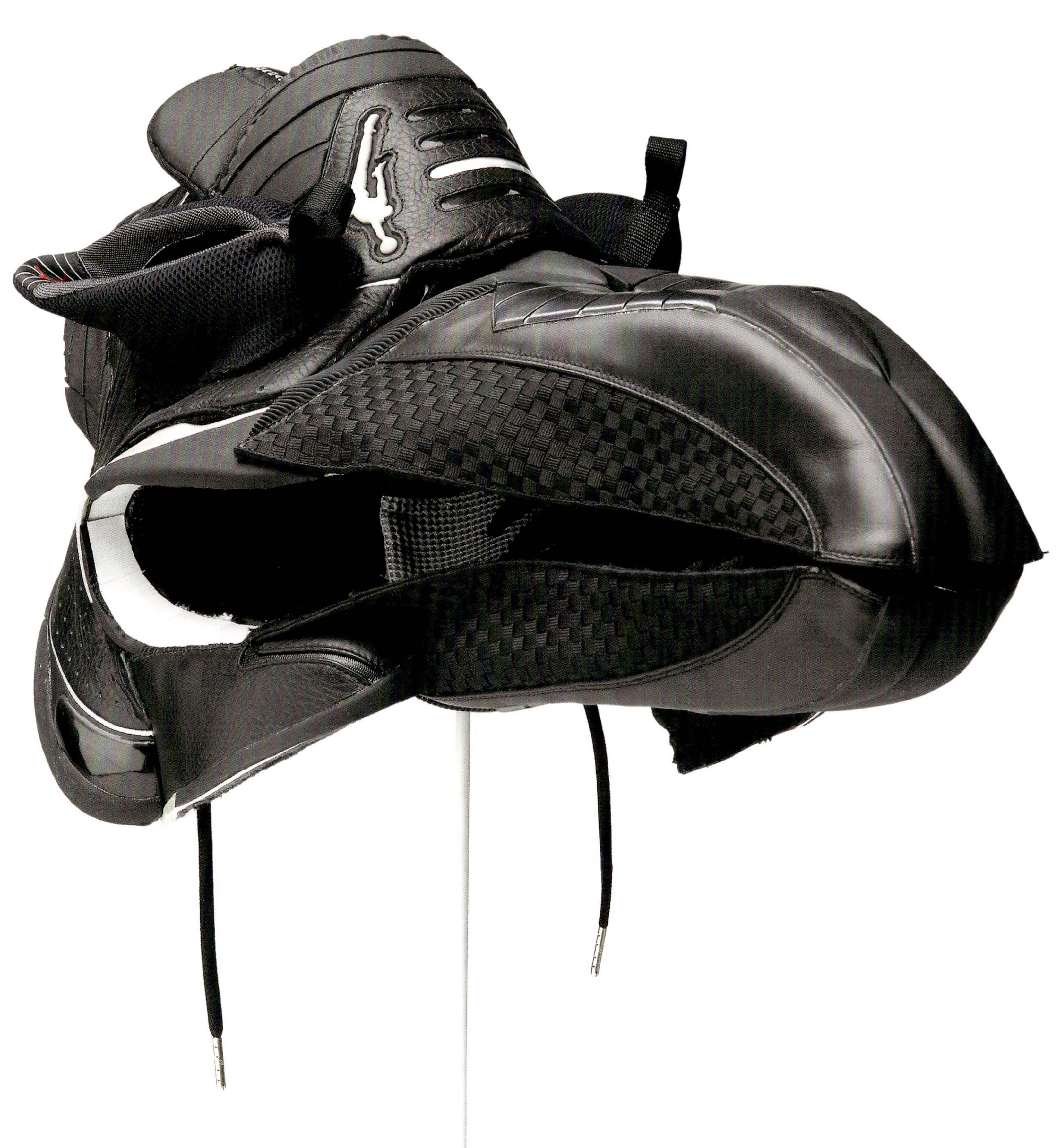

Prototype for New Understanding #10, 2001
Nike Air Jordans
27.9 x 35.6 x 58.4 cm (11" x 14" x 23")
Collection of Bob Rennie, Rennie Management Corporation, Vancouver
Photos: Trevor Mills, Vancouver Art Gallery

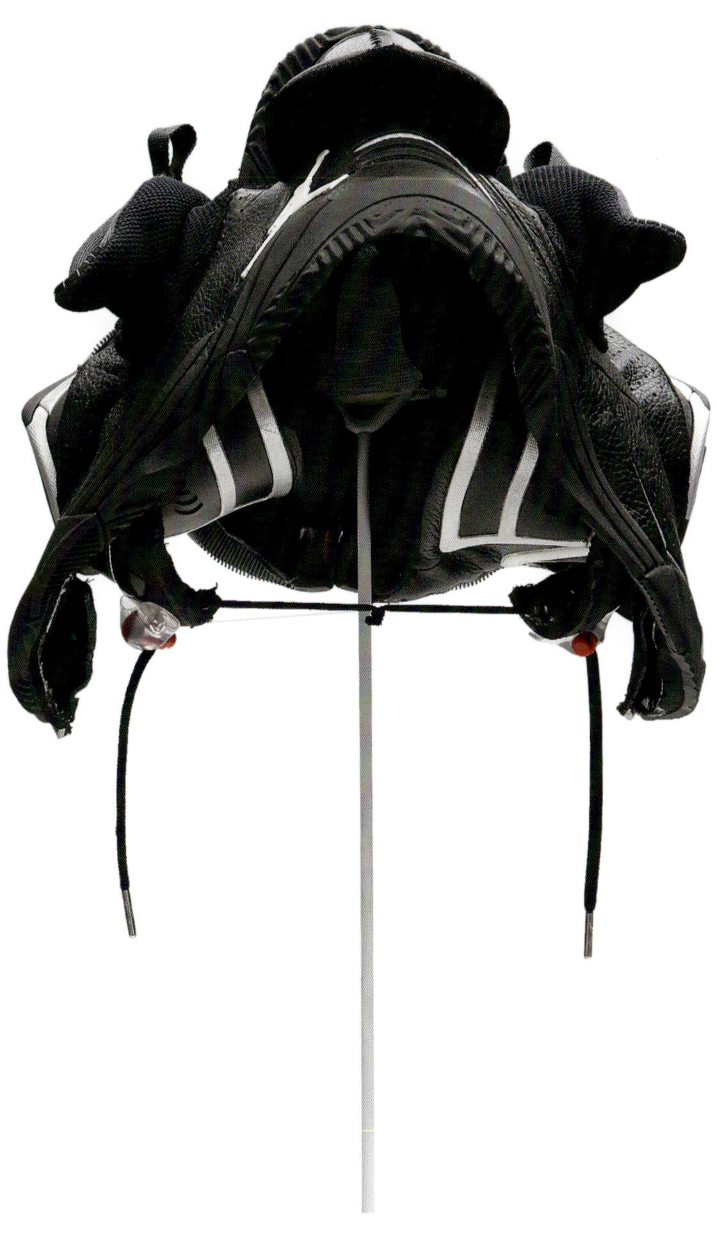

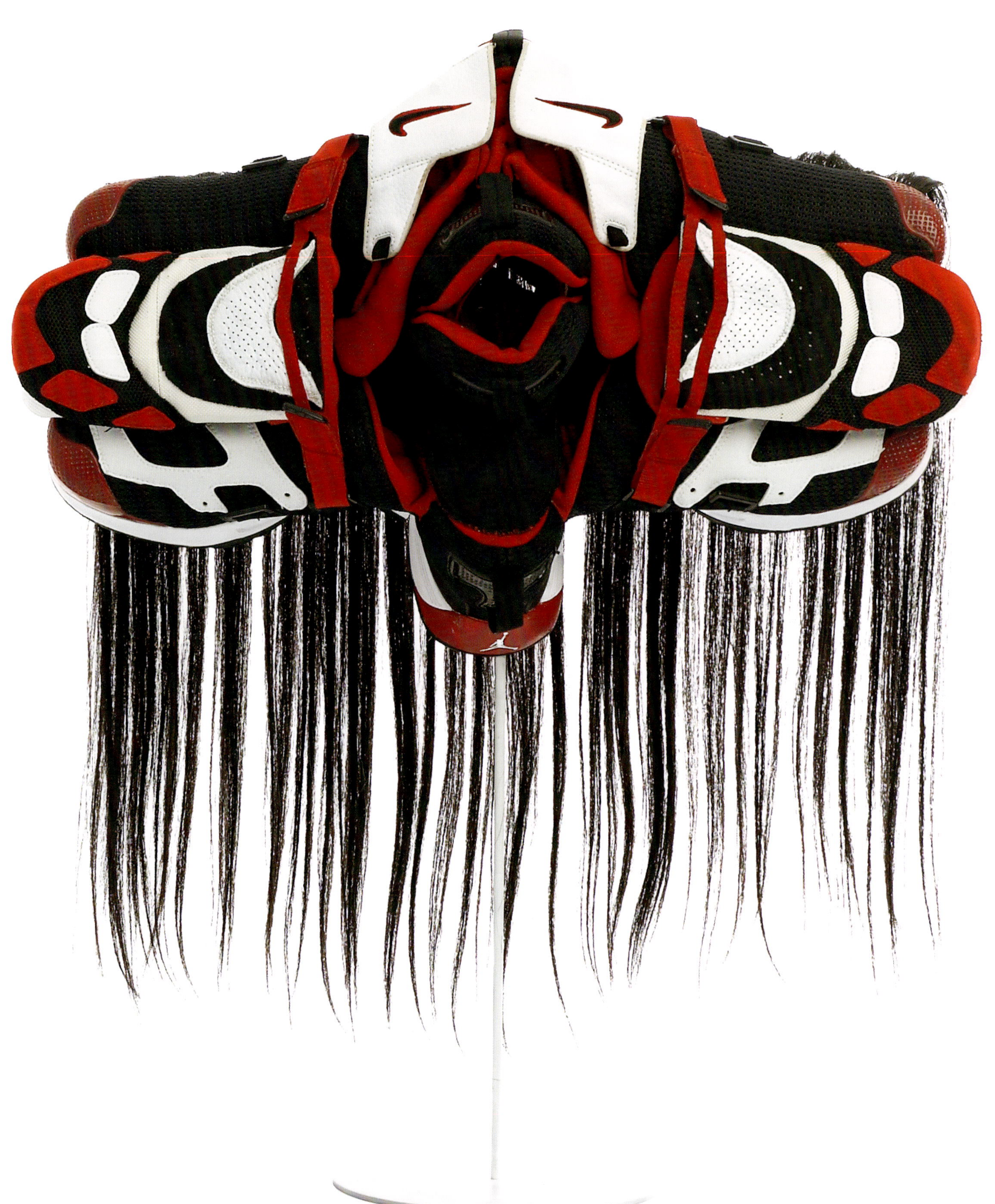

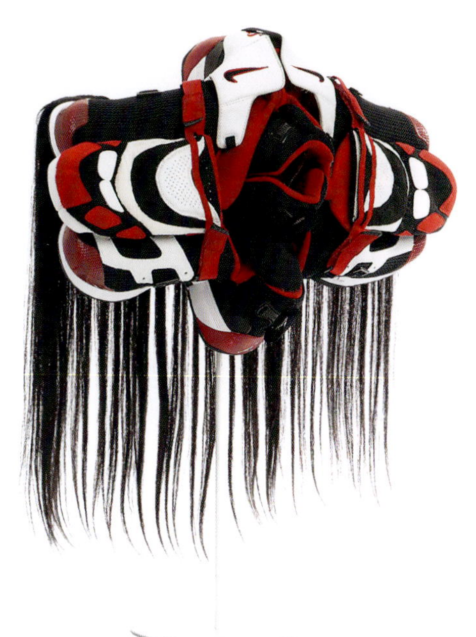 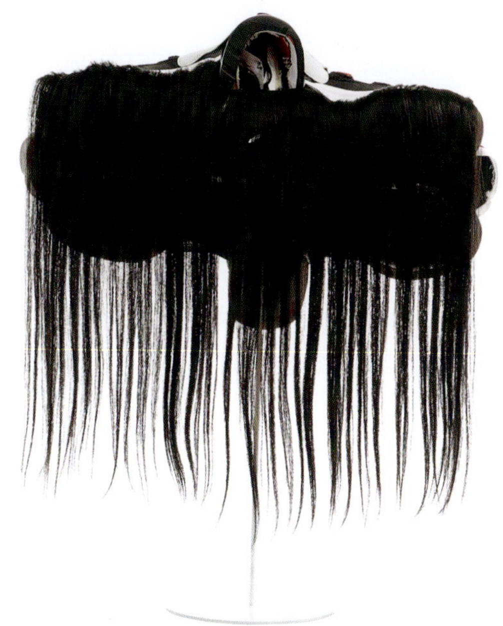 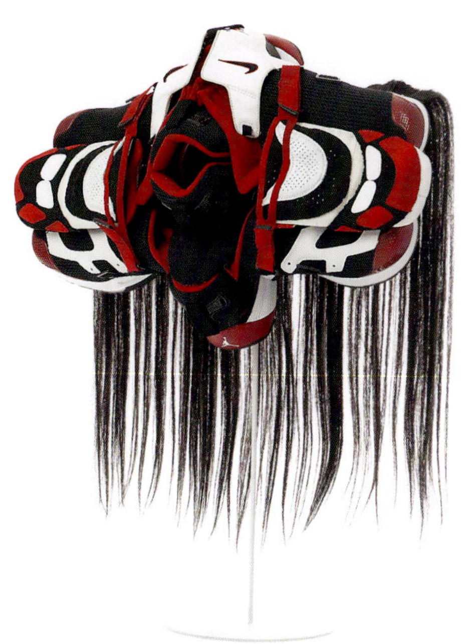

Prototype for New Understanding #11, 2002
Nike Air Jordans, human hair
67.3 x 58.4 x 25.4 cm (26 1/2" x 23" x 10")
Collection of Gilles and Julia Ouellette, Toronto
Photos: Rafael Goldchain

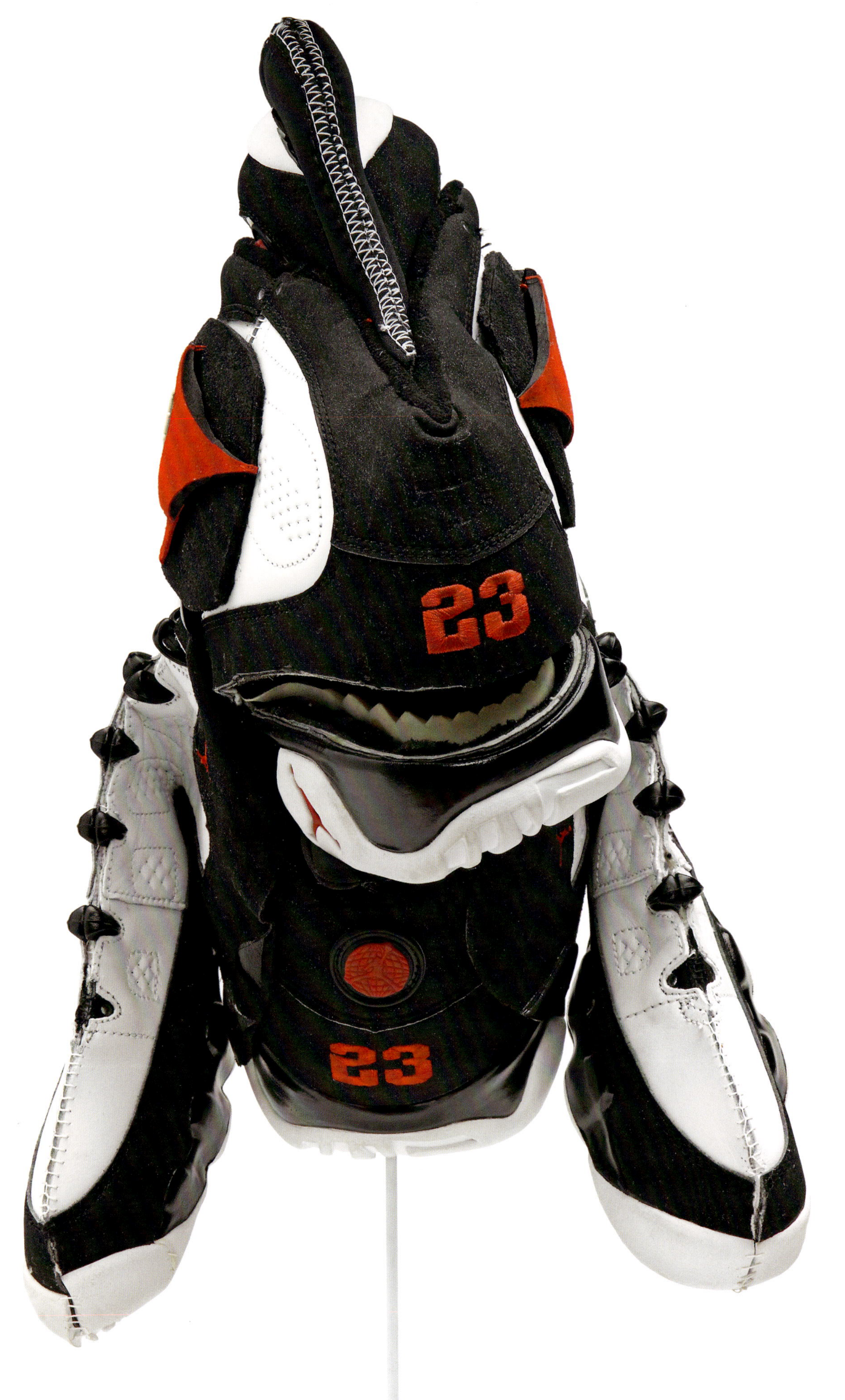

Prototype for New Understanding #12, 2002
Nike Air Jordans
58.4 x 27.9 x 30.5 cm (23" x 11" x 12")
Collection of Ruth and William True, Seattle
Photos: Trevor Mills, Vancouver Art Gallery

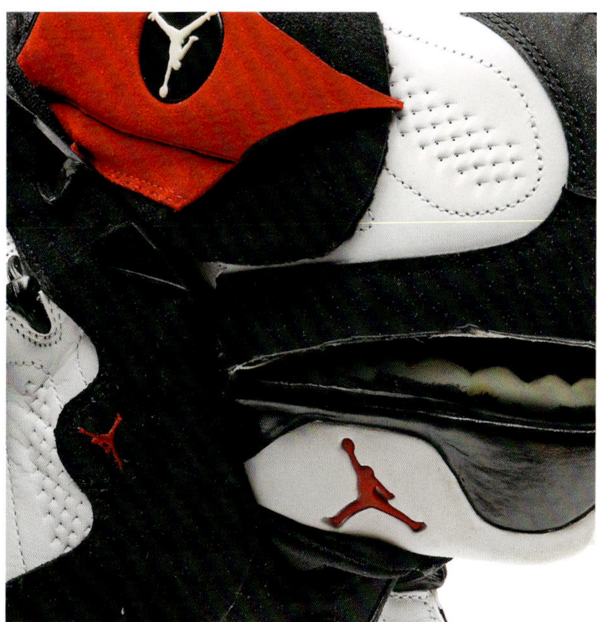

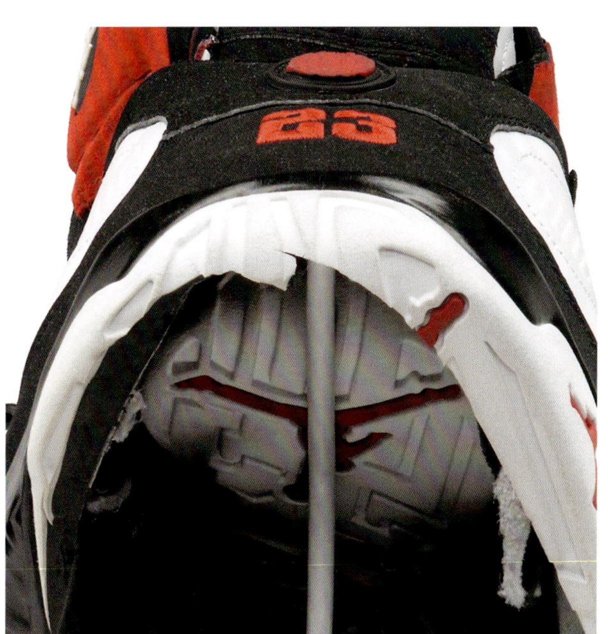

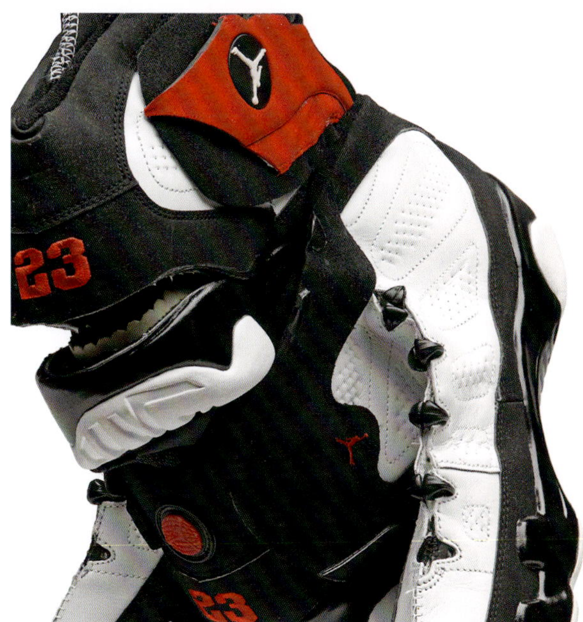

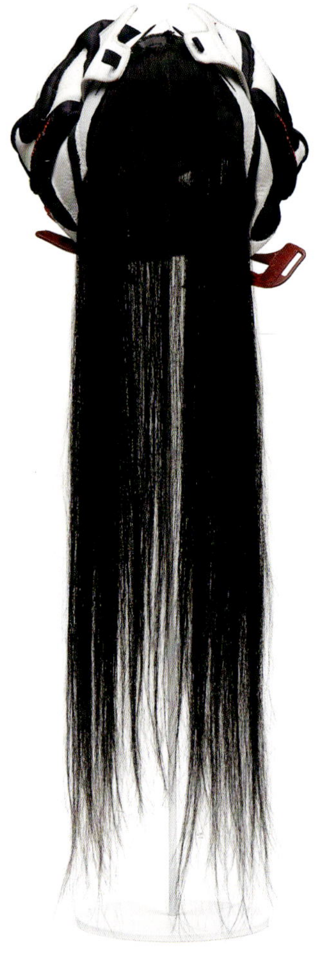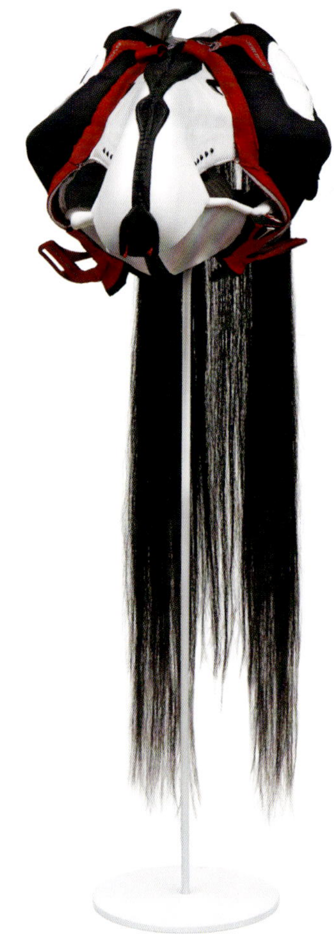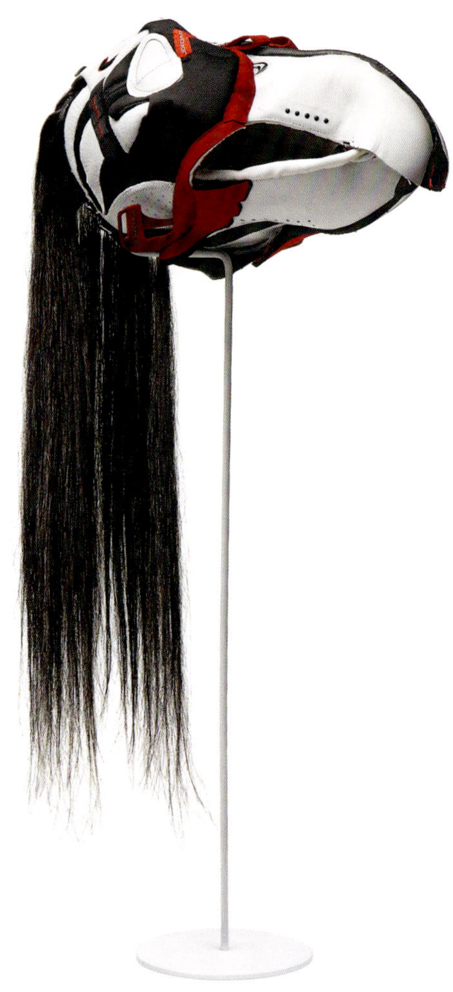

Prototype for New Understanding #13, 2003
Nike Air Jordans, human hair
63.5 x 23.8 x 39.3 cm (25" x 9" x 15 1/2")
Private collection, Vancouver
Photos: Trevor Mills, Vancouver Art Gallery

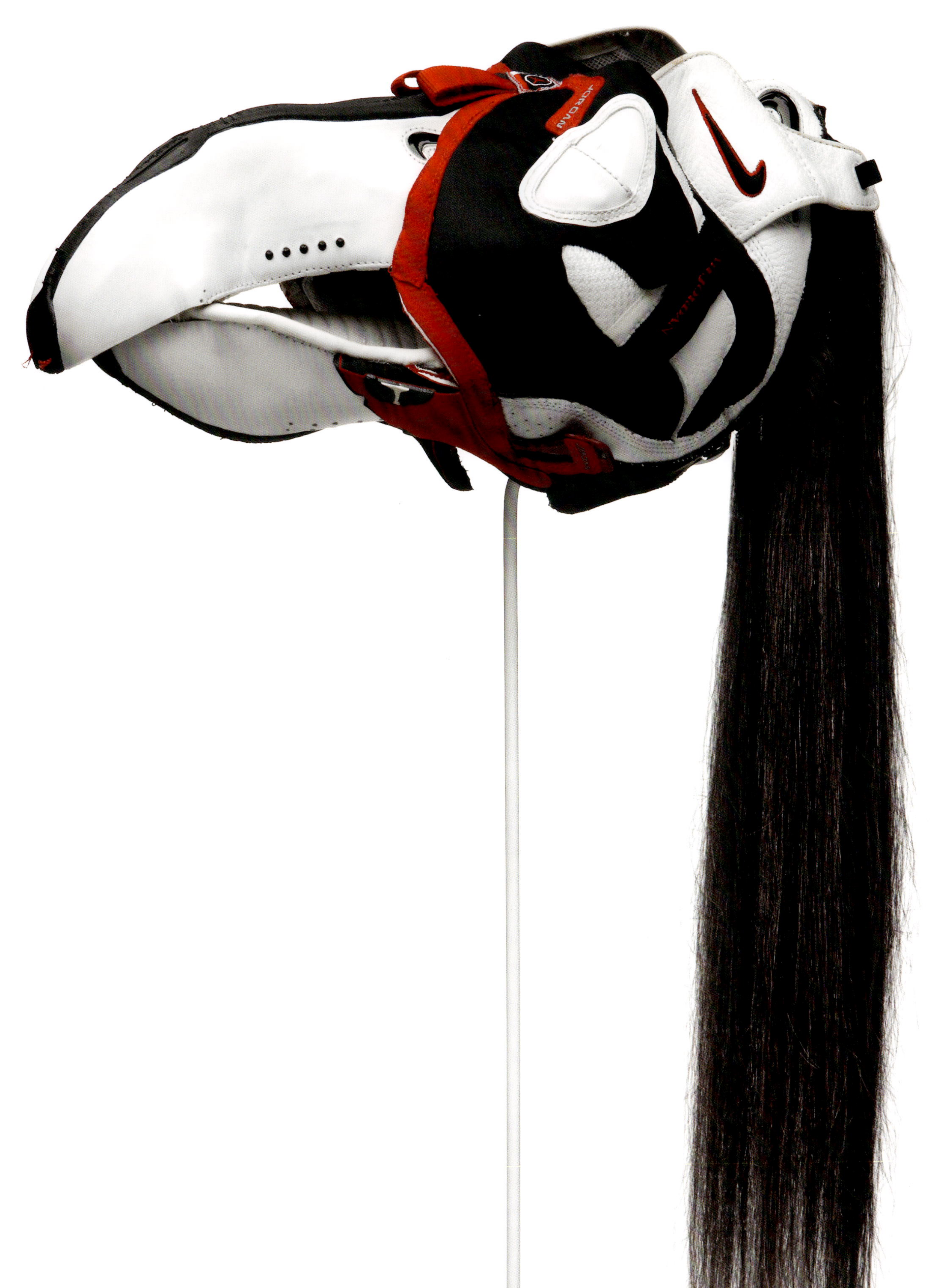

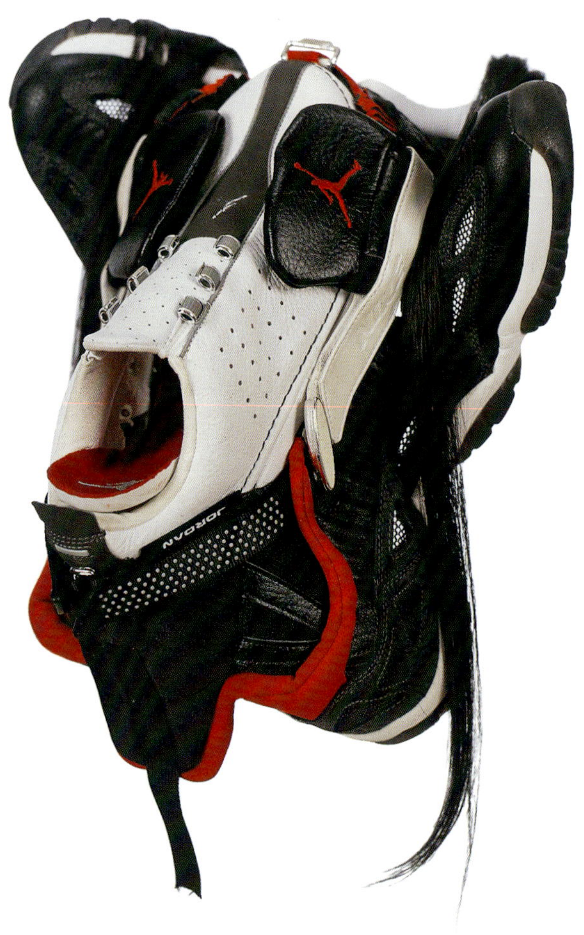

Prototype for New Understanding #14, 2003
Nike Air Jordans, human hair
63.5 x 35.6 x 30.6 cm (25" x 14" x 12")
Collection of Lawrence B. Benenson, New York
Photo: Courtesy of Catriona Jeffries Gallery, Vancouver

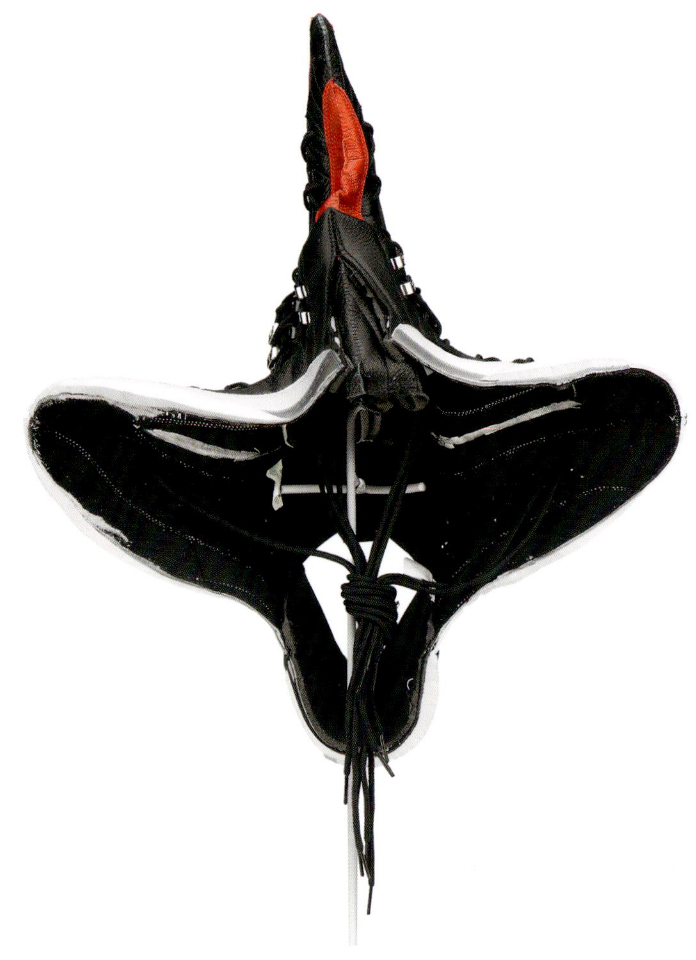

Prototype for New Understanding #15, 2003
Nike Air Jordans, shoelaces
63.5 x 48.9 x 48.9 cm (25" x 19 1/4" x 19 1/4")
Private collection, Toronto
Photos: Trevor Mills, Vancouver Art Gallery

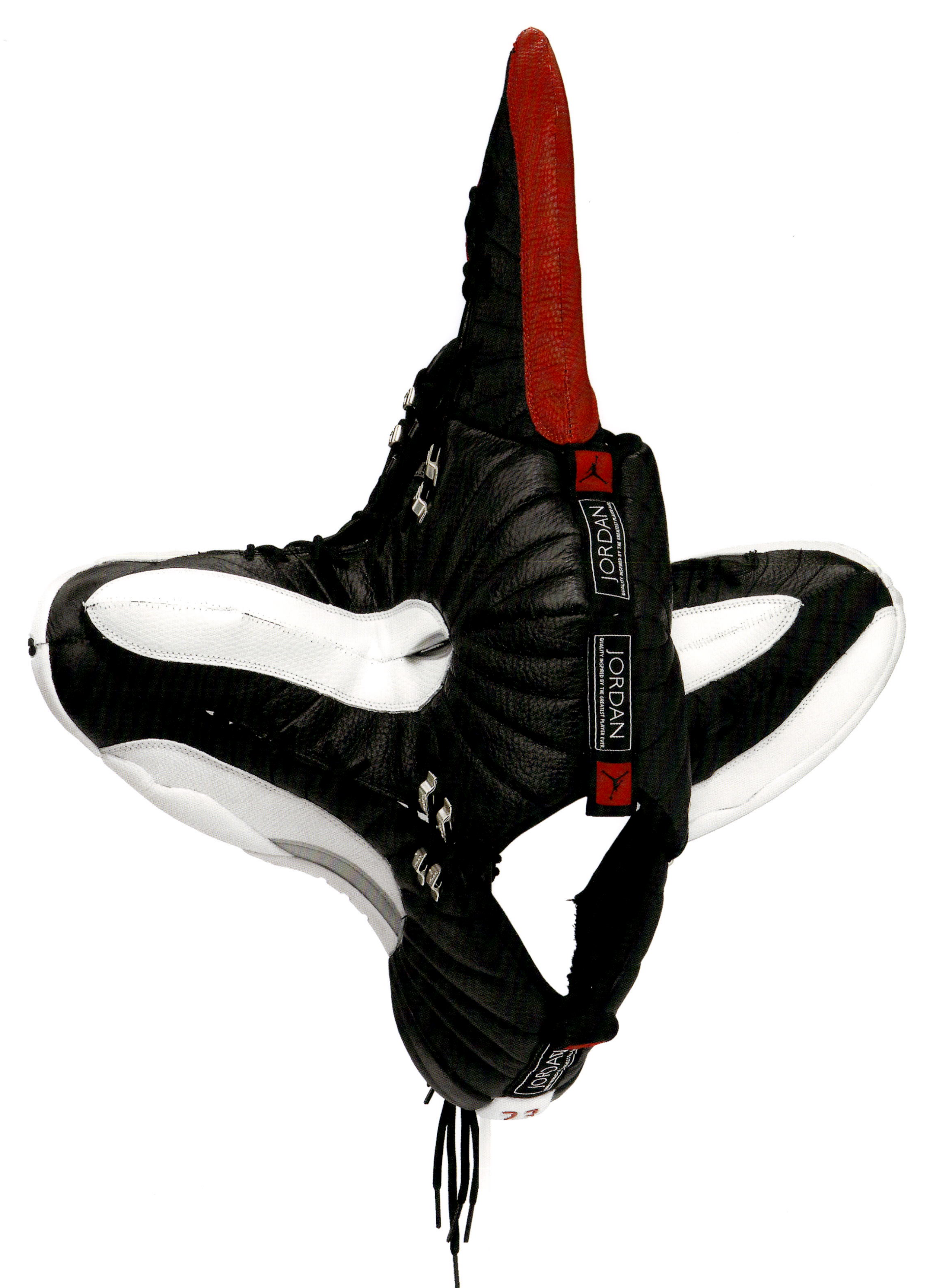

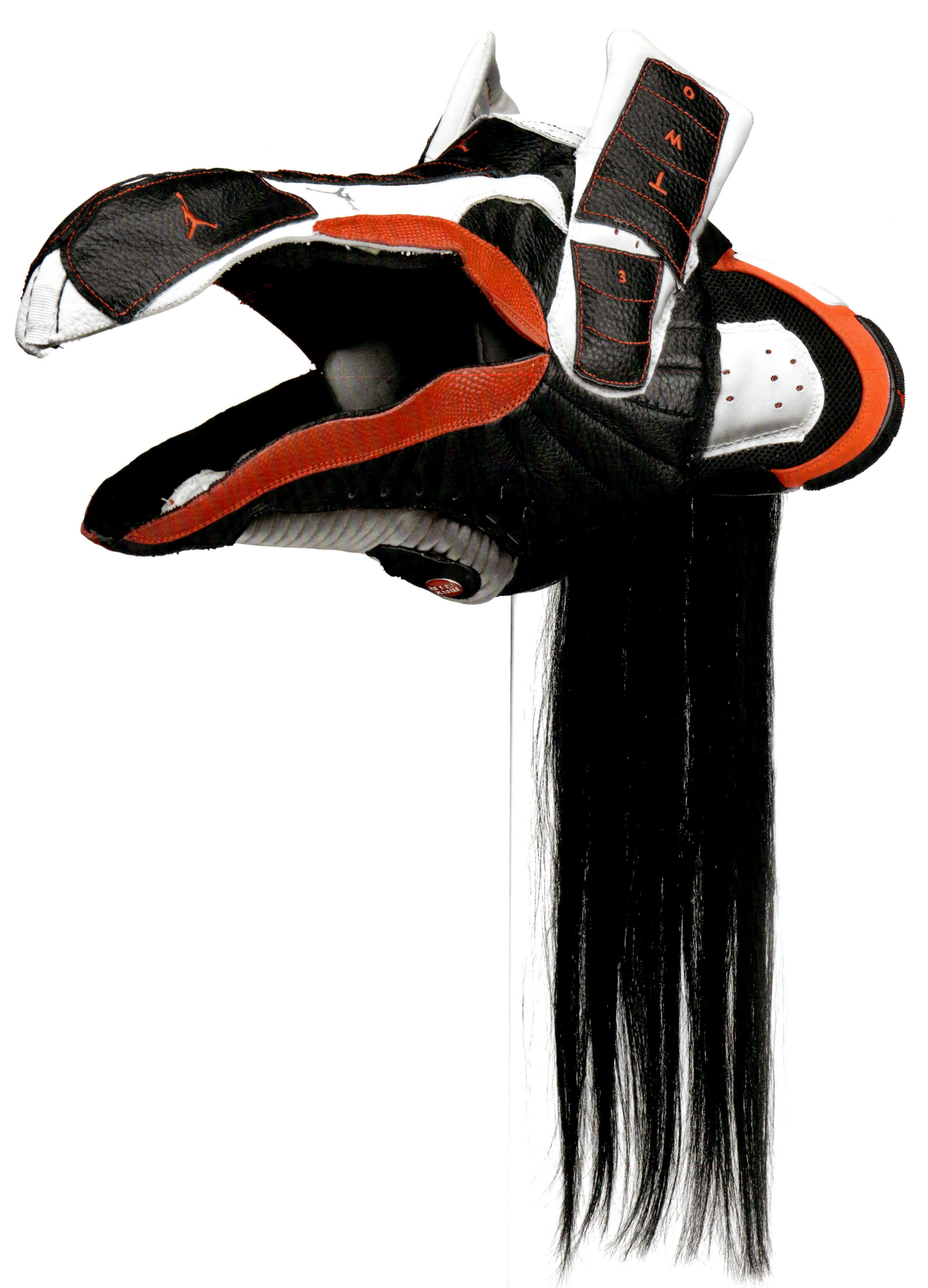

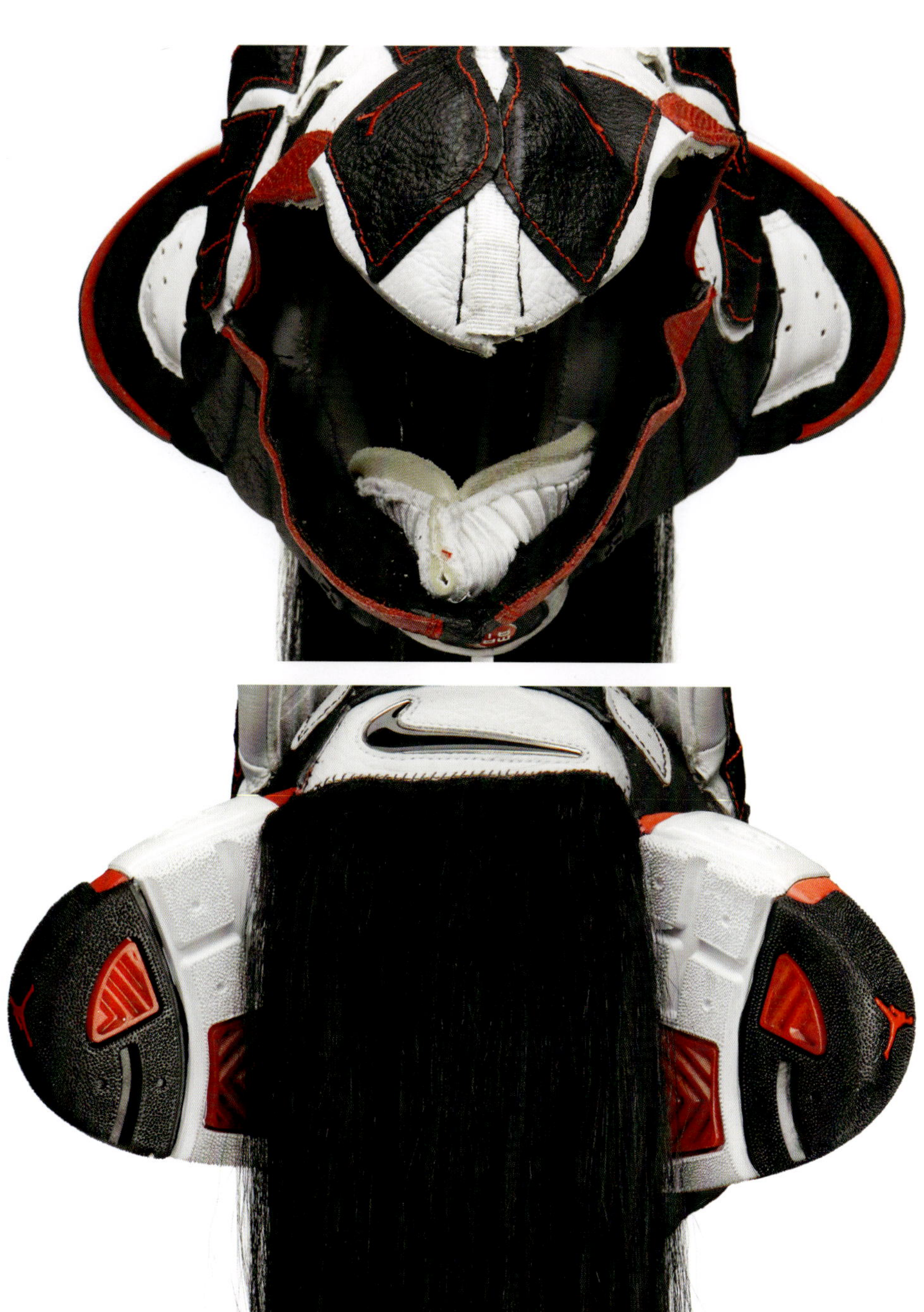

Prototype for New Understanding #16, 2004
Nike Air Jordans, human hair
57.3 x 30.5 x 45.7 cm (22 1/2" x 12" x 18")
Collection of Joel Wachs, New York
Photos: Trevor Mills, Vancouver Art Gallery

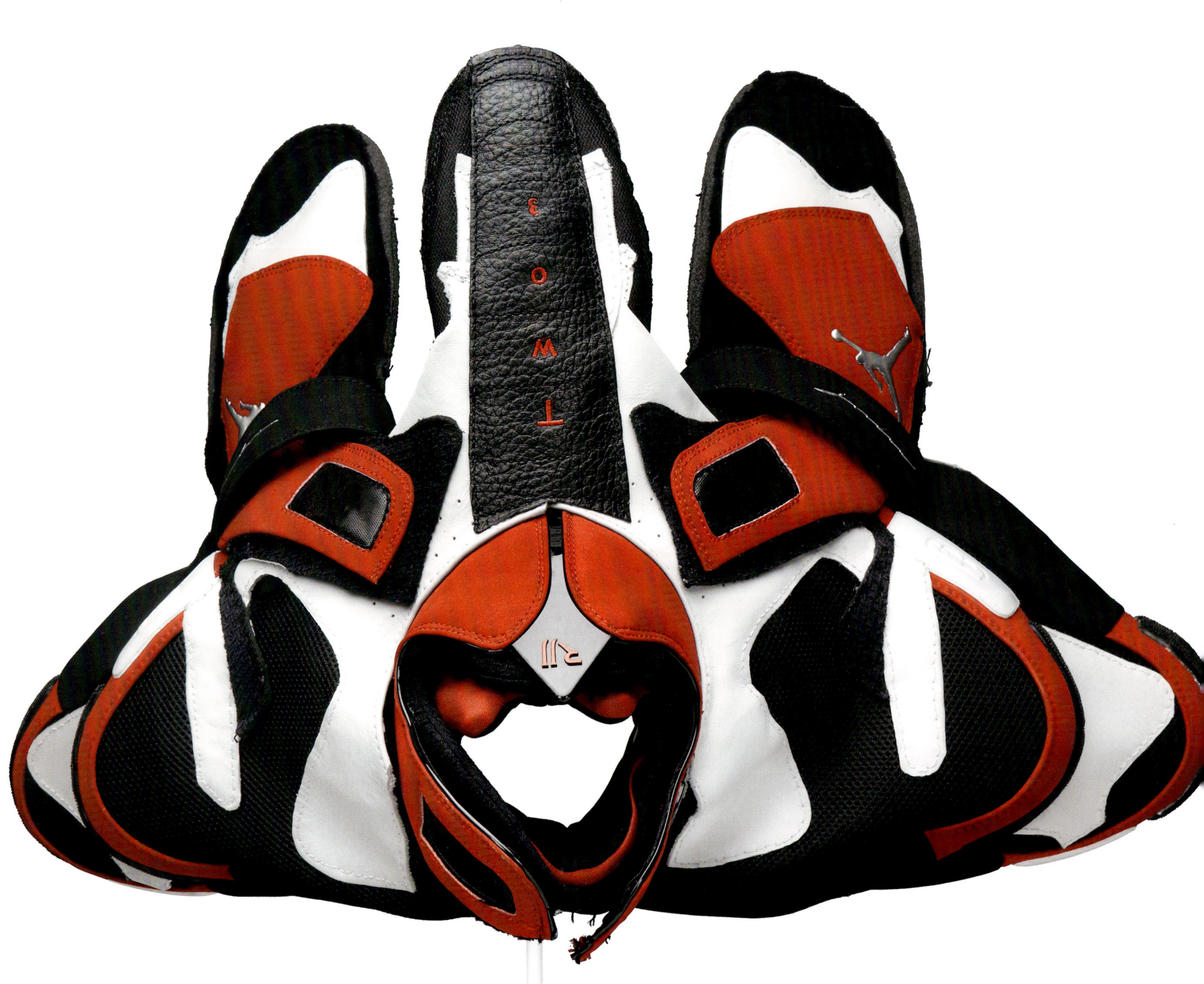
TWO 3
211

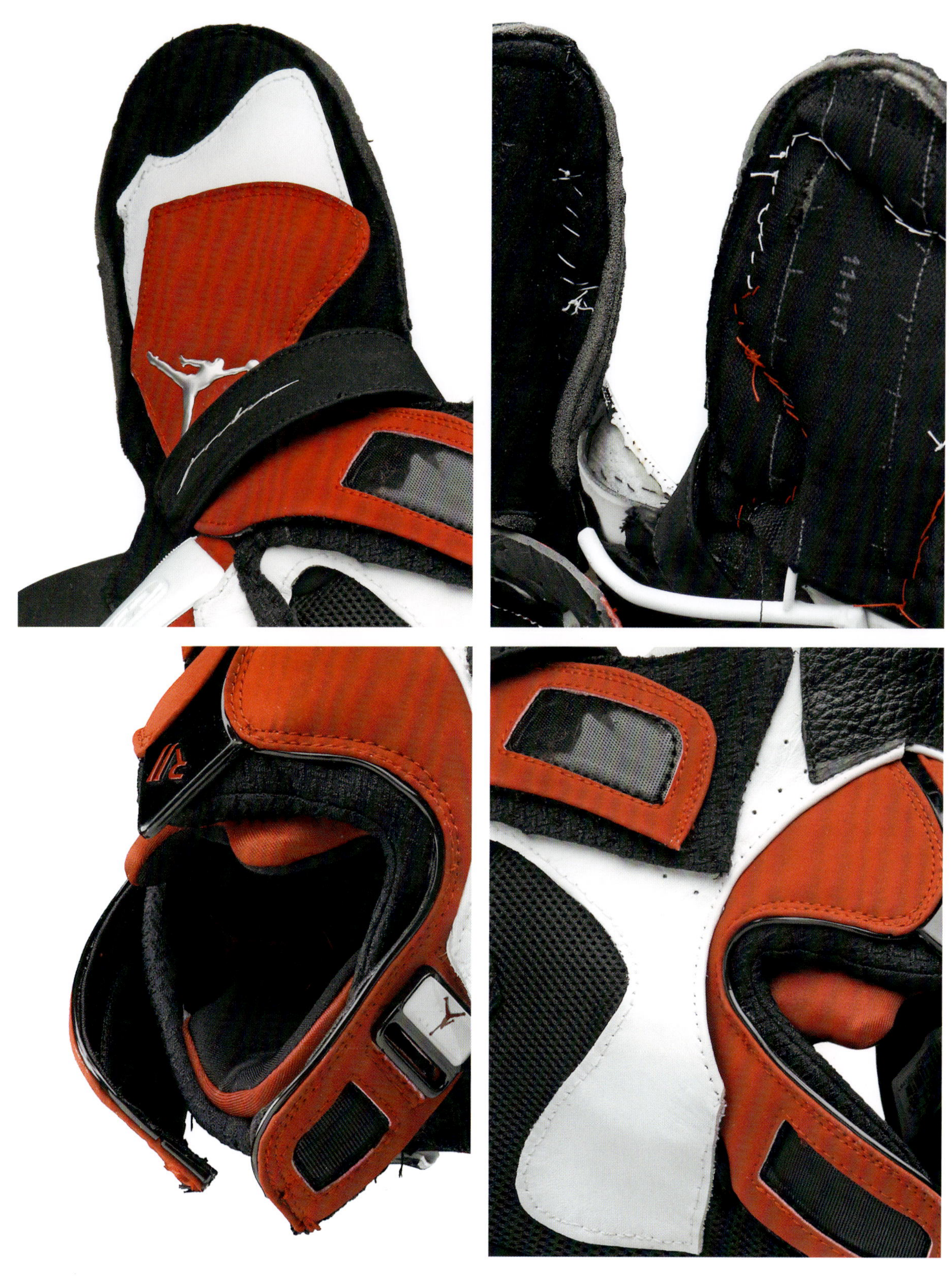

Prototype for New Understanding #17, 2004
Nike Air Jordans
33 x 48.3 x 25.4 cm (13" x 19" x 10")
Private collection, Vancouver
Photos: Trevor Mills, Vancouver Art Gallery

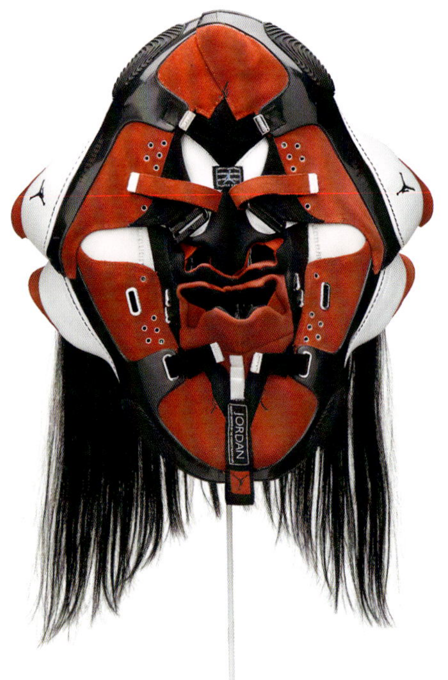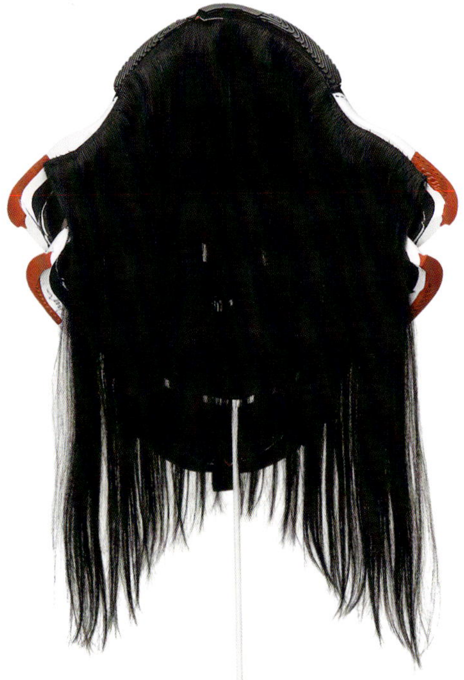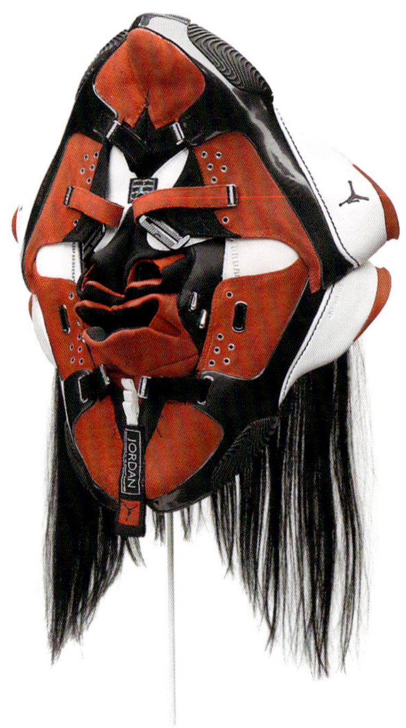

Prototype for New Understanding #18, 2004
Nike Air Jordans
67.5 x 45.7 x 19.7 cm (26 5/8" x 18" x 7 3/4")
Private collection, West Vancouver
Photos: Trevor Mills, Vancouver Art Gallery

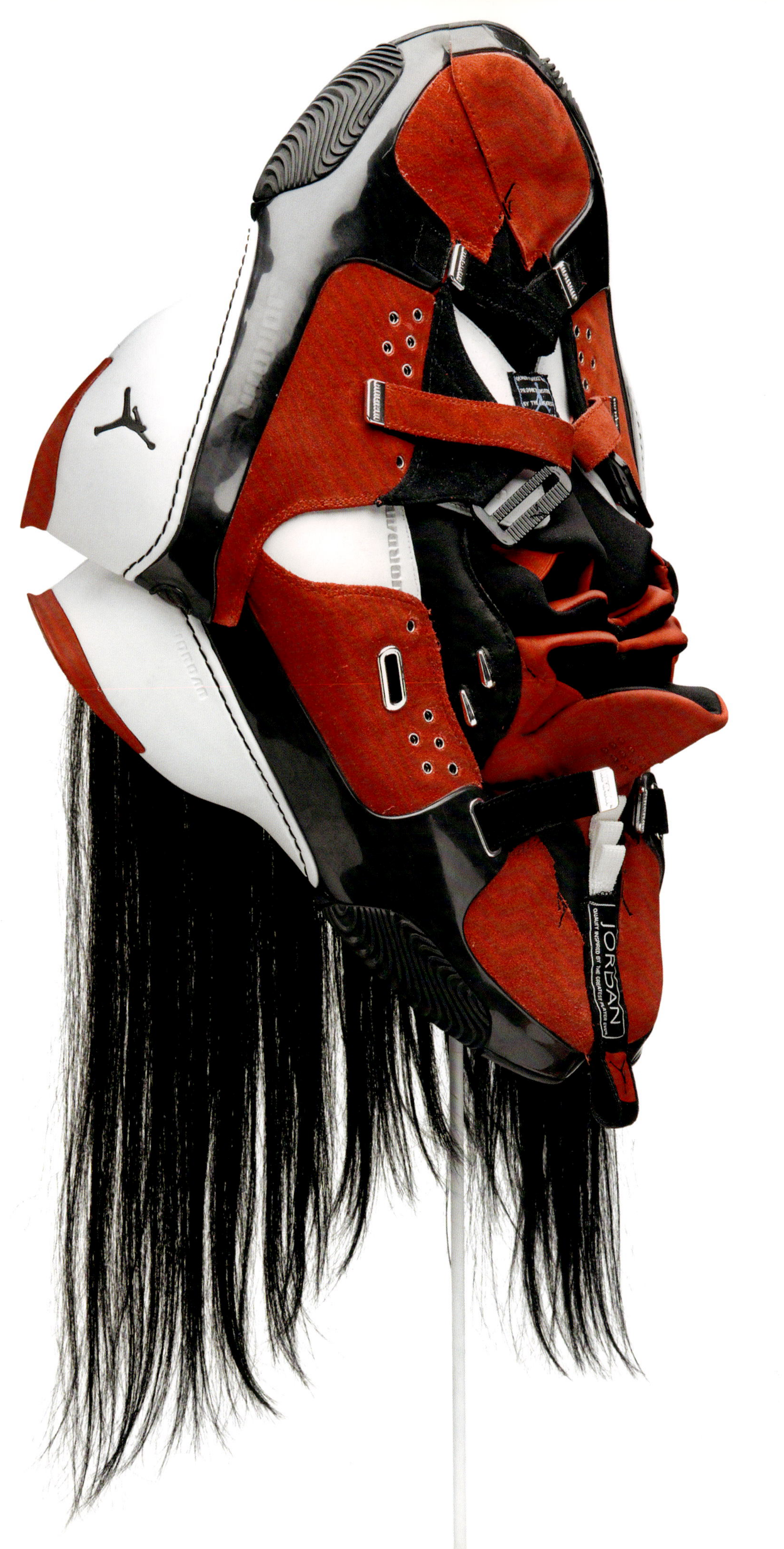

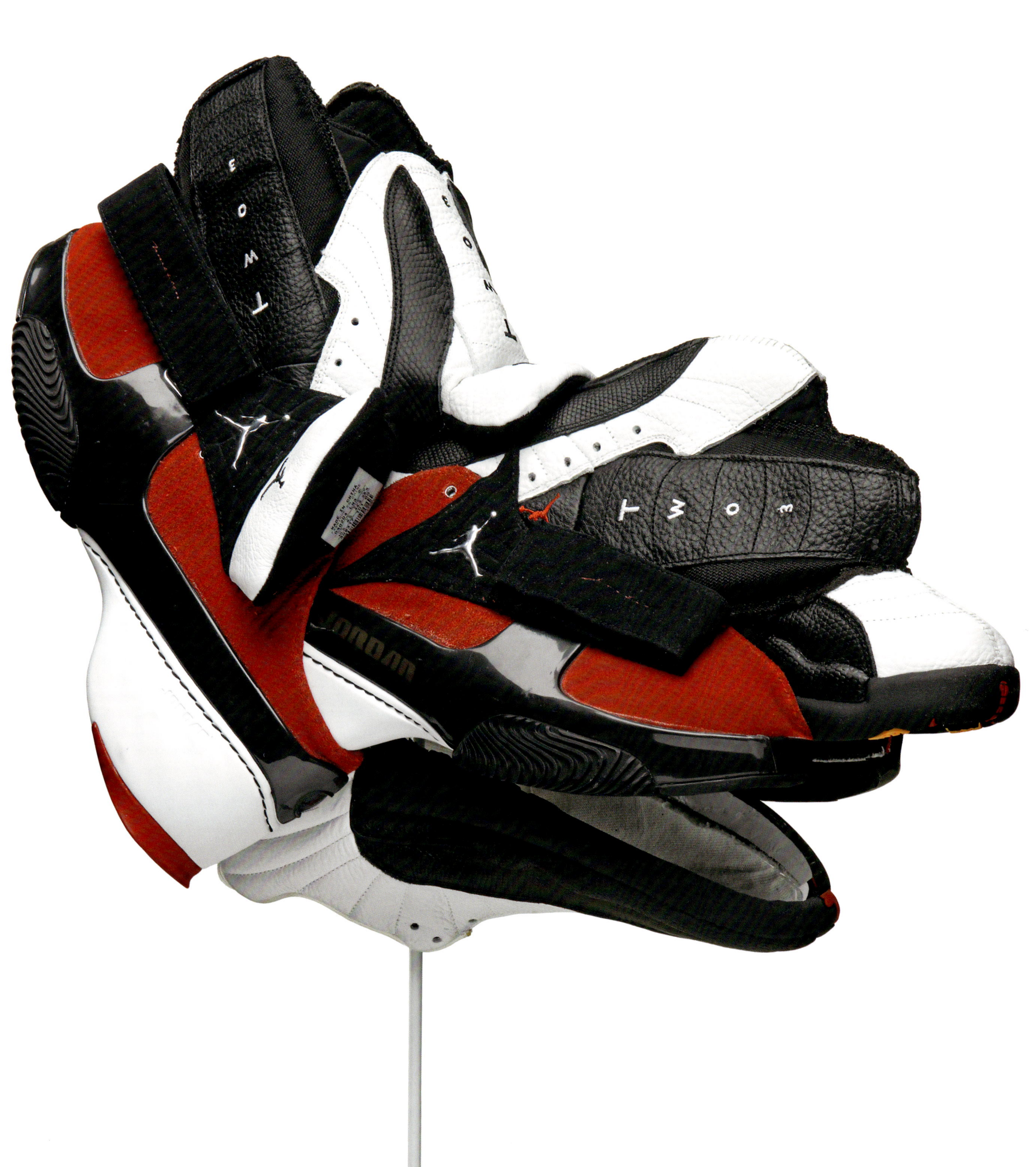

Prototype for New Understanding #19, 2004
Nike Air Jordans
61 x 61 x 20.3 cm (24" x 24" x 8")
Collection of Donald R. Sobey, Stellarton, Nova Scotia
Photos: Trevor Mills, Vancouver Art Gallery

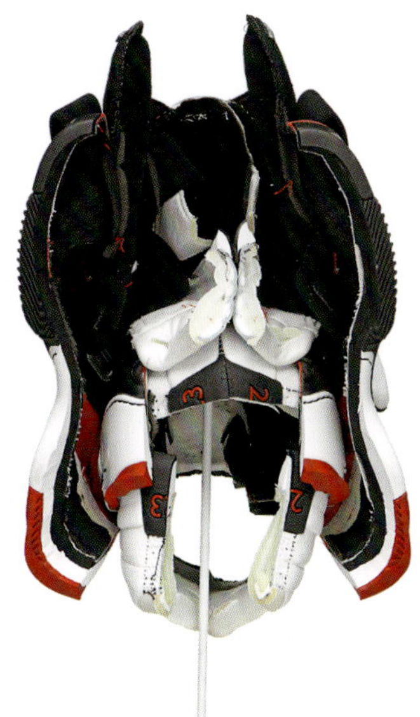 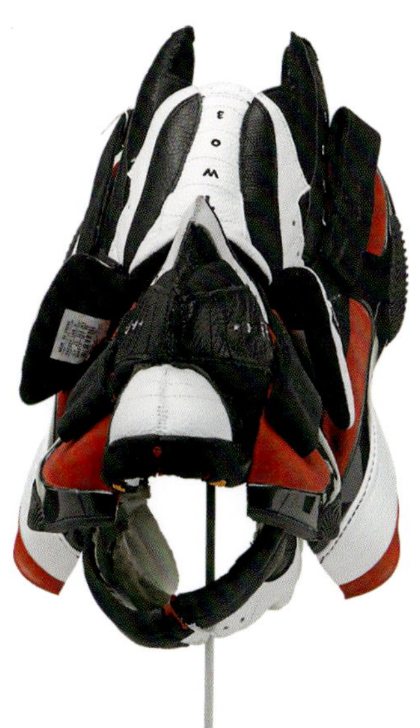 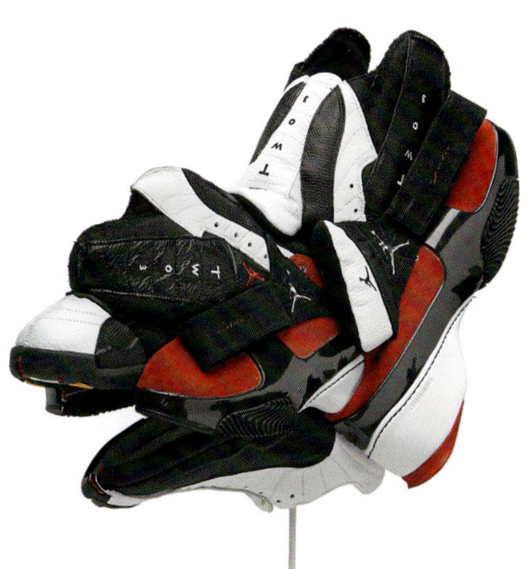

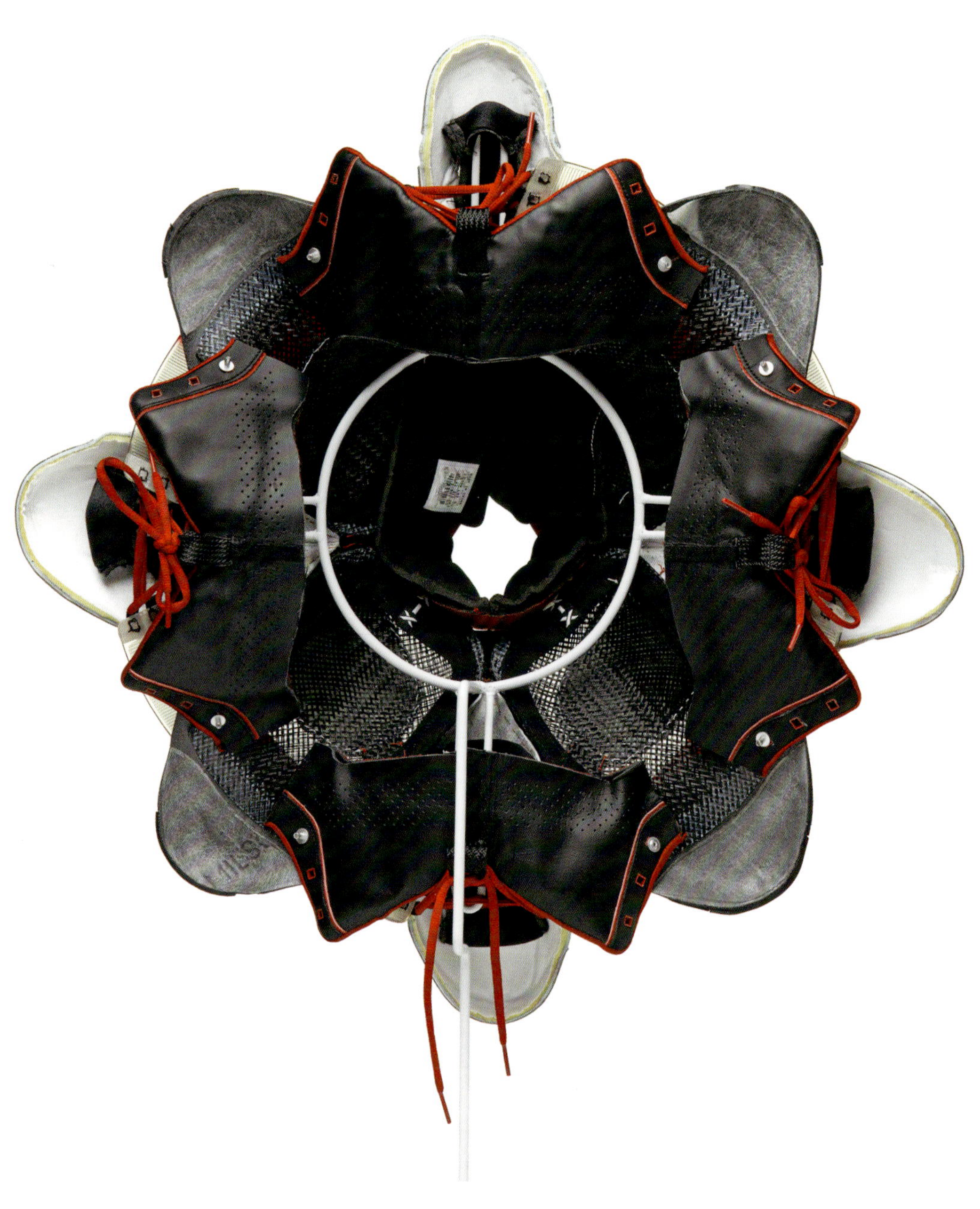

Prototype for New Understanding #20, 2004
Nike Air Jordans
43.2 x 25.4 x 50.8 cm (17" x 10" x 20")
Collection of Alexandre Taillefer and Debbie Zakaib, St. Lambert, Quebec
Photos: Trevor Mills, Vancouver Art Gallery

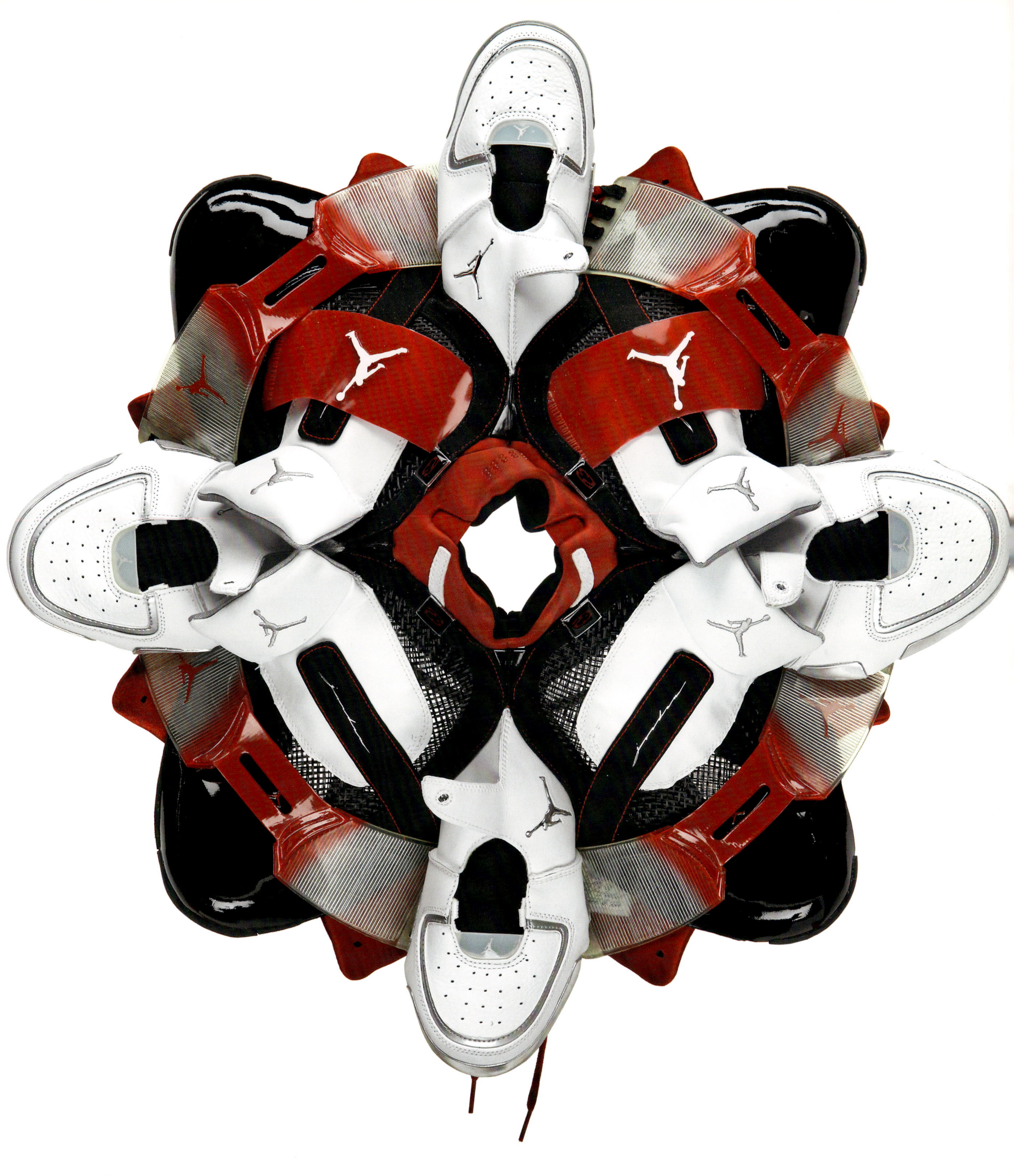

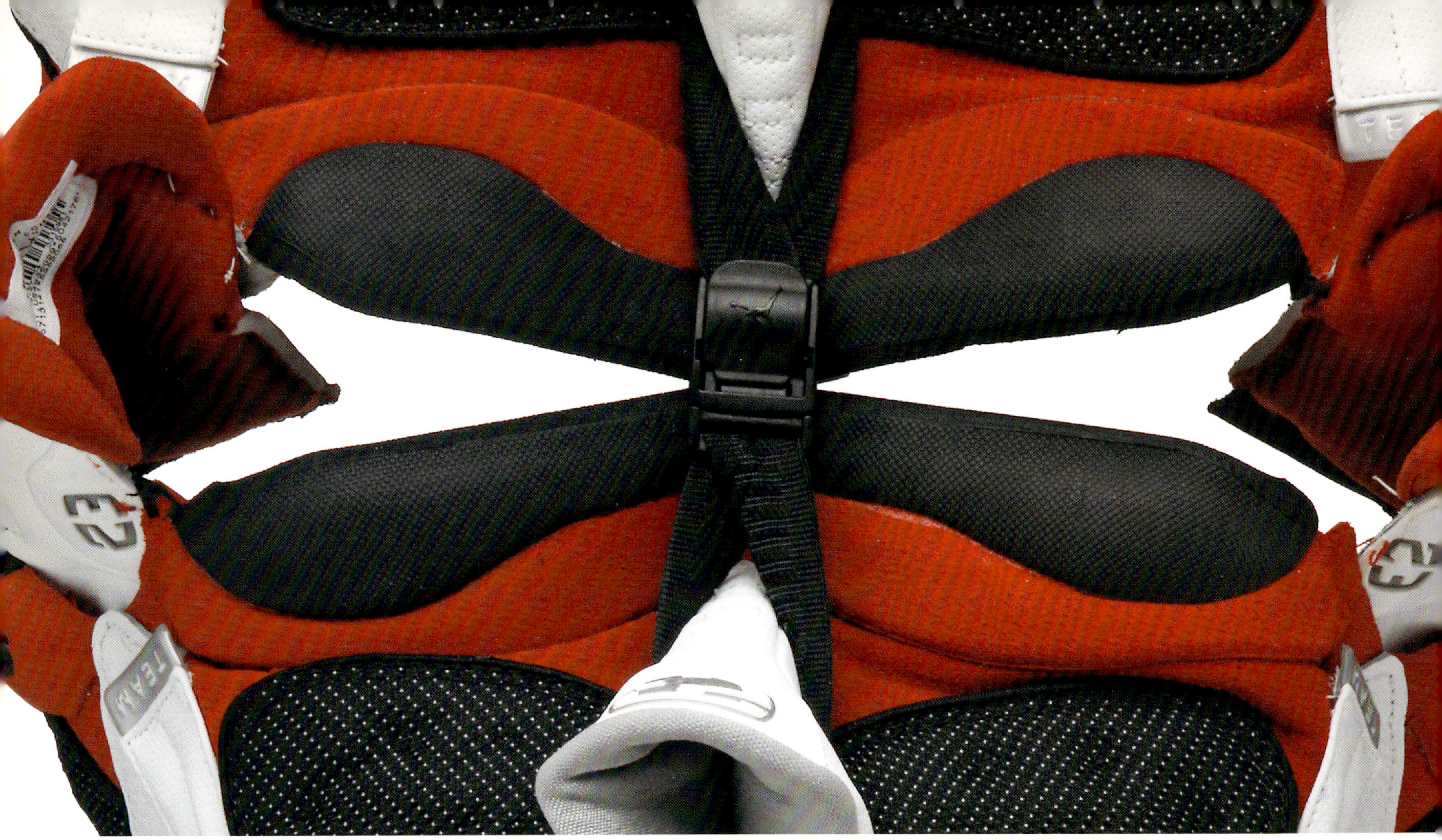

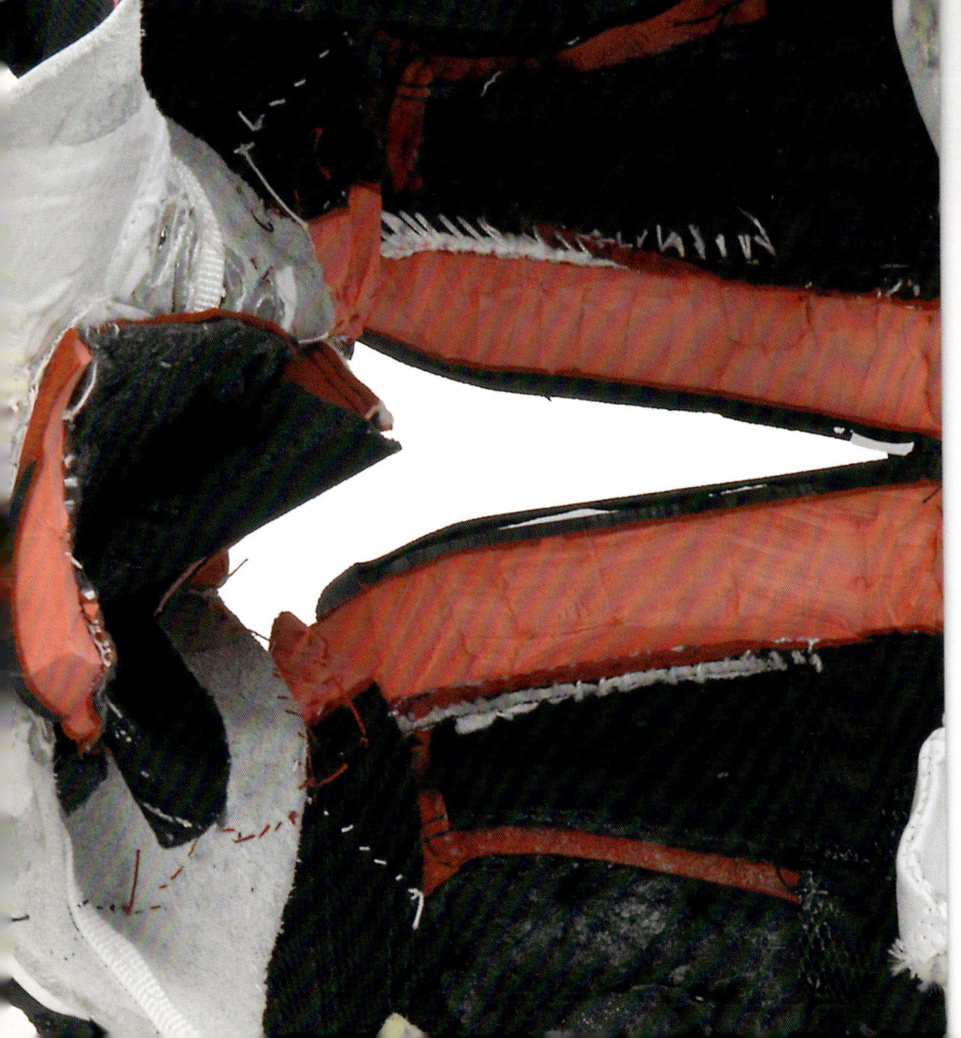
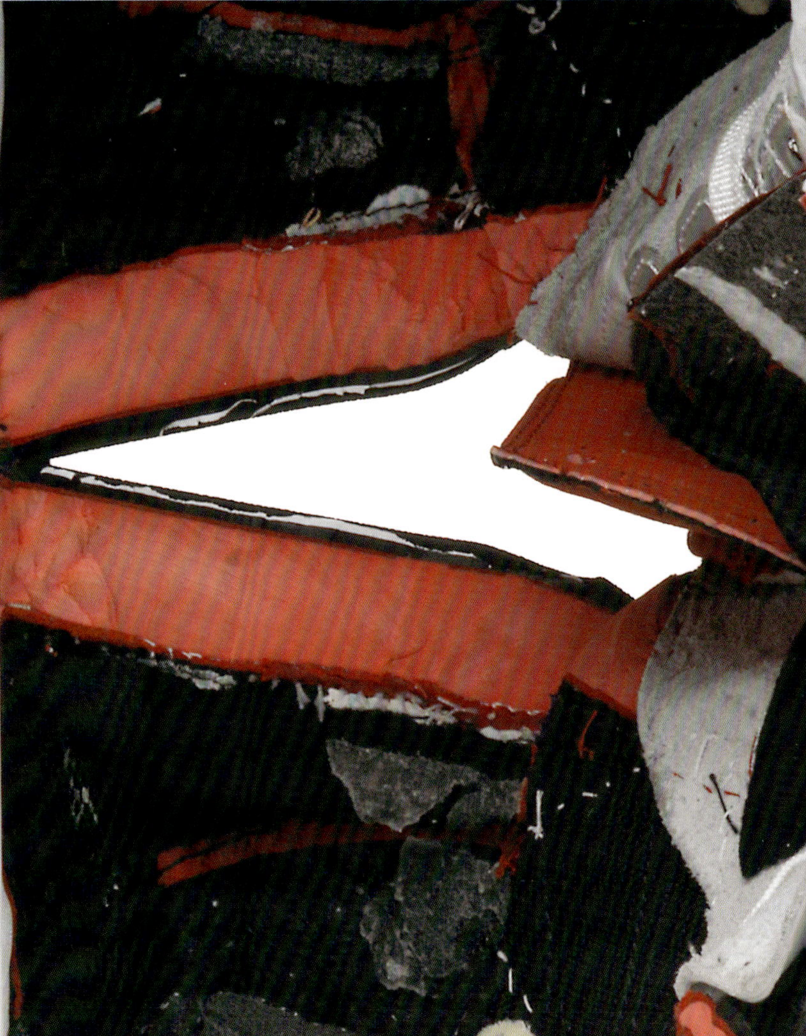

Prototype for New Understanding #21, 2005
Nike Air Jordans
50 x 36 x 33 cm (19 3/4" x 14 1/8" x 13")
Private collection, New York
Courtesy of the artist and Casey Kaplan Gallery, New York
Photos: Trevor Mills, Vancouver Art Gallery

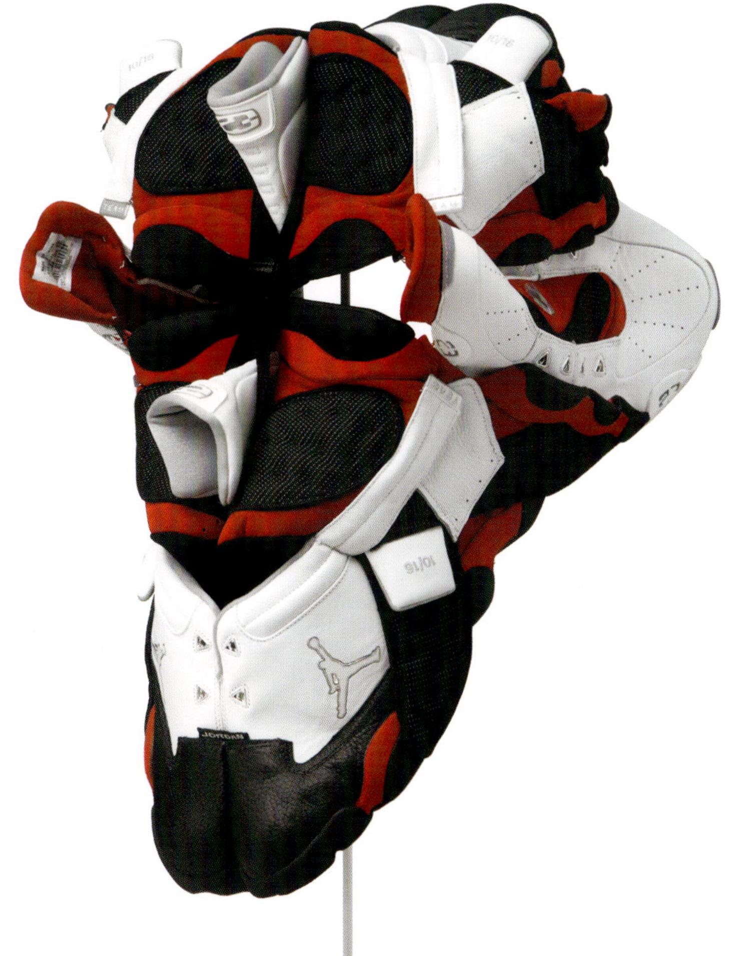
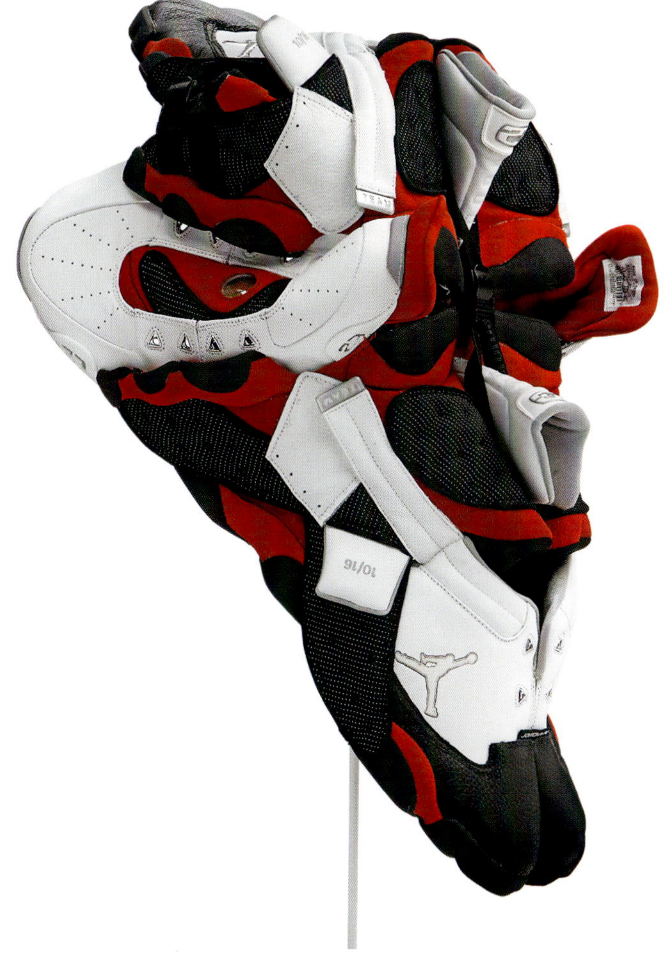

Prototype for New Understanding #22, 2005
Nike Air Jordans
49 x 51 x 21 cm (19 1/4" x 20" x 8 1/4")
Collection of Glenn Fuhrman, New York
Courtesy of the artist and Casey Kaplan Gallery, New York
Photos: Trevor Mills, Vancouver Art Gallery

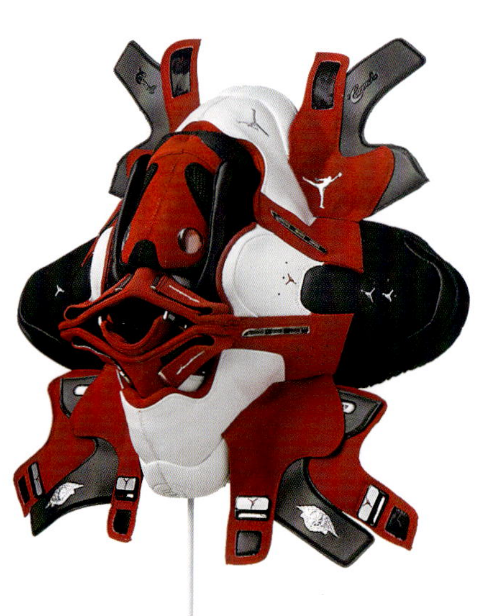
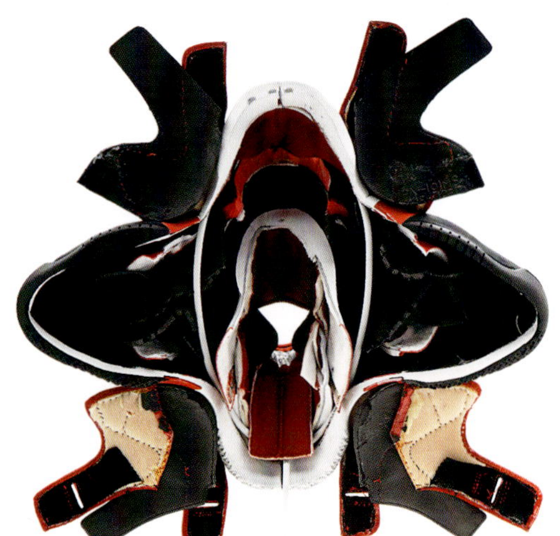
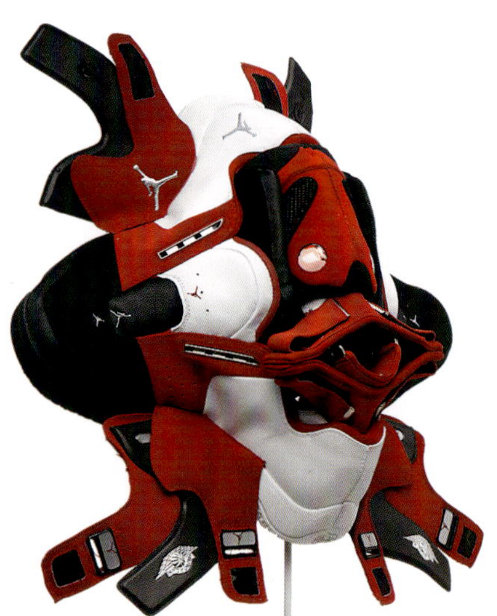

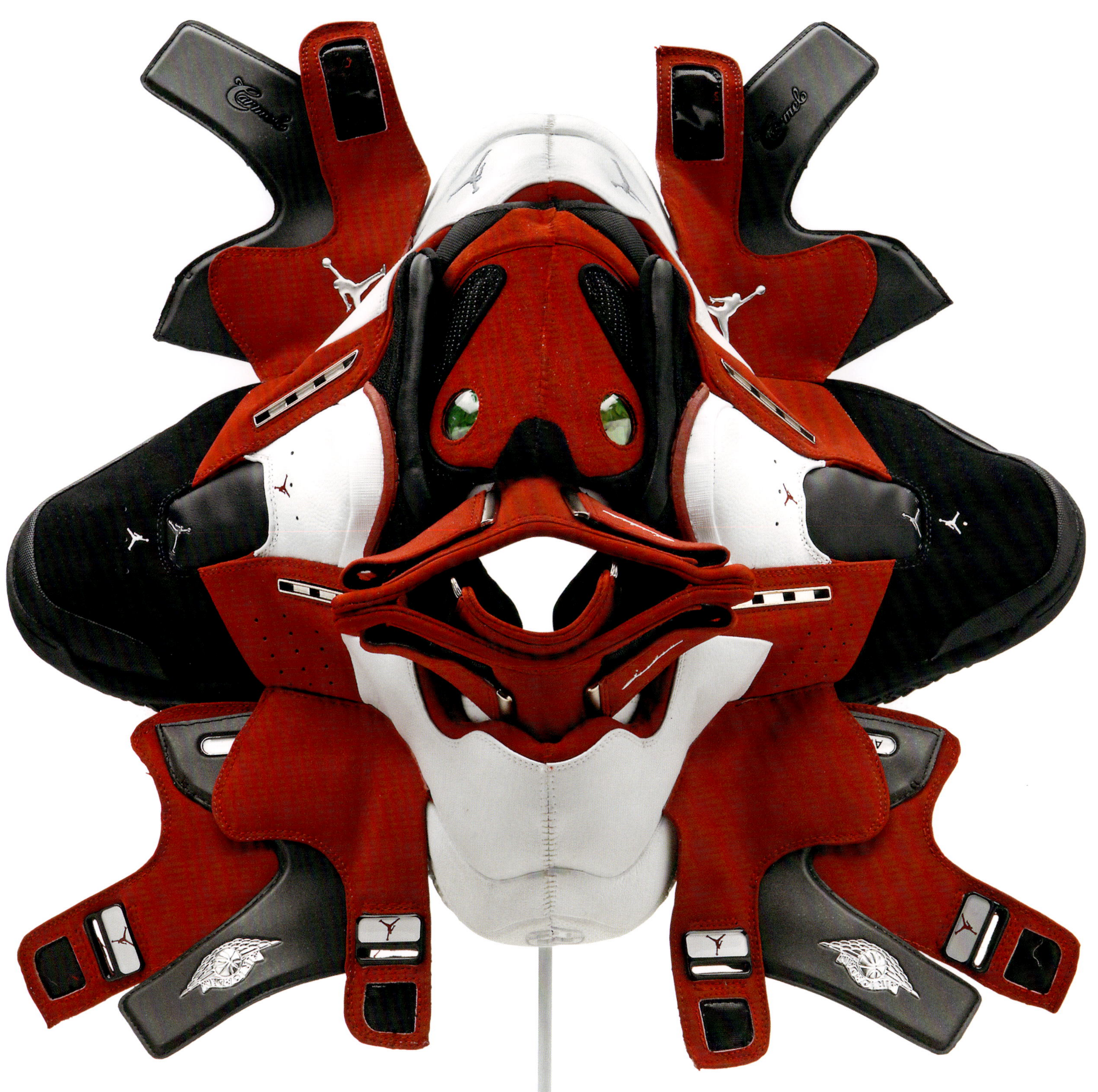

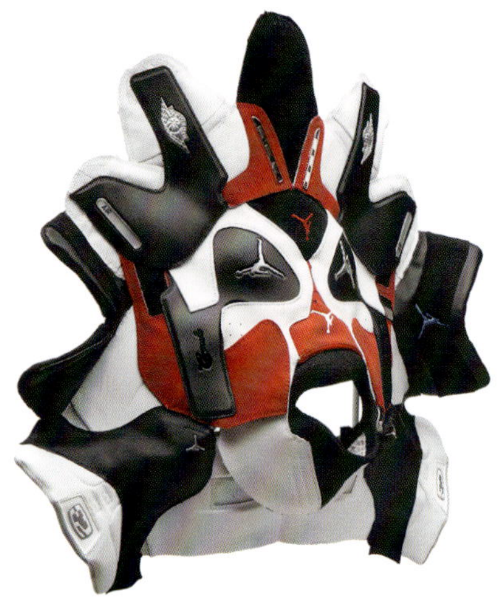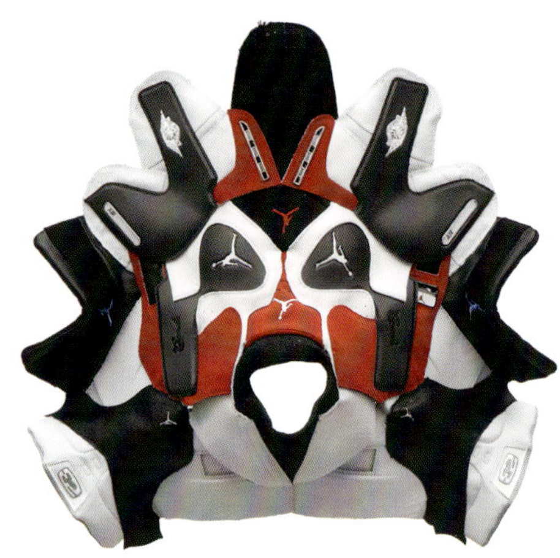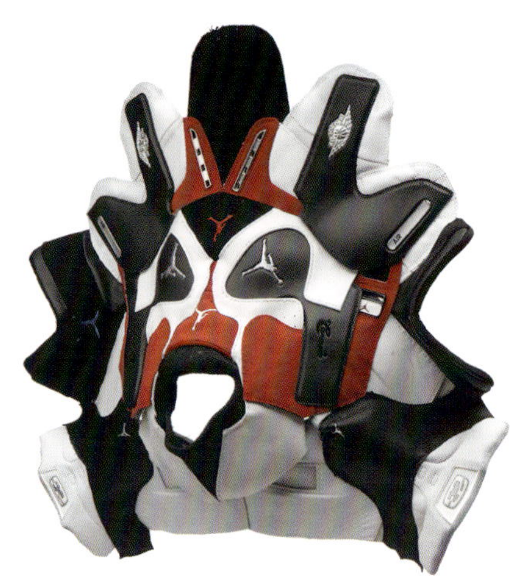

Prototype for New Understanding #23, 2005
Nike Air Jordans
47 x 52 x 15 cm (18 1/2" x 20 1/2" x 5 7/8")
Collection of Debra and Dennis Scholl, Miami Beach, Florida
Courtesy of the artist and Casey Kaplan Gallery, New York
Photos: Trevor Mills, Vancouver Art Gallery

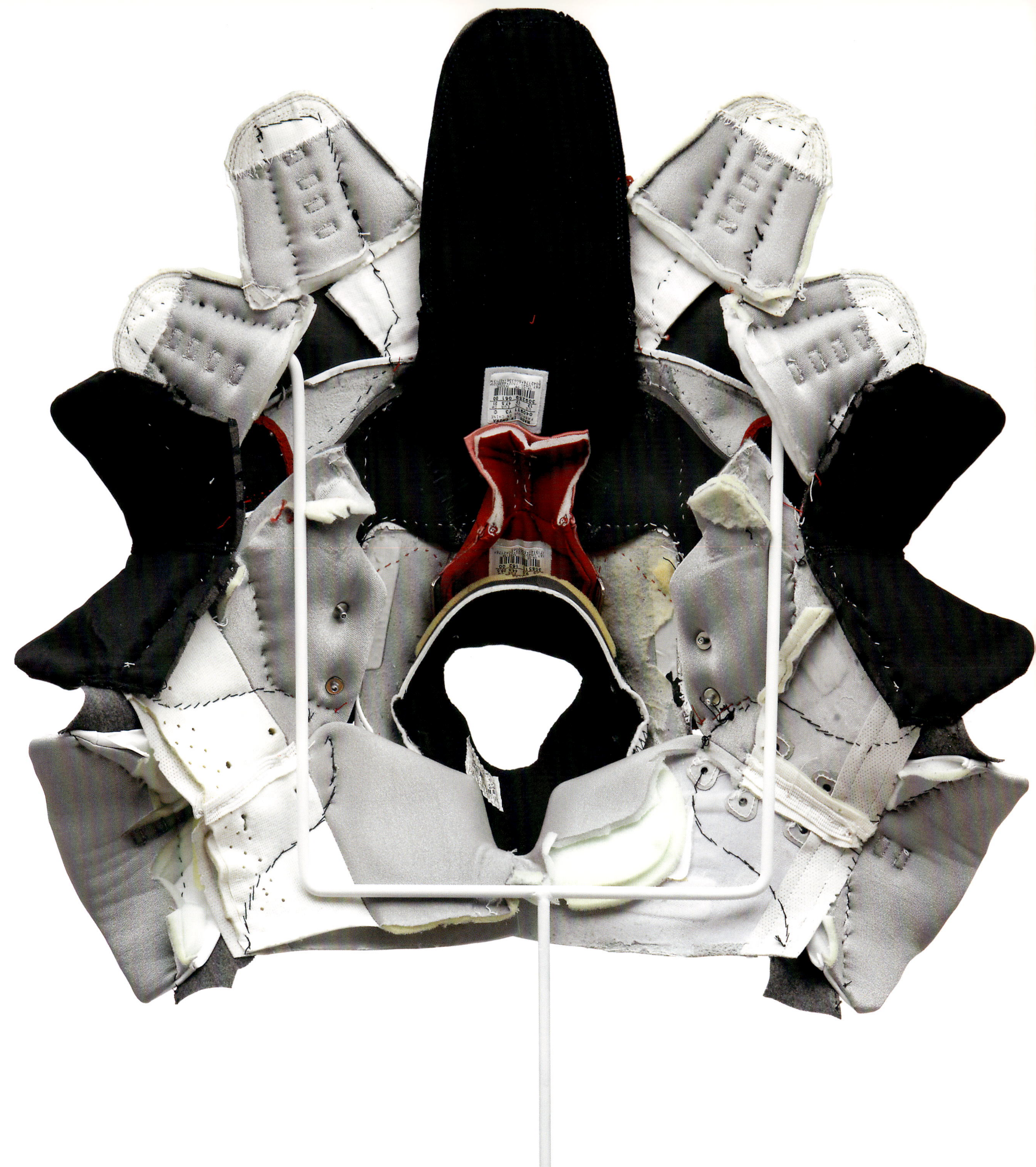

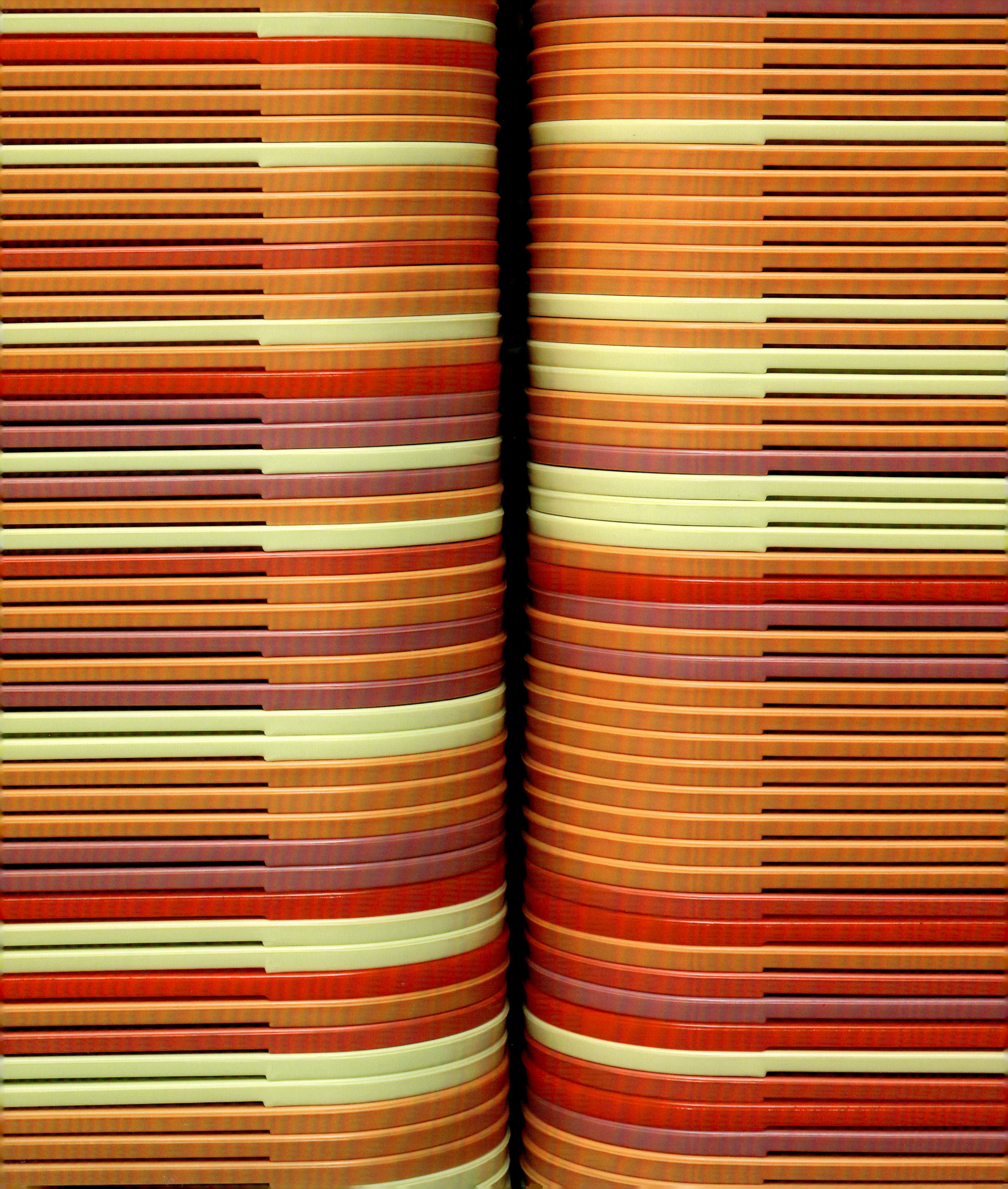

Collapsing Utopias:
Brian Jungen's Minimalist Tactics
Trevor Smith

My approach to working with existing objects and altering
them is directly related to a material sensibility I experienced in
my childhood, the way my mother's family would use objects
in ways that weren't originally intended, a kind of improvisatory
recycling that was born out of both practical and economic
necessity. Witnessing that resourcefulness continues to exert
a deep influence on how I relate to the world as an artist.[1]
—Brian Jungen

In the late 1940s, engineer and architect Buckminster Fuller applied the principles
of the geodesic dome to prototypes of rapid-construction dwellings. At that time,
the United States was in the midst of a housing shortage, and these dwellings
could be made efficiently from the same equipment that was used to build
airplanes during wartime; indeed, Fuller understood how advancing technology
had the potential to decrease the relationship between human culture and
geographical place, and he imagined the houses being delivered by airplane to
address the need for shelter in remote or inaccessible regions of the world.
However, by 1967, just a single generation later, Fuller's dream of advancing the
welfare of all humankind through more efficient and affordable housing had
not found large-scale practical application. Instead, the dome's most resonant
expression became its use as the United States Pavilion at Expo 67 in Montreal—
an unqualified success as a spectacle of American ingenuity and engineering but
a tragically hollow testament to Fuller's utopian vision.

Thirty-six years later, at his first international solo exhibition at the Secession in Vienna in 2003, Vancouver-based artist Brian Jungen presented a sculpture in the form of a geodesic dome. Whereas Fuller's design of the American pavilion for Expo 67 was an awe-inspiring construction whose transparent skin engulfed and surrounded the viewer, even the smallest of viewers towers over *Little Habitat I* (2003). Jungen's geodesic domes (a second version was created in 2004) are only 30 centimetres tall and have been constructed by cutting, scoring and reassembling the black-and-silver display boxes for Nike Air Jordan running shoes. These boxes are emblazoned with a portrait of Michael Jordan, one of the greatest (and most highly branded) athletes of our time. Jungen multiplies and fragments Jordan's determined gaze across the surface of the *Little Habitats,* pointedly creating a utopian form from the detritus of brand identification. In light of Karl Marx's famous dictum that history repeats itself first as tragedy and then as farce, Jungen's *Little Habitats* might be understood as a travesty, a farcical monument to the collapse of idealistic aspirations.

Like many of Jungen's works, the *Little Habitats* reference architecture and are constructed in a tensile relationship to the viewer's body. That is, their scale invites emotional responses that might oscillate between contempt (the domes are on the floor, alone in a corner) and empathy (they're small, fragile, in need of protection). Given that Jungen often produces very large-scale work, one's response to the *Little Habitats* does not simply register the difference between sculptural and architectural scale. Instead, Jungen's work is embodied not only by calibrating the scale of the sculpture to the scale of the viewer, as might be expected of an artist engaging with the legacies of minimalism, but also by using objects and materials usually associated with food, clothing, furniture and shelter.

Art historian and theorist Hal Foster describes how minimalism announces its interest in the body "not in the form of an anthropomorphic image or in the suggestion of an illusionist space of consciousness, but rather in the *presence* of its objects, unitary and symmetrical as they often are (as art historian and critic Michael Fried saw), just like people." Foster suggests that "a problem emerges here too, for minimalism considers perception in phenomenological terms, as somehow before or outside history, language, sexuality and power... If minimalism does initiate a critique of the subject, it does so in abstract terms, and as subsequent art and theory develop this critique, they also come to question minimalism... "[2] Over the past decade, Jungen has tactically deployed minimalist strategies—a theatrical use of scale, the multiplication of integers (permutations of multiple identical objects), the use of industrial materials—in his embodied forms, not to fetishize the abstract forms of minimalism but to refocus their potential to critique social realities.

Many of Jungen's best-known works involve integers: running shoes in *Prototypes for New Understanding* (1998–2005), plastic chairs in *Shapeshifter* (2000), *Cetology* (2002) and *Vienna* (2003), pallets in *Untitled* (2001), cafeteria trays in *Isolated Depiction of the Passage of Time* (2001), replicas of Air Jordan boxes in *Michael* (2003). With these pieces, Jungen has been intensively mapping

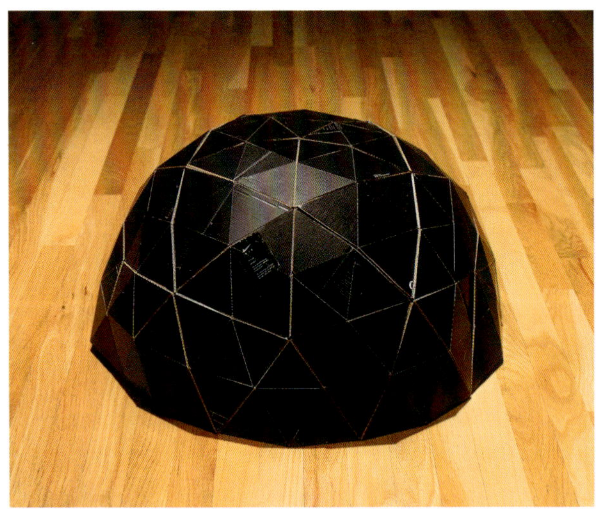

Little Habitat II, 2004
Installation view at Walter Phillips Gallery,
Banff, Alberta, 2004
Nike Air Jordan boxes
65 x 65 x 30 cm (25 1/2" x 25 1/2" x 11 3/4")
Collection of Brett Shaheen, Cleveland
Photo: Courtesy of Walter Phillips Gallery,
Banff, Alberta

what photographer Roy Arden has termed "the landscape of the economy"—by exploring the effects of neo-colonial and global economic forces on the construction of social space and representation. For example, *Untitled* is a stack of ten identical replicas of industrial pallets. *Isolated Depiction of the Passage of Time* uses one of these pallets as a base and on it tightly stacks rectangular plastic cafeteria trays to a height of about a metre. *Michael* reproduces in cast aluminum copies of the Air Jordan display box. Finally, *Court* (2004) is a scale model of a basketball court produced with 224 sweatshop sewing tables. All these works use the raw materials of economic production and marketing as their foundation, and they might be understood as tracing the production cycle and its effects.

Jungen's sculptures and installations summon up a range of references. By evoking the landscape of the economy, Jungen claims a place in an important genealogy of artists from British Columbia who have depicted the local environment not as the picturesque landscape of tourist brochures but as a site riven by vectors of economic power and social consequences. This lineage reaches back through Roy Arden, Stan Douglas, Jeff Wall, Ian Wallace—some members of the so-called Vancouver School—to others, even as far as the modernist painter Emily Carr in the early part of the twentieth century.[3] However, whereas the works by Jungen's Vancouver predecessors are predominantly photographic or at least photo-based, Jungen and his generational peers, including Geoffrey Farmer, Myfanwy MacLeod, Damian Moppett and Ron Terada, have invested much more heavily in sculpture, and much of their work relates in various ways to found or

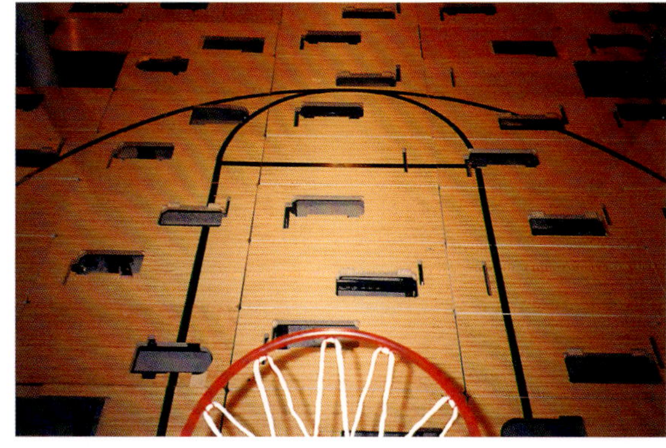

Installation views of *Court* at
Triple Candie, New York, 2004
224 table tops, basketball hoops, paint
37.6 x 85.3 x 215.1 m (12' 4" x 28' x 70' 7")
Collection of Bob Rennie, Rennie Management
Corporation, Vancouver
Photos: Courtesy of Catriona Jeffries Gallery,
Vancouver

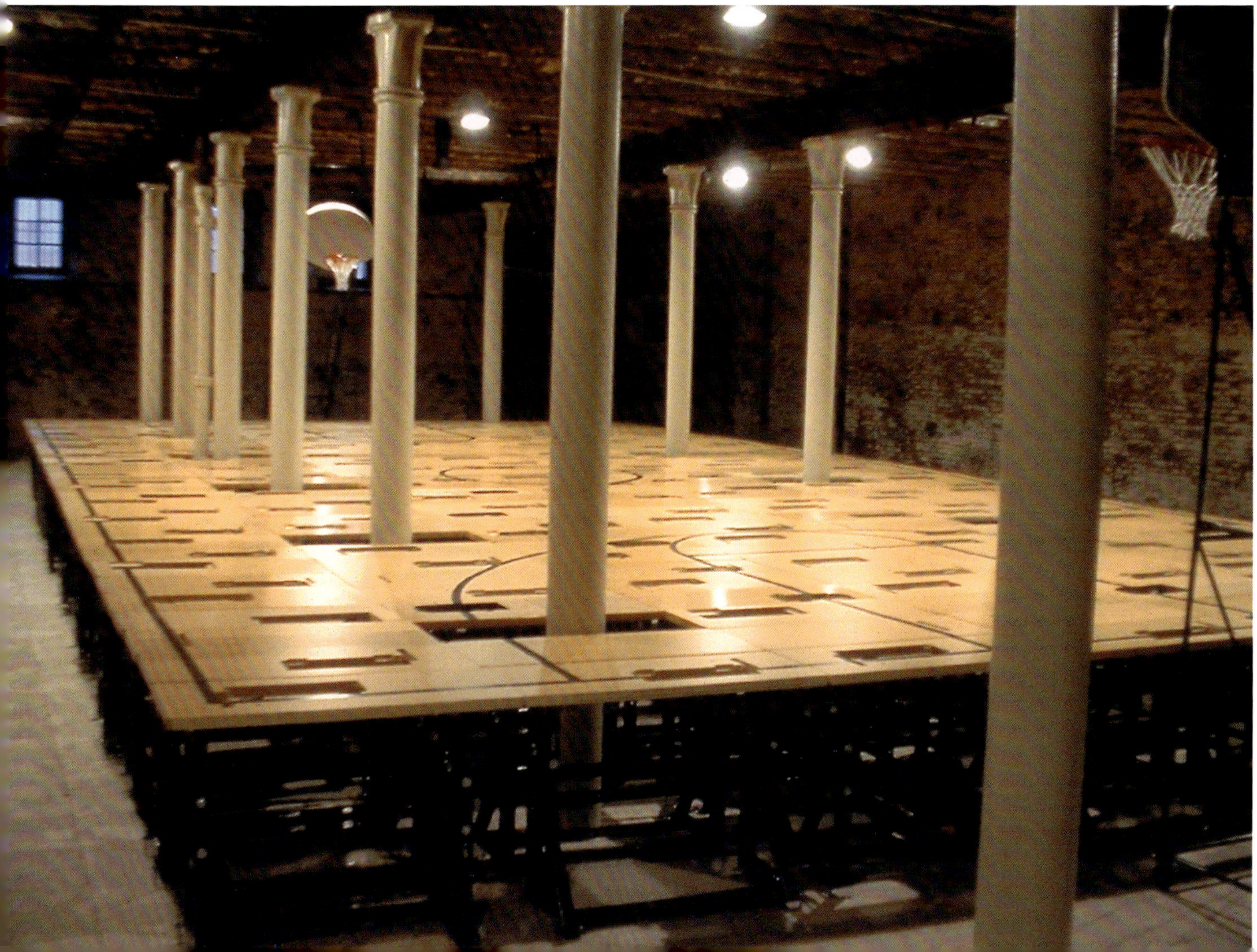

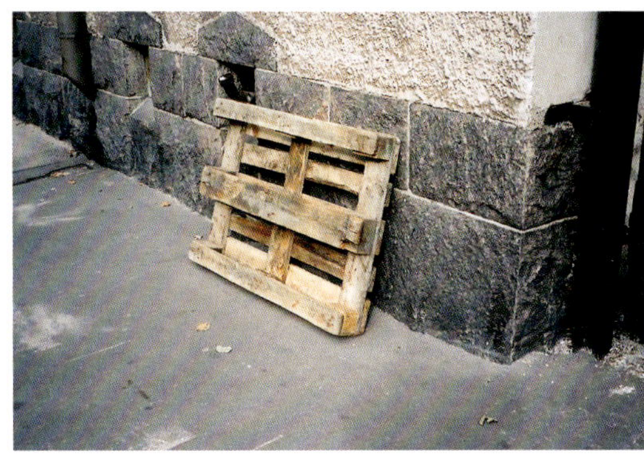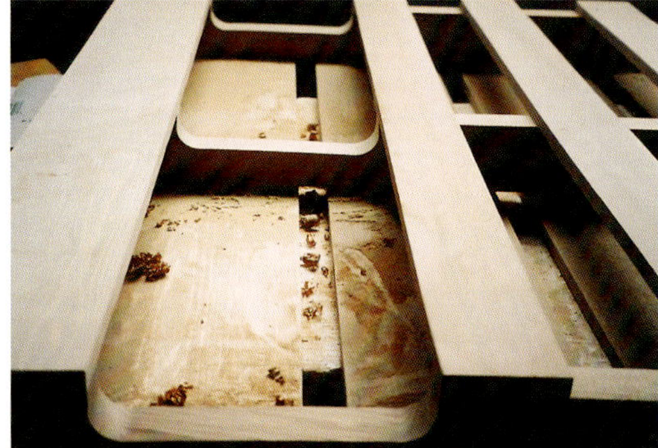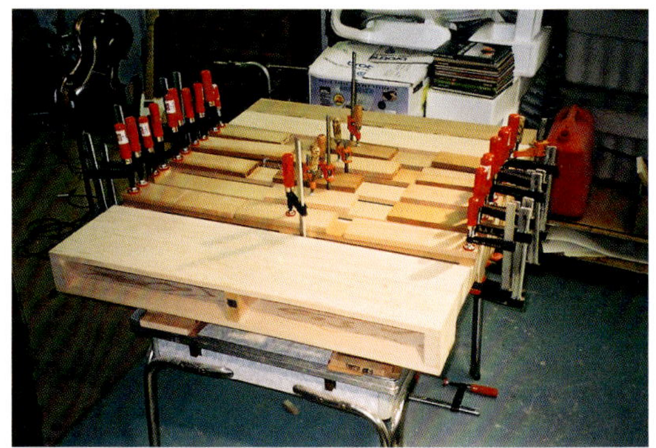

store-bought objects—ready-mades—a concept first employed by Marcel Duchamp in his *Fountain* (1917)—a urinal presented, physically unaltered except as to its orientation, as a sculpture. Jungen's art recalls the work of Carl Andre and Andy Warhol in the early 1960s and of Ashley Bickerton, Jeff Koons and Haim Steinbach in the mid- to late 1980s, artists whose work questions the opportunistic and hypocritical view of the art market as somehow more elevated and pure than other arenas of marketing and exchange.

In this generational shift of emphasis from photography to sculpture, it is tempting to recall artist and critic Robert Morris's trenchant observation that sculpture has the potential to take a position "absolutely opposed to the meaning of photography."[4] Morris was particularly interested in the way the phenomenological space of some sculpture was resistant to being captured and frozen in a photographic image. Although Jungen appears to have rejected photography as his means of expression, he nonetheless continues the local tradition of engaging in a critique of representation as a form of social criticism: he further invests minimalism's deceptively abstract forms with social implications. For example, the pallets Jungen uses in *Untitled* and *Isolated Depiction of the Passage of Time* are not real: carefully handcrafted from cedar, assembled with pegs rather than nails and finished by hand, these pallets and their fragile surfaces are not meant to be sullied. They stand before us like a stage prop that cannot be used without being destroyed.

Similarly, *Court,* a more recent work that premiered at Triple Candie, an alternative space in Harlem, New York, is constructed from a field of sweatshop sewing tables and suggests that the economy might be understood as a sweatshop of desire. Instead of Michael Jordan's intent silvery visage on the simulated display boxes in *Michael, Court* leads viewers back to the basketball court from which Michael Jordan came, where the dream of the flight to a better life might only be a slam dunk away. However, Jungen's court is pockmarked with holes originally cut to hold the industrial sewing machines that might have produced Air Jordans or other articles of apparel. Any attempt at a slam dunk might well result in a broken ankle.

Unlike photographer Jeff Wall's backlit transparency *Outburst* (1989), which dramatizes a confrontation in a sweatshop that might take place in any

Abandoned pallet and production stills
of *Untitled,* 2001
Photo: Courtesy of Brian Jungen

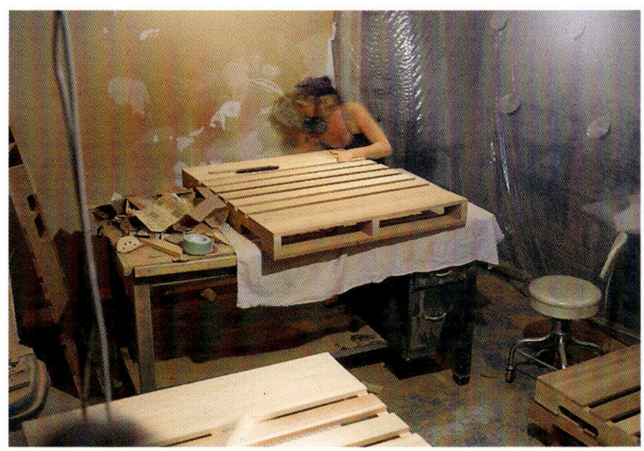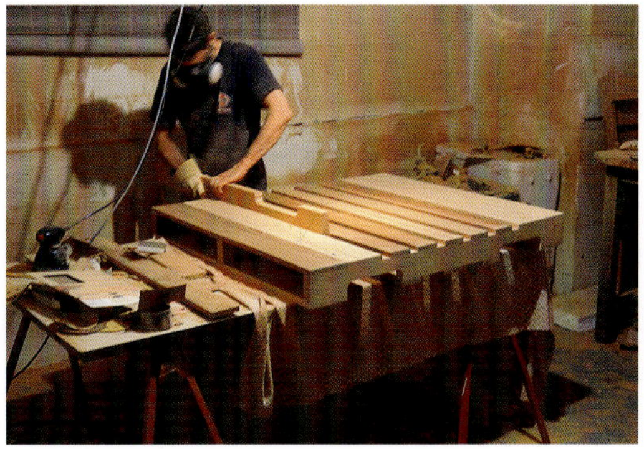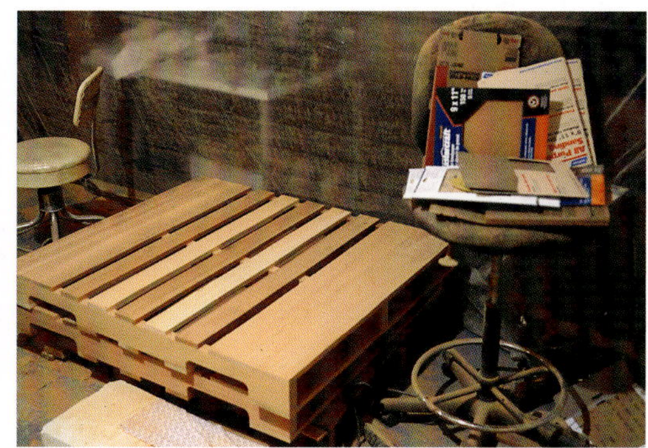

large industrial city, Jungen's *Court* merely provides a stage set, a set constructed of sewing-machine tables that foregrounds the gap between aspirational lifestyle and material realities. Jungen's sculptures position viewers not as silent subjects of photography but as actors upon a stage. It remains to be seen, however, what role the viewers might be able to play. Jungen's *Court* continues the trajectory of theatricality that Michael Fried observed as a constituent quality of minimalism, where a sculpture's mute surfaces are largely activated through a somatic relationship with the beholder. As such, Jungen's installation operates from a different perspective from the absorptive composition of Wall's *Outburst,* whose protagonists enact their drama with no awareness of being observed. By absenting the literal representation of the body, Jungen subtly shifts the beholder from a position of observing a parallel universe to occupying a space of simultaneous awareness.

Although the consistent use of multiple integers of identical objects in Jungen's sculpture, reaching its apotheosis in *Court,* implies a minimalist legacy, this connection can also be drawn back in relation to Jungen's choice of materials. His use of Western red cedar in *Untitled* alludes not only to Northwest Coast Native carving traditions but also to the work of Carl Andre, an artist whose early work came to be identified with minimalism.[5] In those early pieces Andre set out, in grids or other formations, industrial materials such as sheets of metal or blocks of wood. Several of his signal works consisted of arrangements of untreated, unfinished blocks of cedar;[6] for example, *Pyre (Element Series)* (1960/1971) is a stack made by alternating layers of cedar blocks. Each layer consists of two blocks laid one block width apart and arranged perpendicular to the blocks below them, creating a volume whose surfaces rhythmically alternate between solid and void.

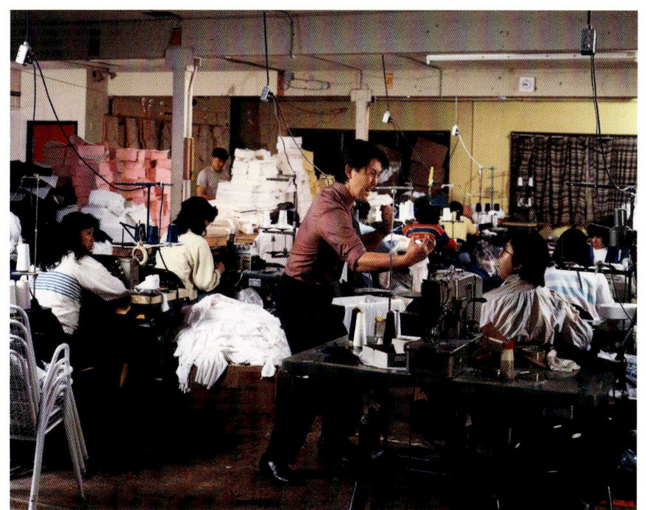

Jungen's *Untitled* is also, materially speaking, a cedar stack and has something of a human presence about it. However, where Andre's rough-hewn blocks are arranged precisely, Jungen's pile of beautifully finished pallets is slightly ragged, as if someone had casually but efficiently left them stored there. As with most but not all of Andre's work, Jungen's accumulation of pallets offers no implication of progression or other structuring device. Both artists' works speak to an interest in commodities and the landscape of industrial manufacture.

Andre described how his "particles" are "all more or less standards of the economy because I believe in using the materials of society in the form that society does not use them."[7] The elements of Jungen's sculpture are precisely standards of the economy—pallets are used around the world to store and ship commodities of all kind.

Jungen's pallets are simulacra whose finely tuned craftsmanship (almost fine cabinetry) might be seen as a wry misreading, or misprision, of Andre's description of himself as "an artisan."[8] I say "misprision" because Andre described himself in the context of an economic—not an aesthetic—judgement: "I've never minded somebody buying works at all. My social position really, in classic Marxist analysis, is I'm an artisan. That is, a worker who employs himself essentially as his own tool to produce goods that he exchanges for other people's goods. This is different from a worker who is employed by somebody else. So technically this business about the art object being corrupt or uncorrupt is simply not an issue."[9]

With *Isolated Depiction of the Passage of Time,* Jungen can be said to have shifted his focus from Roy Arden's landscape of the economy to Robert Morris's "realm of the carcereal." In fact, Jungen's piece was inspired by "one of the most infamous objects" in the Correctional Service of Canada Museum, "an escape pod fashioned from a hollowed-out stack of lunch trays clandestinely hoarded from the prison cafeteria.[10] The object was built in 1980 by a prisoner from Millhaven Maximum Security Institution who knew that trays and dishes were sent for cleaning at Bath, a minimum-security facility thought to be an easier launch for escape."[11] *Isolated Depiction* was the first of Jungen's works to be almost entirely composed of ready-made integers: the colour and number of trays in the work stand for "the number of Aboriginal males incarcerated in Canadian penal institutions. Each tray represents an individual, and the five colours (orange, light pink, pink, mustard, yellow) correspond to the sentences meted out (life, ten or more years, six to ten years, three to six years, and less than three years, respectively)."[12] In the centre of Jungen's stack is a hollow, just like the one that secreted the prisoner in the original pod, and into it Jungen has inserted a television—whose presence is given away only by a murmur and a blue glow.

The idea of sculpture volumetrically implying a body might be traced back to Carl Andre's *Well* (1964/1970), in which blocks are stacked to create an implied but invisible hollow centre big enough for a person to stand in unseen, or to Robert Morris's *Box for Standing* (1961), in which Morris constructed from pine boards a rough-hewn, open-fronted box whose horizontal and vertical dimensions perfectly contained the artist's body and might also evoke a vertical coffin. Unlike these two works, Jungen's *Isolated Depiction* does not so much suggest human storage as it copies a structure that somebody actually built in order to hide. It also continues a critical trajectory of sculpture that has used minimalism's forms to speak to issues around violence and incarceration.

In 1978, influenced by French philosopher Michel Foucault's book *Discipline and Punish: The Birth of the Prison,* Robert Morris produced a set of drawings of walls, cells, containers and stockades suggesting containment or imprisonment that he called *In the Realm of the Carcereal.* More recently, Hans

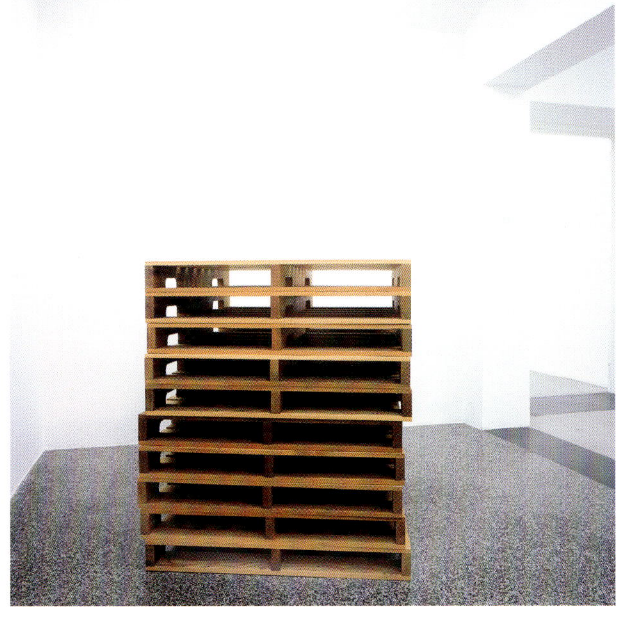

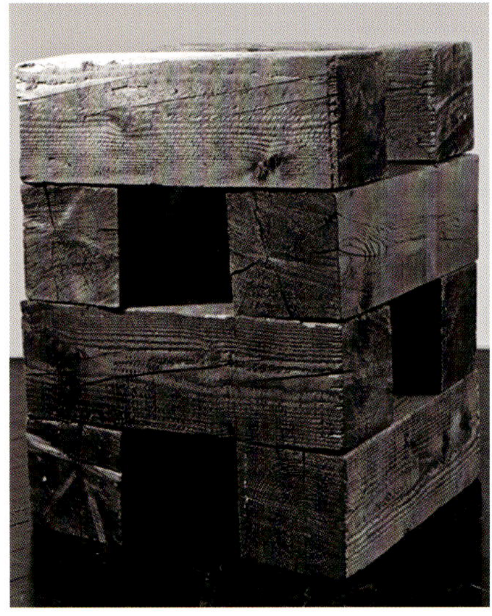

Untitled, 2001
Installation view at Secession, Vienna, 2003
red cedar
116.2 x 119.4 x 101.6 cm (45 3/4" x 47" x 40")
Collection of Bob Rennie, Rennie Management Corporation, Vancouver
Photo: Matthias Herrmann, Secession

BELOW:
Carl Andre
Pyre (Element Series)
New York 1960 (proposed) / Minneapolis 1971 (made)
wood
8-unit stack, 4 tiers of 2 timbers each alternating
30.5 x 30.5 x 91.4 cm (12" x 12" x 36") each
121.9 x 91.4 cm x 91.4 cm (48" x 36" x 36") overall
Private collection
© Carl Andre/Licensed by VAGA, New York, NY
Photo: Courtesy of Paula Cooper Gallery, New York

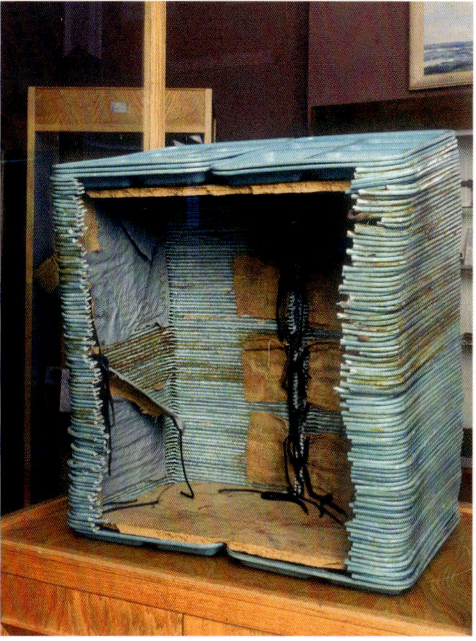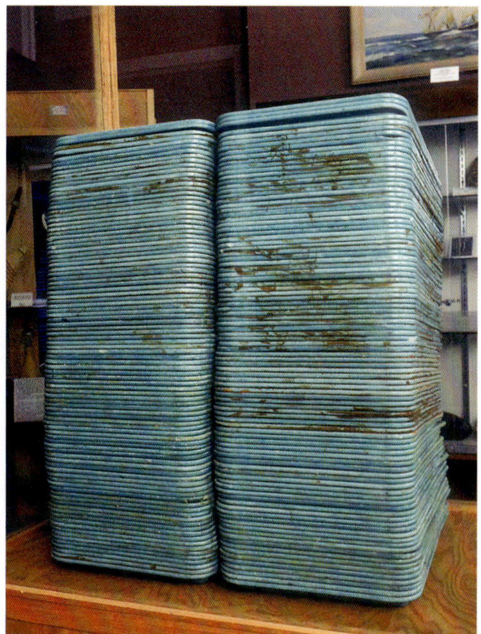

Millhaven Escape Trays, 1980
glued and hollowed-out stack of food
trays
68.6 x 58.5 x 38 cm (27" x 23" x 15")
Collection of Correctional Service of Canada
Museum, Kingston, Ontario
Photo: Cheryl O'Brien

Haacke's *USA Isolation Box, Grenada 1983* reproduced a wooden crate used by
the U.S. military to store prisoners. And Theresa Margolles, who works in a
morgue in Mexico City, has often used the by-products of autopsies (such as the
water used to wash unidentified corpses which she adds to concrete mix) to
produce her minimalist forms. In this context, Jungen's *Isolated Depiction of the
Passage of Time* portrays dead weight by bearing witness to prisons as human
storage and to Aboriginal males as integers in a carcereal economy.

    Although Jungen's use of the ready-made has few earlier exemplars in
Vancouver art, Ken Lum's early 1980s sculptures used mass-produced furniture as
domestic minimalist integers. Often these sculptures refused their original
function: couches were tipped on one end or sectional components were placed
to form completely enclosed circles. In a similar sense, Jungen's *Prototypes*
remain recognizable as running shoes, but they could never be used as footwear.
Jungen has described how he uses the ready-made object "as a device to merge
paradoxical concepts. Often, such concepts have raised questions of cultural
authenticity and authority while simultaneously comparing the handmade over
the mass-produced. I attempt to transform these objects into a new hybrid
object, which both affirms and negates its mass-produced origin, and charts an
alternative destination to that of the landfill."[13]

    If Jungen's *Little Habitats* originated from an impulse to reuse discarded
material, *Michael* consists of a stack of cast aluminum replicas of Nike Air Jordan
display boxes. Jungen's fetishistic mimesis of the display boxes elevates and
makes permanent what would usually be temporary and discarded. Unlike Andy
Warhol's screen-printed facsimiles of Brillo boxes or Campbell's soup cans that
amplify the glitches of an imperfect screen-printing process, Jungen's luxurious
Air Jordan boxes fetishize the perfect reproduction of the Nike logo and Michael

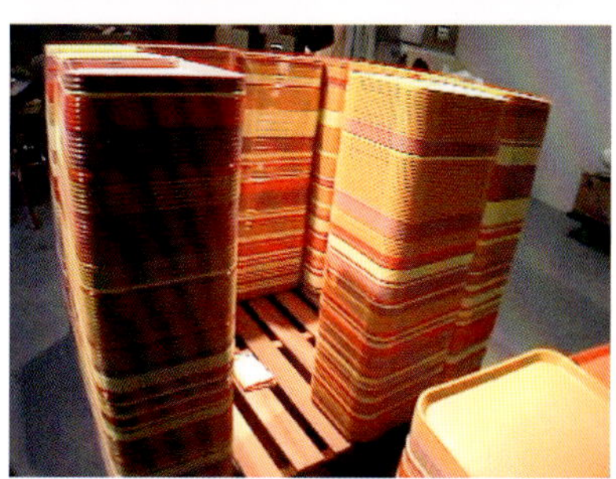

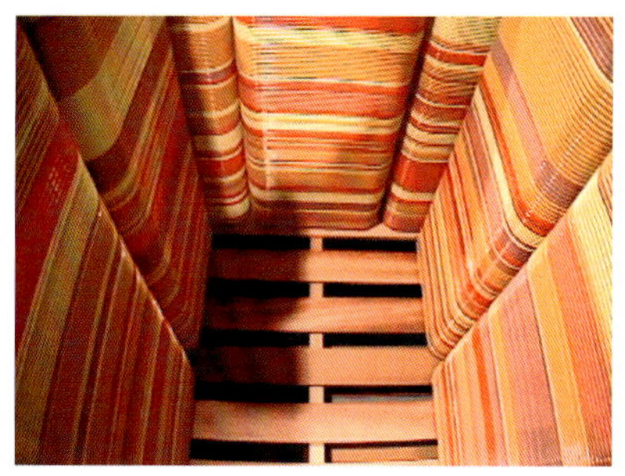

Video stills of Brian Jungen's
*Isolated Depiction of the
Passage of Time,* 2001, being
installed at Agnes Etherington
Art Centre, Queen's University,
Kingston, Ontario, 2001
Photos: Courtesy of Brian Jungen

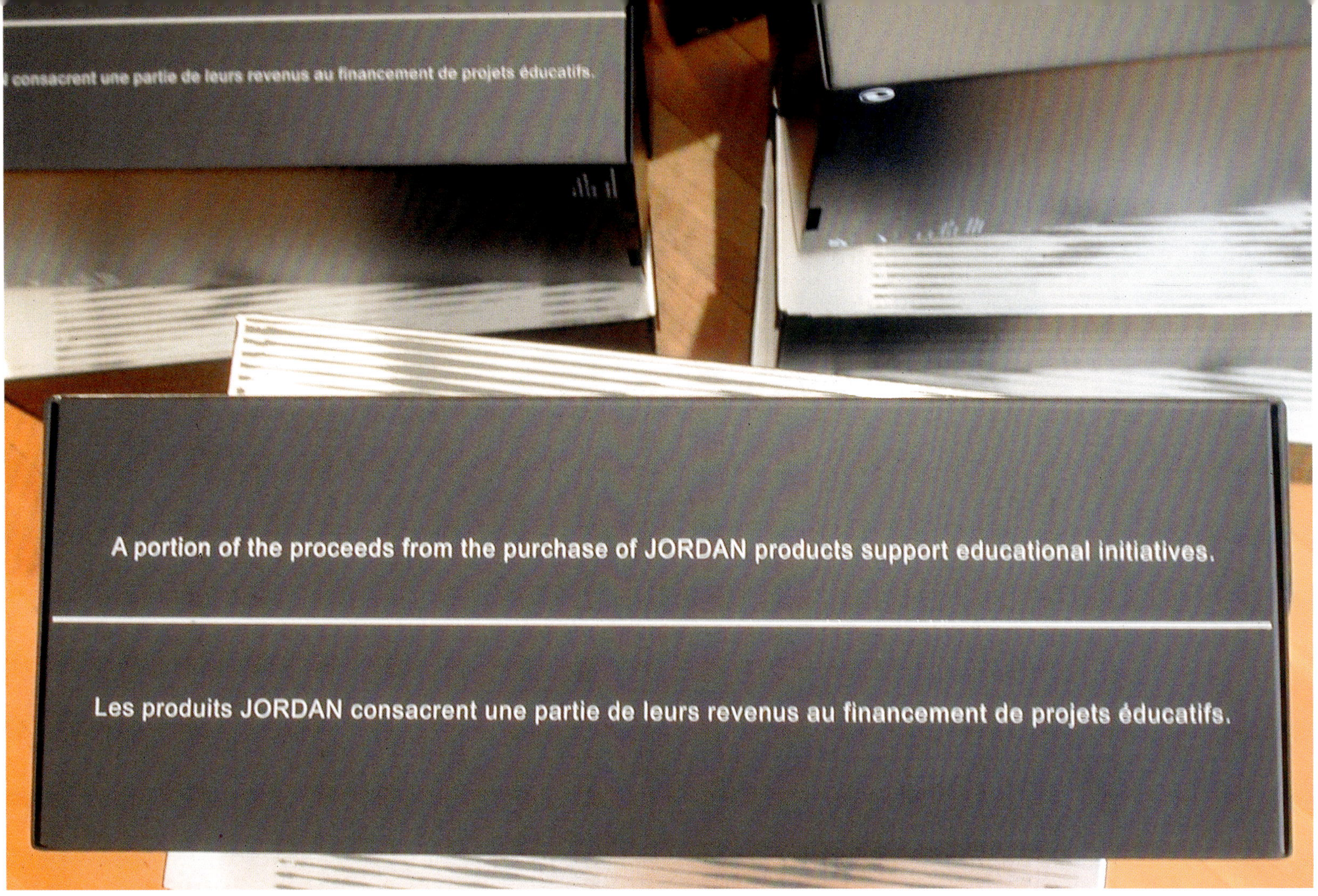

Michael, 2003 (detail)
screen print on powder-coated
aluminium, 10 boxes
86.4 x 117.8 x 83.8 cm (34" x 44" x
33") approximate installation
dimension
24.1 x 38.1 x 13.3 cm (9 1/2" x 15" x
5 1/4") each box
Collection of Bob Rennie, Rennie
Management Corporation, Vancouver
Photo: Courtesy of Catriona Jeffries Gallery,
Vancouver

Jordan as forms of brand identification. If Haim Steinbach's sculptures between about 1984 and 1986 placed consumer objects onto raised shelves to slow down the viewer's gaze (which generally scans these objects in store aisles), and if Ashley Bickerton's sculptures of the late 1980s were emblazoned with real and imagined logotypes from high fashion, banks, artists and galleries that, with their surfeit of fasteners and coverings, looked like minimalist sculptures held up in bondage, then, stacked on the floor, Jungen's *Michael* intensifies and magnifies the aspirational aspects of the Air Jordan boxes. Made from cast aluminum and placed on the floor, they are both weighed down and laid low.

If Jungen's work manipulates our desire for brands and consumer goods, he also encodes a skepticism towards its promises. His sculptures critique minimalism's socially opaque forms, yet they employ its gestalt, its use of integers and its qualities of embodiment to situate his viewers in the landscape of the economy far from the utopian promise of Buckminster Fuller's geodesic dome. In doing so, his work also takes its distance from the pictorial legacy of the Vancouver School, even as it extends its tradition of thinking through issues of representation and social critique.

NOTES

1. Brian Jungen, "Brian Jungen in conversation with Matthew Higgs" in *Brian Jungen* (Vienna: Secession, 2003), 29.

2. Hal Foster, "The Crux of Minimalism" in James Meyer, *Minimalism* (London: Phaidon, 2000), 271.

3. Emily Carr was a pioneering modernist painter who lived most of her life in British Columbia. Several generations of West Coast artists have been influenced by her work, especially by *Scorned as Timber, Beloved of the Sky* (1934), her depiction of a lone, scraggly tree in the midst of a clear-cut, which has been a particular touchstone for many Vancouver artists. It is interesting to consider Jungen's pieces in relation to Carr's early paintings of decaying totem poles in the Queen Charlotte Islands (Haida Gwaii), which trace an earlier colonialist chapter of globalization and its effect on First Nations peoples. If Carr's emblems suggested a civilization on the verge of extinction, Jungen's masks suggest several vectors on which the struggle in fact continues.

4. Robert Morris, "The Present Tense of Space" in Robert Morris, *Continuous Project Altered Daily, The Writings of Robert Morris,* An October Book (Cambridge: MIT Press, 1993), 201.

5. Lindsay Brown, "Entitlement: Brian Jungen's *Untitled*" in *Brian Jungen* (Vancouver: Contemporary Art Gallery, 2002), 25.

6. One of the works in the Vancouver exhibition was *The Way North, East and South (Uncarved Blocks)* (1975). Andre was also included in *955,000,* an international exhibition of conceptual art curated by Lucy Lippard. This was the second venue for an exhibition that began life in Seattle as *577,087.* The number refers to the population of the host city at the time of the exhibition.

7. Quoted in David Bourdon, *Carl Andre Sculpture 1959–1977* (New York: Jaap Rietman Inc., 1978), 14. Andre had two solo exhibitions at the Ace Gallery in Vancouver in 1974 and 1975; the latter included his signature arrangements of cedar blocks.

8. Carl Andre, "Artworker: Interview with Jeanne Siegel [1970]" in James Meyer, *Minimalism* (London: Phaidon Press, 2000), 252.

9. Ibid.

10. *Museopathy,* curated by Jim Drobnick and Jennifer Fisher, Agnes Etherington Art Centre, Queen's University, Kingston, Ontario, in association with Displaycult, 2002.

11. Ibid.

12. Ibid.

13. Jens Hoffmann, "Brian Jungen," *Flash Art* 36, no. 231 (July–September 2003): 86.

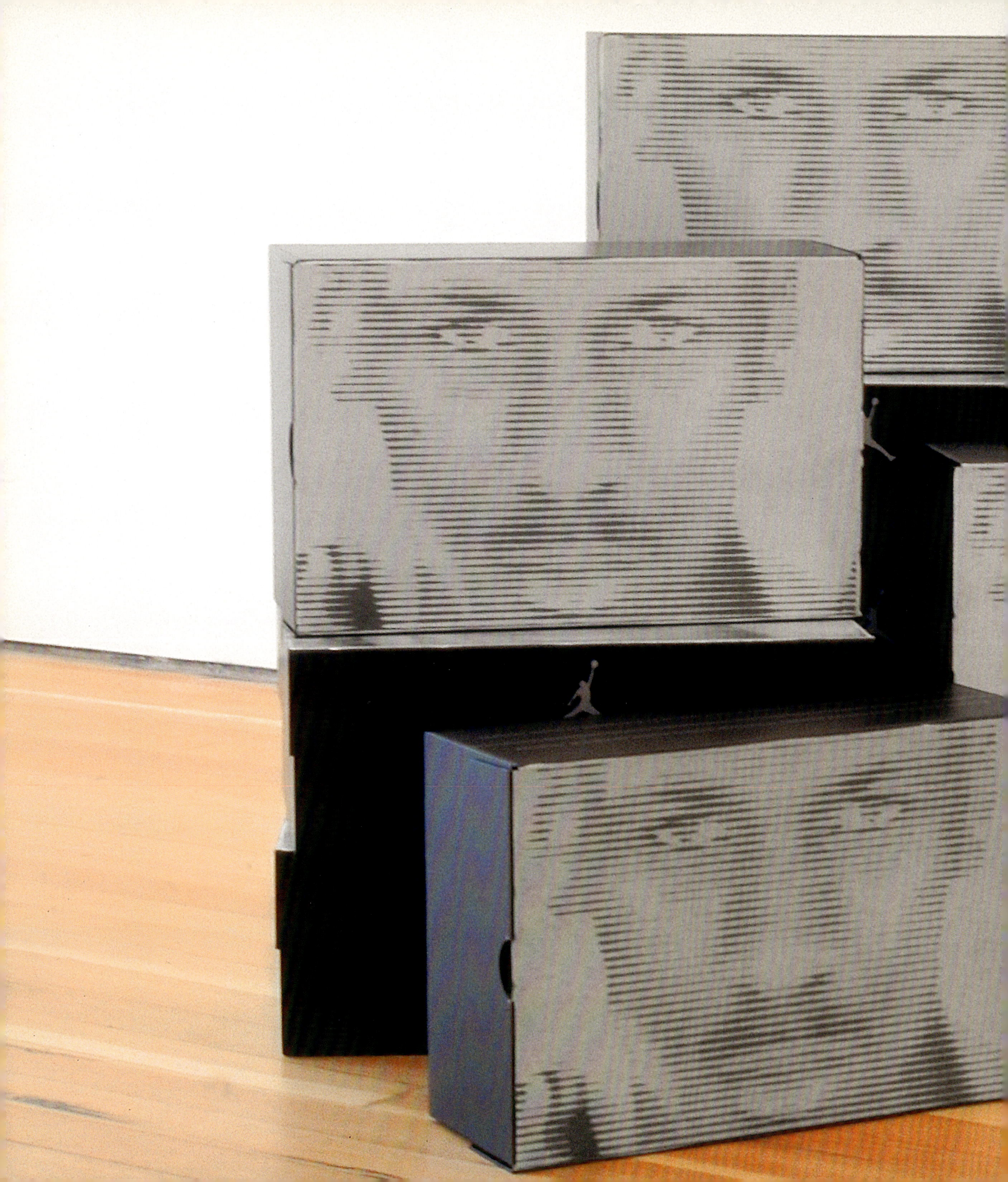

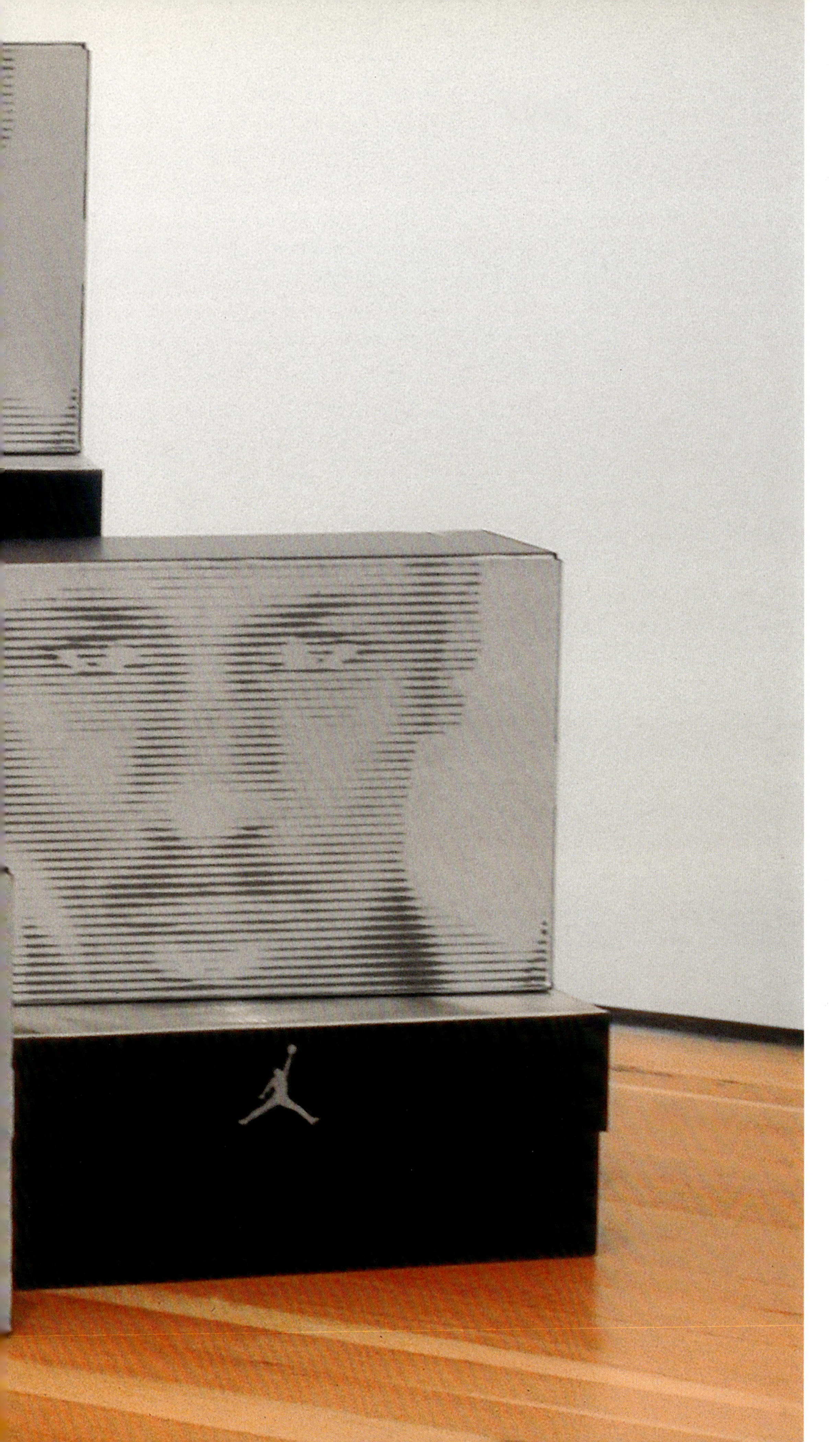

Michael, 2003
screen print on powder-coated aluminium, 10 boxes
86.4 x 117.8 x 83.8 cm (34" x 44" x 33") approximate
installation dimension
24.1 x 38.1 x 13.3 cm (9 1/2" x 15" x 5 1/4") each box
Collection of Bob Rennie, Rennie Management Corporation,
Vancouver
Photo: Courtesy of Catriona Jeffries Gallery, Vancouver

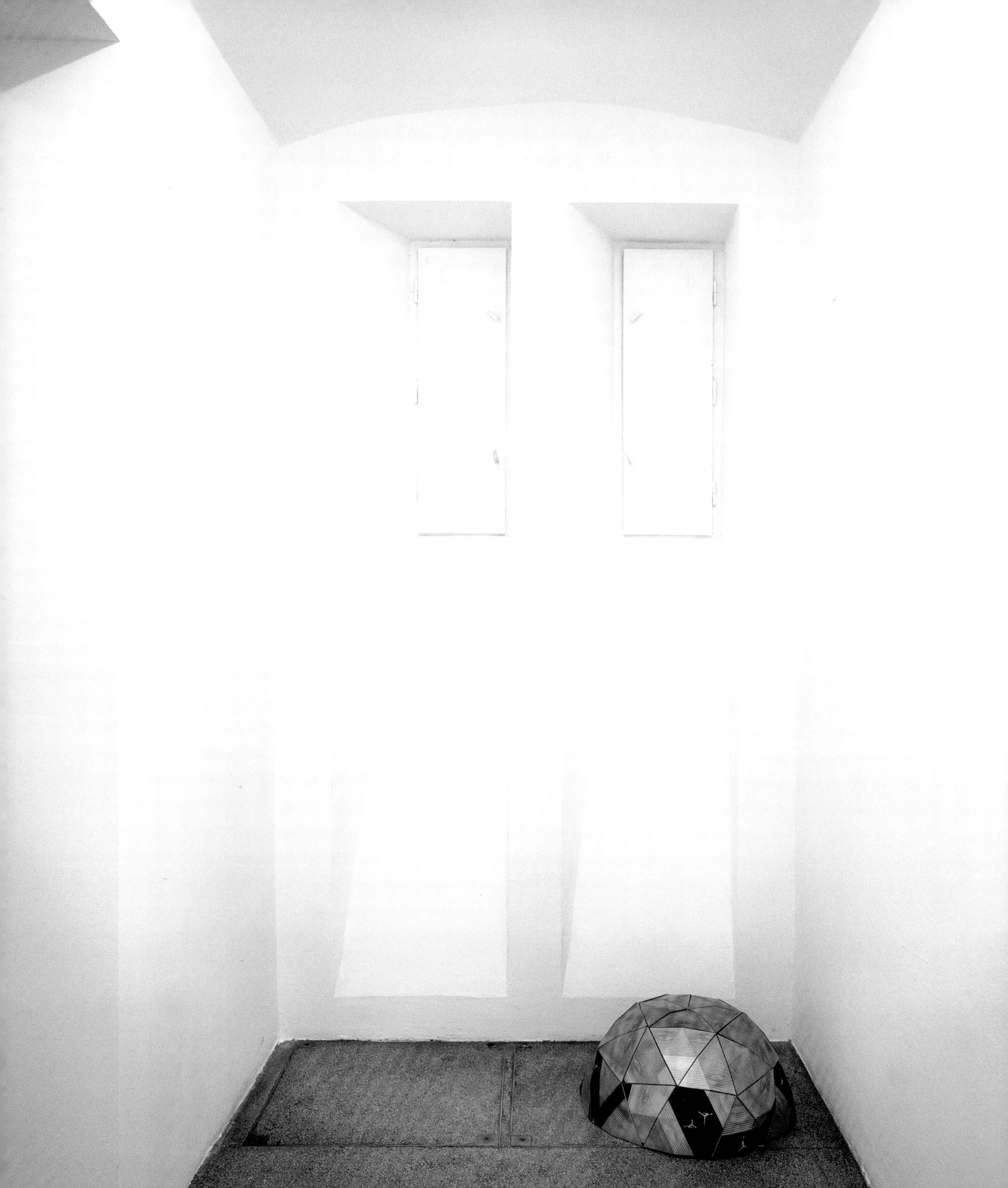

OPPOSITE:
Little Habitat I, 2003
Installation view at Secession, Vienna, 2003
Nike Air Jordan boxes
65 x 65 x 30 cm (25 1/2" x 25 1/2" x 11 3/4")
Collection of Secession, Vienna
Photo: Matthias Herrmann, Secession

Little Habitat II, 2004
Nike Air Jordan boxes
65 x 65 x 30 cm (25 1/2" x 25 1/2" x 11 3/4")
Collection of Brett Shaheen, Cleveland
Photo: Courtesy of Walter Phillips Gallery, Banff, Alberta

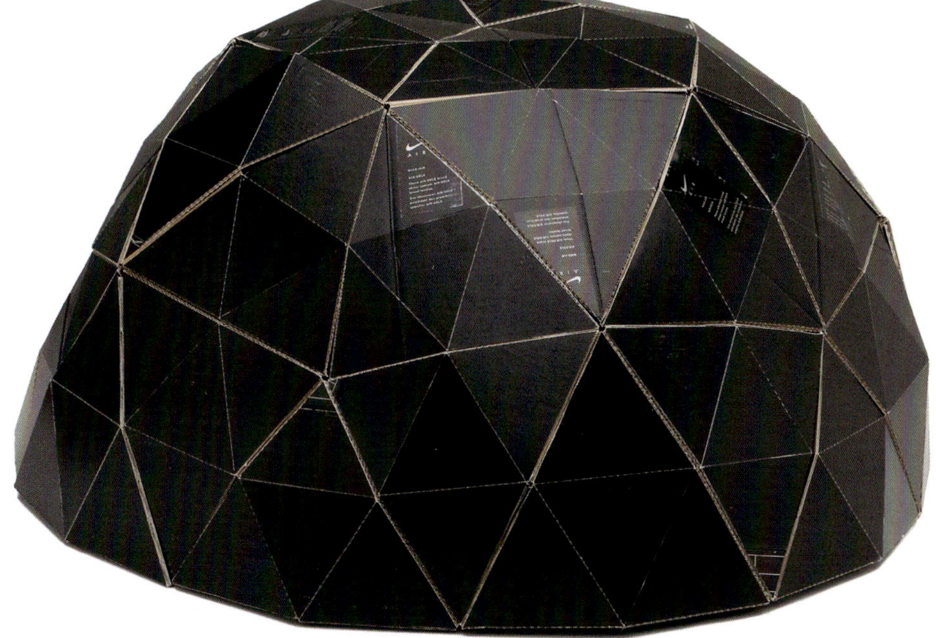

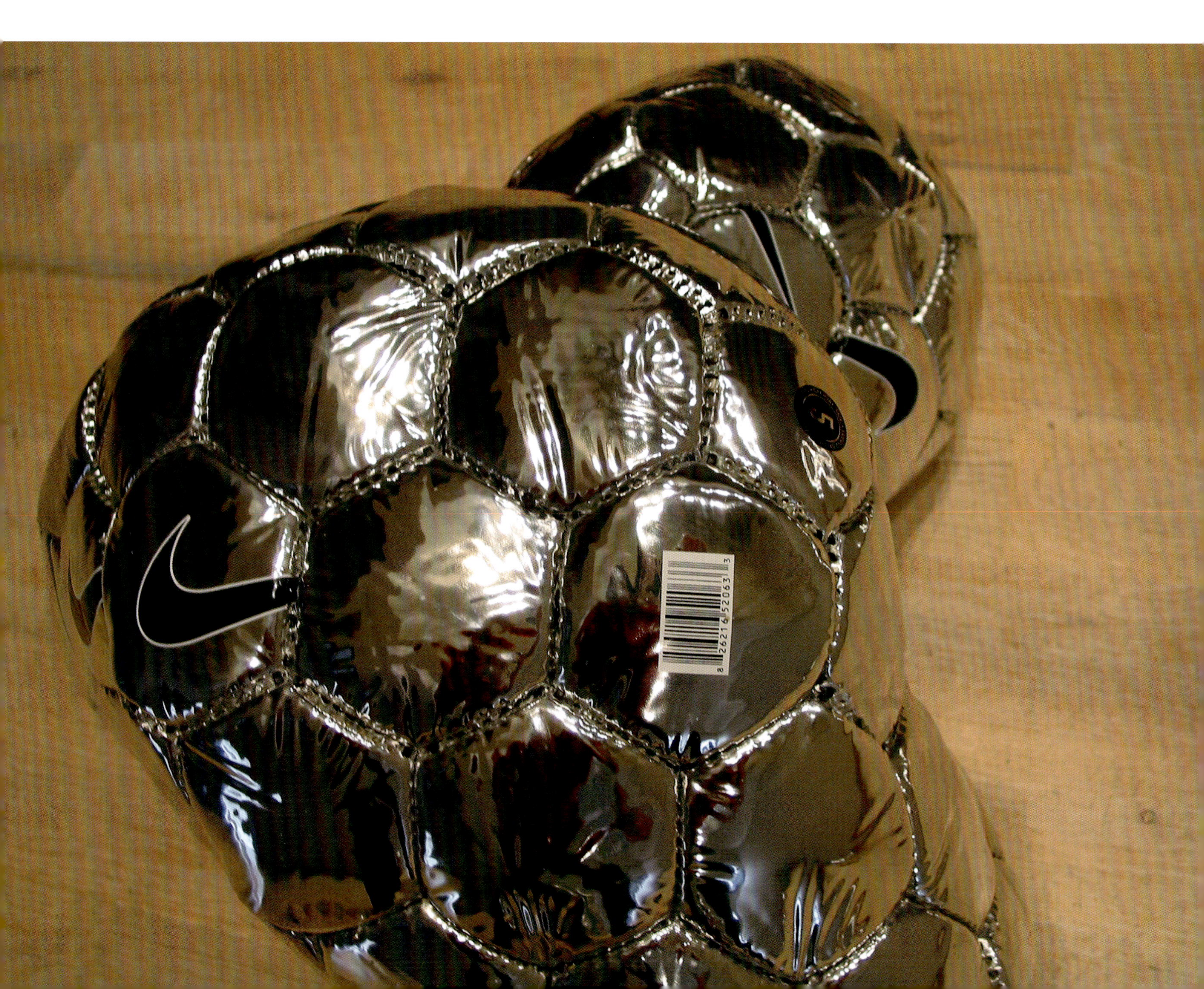

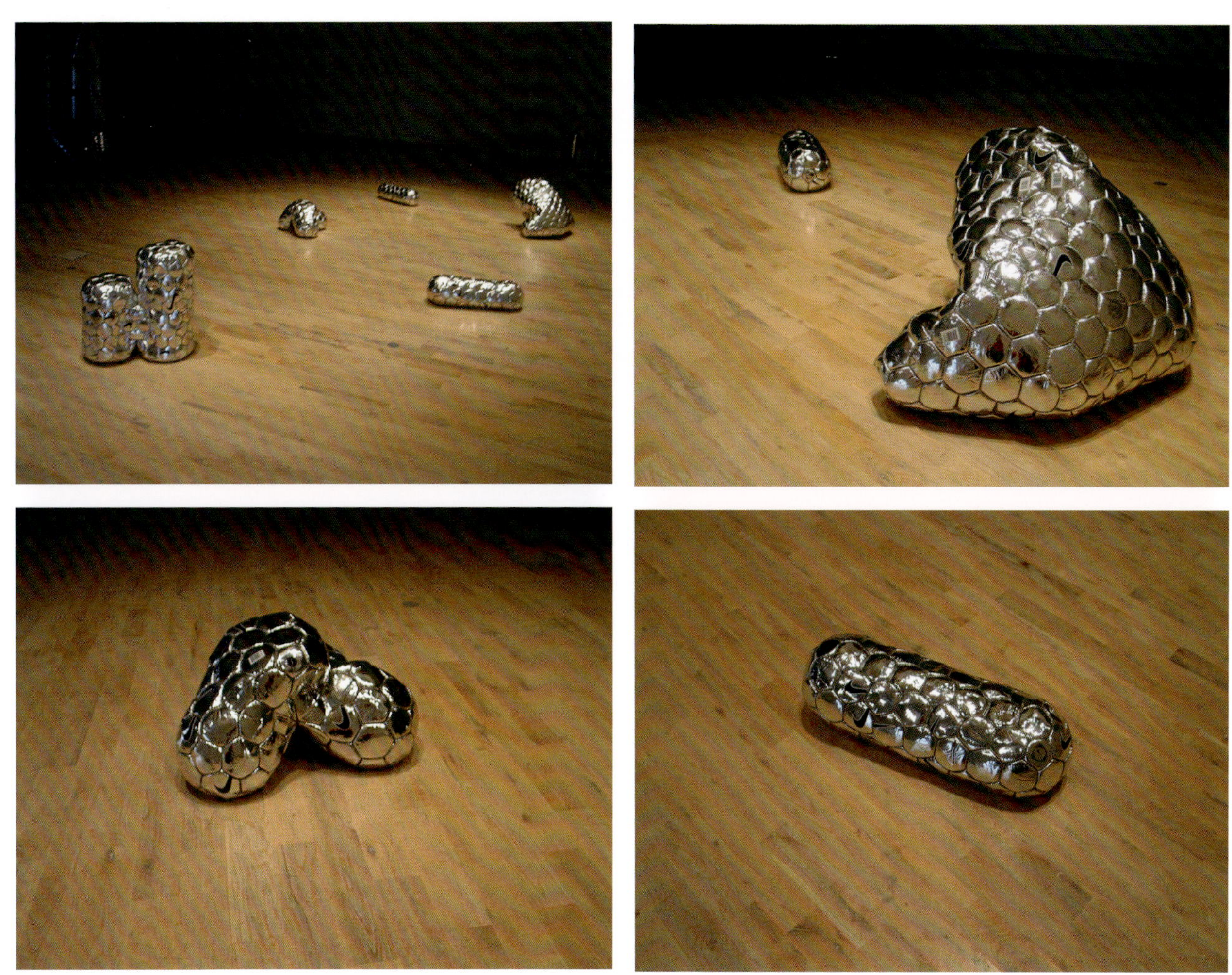

Modern Sculpture, 2005
Installation view at Reykjavik Arts Festival, 2005
soccer balls and lava rocks
installation dimensions variable
Collection of the artist
Photos: Brian Jungen

Beer Cooler, 2002
Installation views at Art Gallery of Nova Scotia, Halifax, 2004
Photos: Sue Klabunde, Art Gallery of Nova Scotia

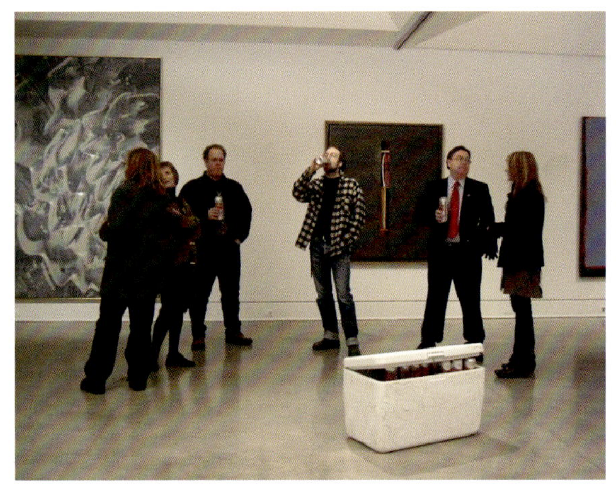
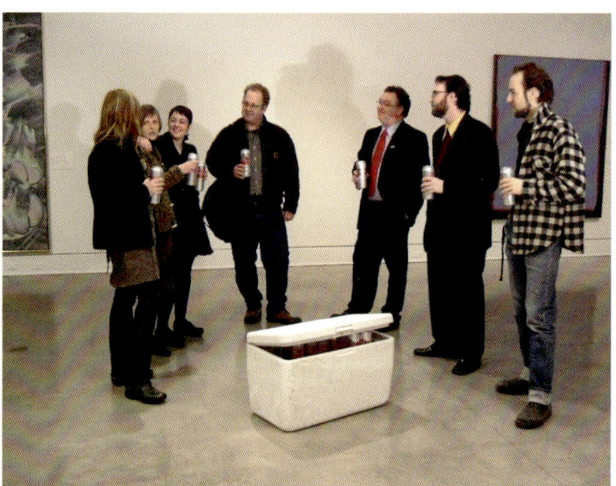
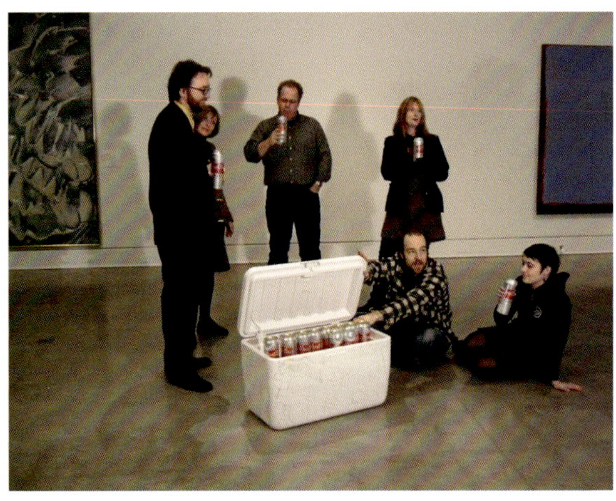
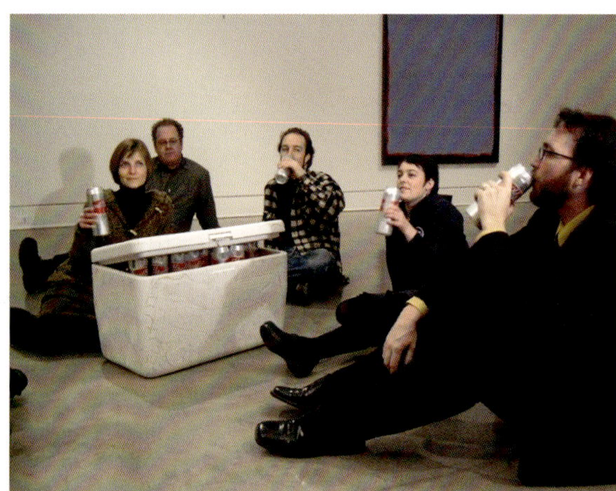

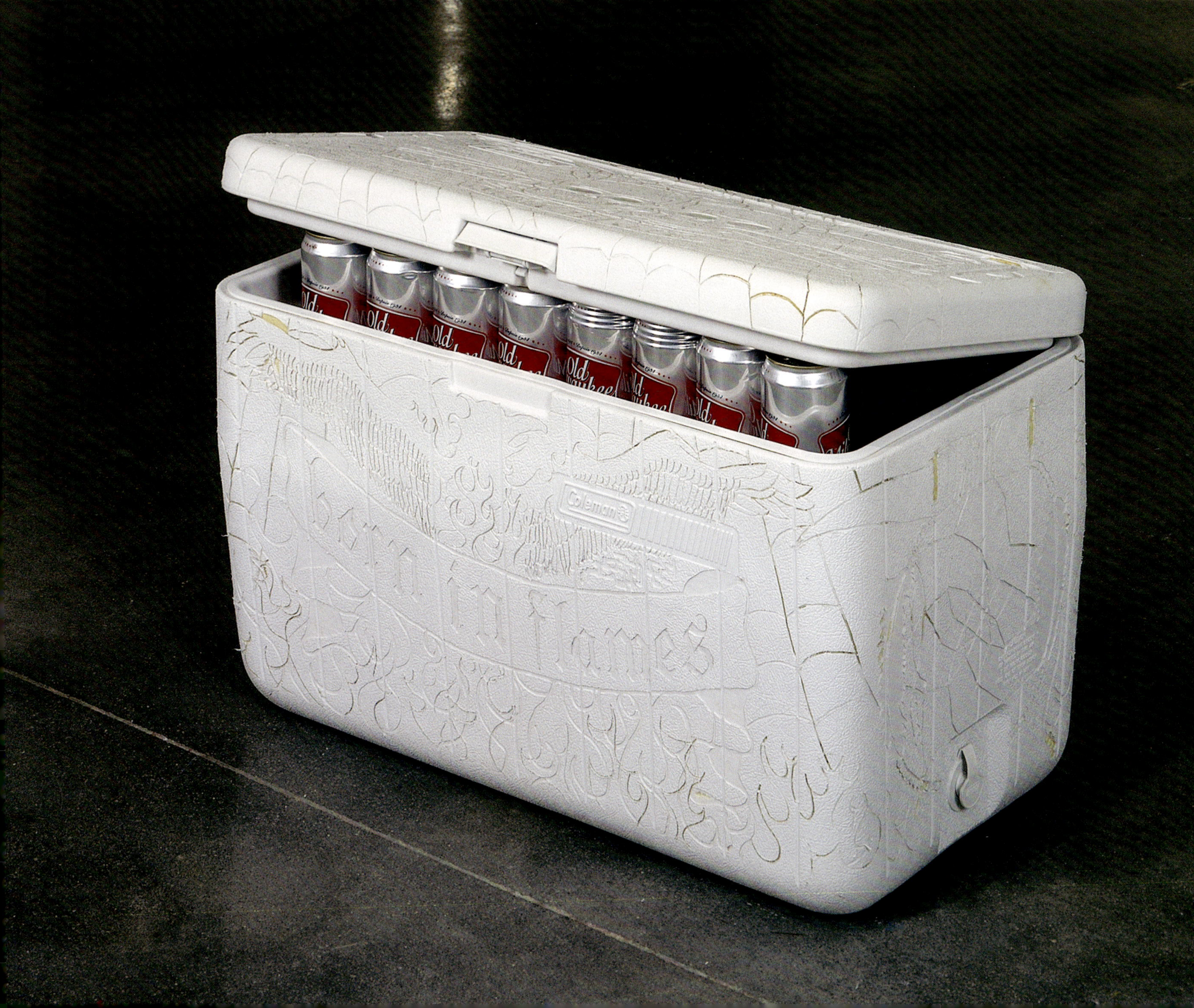

Beer Cooler, 2002
cooler, beer cans
40.6 x 71.1 x 40.6 cm (16" x 28" x 16")
Collection of the Art Gallery of Nova Scotia, Halifax
Photo: Steve Farmer

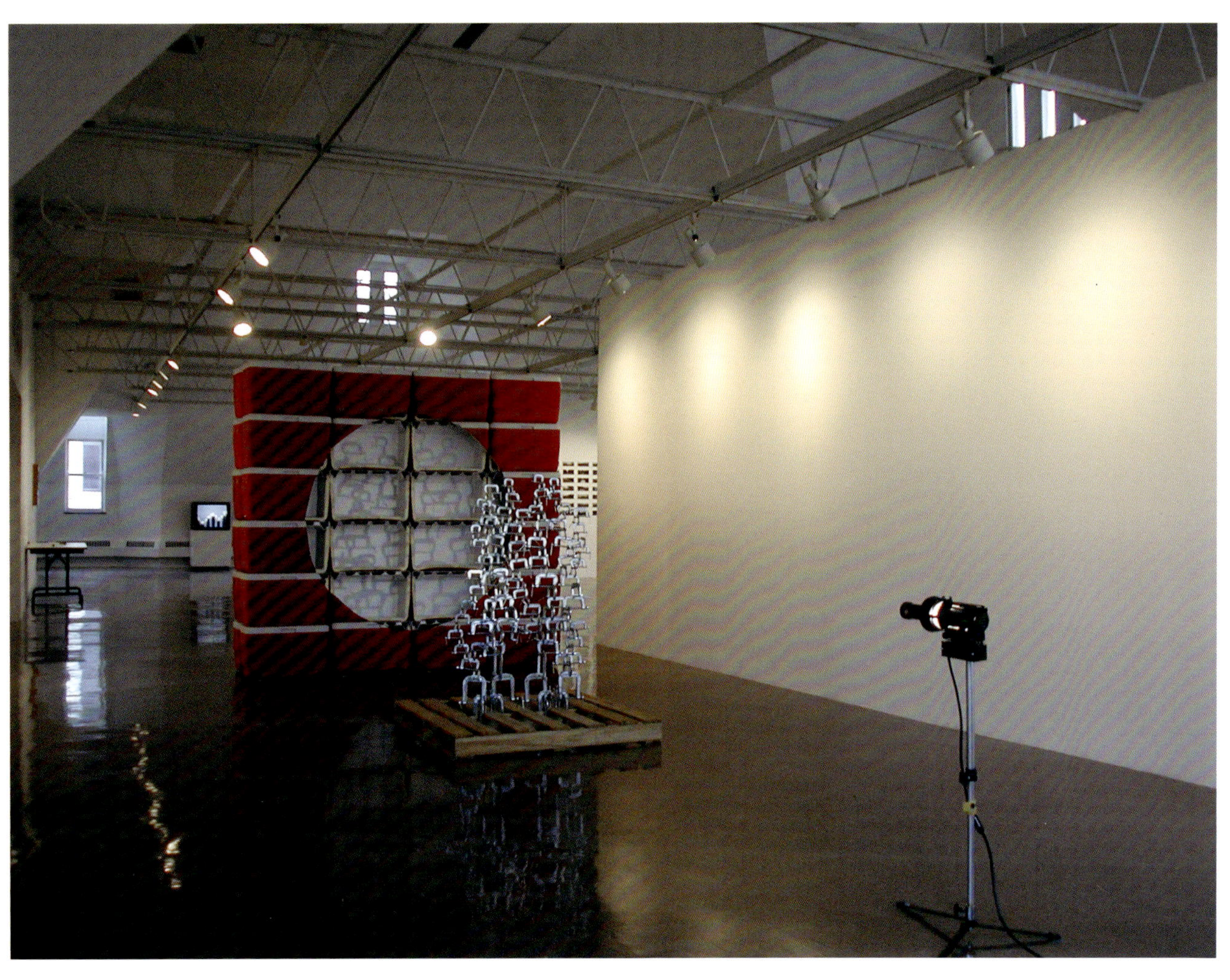

Void, 2002
Installation view at Renaissance Society, Chicago, 2002
Coleman coolers, wooden pallet, light, metal clamps
221 x 244 x 69 cm (87″ x 90 1/16″ x 27 1/8″)
Collection of Bob Rennie, Rennie Management Corporation, Vancouver
Photo: Courtesy Catriona Jeffries Gallery, Vancouver

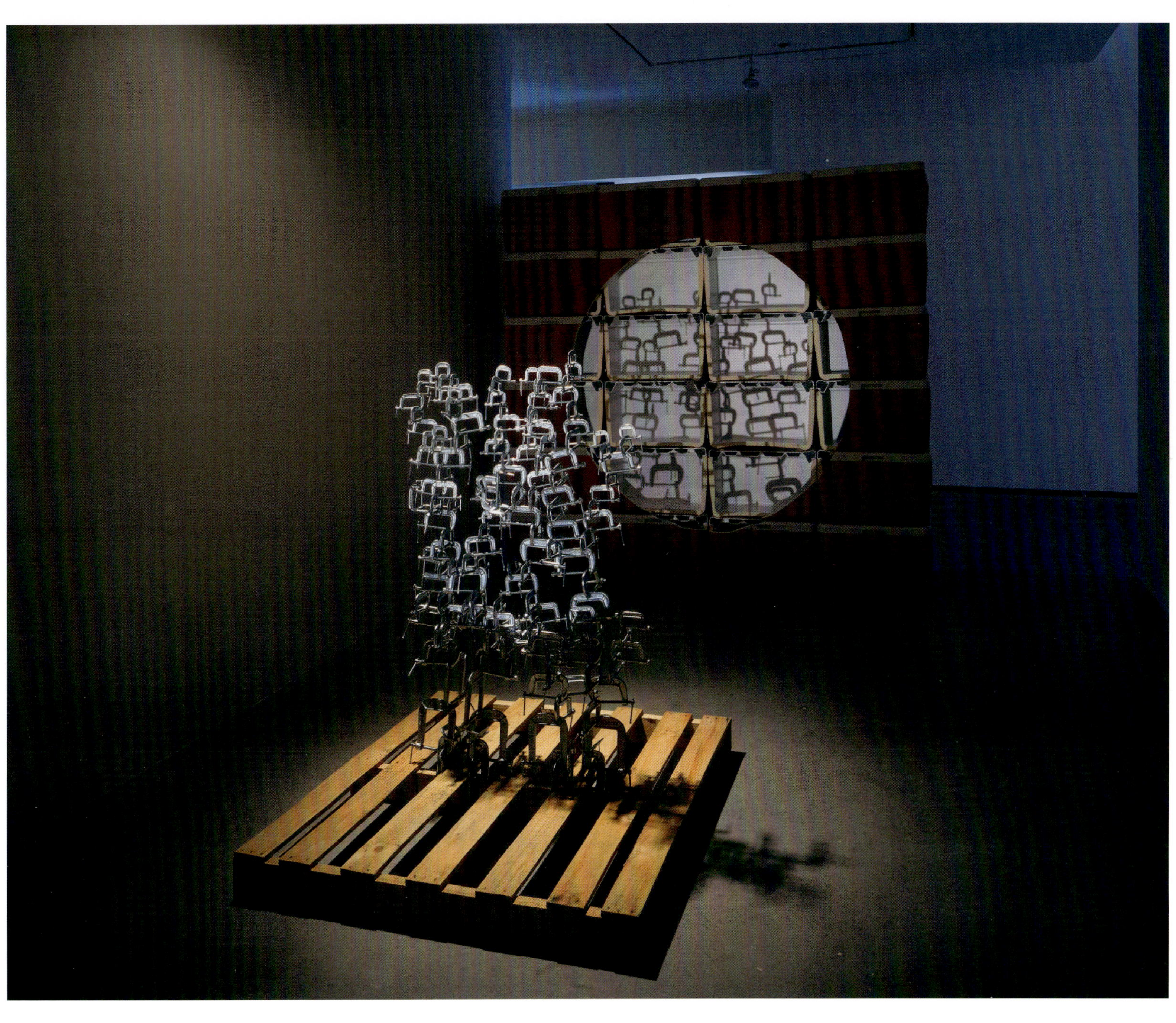

Void, 2002
Installation view at The Power Plant, Toronto, 2002
Photo: Cheryl O'Brien, Courtesy of The Power Plant, Toronto

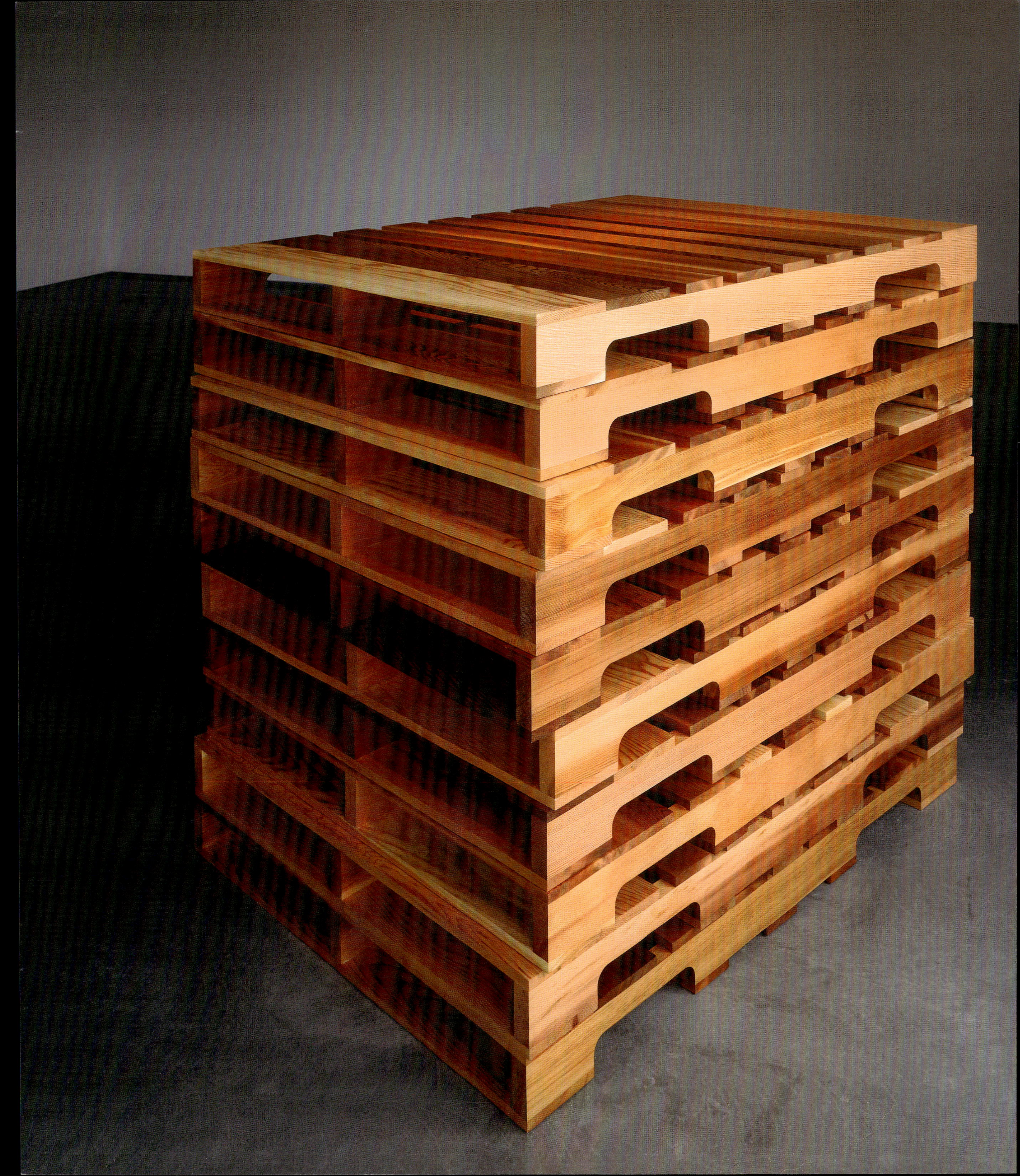

OPPOSITE AND BELOW:
Untitled, 2001 (with detail)
Installation at Contemporary Art Gallery, Vancouver, 2001
red cedar
116.2 x 119.4 x 101.6 cm (45 3/4" x 47" x 40")
Collection of Bob Rennie, Rennie Management Corporation, Vancouver
Photos: Kim Clarke

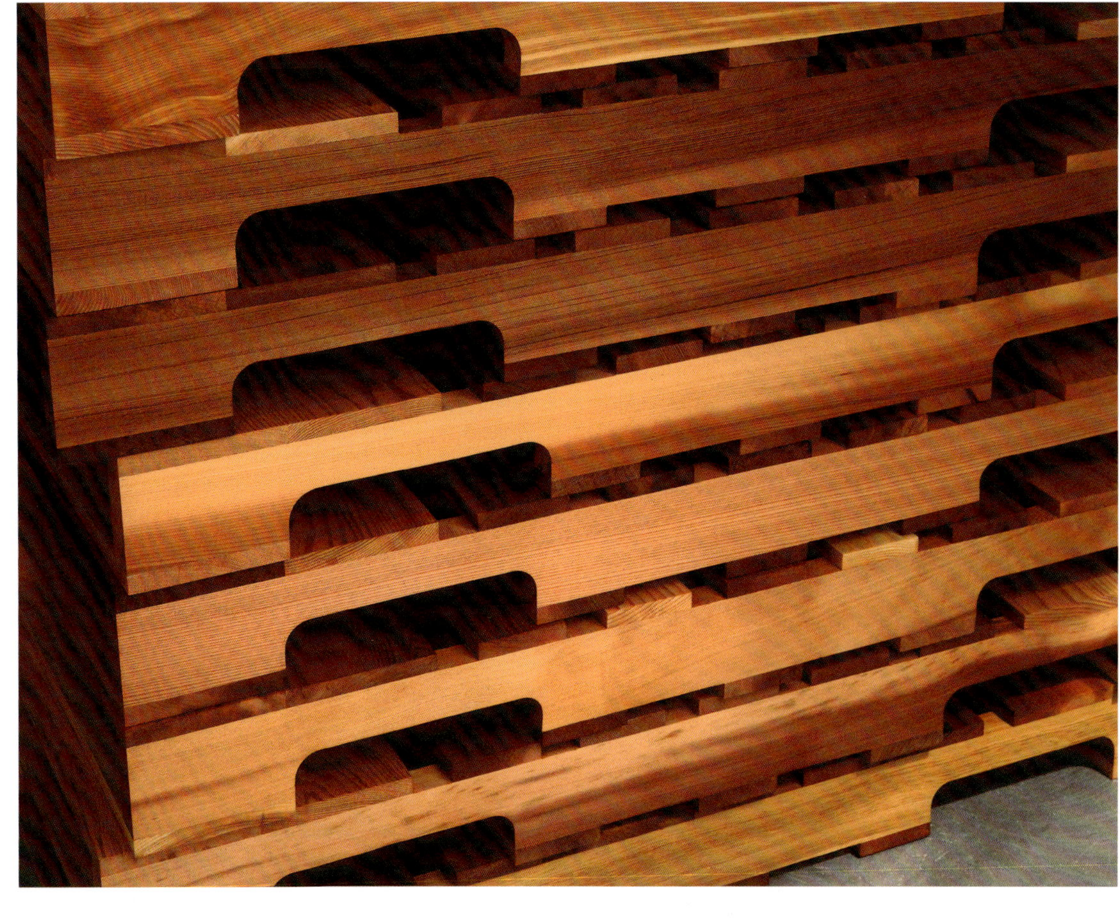

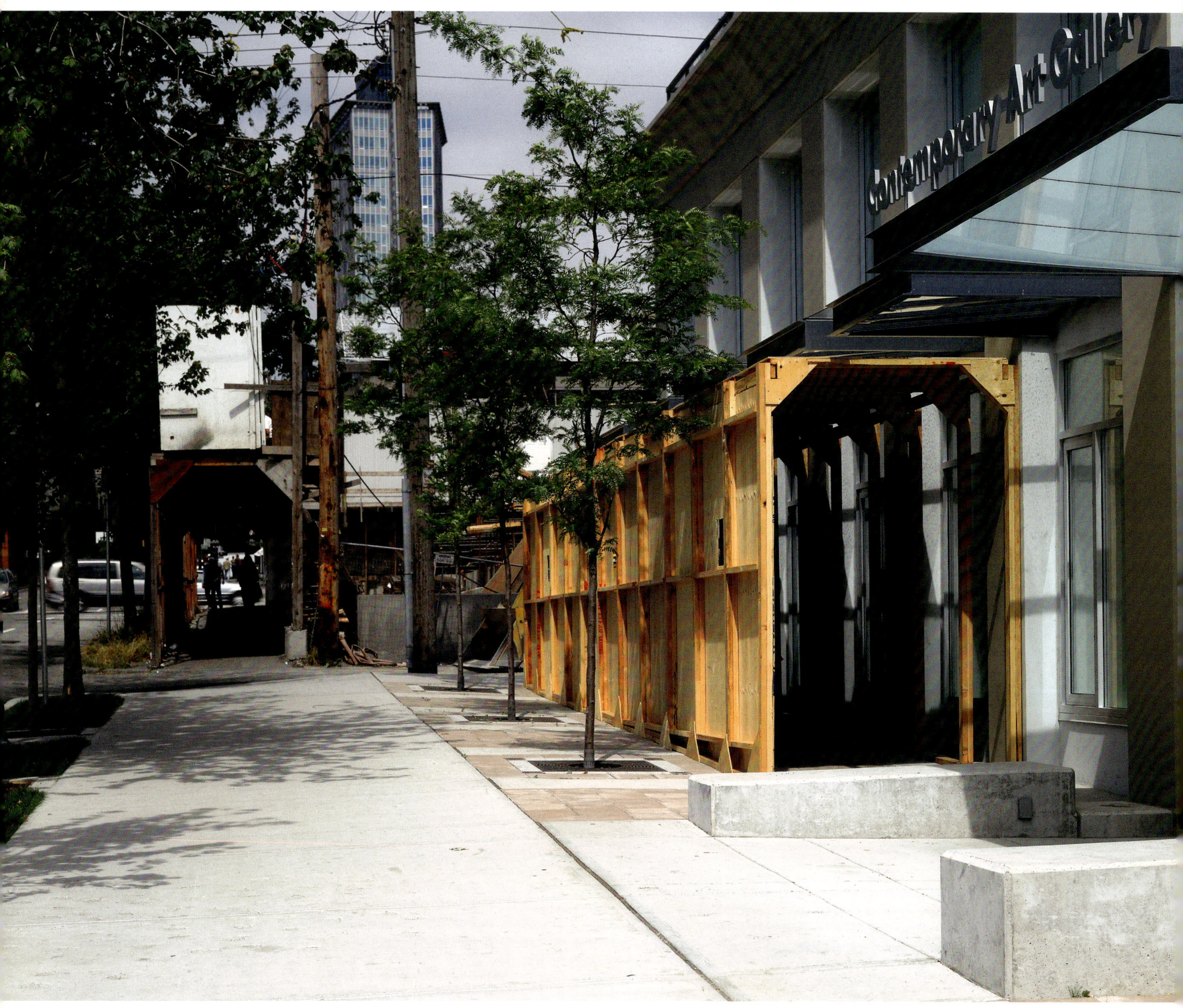

ABOVE AND OPPOSITE:
Unlimited Growth Increases the Divide, 2001 (with detail)
Installation view, exterior of Contemporary Art Gallery, Vancouver, 2001
wood and posters
243.8 x 121.9 x 182.9 cm (8' x 4' x 6')
Photos: Kim Clarke

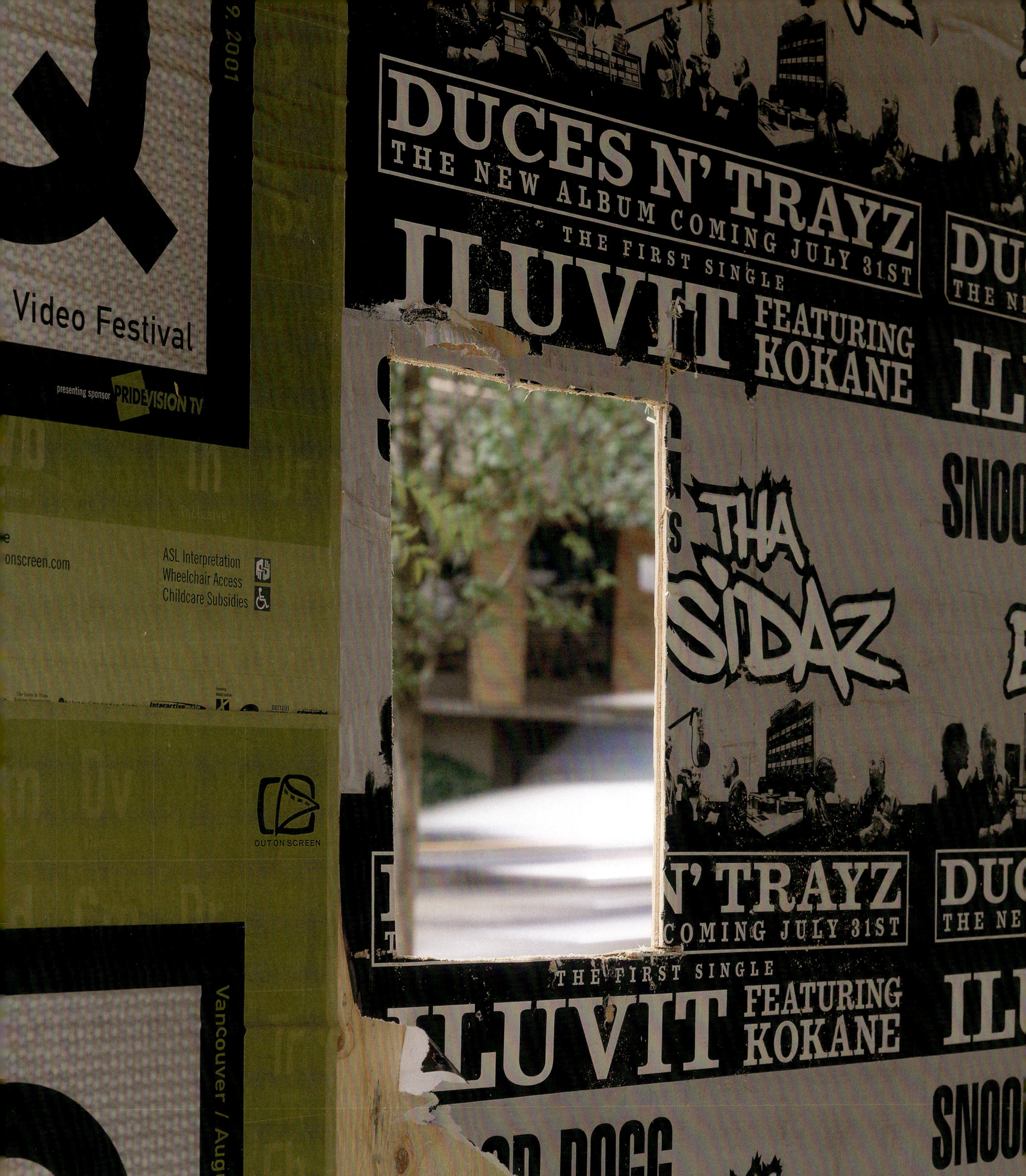
9. 2001
Video Festival
presenting sponsor PRIDEVISION TV
onscreen.com
ASL Interpretation
Wheelchair Access
Childcare Subsidies
OUT ON SCREEN
Vancouver / August
DUCES N' TRAYZ
THE NEW ALBUM COMING JULY 31ST
THE FIRST SINGLE
ILUVIT FEATURING KOKANE
THA SIDAZ
SNOO
DU
N' TRAYZ
COMING JULY 31ST
THE FIRST SINGLE
ILUVIT FEATURING KOKANE
DUC
SNOO
DOGG

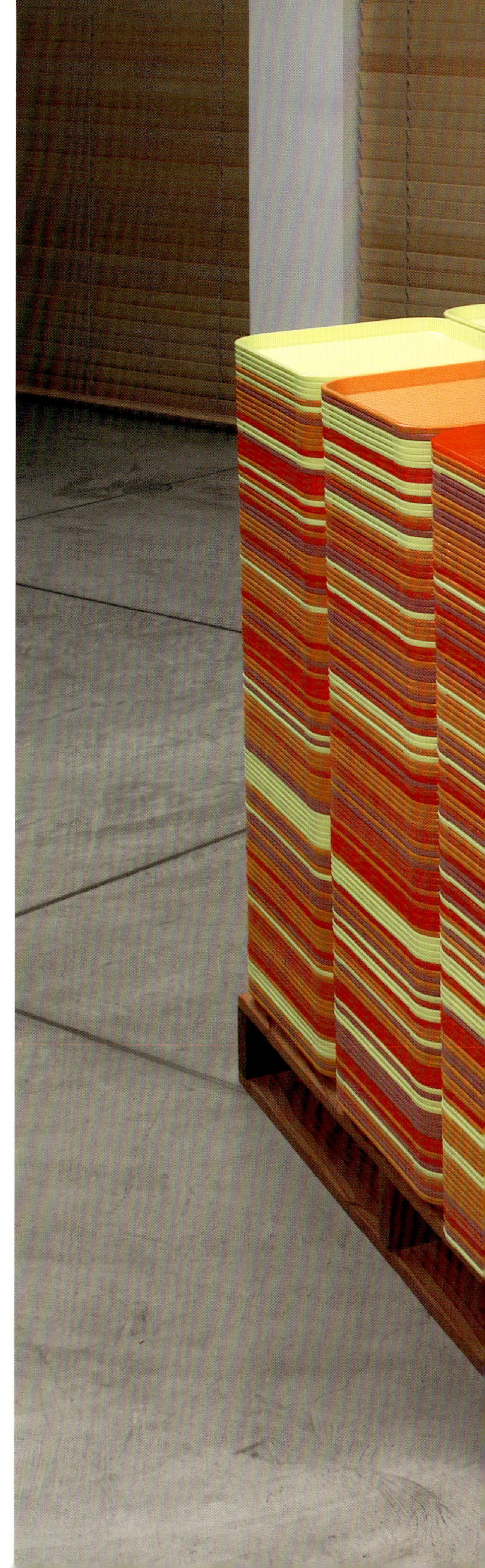

Isolated Depiction of the Passage of Time, 2001
plastic food trays, television monitor, VCR, wood
112.5 x 117.5 x 100 cm (44 1/4" x 46 1/4" x 39 1/4")
Collection of Bob Rennie, Rennie Management Corporation, Vancouver
Photo: Trevor Mills, Vancouver Art Gallery

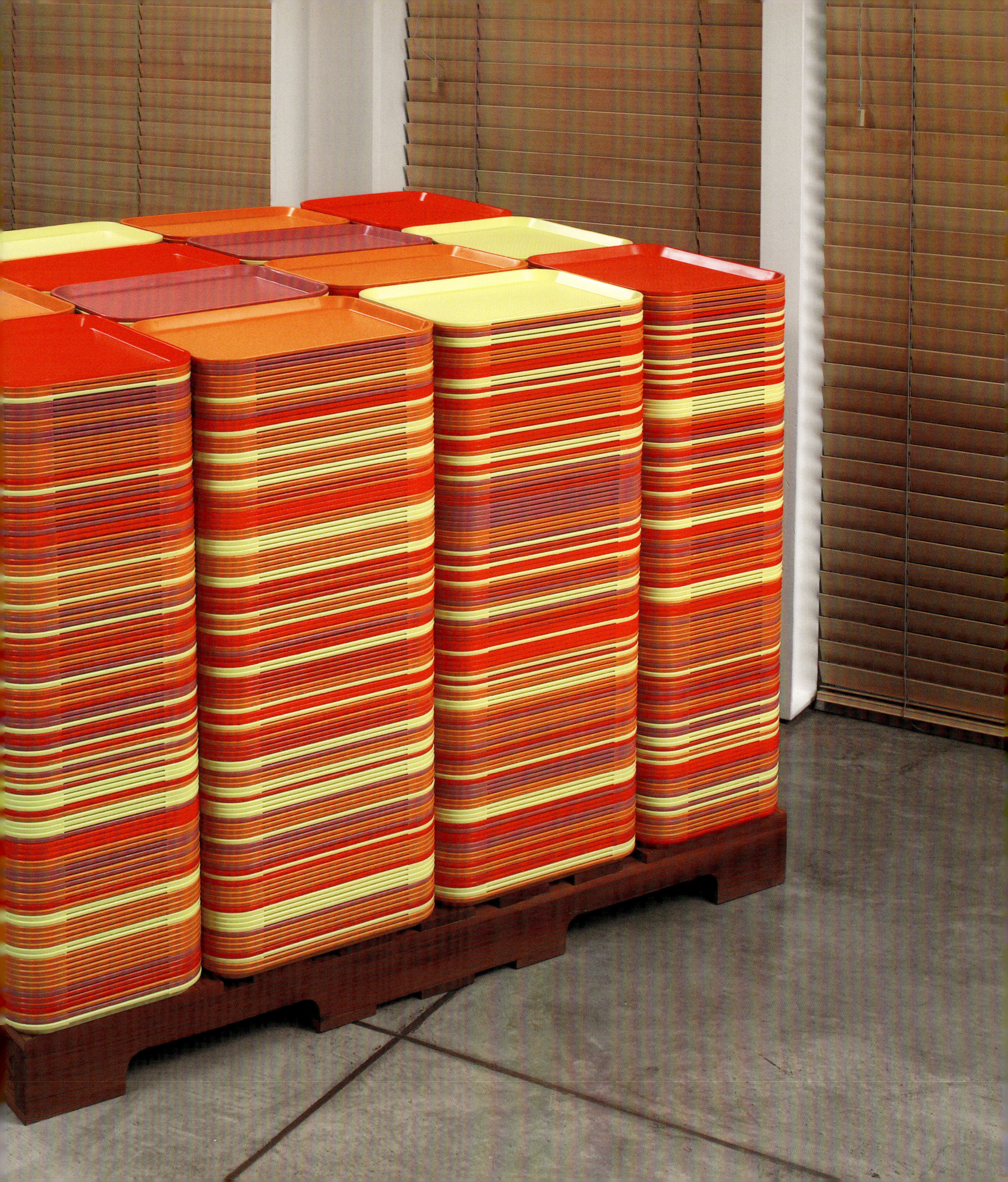

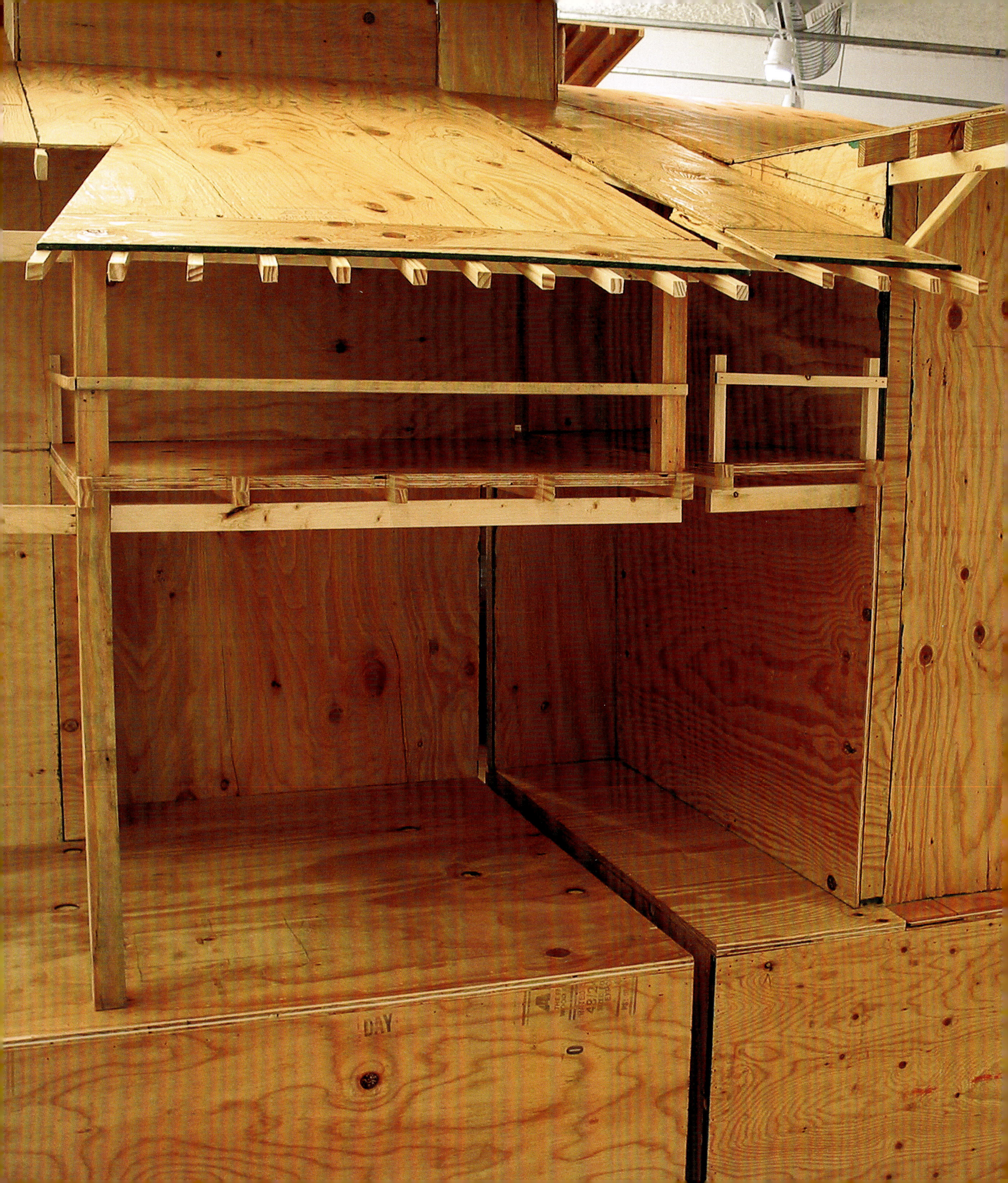

Capp Street Project
Ralph Rugoff

Brian Jungen's approach comprises a rhetorical mode of art making. It troubles, and complicates, the ways in which we assign identity and meaning to material objects and visual codes. It questions the categories we use to make sense of our culture(s), and of contemporary art as well. In the process, it also communicates a heady sense of the impurity of all aesthetic and cultural production, including our most cherished models of authenticity.

Jungen's *Arts and Crafts Book Depository/Capp Street Project 2004* (2004) elaborates this hybrid approach of artistic and social inquiry. It is inspired by an unlikely pair of artistic and architectural monuments from the twentieth century: Charles and Henry Greene's 1908 Arts and Crafts–style Gamble House and Gordon Matta-Clark's 1974 *Splitting*, a New Jersey suburban home that the artist cut in two, from top to bottom. The Gamble home provides the basic blueprint: Jungen's project is essentially a crude scale model of the house's exterior, constructed with inexpensive plywood sheeting and bereft of even major details such as windows and doors. Additionally, Jungen's model has been roughly quartered, with each section placed atop two-foot-high plywood pedestals that are equipped with casters. When pulled apart from each other, the four sections suggest an exploded architectural model. The structure's interior has been turned into an idiosyncratic library housing materials on architecture and crafts. Shelves and glass-encased cabinets, as well as upholstered plywood reading benches and a study table, have been built into the scale model's existing nooks and corners. The books on display include rare publications lent by the artist, in addition to bound volumes of periodicals and various tomes borrowed at the time from the California College of the Arts library.

*Arts and Crafts Book
Depository/Capp Street Project
2004,* 2004 (detail)
Installation view at CCA Wattis
Institute, San Francisco, 2004
Architectural model (scale 1:5 of
Greene and Greene's Gamble House)
made of plywood sectioned into four
quadrants, locking casters, built-in
bookshelves, two framed glass
cabinets with electrical source and
lighting unit, hand-made fabric
pillows for seating benches, video
monitor, ongoing accumulation of
library inventory of magazines,
journals, books and videos
255.2 x 422.4 x 554.4 cm (108" x 192"
x 252") approximate installation
dimensions
255.2 x 185 x 185 cm (108" x 84" x 84")
approximate dimensions for each
quadrant
Collection of Pamela and Richard Kramlich,
San Francisco
Photo: Brian Jungen

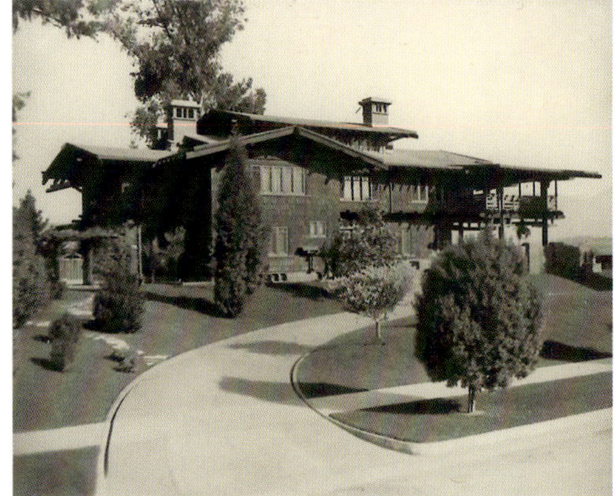
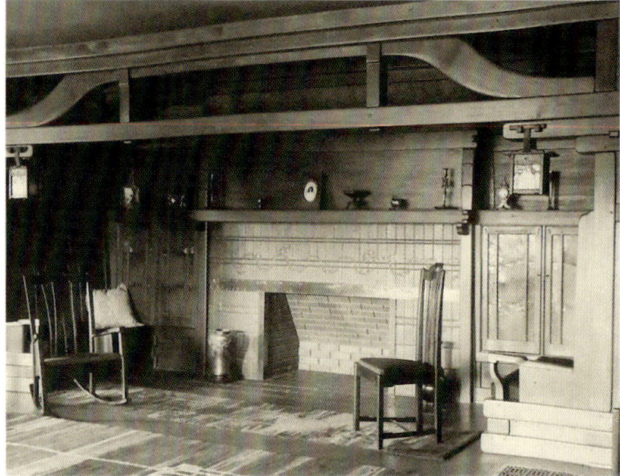

Capp Street Project was first installed at the California College of the Arts' Logan Galleries, where students and faculty who wished to read these publications could use Jungen's installation as a study centre. Thus his project partially transformed the function of the galleries: no longer were they simply a space for exhibiting contemporary art, they served as an integral part of the school's research facilities, a place where people went to study the recent history of crafts and architecture. At the same time, Jungen's sculpture-cum-library indirectly raised questions concerning the educational value of contemporary art itself, while reminding us that we inevitably "read" aesthetic artifacts through our knowledge of the past.

Beyond doubling the gallery's functional identity, Jungen's project provokes us to reconsider the ways that we categorize or pigeonhole works of art. His *Capp Street Project* confounds such attempts on account of its ambiguous, multiple identity: it is at once a contemporary art installation, a library annex, a type of hybrid furniture that includes seating and shelving, and an architectural model. Its composite aesthetic is equally difficult to pin down. Though based on the Gamble House, the structure's walk-in scale removes it from the realm of conventional architectural models, leaving its appearance in a kind of no man's land between playhouse, shelter and three-dimensional representation. Its windowless exterior, meanwhile, gives the impression of a slightly abstracted form, evoking an eccentric wooden crate as much as a house.

The work's most jarring aesthetic fusion, though, is its use of raw, factory-produced plywood to represent an icon of Arts and Crafts architecture. With the Gamble House, Greene and Greene had sought to elevate a "low" architectural form, the bungalow, into a kind of protomodernist *Gesamtkunstwerk,* a complete artwork in which every meticulously crafted detail and hand-finished surface served a unified design statement. In contrast, Jungen's model evinces a funky, lumpenproletariat demeanour: instead of intricate joinery, its structural

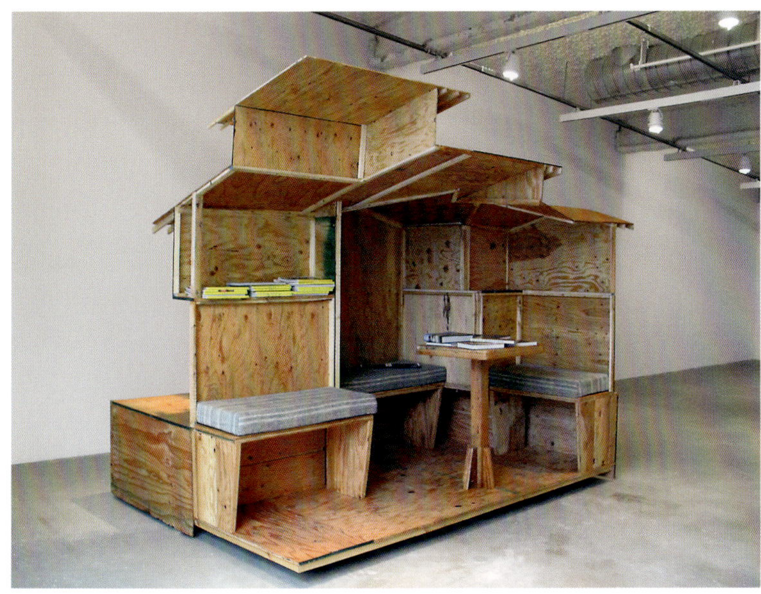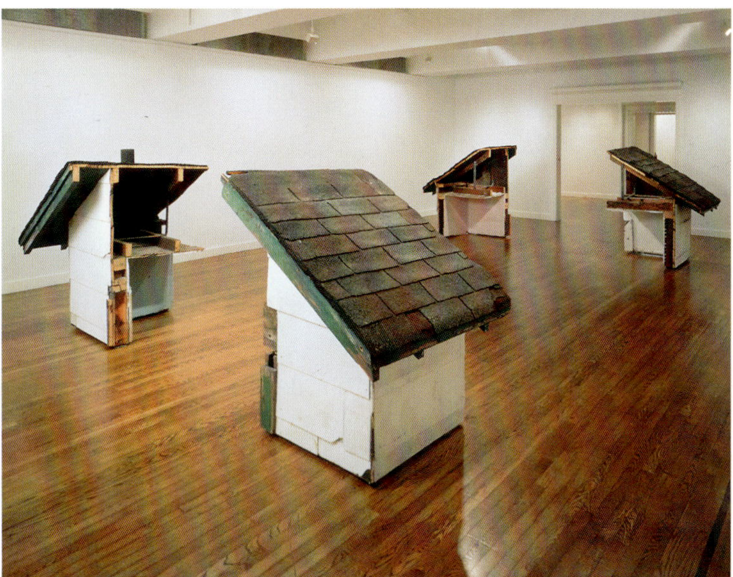

seams betray the use of nail guns and glue. Rather than offering a symphony of rare woods such as the mahogany, redwood, maple and cedar employed by Greene and Greene, it presents a haphazard medley of knotty, spray-painted and stencilled plywood sheets.

Initially, this aesthetic reversal might seem an ironic gesture—as if the artist were mocking the naive idealism of a movement that protested the dehumanizing effects of industrialization by reviving the production modes of medieval guilds. Against this blinkered and impractical utopianism, Jungen's industrialized version of an Arts and Crafts landmark spins the high-low dial yet again and wryly returns the bungalow to its working-class roots.

At the same time, however, Jungen's hybridizing approach looks back to, or elaborates upon, the kind of stylistic morphing practised by Greene and Greene, whose architecture amalgamated such diverse influences as Swiss chalets, Japanese temples, English cottages and Adirondack camps. (In fact, it is precisely this aspect of their work that initially intrigued the artist.) Instead of merely poking fun, Jungen's model denatures our stereotypical image of Greene and Greene's work and reinvents its polyglot character as a contemporary figure of cultural impurity.

An underlying irony here is that Greene and Greene's bungalow architecture currently functions as an emblem of an "authentic" California aesthetic, providing a template for countless real estate developers (as well as for the hotel Disney recently built alongside its California Adventure theme park). This kind of commodification of cultural history, with its attendant gross simplification of meaning, provides a background for Jungen's reference to Matta-Clark's *Splitting*. In cutting open a prosaic, boxlike house, Matta-Clark put into question the seemingly "transparent" values represented by such a single-family residence, transforming the image of a suburban home into something defiantly ambiguous. Was it a cradle for the sanctity of domestic life, or an isolating container for

LEFT:
Arts and Crafts Book Depository/Capp Street Project 2004, 2004 (detail)
Photo: Brian Jungen

RIGHT:
Gordon Matta-Clark
Splitting: Four Corners, 1974
building fragments
dimensions variable
San Francisco Museum of Modern Art Purchased through a gift of Phyllis Wattis, the Art Supporting Foundation to the San Francisco Museum of Modern Art, the Shirley Ross Davis Fund, and the Accessions Committee Fund: gift of Mimi and Peter Haas, Niko and Steve Mayer, Christine and Michael Murray, Helen and Charles Schwab, Norah and Norman Stone, and Danielle and Brooks Walker, Jr.
© Gordon Matta-Clark Estate/SODRAC

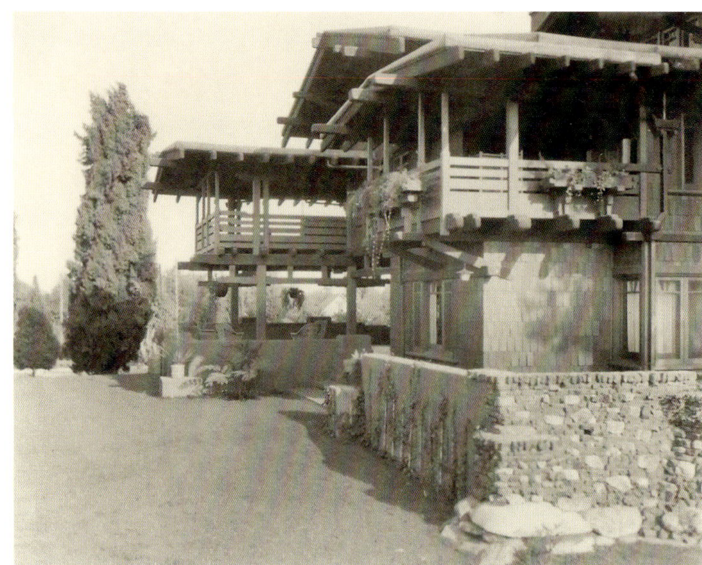

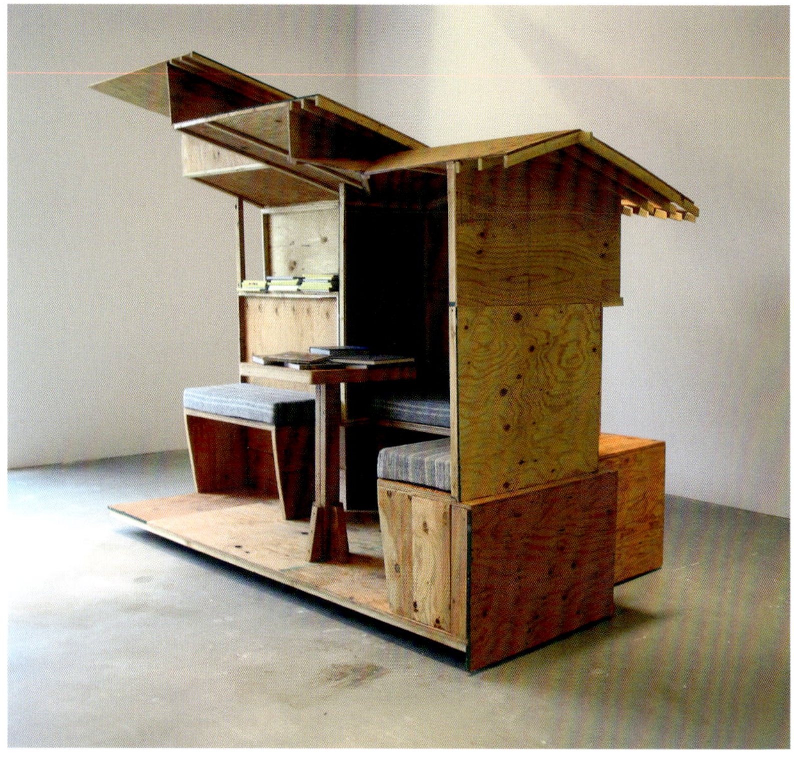

passive consumers? Matta-Clark's disorienting cuts opened up its potential meanings in a dialogue around terms such as "public" and "private," "urban" and "suburban," "stability" and "instability."

Physically as well as conceptually, *Splitting* created a type of "mutable space."[1] Jungen's *Capp Street Project* echoes this approach in different ways, including in its nomadic mode of display at the California College of the Arts: taking advantage of his sculpture's mobile pedestals, the artist periodically changed the orientation of its different sections. Occasionally they were shown with their interiors facing out—an arrangement that made it extremely difficult to read the four sections as pieces of a single architectural model. Through this ongoing spatial recontextualization, Jungen routinely unsettled the appearance of his "model," as if subverting its capacity to function as a representation, while making certain that its visual identity was as diverse as the many rooflines that enliven its upper structure.

The intertwined and concatenated logic of Jungen's work ensures that there is no central reference or issue around which its significance revolves. Although it plays with ideas associated with "social sculpture," its impact is not determined by its use as a prop of conviviality or education. Nor is it ultimately "about" a specific idea or subject. Instead, it forges a visual language that accommodates the contingency of meaning, that foregrounds its cultural and historical variability. The borrowed and conjoined aesthetics that the artist puts into play serve as rhetorical hinges, or turning points, in a conceptual maze of linked ideas and allusions. There is no "solution" that we might discover upon escaping this labyrinth; rather, we are prompted to continually revise and adjust our perceptions as we proceed through it.

This process includes our re-evaluation of a term such as "crafts." In developing *Capp Street Project,* Jungen was initially inspired by the name change of California College of the Arts (formerly California College of Arts and Crafts). The decision to drop the word "crafts" reflected, in part, a growing suspicion that it conjured anachronistic and negative associations for prospective applicants to the school. With its tree-fort funkiness, however, Jungen's installation reframes the meaning of "craft," aligning it with a do-it-yourself anti-aesthetic that stands in stark contrast to the sheen and gloss of high-tech culture. On another level, this project also rewrites Jungen's own history—or at least the critical reception of his earlier work that stressed the value of the artist's painstaking craftsmanship. Here it is obvious that what distinguishes Jungen's approach is not a fetishistic mode of manufacture but a conceptual craftiness and a strategic engagement with the volatile nature of cultural identities.

That engagement entails, naturally enough, overturning, or commingling, many of our seemingly autonomous and clear-cut categories. And though the blurring of distinctions typically suggests a type of entropic activity, a passage from order to disorder, in Jungen's work it is ultimately a tool of critical and creative inquiry, provoking us to look, and think, with a curious, hybridizing vision of our own. It is a perspective from which no aesthetic language appears to be pure or authentic or natural, but from which, instead, we glimpse culture's profound intimacy with struggle and perpetual change.

This essay is an edited version of one that first appeared in an exhibition brochure published on the occasion of Capp Street Project 2004, by the Wattis Institute for Contemporary Arts, California College of the Arts, San Francisco.

NOTES

1. Gordon Matta-Clark, quoted in Pamela M. Lee, *Object to Be Destroyed: The Work of Gordon Matta-Clark* (Cambridge: MIT Press, 1999), 15.

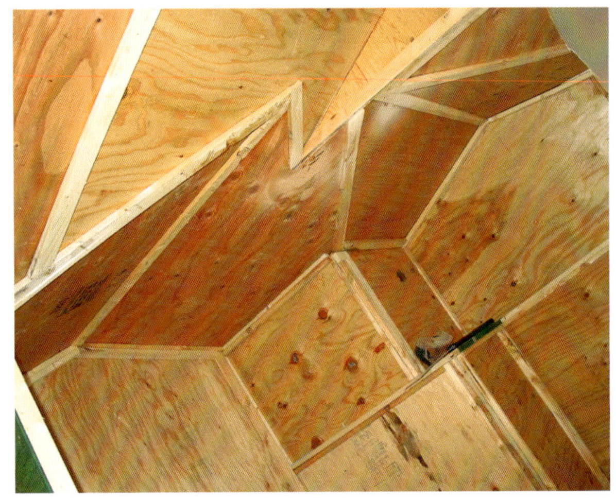

*Arts and Crafts Book
Depository/Capp Street Project
2004*, 2004
Installation views at CCA Wattis Institute,
San Francisco, 2004
Architectural model (scale 1:5 of Greene
and Greene's Gamble House) made of
plywood sectioned into four quadrants,
locking casters, built-in bookshelves, two
framed glass cabinets with electrical
source and lighting unit, hand-made
fabric pillows for seating benches, video
monitor, ongoing accumulation of library
inventory of magazines, journals, books
and videos
255.2 x 422.4 x 554.4 cm (108" x 192" x
252") approximate installation dimensions
255.2 x 185 x 185 cm (108" x 84" x 84")
approximate dimensions for each
quadrant
Collection of Pamela and Richard Kramlich,
San Francisco
Photos: Brian Jungen

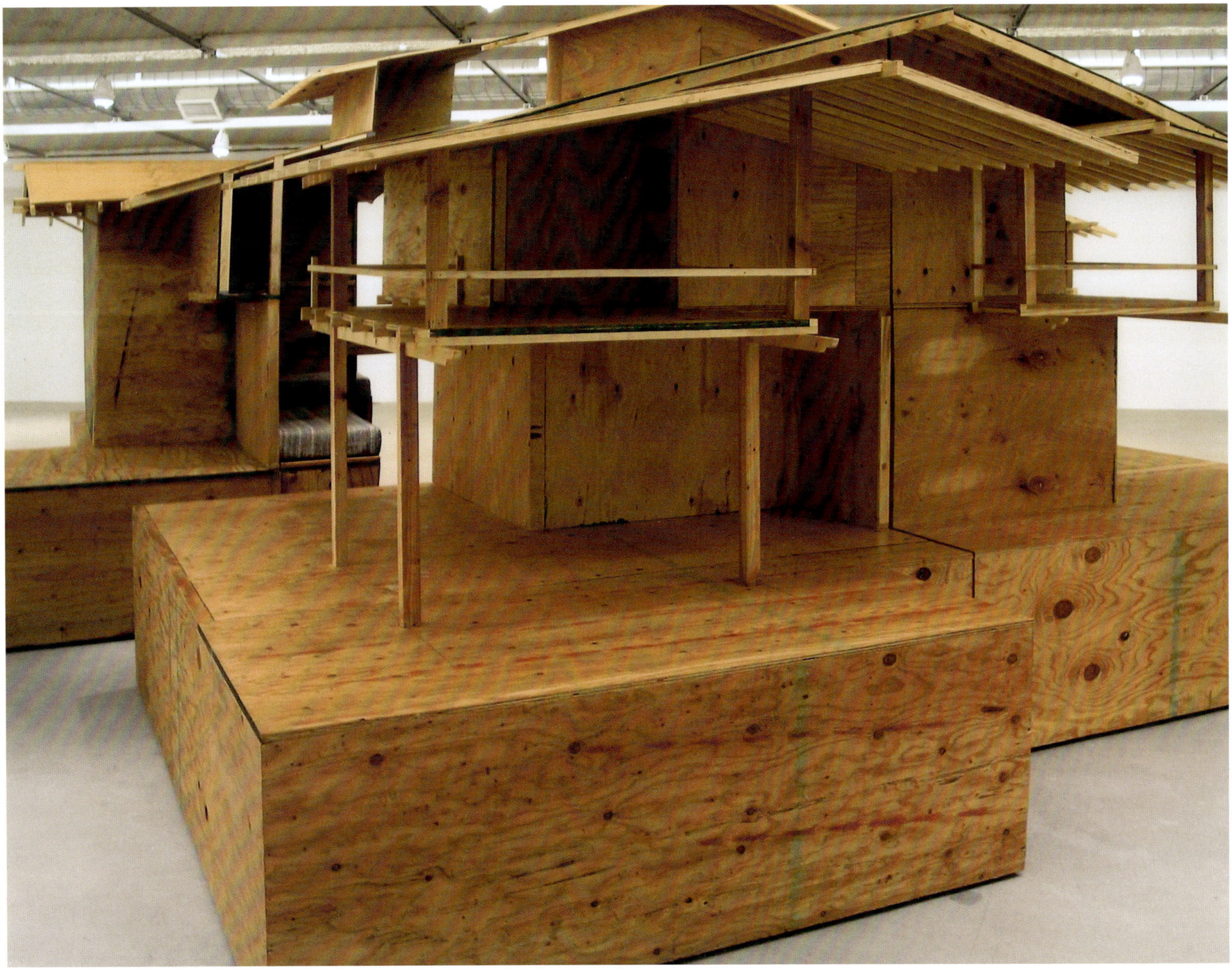

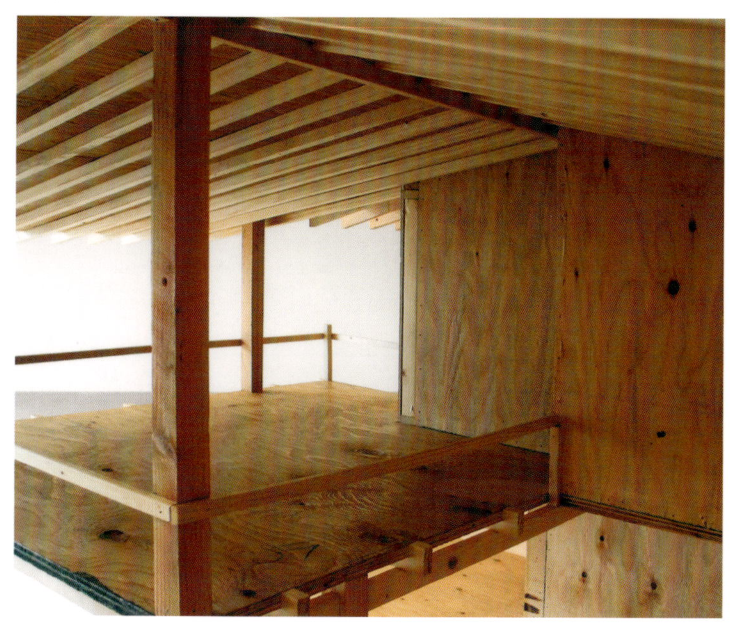

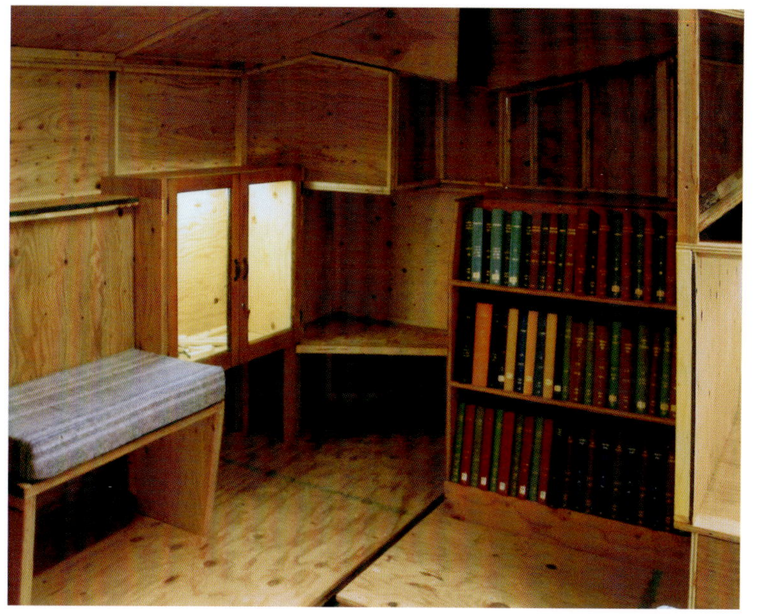

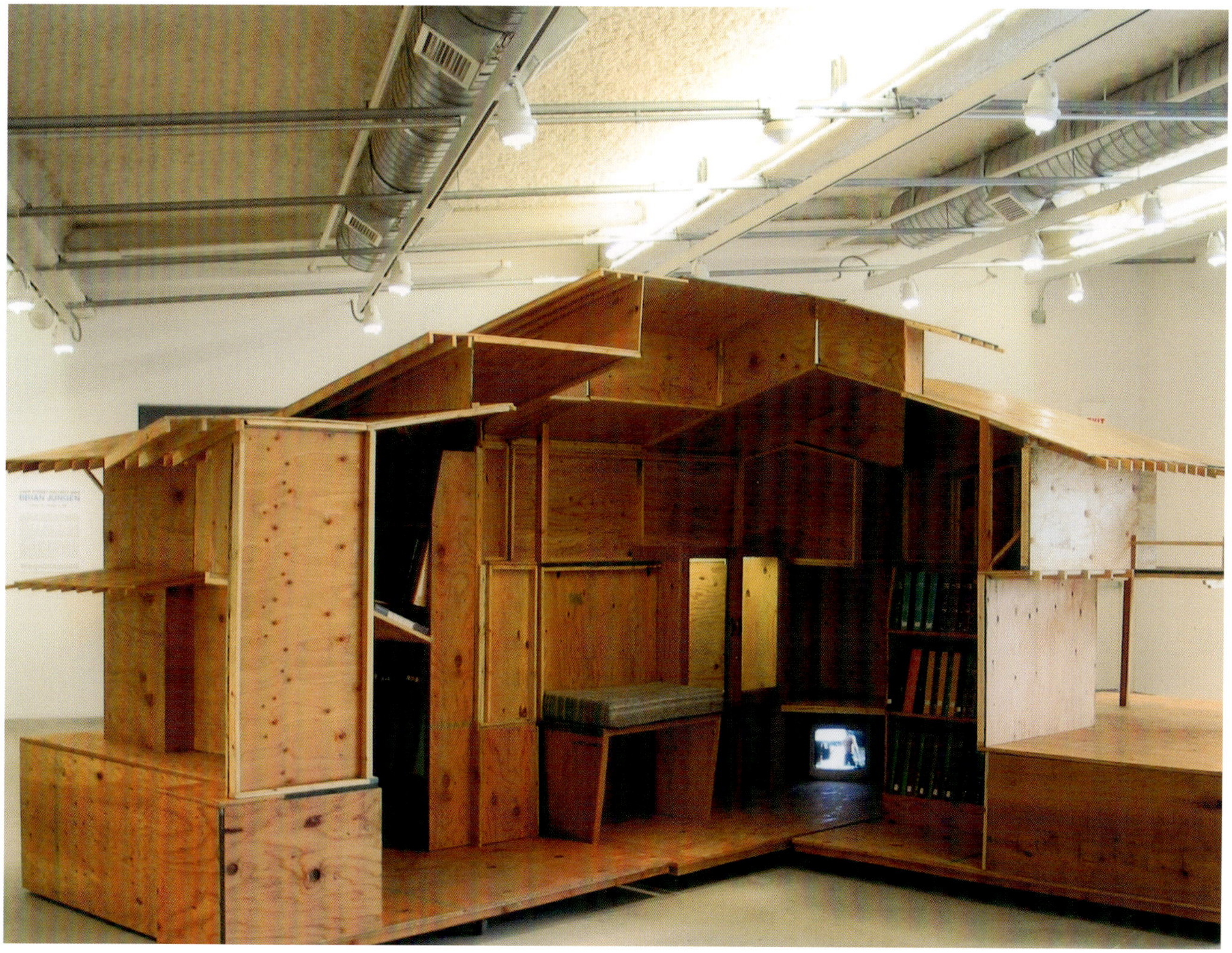

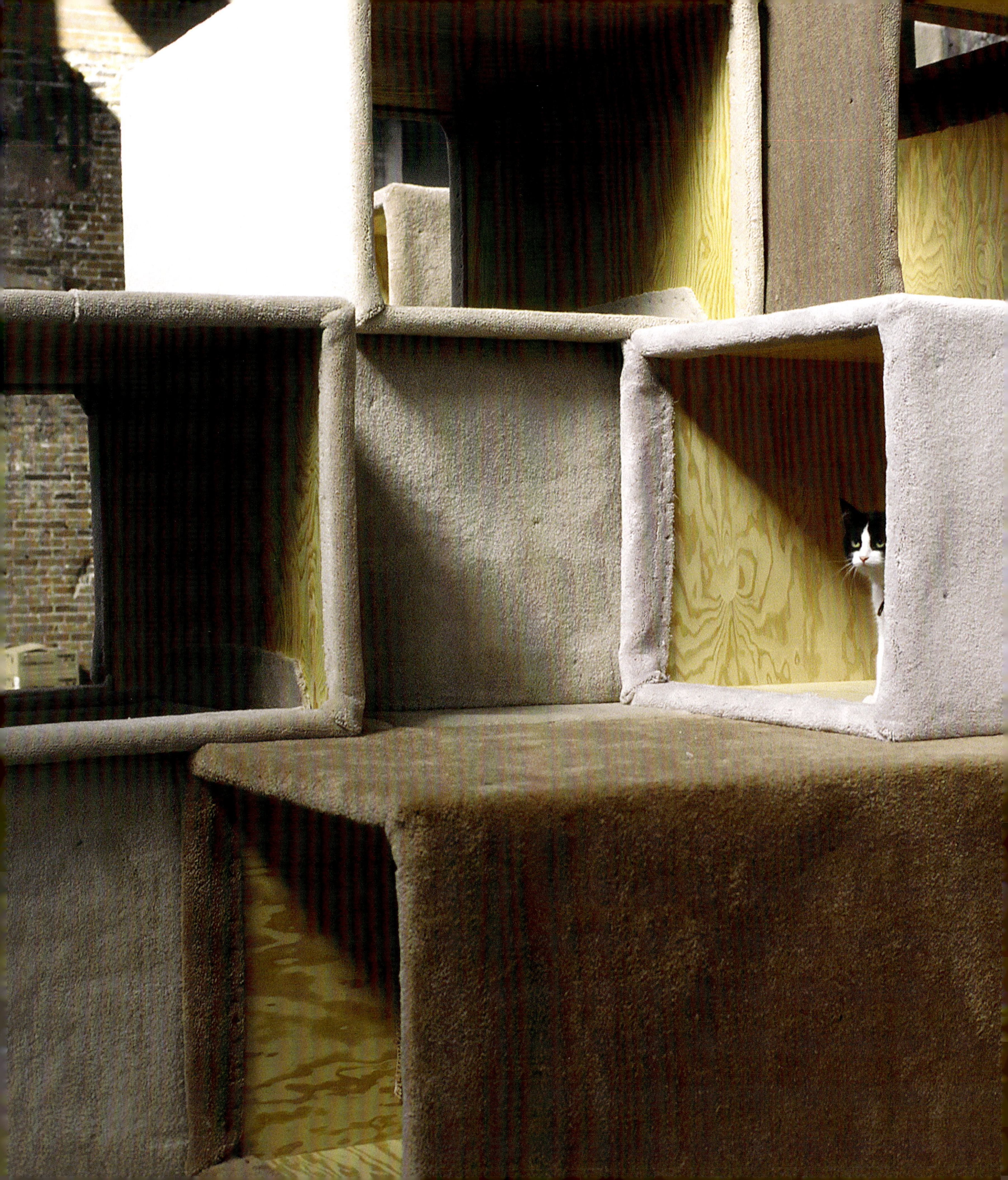

Habitat 04
Kitty Scott

Habitat 04—Cité radieuse des chats/Cats Radiant City, 2004 (detail)
Installation view at Darling Foundry, Quartier Éphémère, Montreal, 2004
plywood, carpet, cats
3.35 x 4.57 x 8.53 m (11' x 15' x 28')
Courtesy of Catriona Jeffries Gallery, Vancouver
Photo: Guy L'Heureux

On Parliament Hill in Ottawa, there are a surprising number of haphazardly sited and traditional commemorative bronzes. Among the many figures is a larger-than-life statue of Queen Elizabeth II on horseback and an equally sizable suited and seated Lester B. Pearson (1897–1972). As the symbolic head of state, Queen Elizabeth is familiar; for those who may not remember Pearson, he was Canada's fourteenth prime minister. One of his great earlier achievements, while serving as president of the General Assembly of the United Nations, was winning the Nobel Peace Prize in 1957 for proposing a United Nations peacekeeping force to ease tensions during the 1956 Suez crisis. Another accomplishment was his furthering of the Canadian welfare state: his Liberal administration instituted such important social programs as the Canada Pension Plan, the national system of universal medicare and student loans, the building blocks of the so-called social safety net that today distinguishes us from our neighbour to the south and is frequently described as "unravelling." Pearson, before retiring, also participated in Canada's centennial celebrations, including Montreal's Expo 67, which affirmed Canada's new-found internationalism.

Other statues in this garden of oft-forgotten personages are markers of rarely remembered histories; still, there is another monument, hardly ever discussed, that is arguably the most complex. In this scenic location overlooking the Ottawa River, and set behind a stone-and-wrought-iron fence demarcating the grounds, stand two crudely built, miniature, mansard-roofed plywood houses reminiscent of the Parliament Buildings. Several arched entrances articulate the façade of each shelter, and bowls overflowing with food are scattered about. Within the rustic enclosure, a tabby sleeps ensconced in an old rocking chair while

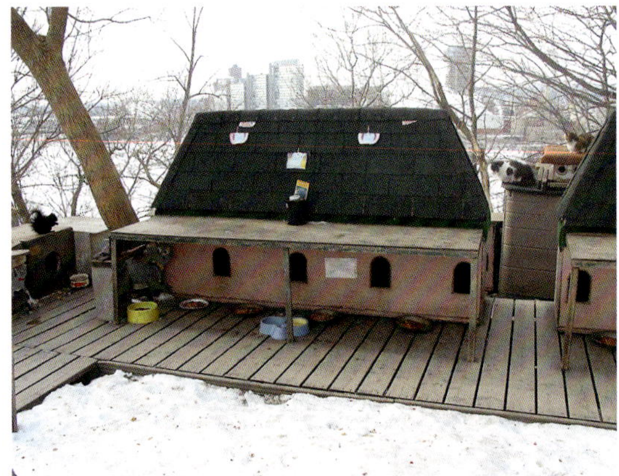

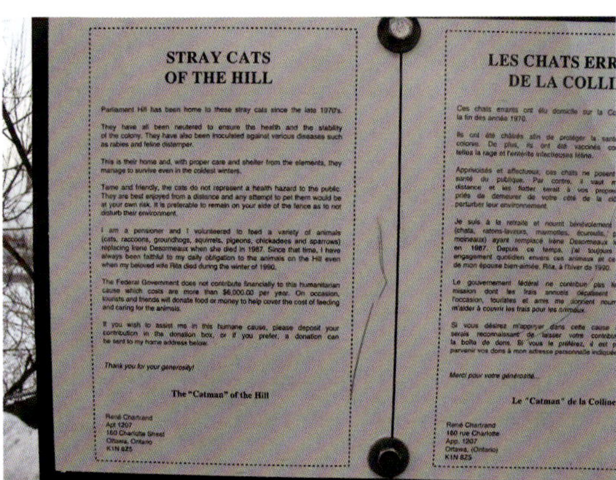

another sits perfectly still, like a nesting hen, watching the birds, squirrels and groundhogs as they come to feed. On one of the most widely used maps of the city this compound is identified as "Cat Condos," in contrast to the more humane terminology used by the Government of Canada's Parliament Hill Web site, which refers to the location as "Cat Sanctuary."

This unusual squatter community and its keeper intrigue tourists and local visitors alike. The cats are apparently descendants of feral animals introduced to the area in 1877 to counter the local rodent population. In the 1970s, Isabelle Desoreaux began feeding and caring for these animals. After she passed away, her neighbour René Chartrand, now known as "the Catman," took over. He built the shelters and looks after the cats every day. Signage, in English and French, describes the mission and informs readers of the annual maintenance cost of $6,000. Chartrand's address is posted on the sign, as he depends on passersby who want to donate to the cause, since the federal government does not appear to financially support the endeavour. Given that all the sculptures on Parliament Hill commemorate some aspect of Canadian identity and history, it is conceivable that the Cat Sanctuary and its residents are permitted to stay because they represent a democratic and positive image of Canadian society: humane, tolerant and generous. As the government's Web site states, "The contrast between these modest shelters and the formality and tradition of the Parliament Buildings is a symbol of compassion, one of the most important elements of Canadian society."[1]

In the spring of 2004, Brian Jungen, partly inspired by the Cat Sanctuary, produced the site-responsive *Habitat 04: Cité radieuse des chats/Cats Radiant City* in the gallery of the Darling Foundry, a former industrial space in Old Montreal.[2] Rather than creating a conventional exhibition—a contemplative display of objects, such as sculptures, made under his direction—Jungen conceived of *Habitat 04* as a much-needed service in support of the Society for the Prevention of Cruelty to Animals (SPCA). For the duration of the exhibition, the artist collaborated with the office of the Darling Foundry and the SPCA to establish a new network of relations for the purposes of finding homes for a few of Montreal's escalating population of stray cats and fundraising for the SPCA. For example, instead of an opening with the Montreal art crowd, a fundraising dinner was held in the gallery. Pierre Barnoti, director of the Montreal branch of the SPCA, gave a speech in English to the patrons of the charitable organization concerning his current activities, and Jungen made available a limited edition of welcome mats inscribed with his Habitat logo. The event found its way onto the society page of the *Montreal Gazette.*

As a temporary and ephemeral artwork made for the gallery, *Habitat 04* possessed a "relational" currency not easily disregarded. The French critic Nicolas Bourriaud maps out "relational aesthetics," a much-debated and newly minted category of art that some consider to be the definitive art of the nineties, a time that coincides with Jungen's art school education and emergence as an artist. Bourriaud remarks, "Its basic claim—the sphere of human relations as artwork venue—has no prior example in art history, even if it appears, after the fact, as the obvious backdrop of all aesthetic praxis, as a modernist theme to cap all

Cat Sanctuary, Parliament Hill,
Ottawa
Photos: Courtesy of Brian Jungen

modernist themes."[3] He continues, "It [its novelty] resides in the fact that this generation of artists considers inter-subjectivity and interaction neither as fashionable theoretical gadgets, not as additives (alibis) of a traditional artistic practice. It takes them as a point of departure and as an outcome, in brief, as the main informers of their activity."[4] The artist Rirkrit Tiravanija, an agent of conviviality who in his well-known works has served meals to people gathered in the gallery, perhaps best exemplifies this artistic attitude. Relational works are often ephemeral, celebratory, open-ended, collaborative and use the installation format. As critic Hal Foster states, "Discursivity and sociability are central concerns of the new work, both in its making and in its viewing."[5] Within the rhetoric of the relational, all these characteristics represent something good and something supposedly democratic.

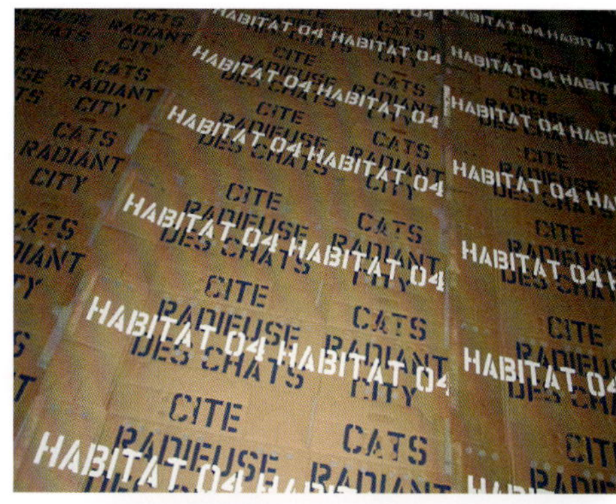

Habitat 04 embodied many of the aspects of relational aesthetics. It involved the conjoining and collaboration of previously unrelated institutions and demanded a complete transformation of the gallery. In what was both a practical and utopian perspective, the new space existed primarily to facilitate bonding between cats and people in the hope that some cats would find homes. In its attempts to foster closer relations between animals and humans, *Habitat 04* represented a new direction for Jungen, who had, for the most part, been making wall paintings, drawings, sculptures and site-specific installations.

Much of Jungen's well-known early work hinged on the simple act of transforming banal consumer goods into discrete art objects. For his *Prototype* series (1998–2005), Nike running shoes deconstructed and then reconstructed into objects similar to West Coast First Nations masks, and his monumental, suspended, skeletal, whale-like sculptures—such as *Shapeshifter* (2000), *Cetology* (2002), *Vienna* (2003)—were fabricated from fragments of common white plastic patio chairs.[6] With these works, Jungen's aesthetic language resides in the tensions sounded by the coming together of disparate ideas and ready-made objects.

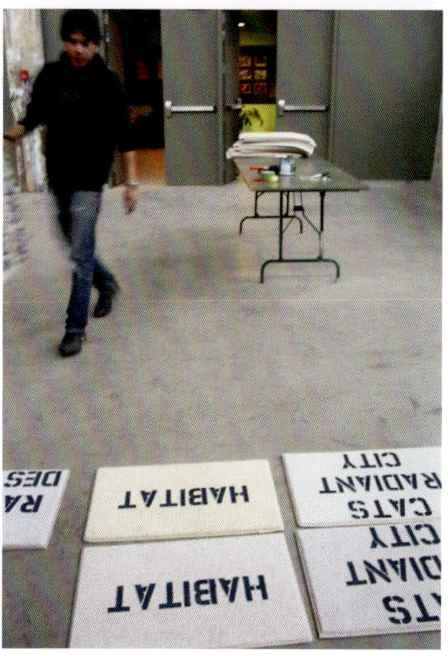

It is possible to detect the seeds of a relational practice in Jungen's early wall paintings. First exhibited in 1997, these works are representative of the artist's attempts to address the identity politics of the late eighties to the mid-nineties. To make these conceptual paintings, Jungen instructed volunteers to solicit drawings from non-Aboriginal people in the street. The volunteers asked the participants to draw their own versions of Native art. The artist then selected a series of these mostly abject and sometimes racist images and reproduced them as wall paintings.[7]

Jungen's *Arts and Crafts Book Depository/Capp Street Project 2004* (2004), inspired by two icons of twentieth-century architecture—Charles and Henry Greene's Arts and Crafts–style Gamble House of 1908 and the suburban New Jersey home that American artist Gordon Matta-Clark cut in two in *Splitting* (1974)—is a later example of a more fully fledged relational project. The installation takes the form of a quartered, miniaturized Arts and Crafts house filled with books and periodicals on architecture and crafts, which at the California College of the Arts were borrowed from the host school's library and from the artist. The semi-comfortable interior was also a screening space for Matta-Clark's video

117

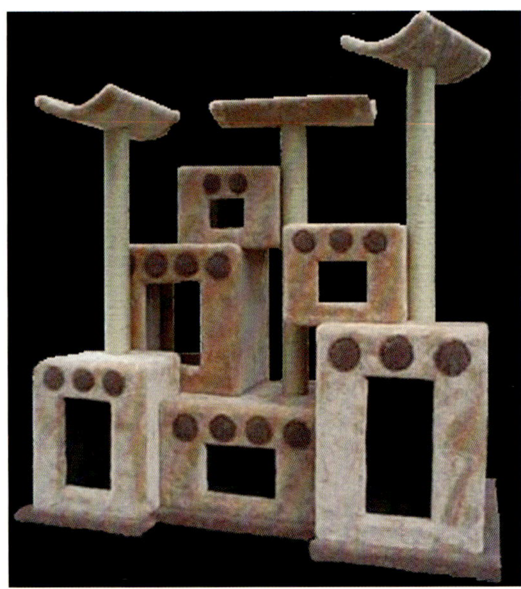

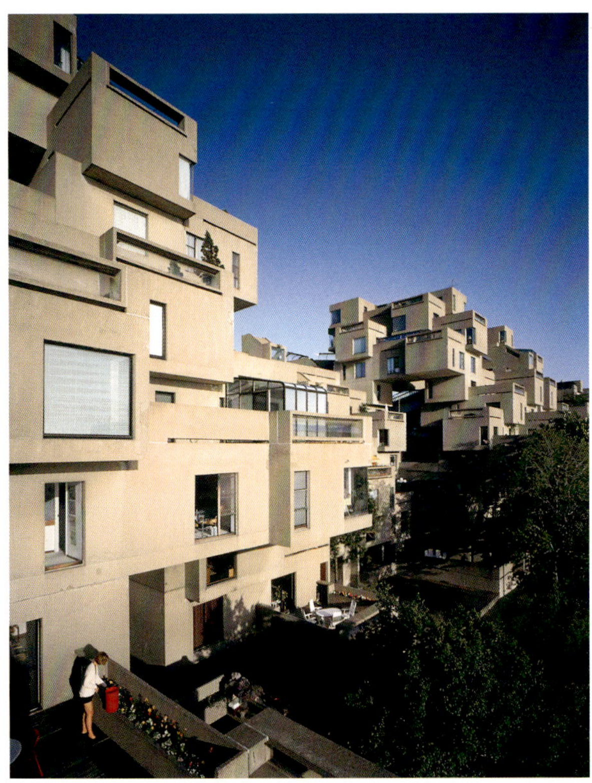

version of *Splitting.* As art writer and curator Ralph Rugoff has observed, Jungen altered the function of the college's Logan Galleries for the duration of the exhibition so that it was no longer simply a place for exhibiting contemporary art, it also served as an integral part of the school's research facilities, a place where people went to study the recent history of crafts and architecture.[8]

Although the relational spaces of *Habitat 04* and *Arts and Crafts Book Depository* are sites for encountering history through the reactivation of architectural forms, it is perhaps equally enlightening to situate Jungen's oeuvre, as Vancouver curator Scott Watson does, within the project of retooling the minimalist gesture. Watson cites work from the late eighties and nineties by Felix Gonzales-Torres and Roni Horn, which he claims is indebted to an earlier critical minimalism as practised by Dan Graham, Gordon Matta-Clark and Robert Smithson, and which arose out of a reaction to the neo-conservatism of the Ronald Reagan administration. In this context, Watson elaborates on Jungen's practice: "It is an investigation of sculpture as it impinges on modes of production, implicates architecture, asks questions about how we organize shelter, exposes the truth of materials, and also takes on the theme of identity."[9] Of *Isolated Depiction of the Passage of Time* (2001), a work by the artist documenting the number of Aboriginal people in Canadian jails, Watson's discussion introduces a darker, critical dimension that is unusual in the field of relational aesthetics and that has implications for a broader understanding of *Habitat 04:* "Jungen brings to the vocabulary of sculpture new strategies of representation and new thoughts on the condition of alienation."[10]

Instead of mining consumer culture's ready-mades, *Habitat 04* followed a logical trajectory that, as the title of the work suggests, looked to resuscitate, if only partially, a pursuit of the modernist ideals set forth by artist and architect Le Corbusier in his visionary but unrealized Radiant City and the exuberant utopian promise of Expo 67 as embodied by architect Moshe Safdie's signature Habitat housing development, sited on a peninsula in the St. Lawrence River. Both Le Corbusier and Safdie attempted to solve the problem of providing shelter for large numbers of people, and each proposed a radical solution whereby sunshine, fresh air, density with privacy, and a strong sense of the social and communal would be privileged.

In dreaming up his Radiant City, Le Corbusier sought to make affordable and livable spaces, rather than luxury dwellings signifying status. In 1935 the egalitarian Le Corbusier wrote, "My own thinking is directed toward the crowds in the subway who come home at night to dismal dwellings. The millions of beings sacrificed to a life without hope, without rest—without sky, sun, greenery."[11] Concerning apartment design, Le Corbusier stated that he "thought neither of rich nor of poor but of man."[12]

The intention behind Safdie's stunning modular building, whose forms were influenced by vernacular Mediterranean hilltop homes, was to make economical, high-density, community-oriented, mass-produced housing using a prefabrication process. Supposedly, this method of building would solve the worldwide problem of housing the masses—in countries such as India and Ghana

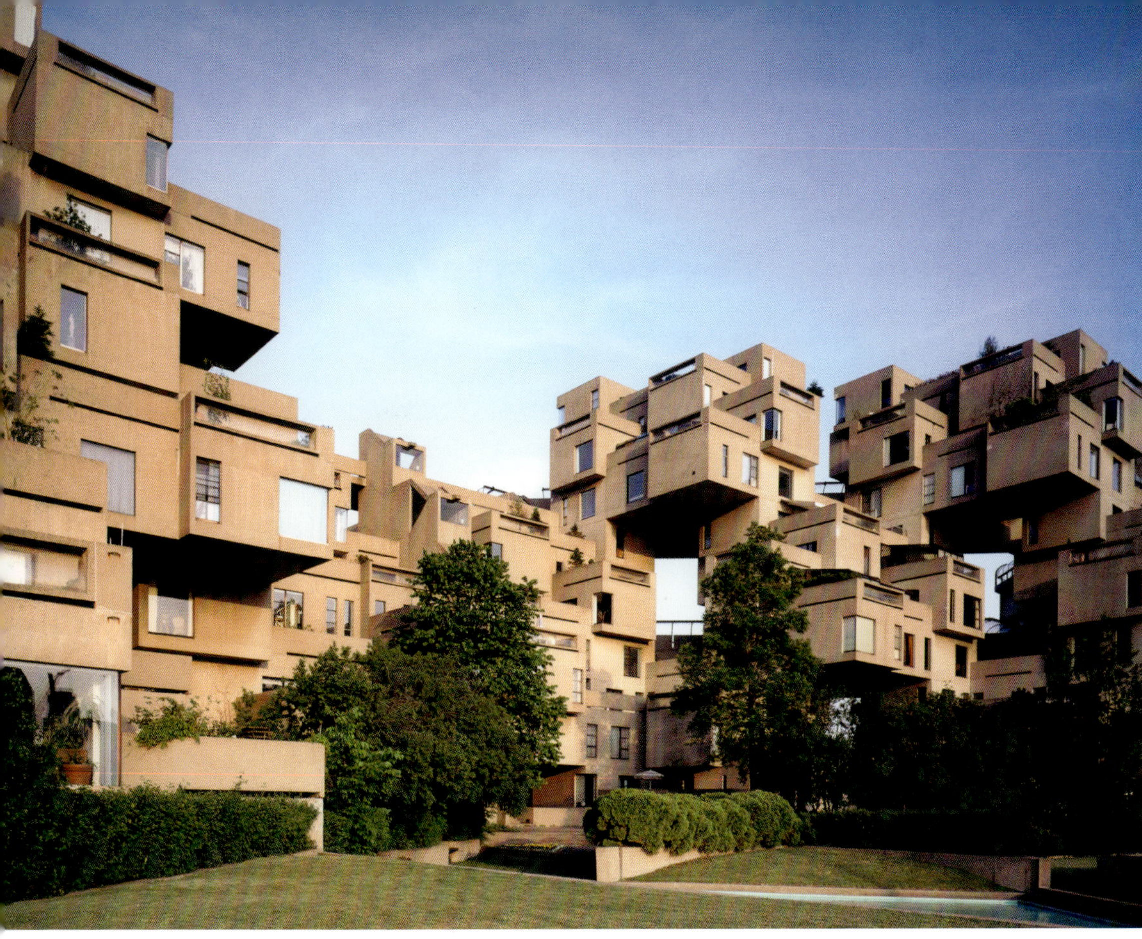

as well as in cities like Detroit.[13] However, the units were incredibly expensive to produce and, paradoxically, Montreal's Habitat is now an exclusive condominium community. Still, after Habitat was completed, Safdie did not let go of the potential for change offered by the project's failure:

> Habitat reminds us that a major reorganization in the technical field requires a major reorganization among the professions. Architect, researcher, manufacturer must all be a single entity working to a common goal. This will take place eventually, but it will take a revolution to bring it about. And this is where the large-scale prototype produces the shock treatment needed to bring about change.[14]

Habitat 04—Cité radieuse des chats/Cats Radiant City, 2004
Installation view at Darling Foundry, Quartier Éphémère, Montreal, 2004
plywood, carpet, cats
3.35 x 4.57 x 8.53 m (11' x 15' x 28')
Photo: Guy L'Heureux

Situated in the largest gallery of the Darling Foundry, and just a stone's throw from the original Habitat and the monumental industrial concrete grain silos built in the early 1900s and cited by Le Corbusier in his book *Towards a New Architecture* as embodying the spirit of a new age, the nexus of Jungen's project was an ingenious, scaled-down sculptural interpretation of Habitat occupied by eight young, highly seductive but formerly abandoned cats who, when not lounging about or sleeping, were curiously exploring their limited territory and visitors alike. Their activities alone—be they eating, sleeping or playing together—constituted a whimsical gloss on the sociability that is at the heart of relational aesthetics.[15]

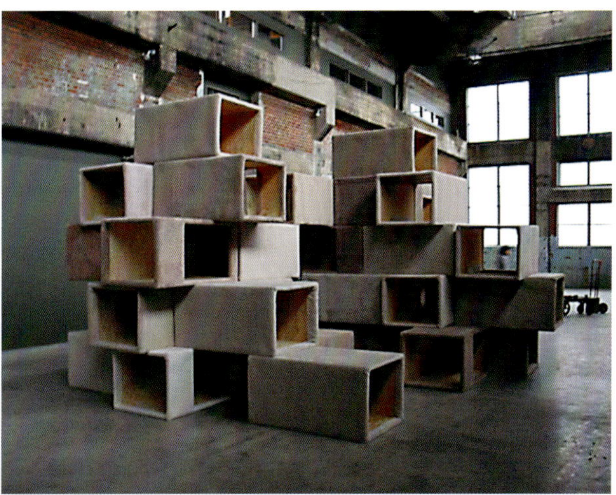

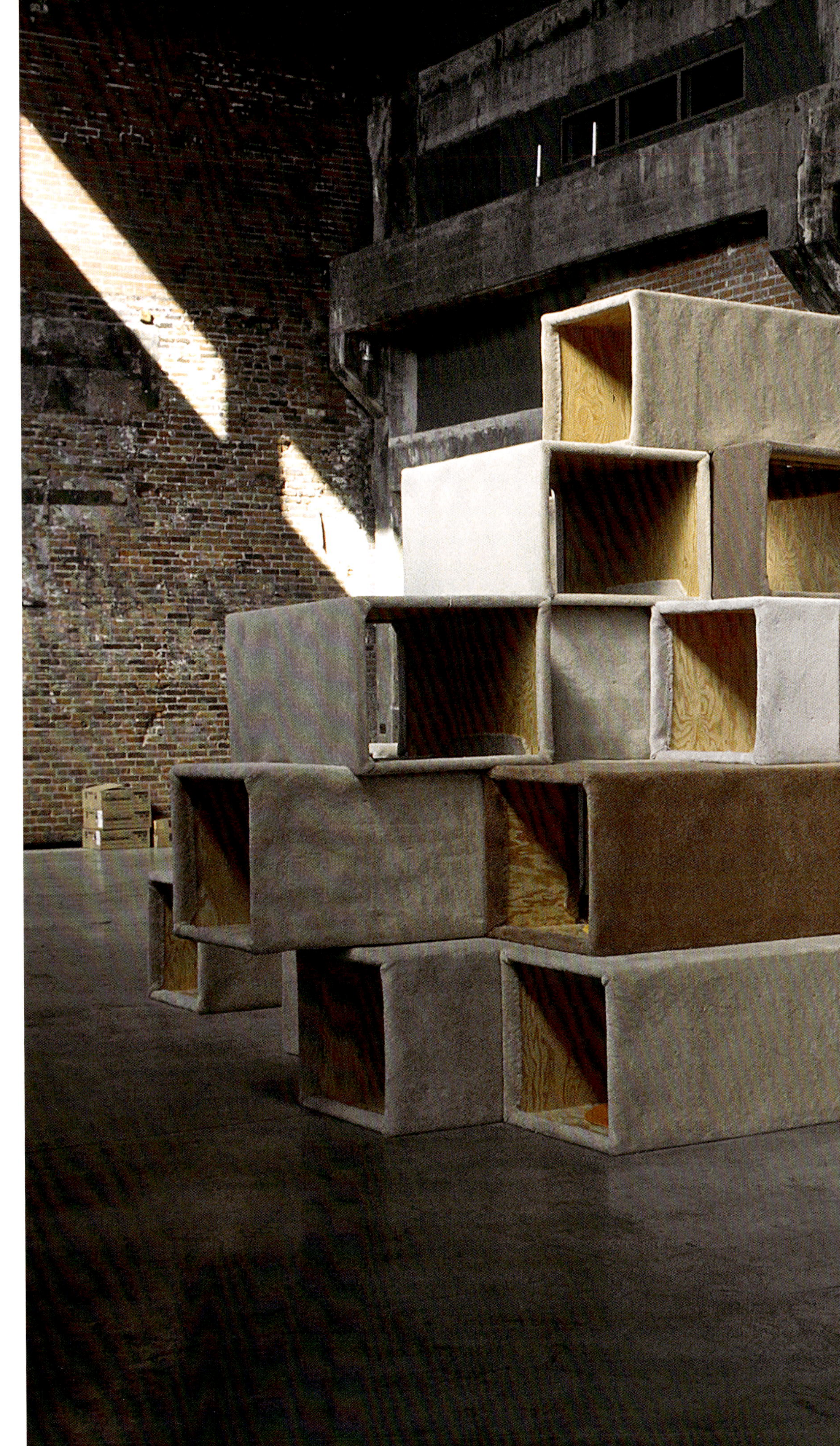

*Habitat 04—Cité radieuse des
chats/Cats Radiant City*, 2004
Installation view at Darling Foundry,
Quartier Éphémère, Montreal, 2004
plywood, carpet, cats
3.35 x 4.57 x 8.53 m (11' x 15' x 28')
Photo: Guy L'Heureux

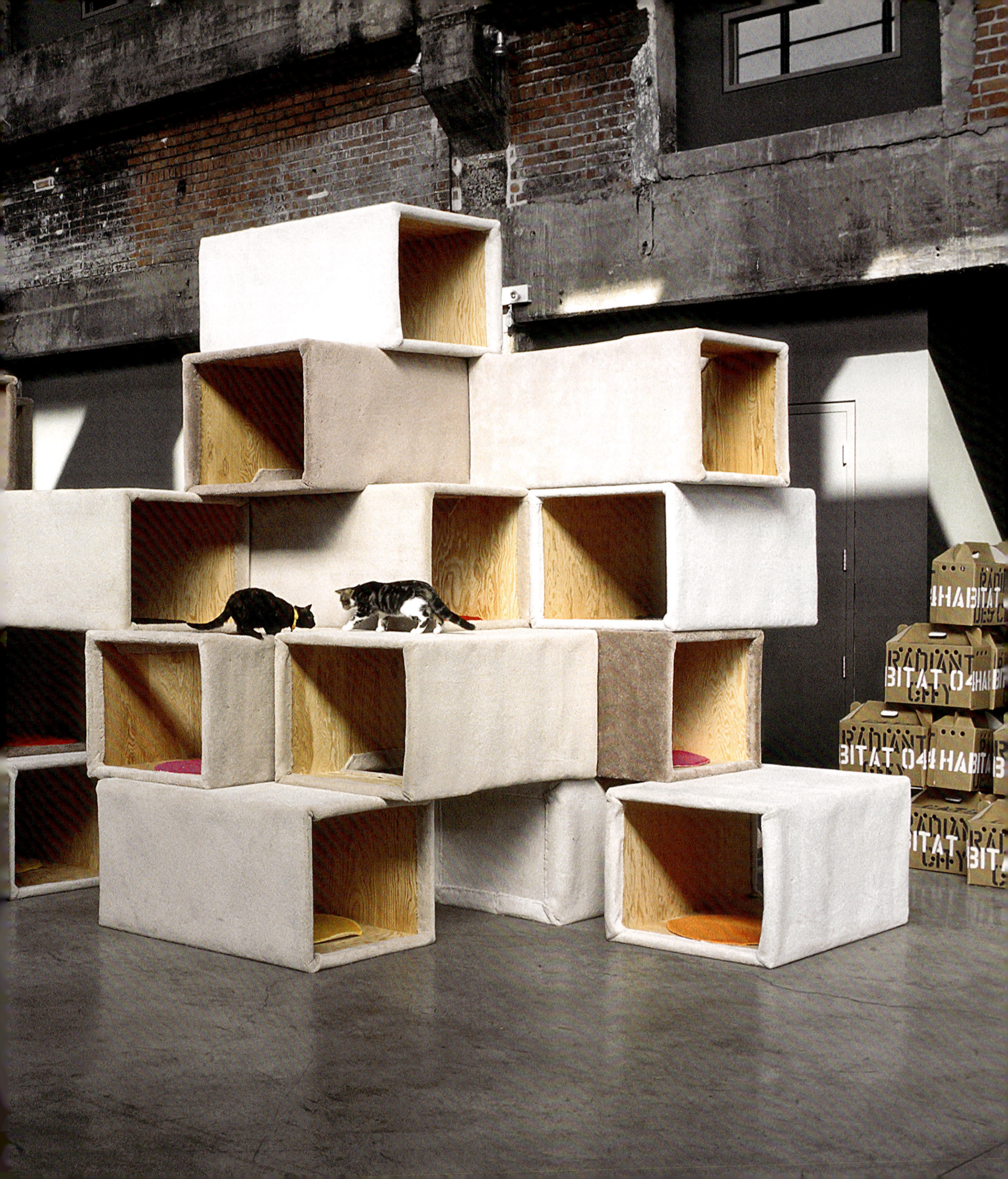

RADIANT
4 HABITAT
BITAT 04 HABITAT
RADIANT CITY
BITAT 04 HABITAT
HABITAT
BITAT

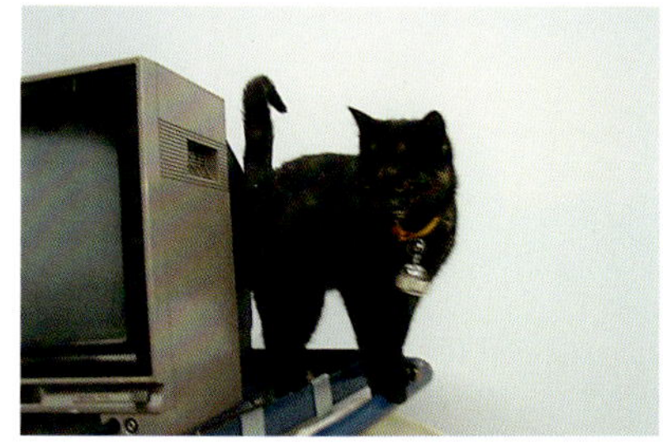
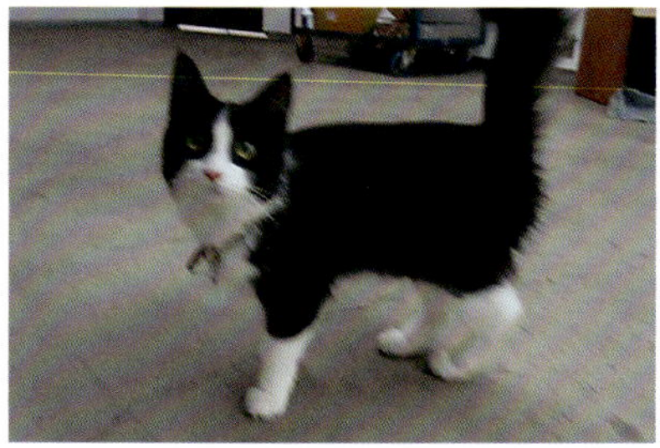
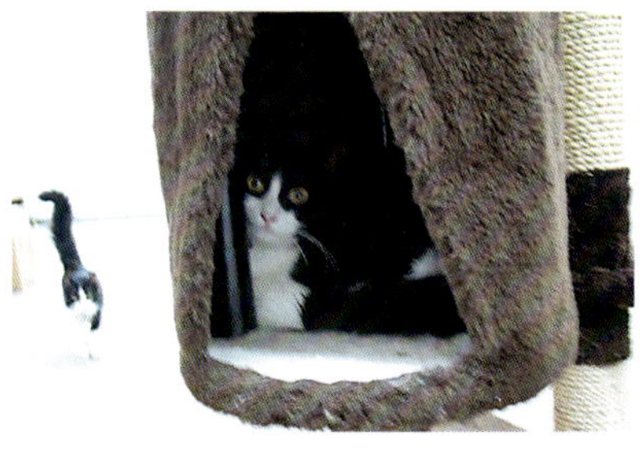
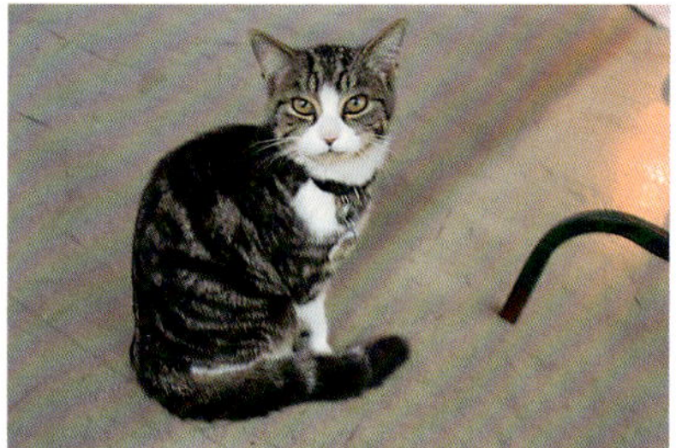

Fabricated from stacked plywood boxes covered with warm pink- and beige-coloured carpet rather than the harsher concrete associated with modern architecture, this softer Habitat functioned as a humane and highly styled SPCA-approved cat's jungle gym while simultaneously referencing, albeit playfully, cat furniture as sold in pet stores and minimalism as elaborated by Donald Judd's sculptures and the International style. The interiors of the individual modules were appointed with brightly coloured round mats from IKEA, trays of catnip and the occasional toy. *Habitat 04* also incorporated a human presence, a volunteer from the SPCA, who watched over the animals and, if requested or required to, educated visitors about the SPCA and facilitated adoptions. For adoptees, the artist designed a series of takeaway boxes adorned with the same Habitat logo that was inscribed on the welcome mats. With *Habitat 04,* Jungen appeared to be salvaging the promises of Le Corbusier and Safdie's projects, though what precisely was he doing populating a symbolic version of Habitat with disadvantaged and otherwise homeless creatures?

One of the primary reasons the artist and the SPCA concern themselves with the welfare of cats is that the supply of animals far outweighs the demand. For example, in Quebec there are approximately 1.6 million stray cats and, at the time these statistics were collected, 65 per cent of the animals at the SPCA shelters were cats.[16] One of the SPCA's goals is to find prospective homes for cats and so those brought to the Darling Foundry remained there until they were adopted. New ones replaced those that left. During the course of Jungen's project, twenty cats found new homes. At first glance, the entire scenario at the Darling Foundry looked to be altruistic, as *Habitat 04* presented itself as an exemplary solution to Montreal's homeless cat problem. For the cats adopted, *Habitat 04* effectively extended their lives and offered companionship and perhaps even love both to the animals and their new keepers.[17]

On closer inspection, the system Jungen put in place revealed a far more frightening and contradictory reality. Tiny surveillance cameras discreetly placed throughout the central platform captured, in real time, close-up views of the cats' activities and displayed them via individual quadruple-split screens in Cluny (a restaurant attached to the venue) and in the small, closed-off "backstage" gallery.[18] On the one hand, this gesture seemed relatively democratic and benign as it increased and dispersed the portals for viewing the project. On the other hand, this so-called model community with its architecture, population and hidden cameras spoke metaphorically of the systemic and sinister workings of power and surveillance. In contrast to the Cat Sanctuary, *Habitat 04* can be interpreted as a dystopia, a modern model of social control, a kind of death camp whose inmates have no knowledge of their fate—for those left behind are, euphemistically speaking, put to sleep.

Although *Habitat 04* married two failed examples from French and Canadian architectural history to a contemporary Canadian version of the SPCA, the latter is the one project of these three whose vision—the long-standing concern for animal welfare—remains tenable and true to its origins. The SPCA's mission to provide humane conditions for animals resembles the architects'

SPCA cats in *Habitat 04*
Photos: Guy L'Heureux

desires to provide humane conditions for people,[19] and its history coincides with Jungen's interest in labour and particularly with issues of exploitation and commodification as they relate to mass production in capitalist societies.[20]

In particular, the title *Habitat 04* and the actual work, when discussed in relation to the venue, throw the city of Montreal's ostensible progress and inevitable failures into relief through historical moments that span more than a century of change. Montreal's industrial past is visible in the architecture of the Darling Foundry, which was established in Griffintown in 1888, when Montreal was an important centre of the metallurgy industry in North America, but the business fell into decline and closed its doors in 1991.[21] Expo 67, as evoked by Habitat and the idealism of Safdie, sought to promote a modern, progressive, postindustrial Montreal. The city was on the global stage, and it was a cool, cosmopolitan place that had yet to experience the countercultural unrest of the late sixties and the Front de Libération du Québec (FLQ) crisis of 1970. Much of the neighbouring real estate, consisting of the former factory and warehouse buildings that were once home to artists and other creative individuals, has been converted into offices servicing the high-tech industry, and such places are commonly referred to as "digital corridors." Jungen's live video feeds threaded through the Darling Foundry evinced the technological era's superseding of the industrial past.

Habitat 04 is at once a contemporary work of art, a charitable organization, cat furniture, a historical cipher, a portrait of the oppressed and an architectural model. Perhaps the greatest strength of this contradictory work is its lack of didacticism. From the artist's perspective, *Habitat 04* as staged in Montreal was simply a solution to that city's cat problem.[22] For others, it was and is at once emblematic of the easy togetherness characteristic of relational aesthetics and the critical position delineated by the minimalist reformation. As political allegory, *Habitat 04* can be interpreted within a broad spectrum ranging from a utopia for the disenfranchised to an experiment in social engineering to a death camp filled with detainees. Still, as much as *Habitat 04* seeks to salvage utopian narratives, it points to the absurdity of this type of thought. Does Jungen really believe that the adoption of twenty cats represents a solution? And is the cat surplus really the problem? Perhaps Jungen is pointing to the transformations that have taken place in Canadian society during our lifetime. For example, the current federal government's refusal to cover the minute cost of the cats living in the Cat Sanctuary is symptomatic of the much broader and systemic disintegration of Canada's social safety net. As the humane social programs that politicians like Lester B. Pearson put in place in the sixties are being dismantled bit by bit, less and less do we have the right to call ourselves a truly compassionate people.

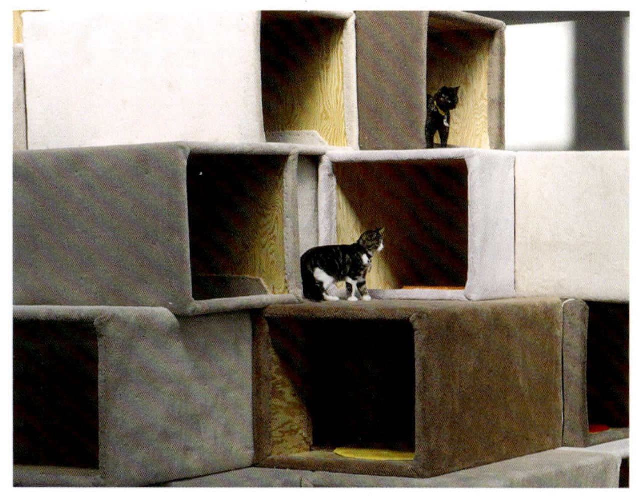

Habitat 04—Cité radieuse des chats/Cats Radiant City, 2004 (detail)
Installation view at Darling Foundry, Quartier Éphémère, Montreal, 2004
plywood, carpet, cats
3.35 x 4.57 x 8.53 m (11' x 15' x 28')
Courtesy of Catriona Jeffries Gallery, Vancouver
Photo: Guy L'Heureux

NOTES

1. See http://www.parliamenthill.gc.ca/text/explorecatsanctuary_e.html (accessed 10/28/2004).

2. The exhibition ran from March 12 to May 9, 2004.

3. Nicolas Bourriaud, *Relational Aesthetics* (Dijon-Quetigny: les presses du réel, 2002), 44.

4. Ibid.

5. Hal Foster, "Arty Party," *London Review of Books,* December 4, 2003: 21.

6. It is interesting to note here that Jungen appears to be drawn to the vulnerable. The cats he is working with have been abandoned, and many whale species are endangered. Both examples, though very different, point to societal apathy with respect to the environment and animal populations.

7. For a more detailed description and interpretation of these works, see Scott Watson, "Shapeshifter" in *Brian Jungen* (Vancouver: Contemporary Art Gallery, 2002), 15.

8. Ralph Rugoff, *Capp Street Project 2004, Brian Jungen* (San Francisco: California College of the Arts, 2004).

9. Watson, 23.

10. Ibid.

11. Le Corbusier, *Quand les cathédrales étaient blanches* (Paris: Editions Plon, 1937), 280–81, as quoted in Robert Fishman, *Urban Utopias in the Twentieth Century: Ebenezer Howard, Frank Lloyd Wright, and Le Corbusier* (New York: Basic Books, 1977), 230.

12. Le Corbusier, *La ville radieuse* (Boulogne-Seine: L'Architecture d'aujourd'hui, 1935), 192, as quoted in Fishman, 231.

13. Robert Gretton, *Canadian Architect* 12, no. 10 (October 1967): 31.

14. Moshe Safdie, as quoted in Gretton.

15. It is surmizable that the cats were more captivated by the human visitors than the human visitors were by the art.

16. See http://www.spcamontreal.com/english/pages/resources/know.html (accessed 10/26/2004).

17. Jungen dismantled *Habitat 04* and at time of writing had no plans to restage it. As a network of relations, the artwork exists outside the market with the exception of some possibly commodifiable aspects, namely the cats themselves and the edition of welcome mats, among other things. Arguably, the cats could be described as "living ready-mades." Ready-mades are typically commonplace prefabricated objects that have been isolated from their functional context and elevated to the status of art by the mere act of the artist's selection. A cat, given its astonishing ability to multiply and its condition of oversupply, could be defined as an ordinary, mass-produced (and mass-producing) living thing. By incorporating the cats as a component of the work of art, Jungen selected and displaced the role of the domestic cat and elevated it to the status of art. Every cat passing through the Safdie/Corbusier–inspired compound became a living ready-made imbued with all the worth the artist's name signifies in the current art world. In other words, the value-added or commodified cat became a Jungen artwork, or perhaps a "living multiple" is a better description. Possibly such signification increased the chance a cat would be "collected" and survive.

18. This space was devised by the SPCA as a holding room, beyond the public eye, for cats to rest in and for additional cats to replace those adopted.

19. The mission of the SPCA is to protect animals against negligence, abuse and exploitation; represent their interests and ensure their well-being; raise public awareness and help develop compassion for all living creatures. See http://www.spcamontreal.com/english/pages/resources/know.html (accessed 10/26/2004).

20. See Brian Jungen discussing his *Prototype* series as quoted in "Brian Jungen in conversation with Matthew Higgs" in *Brian Jungen* (Vienna: Secession, 2004), 24: "Sometime later, in 1998, I was on a residency at the Banff Centre and started to investigate the possibility of using athletic equipment as a sculptural medium. Researching into Nike's use of exploited labour—which was being widely discussed in the media—and thinking about the iconic status of their Air Jordan range of shoes fuelled my interest. I started to make connections between the issues of exploitation, production and commodification and started to think about how this might relate to native art generally."

21. According to a pamphlet produced by the Darling Foundry, "The Darling Foundry is a visual arts centre renovated in 2002 by architects of Atelier in situ. It is composed of the Quartier Éphémère offices, two exhibition halls and the ArtBar Cluny. The two exhibition halls were designed very differently so that all manifestations of contemporary artistic creation might be accommodated between them. One measures 5,000 ft^2 and its strong industrial character makes it ideal for large in situ installations. The other is smaller (1,800 ft^2), more classical and museological... The Darling Brothers established their foundry in Montreal in 1888 at a time when the metallurgical industry was in full bloom in the old Griffintown neighbourhood and the foundries were multiplying. At its height, the Darling Foundry was comprised of three buildings, each with a specific technical function: the warehouse (model showroom), the foundry and the assembly factory, for a total of 120,000 ft^2 employing more than 800 people. The vitality of the Darling Foundry demonstrates the importance of metallurgy since the 1850s, an industrial activity which gave Montreal an opening on the whole of North America. It developed the technique known as 'grey iron' and primarily produced industrial equipment. From 1971 it passed into the hands of other companies, resulting in its decline with the closing of the Lachine Canal (1970) and marked the end of the industrial vocation of Griffintown. In 1991, the Darling Foundry finally closed its doors and was effectively abandoned for the next ten years."

22. The artist in conversation with the author, February 5, 2005.

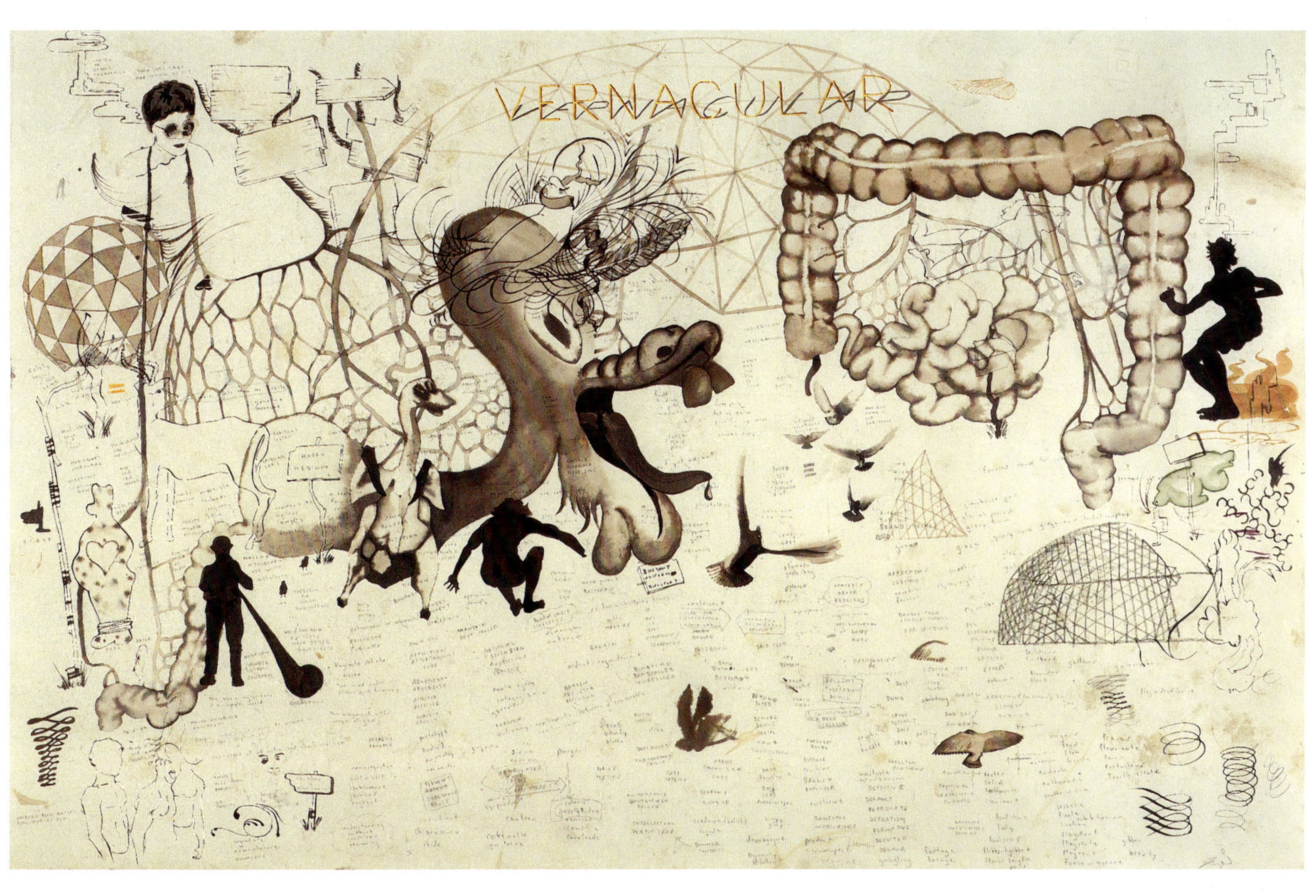

Vernacular, 1998–2001
graphite, watercolour, ink, wax crayon and watercolour on paper
73 x 112 cm (28 3/4" x 44")
Collection of the National Gallery of Canada, Ottawa, Purchased 2002
Photo: Courtesy of Catriona Jeffries Gallery, Vancouver

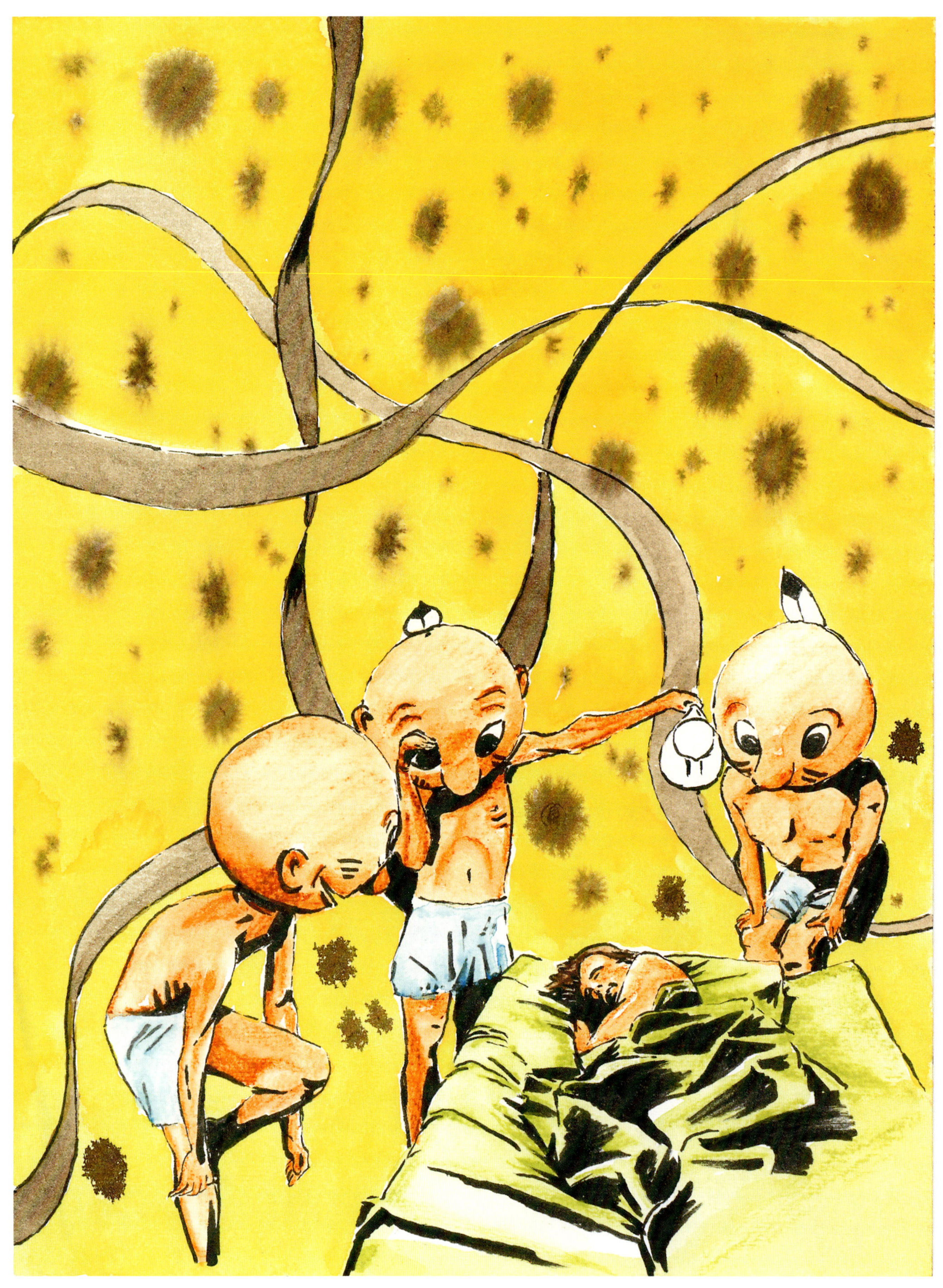

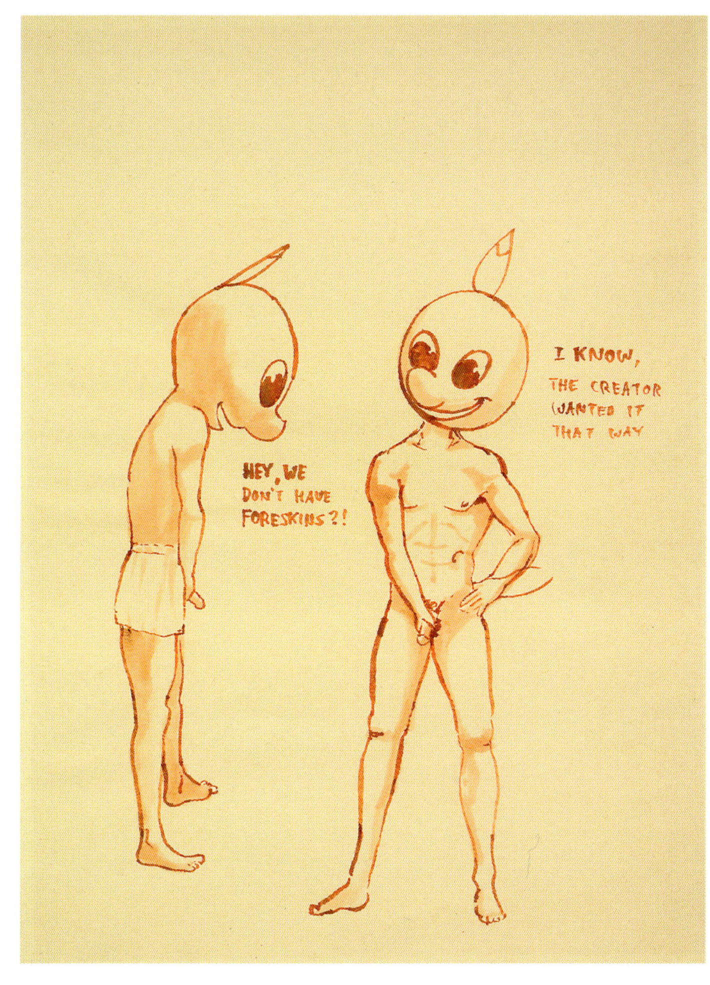

OPPOSITE:
Dream Sequins, 1993
ink and watercolour on paper
30.6 x 23 cm (12" x 9")
Collection of The Morris and Helen Belkin Gallery, Vancouver
Purchased with financial support from the Canada Council for the Arts Acquisition
Assistance Program and the Morris and Helen Belkin Foundation, 1998
Photo: Trevor Mills, Vancouver Art Gallery

Untitled, 1997
ink on manila paper
35.7 x 27.1 cm (14" x 10 1/2")
Collection of The Morris and Helen Belkin Gallery, Vancouver
Purchased with financial support from the Canada Council for the Arts Acquisition
Assistance Program and the Morris and Helen Belkin Foundation, 1998
Photo: Trevor Mills, Vancouver Art Gallery

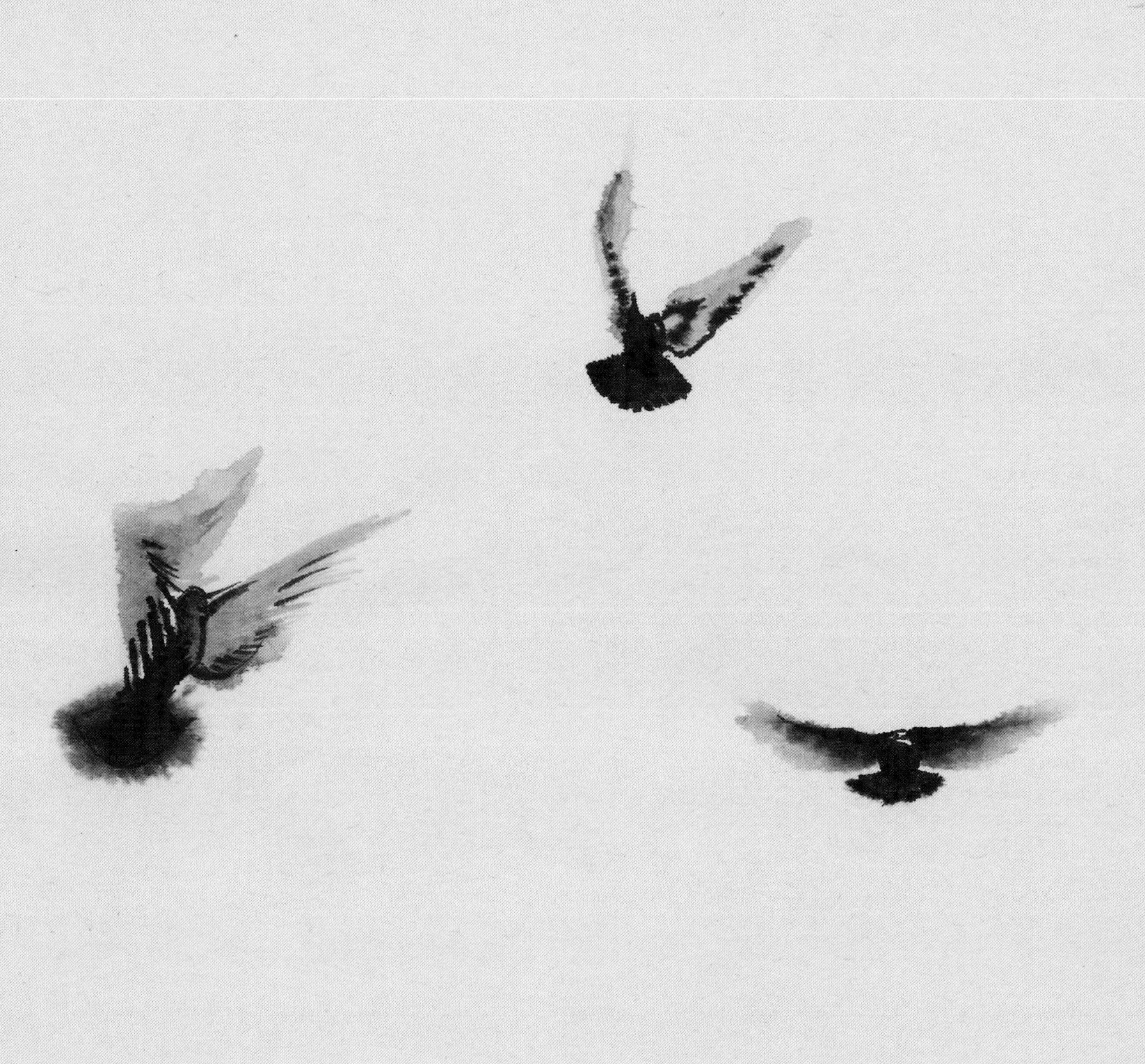

In Conversation
Brian Jungen and Simon Starling

In 2002, the British artist Simon Starling exhibited two models of two modernist concrete houses from Puerto Rico in a New York gallery. Starling's roughly made architectural structures that doubled as birdhouses prompted Brian Jungen, who has recently been developing his own environments for animals, to invite him to take part in a dialogue. What unfolded between January 28 and February 12, 2005, was a wide-ranging discussion around the two artists' practices, their mutual interests in architecture, zoology, ornithology, transmutations and the conflating of diverse culture references.

BRIAN JUNGEN: I recognized some familiar components in your work that I have been investigating, such as environments built for animals, the process of making/transforming objects and modern architecture and design. Of course we have different approaches to these common themes, but let's talk about the points of relation as well as the separations.

Given your surname, I always thought it was sweet that you made these amazing birdhouses. I read that starlings were first imported to New York by a British birdwatcher who released some in Central Park. They now cover the continent and flock together in large numbers. Did you have an interest in a specific type of bird when you made the *Inverted Retrograde Theme, USA* piece?

SIMON STARLING: The idea for the birdhouses developed in a rather convoluted fashion. Essentially the work attempted to collapse two "architectural" forms, the first being the modular concrete houses designed by the Austrian émigré

OPPOSITE:
Untitled, 1997
ink on manila paper
35.8 x 27.3 cm (14" x 10 3/4")
Collection of The Morris and Helen Belkin
Gallery, Vancouver
Purchased with financial support from the
Canada Council for the Arts Acquisition
Assistance Program and the Morris and
Helen Belkin Foundation, 1998
Photo: Trevor Mills, Vancouver Art Gallery

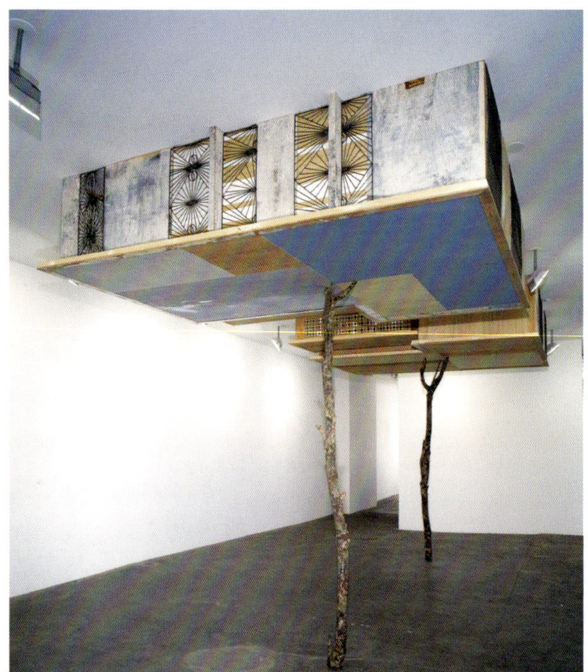

Simon Starling
*Inverted Retrograde Theme, USA
(House for a Songbird)*, 2002
1:5 scale models of No. 2 and No. 4
Calle Victoria, Ville Contessa, Bayamón,
Puerto Rico designed in 1964 by Simon
Schmiderer for the International Basic
Economy Housing Corporation, USA.
Installation view at Casey Kaplan
Gallery, New York 2002
wood, iron, mahogany and birds
337.8 x 309.9 x 355.6 cm (133" x 122" x
140") without tree trunks
Collection of Debra and Dennis Scholl, Miami
Courtesy of the artist and Casey Kaplan,
New York
Photo: Erma Estwick, New York

architect Simon Schmiderer for Rockefeller's International Basic Economy Corporation in Puerto Rico and the other being the modular twelve-tone music of Arnold Schoenberg. The tropical songbirds that I used gave the project its scale, and in a very playful way alluded to music and by association to Schoenberg.

As for the American Starling, it has been a fantastically successful "weed," an "alien" population on the scale of Australia's rabbits, but less damaging. Actually, the flightless Starlings, my Canadian relatives, made it as far as British Columbia. My aunt used to send my grandparents a calendar every year illustrated with images of First Nation masks; your *Prototypes* [*for New Understanding*] were immediately familiar to me on my first encounter with them. I know that animal forms have appeared in your work in the past but in these cases—I'm thinking of the whales you built with plastic garden furniture and the animal-like forms of the masks that inspired the *Protos*—the animals were heavily mediated, shall we say. I sense more of a live engagement with animals in your new work. I know very little about what you are planning for your forthcoming show in Vancouver, and perhaps the best place to start would be to ask you to talk about your current interest in birdhouses.

BJ: I have always had a fascination with animals. It began when I was a child on our family's farm. In terms of art making, there was a huge lapse from when I was a child drawing animals to when I began making the *Prototypes.* This lapse had something to do with the art education that was part of my life from public school through to art school; that is, representations of animals were frowned upon. I began to investigate the animal form when I first started making the *Protos.* Most of these investigations were associated with mythology and storytelling, more specifically with how Aboriginal history is reproduced in the traditional carving of the Northwest Coast nations and in turn how it is represented to the general public through the authority of anthropology and mass media. A lot of this research took place in the Museum of Anthropology at the University of British Columbia, so it was in the context of the museum space that the *Protos* were born.

I also began to look at the Vancouver Aquarium and its exhibits and specimens. I was curious about how these two institutions generated so much identity for the city and the region. I was particularly interested in the mid-twentieth-century architecture of both spaces as some sort of manufactured modernist by-product and began investigating what qualities worked or failed. Perhaps it was in a reaction to this product, but I have an urge to associate and collide seemingly dis-separate but related topics, something I see in your work as well.

When I was hanging out at the aquarium, I discovered a badly neglected and vacant polar bear pit, which is part of an old zoo that used to be adjacent to the aquarium. This sad pit was literally a torturous example of such a failure where polar bears were confined on raw concrete in a mild climate until they died. I have since studied environments and habitats that humans build for animals, in particular how such structures are designed to display the animal for public observation/entertainment or for scientific surveillance.

My first project about this theme was the creation of a shelter and
adoption centre for abandoned cats in Montreal in 2004 [*Habitat 04: Cité radieuse
des chats/Cats Radiant City*]. I have also started designing a park for dogs, and
most recently, birdhouses. I have not engaged in working with wildlife yet but am
thinking that the birdhouse is a step in that direction.

I like how your Schmiderer's houses were perched next to the ceiling so
the songbirds were out of view, as a kind of logic.

SS: I felt most comfortable working with the birds if they had their own space, so
to speak. It's never easy using live animals in this context.

It's interesting to me that you talk about aquarium architecture and the
bear pit in particular. I've just been reading about Bauhaus design in Britain in the
1930s and its relationship to ecology and more specifically animal welfare. The
Norwegian writer Peder Anker is currently developing a historical account of the
relationship between architecture and ecology, and one of his areas of interest
is the collaboration between the Bauhaus (as it regrouped in London in the
thirties) and various ecologists and zoologists of the day. We generally think of
the Bauhaus as having its roots in "Machine Age" thinking, not in the realm of
ecology. I suppose the clearest manifestation of these collaborations would be
the penguin pool in the London Zoo, designed in 1934 by the Tecton Group led
by Berthold Lubetkin. While Lubetkin, who was passionately political, would
have jumped at the chance of displaying modern architectural forms to a mass
audience, he also believed that geometric forms were fundamental building
blocks of nature and, in turn, that forms in nature ought to be the model for
functional design.

Although the penguin pool has been criticized for turning animal welfare
into a "circus act," the relationship between the architects and their client was a
very rigorous and well-intentioned one, and what was produced was a wonder-
fully exuberant modernist jewel of a building dominated by its famous
double-helix ramps. It's interesting that the building was recently in the news
again when, no longer considered to be suitable for penguins—who, according
to the zookeepers, find its pool too shallow—it was turned over to a group of
Chinese alligators. It is clear that in such cases the architects acted largely with
the animals' best interests at heart, and what has changed, perhaps, since the
thirties is our understanding of animals and their needs. Is there a sense that your
Vancouver Aquarium simply developed from a rather half-hearted and less
rigorous deployment of modernism in the service of animals—a sixties prefab
tower block of the zoological world?

BJ: I'm glad you brought up Lubetkin and his Tecton Group. After reading some
of his writing, I was astounded with his approach to zoological design, which
comes across as a slightly corrupt evolutionary manifesto. I think he had a strong
compassion for animals but held tight to the superiority of humans over animals
(and nature), expressing this a bit like the control of a reformist at a prison. I
came across some amazing images of the construction of the penguin pool and
the gorilla house, and I can see why his designs were controversial in his day and

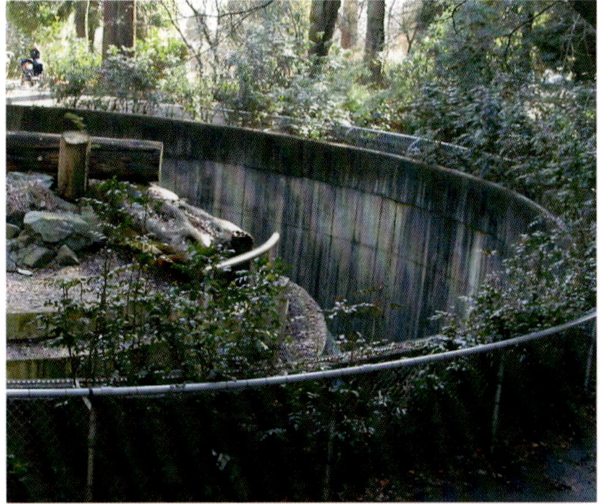

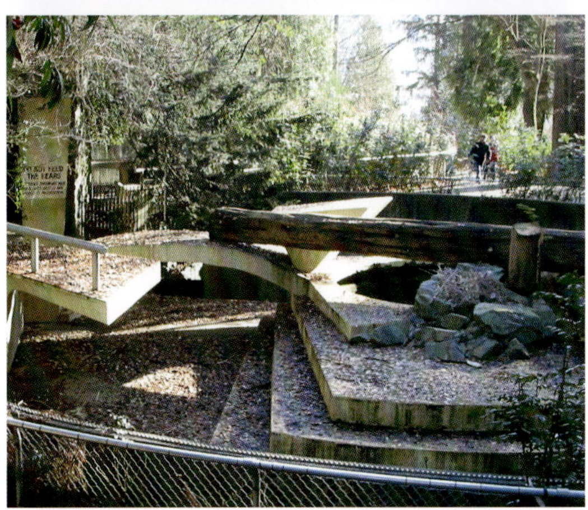

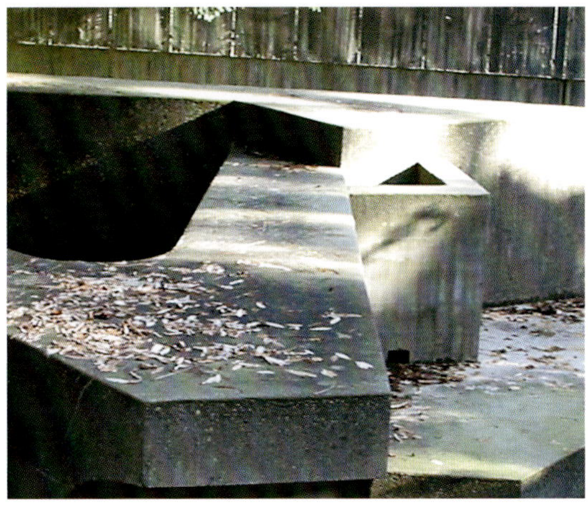

Polar Bear Pit, Vancouver
Aquarium
Photos: Brian Jungen

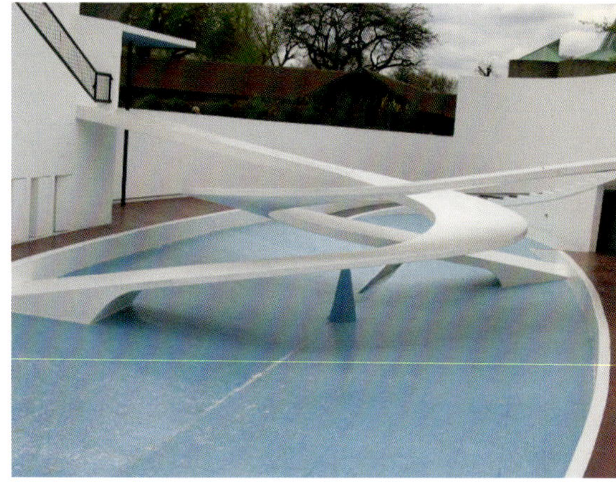

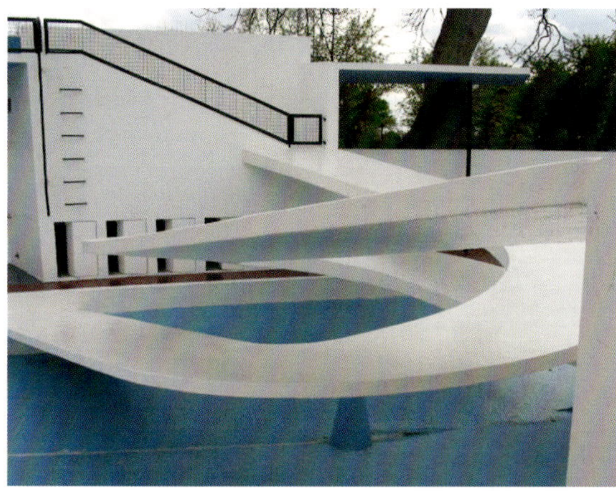

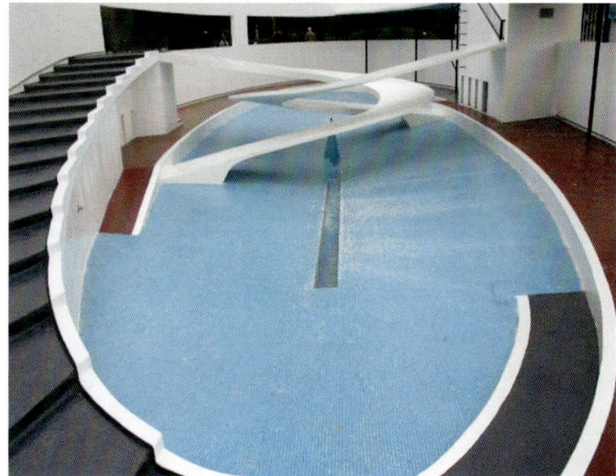

Penguin Pool, Regents Park Zoo
Photos: Brian Jungen

became so influential. When I arrived in London last year for a residency, one of the first places I went to was Regents Park Zoo to see the penguin pool. It had just been painted, and I was surprised (and relieved) not to see any penguins in it. It is a marvellous structure, with a strong sense of incarceration.

I would suggest that the design of the Vancouver Aquarium was a benign version of modernism, attempting to consider the welfare of the animals in its collection. This was a daunting task, as the prime specimens/attractions were killer whales. It is accepted that the global decline of the whale population, and the crisis this generated in the scientific and environmental communities in the sixties, was the key motivation in the development of the aquarium. Vancouver became one of the first centres for marine biologists to study killer whales in the wild, and it also launched the environmental group Greenpeace. Both groups were vocal in creating awareness about the threat of extinction of whales but carried out widely varying strategies on the captivity of whales for research. The aquarium building designed to house sea life looks like a tower block, as you say, but over the decades it has been dressed up to be more friendly. Most of the brutalist concrete has been veneered with colourful panels and imagery of aquatic life. My interest in this place came primarily out of a comparative relationship to the development and inception of the Museum of Anthropology, because I felt that both institutions were born from an impulse to salvage and that both package an idea of nature and this region's "natural history" as cultural commodities.

SS: I would also like to return to your whale skeleton piece, as it is central to the development of your current projects. For me it has a very particular relationship to a series of strange events that occurred in Scotland a few years ago. A male sperm whale was trapped in the upper reaches of the Firth of Forth where, too frightened by the noise from the Forth Road Bridge to reach open water again, he eventually died. The imaginative Scottish press christened him "Moby." Moby's remains ended up in the hands of the Department of Zoology at the National Museum of Scotland and in a matter of days after his death his skeleton was presented in the Edinburgh museum for all to see. The extraordinary thing was that the skeleton was still extremely fresh and not completely clean. What you saw, and more importantly smelled, was a pile of bones in a makeshift piece of exhibition architecture, made by lining the decorative pool and fountain in the museum's magnificent vaulted entrance space with black plastic. It was the middle of the summer and very quickly the entire museum was filled with the stench of Moby's still-fleshy bones. Moby's celebrity had somehow compelled the museum to make him instantly available to the public. It was such a magnificently incongruous image within this otherwise staid institution. Somehow this urgency to assimilate nature into the world of culture seems to have a parallel sense of pathos to your elegantly fashioned whale skeleton constructed entirely from petroleum-based plastics—an opposite but perhaps complementary collision?

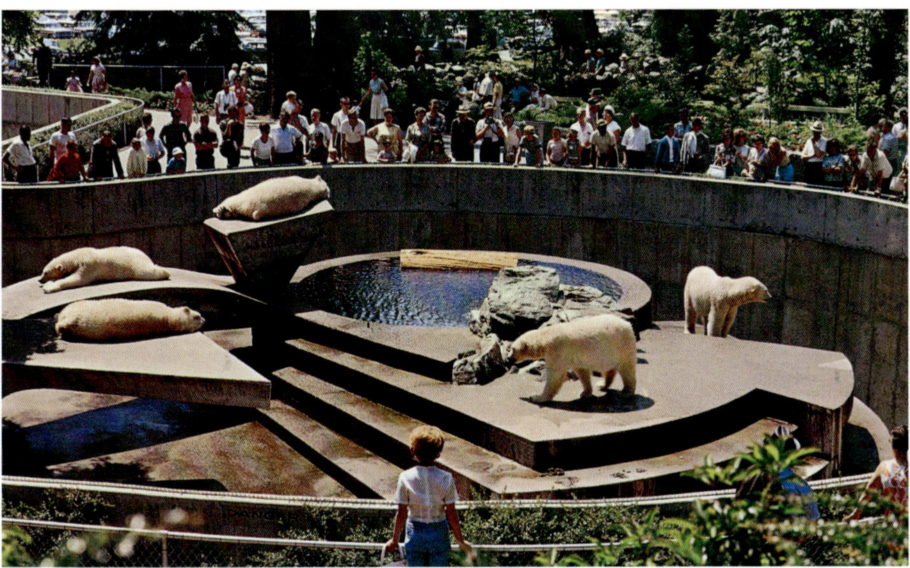

Polar bears at Stanley Park,
c. 1966
Photo: Ted Czolowski, Courtesy of Real
Estate Board of Greater Vancouver

BJ: Your account is quite telling of this salvaging I refer to, although the museum's haste to get Moby's skeleton on display to take advantage of the media's attention adds a revealing twist, that they chose to exhibit the raw bones of this whale as if it were the body of a celebrated public figure lying in state. The public has a strong empathy and respect for whales, and this has been exploited by Hollywood and the news media. It is not surprising that the museum's marketing people would take advantage of such pathos, expediently serving up Moby as a cultural offering to a hungry public. When I made my first whale work, *Shapeshifter* [2000], I was curious to see whether a reproduction of an object from the natural world could be made from something completely inorganic. Using these mass-produced, petroleum-based plastic chairs proved to work well for what I was interested in.

SS: It seems that in many of your previous projects there is a very direct dialogue between a motif and the material that you choose to "reproduce" it in. Is it a way of problematizing a traditional understanding of sculpture, where the material is no longer at the service of the subject but rather in dialogue with it? It's almost as if the work is trying to pull itself apart—and is unstable.

Recently I've been dealing with specific sculptural languages in a very direct way, in works that, perhaps in a similar way, try to collapse art history onto current economic situations. I'm thinking particularly of *Bird in Space* [2004]. I took the story of the importation of [Constantin] Brancusi's 1925 bronze sculpture of the same name into the United States by Marcel Duchamp and the subsequent court case between Brancusi and U.S. Customs, and used it as a framework to investigate the more contemporary story of U.S. steel tariffs. My imported hunk of Romanian steel was pushed into the sculptural realm of Brancusi by simply floating its vast weight on helium-filled cushions—a kind of parody of his attempts

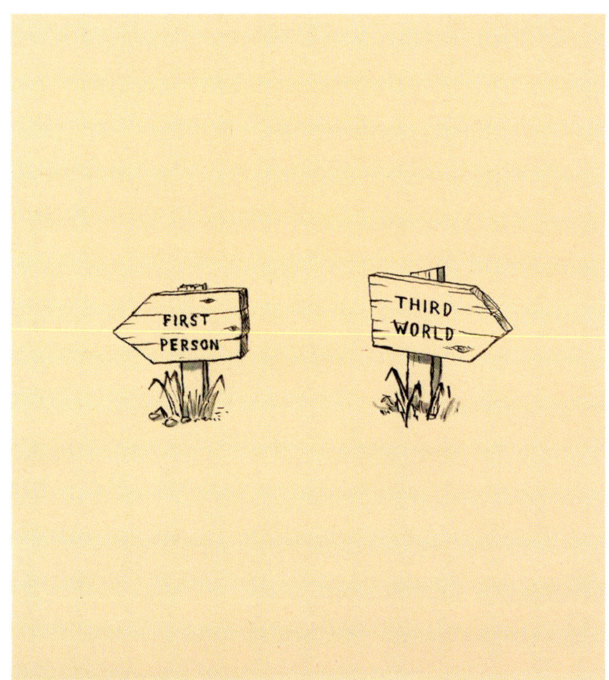

Untitled, 1997
ink on manila paper
35.7 x 27.2 cm (14" x 10 3/4")
Collection of The Morris and Helen Belkin
Gallery, Vancouver
Purchased with financial support from the
Canada Council for the Arts Acquisition
Assistance Program and the Morris and
Helen Belkin Foundation, 1998
Photo: Trevor Mills, Vancouver Art Gallery

to make heavy metal fly. What's interesting about that court case is that on one level U.S. Customs read the work in a very correct way, in that it was indeed an attempt to simulate the perfection of the Machine Age. It was Brancusi's propeller, or so the story goes.

Perhaps it's completely off the mark, but I can't help thinking about Brancusi when I see your *Protos*—of course, Brancusi's materials are there to be transcended and dematerialized, whereas your cut-up Nikes or plastic chairs remain an incisive or even disruptive presence.

BJ: It's an interesting comparison, and I can see how you would be interested in the tension that developed around justifying an artwork in aesthetic/economic terms to a monster like U.S. Customs. I saw an exhibition of Brancusi's work at the Tate Modern last summer, and it led me to consider that the sources for much of his carving were not only from his Romanian heritage but from external influences in Asian and African art—how modern. Brancusi's desire to transcend matter, and the desire to move beyond the material, are qualities that could be applied to the traditional carved masks of the Northwest Coast and the ceremonies they were intended to serve. My *Protos* are built with the understanding that they have a secular existence, that the materials guide the composition and are pushed to the forefront, but not necessarily in a disruptive manner. I am interested in creating and transforming relationships between materials and subjects, but perhaps the polarities in these relationships are not so disparate.

There are plenty of historic examples in the artwork of First Nations cultures where European products were modified and used for their aesthetic qualities, thereby changing the intended use value of these products. This type of exchange accrued as contact with European traders spread across the continent, but I am curious to know why this component of history is not "revived" in today's carving and regalia. It is accepted that the institutionalization of First Nations "artifacts" by the anthropologists in the nineteenth and early twentieth century had the effect of dictating what was to be constituted as authentic. This generally meant that the oldest examples of whatever anthropologists or sociologists could scavenge would become the foundation for theories and be used to identify lineage. Contemporary ways of looking at First Nations art and identifying movements demand that lineages are more fluid and are determined by examining both the similarities and differences in aesthetics, as well as the associative relationships between different cultures, without overtly emphasizing barriers of race, gender or sexuality. Would you agree with this?

SS: Yes, this idea of fluidity is absolutely at the heart of what I do and is reflected almost literally as objects are physically fused, realigned or juxtaposed and both time and space are constantly rejigged, reformulated and collapsed.

BJ: I like to think of my work as a relationship between the accepted idea of a traditional form and the embracing of a very contemporary material. I don't think such relationships create a disruptive or discordant presence, but rather expand parameters and blur some social boundaries. To bring up the natural world again, this is where hybridity often produces endless and harmonious varieties.

SS: Perhaps my projection of a disruptive or unstable sense in the work is not so far from your sense of fluidity and complexity. It is a response in part to what I see as the apparent ease of your work. The key works seem to be persistently bipolar in their structure. From the whale made in plastic garden furniture to the treacherous basketball court laid out with sewing-machine tables, the work has an extreme economy of means. This is both seductive and engaging but also, perhaps on the face of it, seems to run contrary to its potential for the kind of fluidity and complexity of meaning that you propose. One critic has referred it to as a "sleight of hand." In many ways it is formally very stable work—very resolved—and yet it seems able to throw up a wealth of associations, references and meanings.

I'm wondering if when European objects were incorporated into the First Nations sculptural language, were they used for specific critical or reflexive purposes or, rather, were they adopted in the spirit of "making do and getting by"—an opportunistic pragmatism?

BJ: From what I understand, the methods of incorporation of non-Native objects into Native cultures are as diverse as the different cultures of the continent, and varied insofar as the uses to which they were adopted. Some things like tobacco tins were extremely versatile and could be manipulated into many uses, from adornment to utensils. I suppose this is what Claude Levi-Strauss identified as an example of bricolage, as new meanings and narratives were assigned to such objects and motifs. I consider such creative ingenuity to serve a critical purpose, as it represented a counter-logic to colonialists. I also think that this part of the world has a harsh climate and treacherous geography that forced all of its inhabitants to live life with an opportunistic pragmatism of sorts.

SS: I was also very interested to discover Reid Shier's text in the catalogue for your exhibition at the Charles H. Scott Gallery in 1999 and his foregrounding of an economic model in relation to your work in the form of potlatch. I'm interested to know how this text sits with you and your understanding of your work. I suppose [Georges] Bataille's *The Accursed Share,* notably the first volume, has been a big influence on my thinking. Is the notion of the kind of "anti-economy" embodied by the potlatch of interest to you?

BJ: As to Reid's essay and his reading of the Nike work in relation to the potlatch ceremony, I will say that, although there is a parallel in an economic sense, there was no predetermined cultural link that I was trying to make. I read [Franz] Boas and Bataille's enlightening essays about the potlatch, but I have a mixed opinion about the perceived relationship of the potlatch and my work. It has been argued that the potlatch, in its history before it was outlawed between 1884 and 1951, was a resourceful economic system that redistributed goods and commodities to those who had none, and put an emphasis on generosity over accumulation.

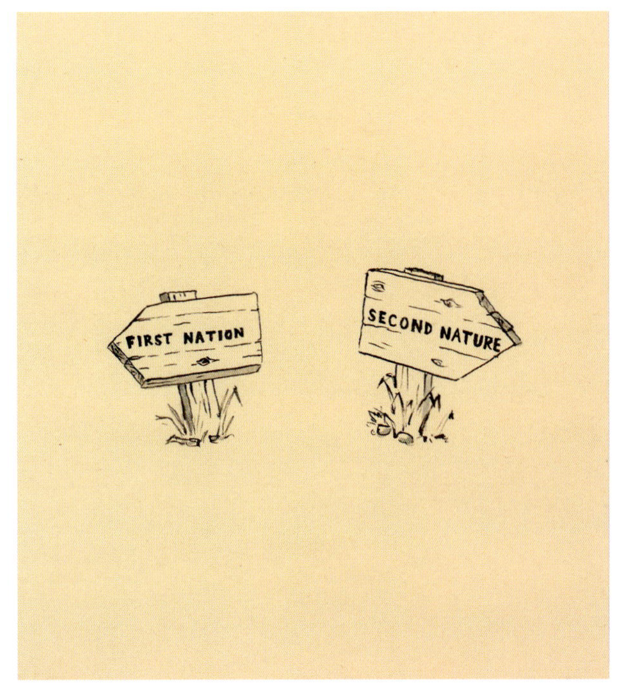

Untitled, 1997
ink on manila paper
35.7 x 27.1 cm (14" x 10 1/2")
Collection of The Morris and Helen Belkin
Gallery, Vancouver
Purchased with financial support from the
Canada Council for the Arts Acquisition
Assistance Program and the Morris and
Helen Belkin Foundation, 1998
Photo: Trevor Mills, Vancouver Art Gallery

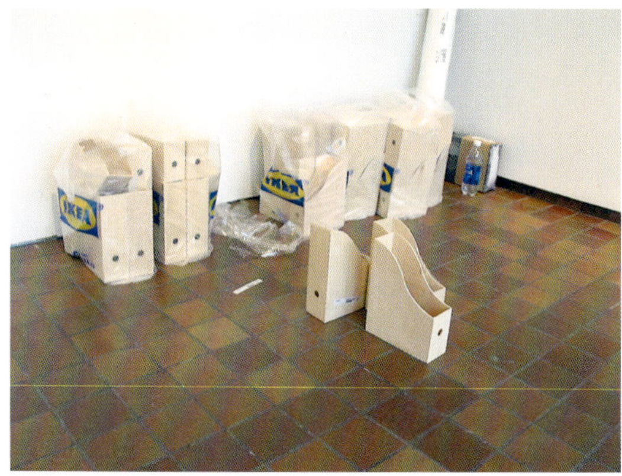

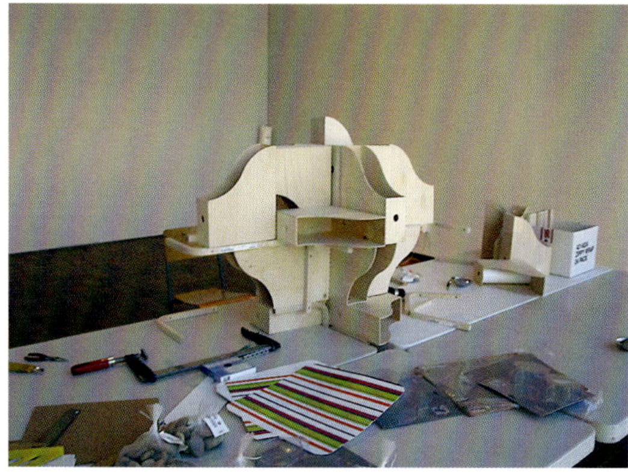

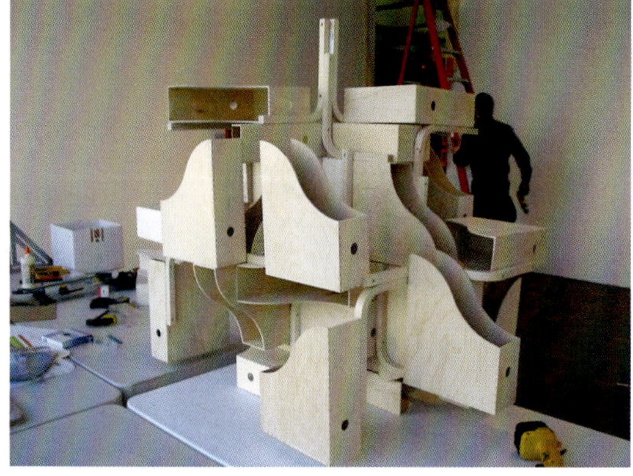

Production of *Inside Today's Home* at The Edmonton Art Gallery, 2005
Photos: Brian Jungen

It was the destruction, or "waste," of goods and the economy that these events represented that was the controversial aspect of the potlatch and that led to the outlawing of this and other ceremonies, [Dan] Cranmer's super-potlatch of 1921 being the ultimate example. It was also this aspect that was the most culturally important, as a means of establishing rank through a kind of competitive waste. The potlatch is very specific in its meaning, and I have been more interested in the diffusion of meaning of coastal First Nations motifs into the public domain. Reid also locates my position as being more about transformation and power, and less (if at all) about humiliation and social status.

SS: Is it possible to talk about the new projects? Are they establishing a new kind of internal logic? I sensed in some of the recent projects that there is a shift of some sort going on, a move towards a more reactive/site-specific practice. Perhaps this is simply another strand in your work that is surfacing again in the new work?

BJ: I was recently in a show at The Edmonton Art Gallery that was looking at how artists interpret architecture. My contribution was an installation that was focussing on the domestic environment and mass-produced, interior-design products. I felt that the show was based around the idea of interiors and the structures marketed to create personal living environments. I thought it would be an interesting opportunity to fuse some of the ideas that I have been speaking to you about. My installation involved creating an aviary for some domesticated finches (mass-produced living products from a pet store), using ubiquitous and identifiable IKEA products. I basically sealed off my designated exhibition space in the museum and built a suspended birdhouse using birch periodical-file boxes and bent-plywood shelf brackets. I did not alter or cut the IKEA products, as I wanted the materials to retain their recognizable and familiar shape, so I suppose this is a new approach for me.

The installation could only be viewed through small peepholes in the plywood barricade, or through closed-circuit television cameras that were attached to the birdhouse. The birdhouse was initially conceived to go outside the museum so that it would be used by chickadees and other wild birds, but it was the wrong season and location for this. By isolating a space inside the museum, I was able to work with the architecture of the building to create a separation similar to an indoor/outdoor thing.

I feel like I have come to a resolution with a way of working that emphasizes a binary, object-viewer relationship. I am curious about some older ideas that I have investigated in past work, in particular ideas that involve some interaction with the public. Having located most of my work in the institutionalized arena of the museum, a new direction will lead me to experiment with less stable environments.

Inside Today's Home, 2005 (detail)
Installation at The Edmonton Art Gallery, Edmonton, Alberta, 2005
IKEA products, video cameras, birds
106.7 x 134.6 x 340.4 cm (42" x 53" x 32")
sculpture only
4.27 x 7.62 x 7.0 m (14' x 25' x 23')
room enclosure
Photo: Hutch Hutchinson, Courtesy of The Edmonton Art Gallery

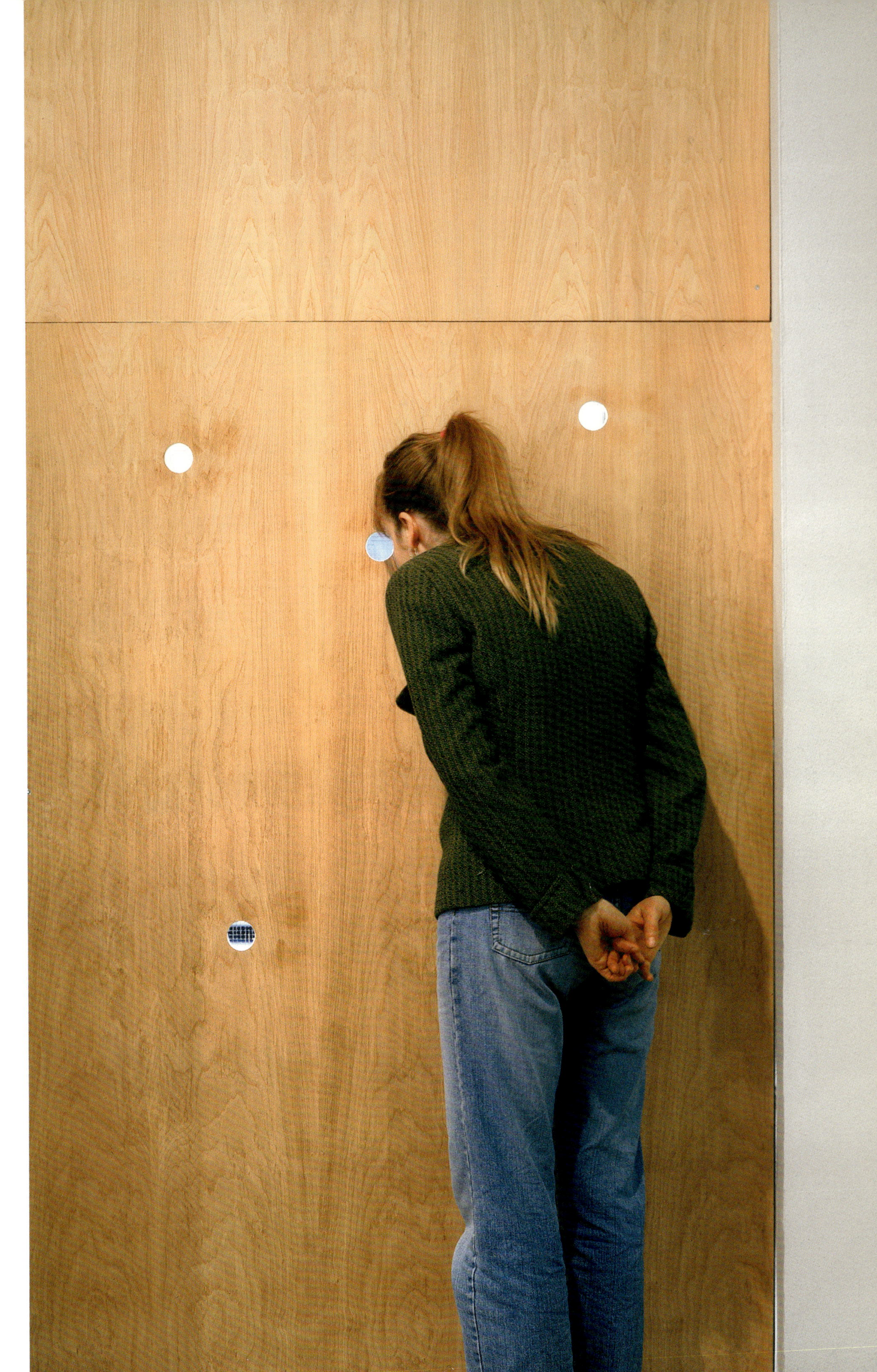

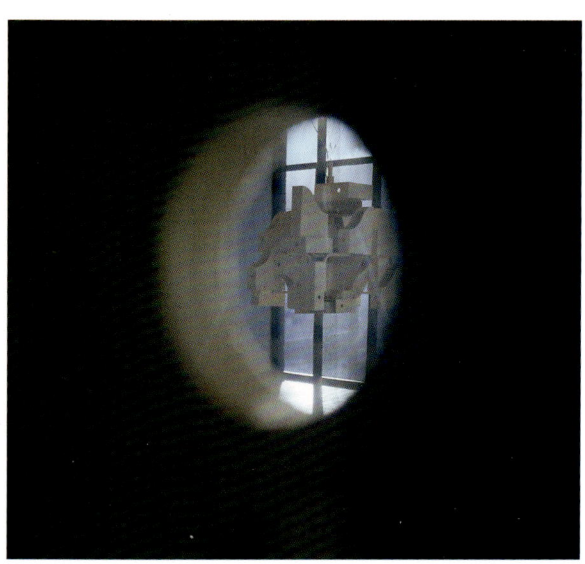

Inside Today's Home, 2005
Installation views at The Edmonton Art Gallery, Edmonton, Alberta, 2005
IKEA products, video cameras, birds
106.7 x 134.6 x 340.4 cm (42" x 53" x 32") sculpture only
4.27 x 7.62 x 7.0 m (14' x 25' x 23') room enclosure
Photo: Hutch Hutchinson, Courtesy of The Edmonton Art Gallery

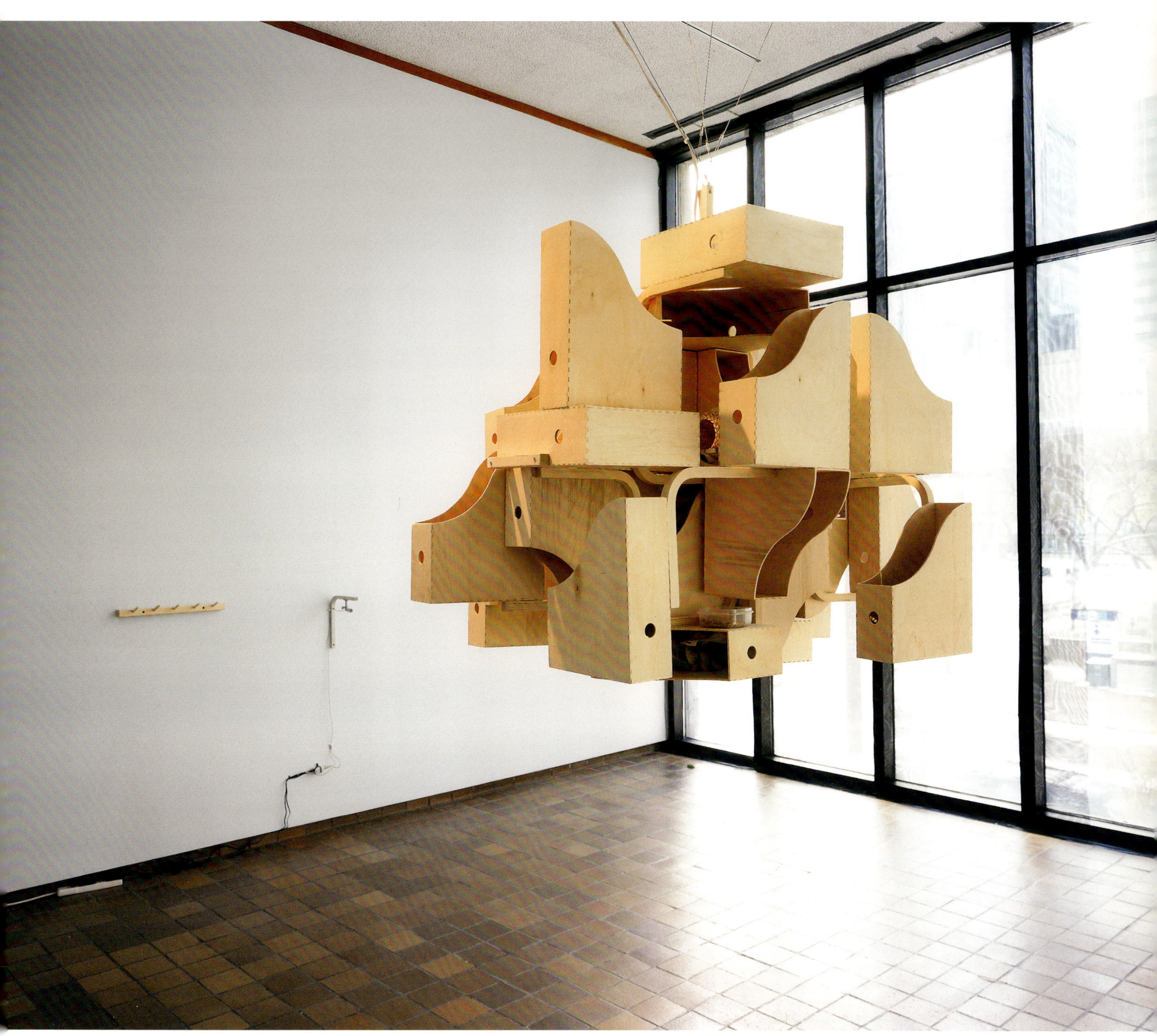

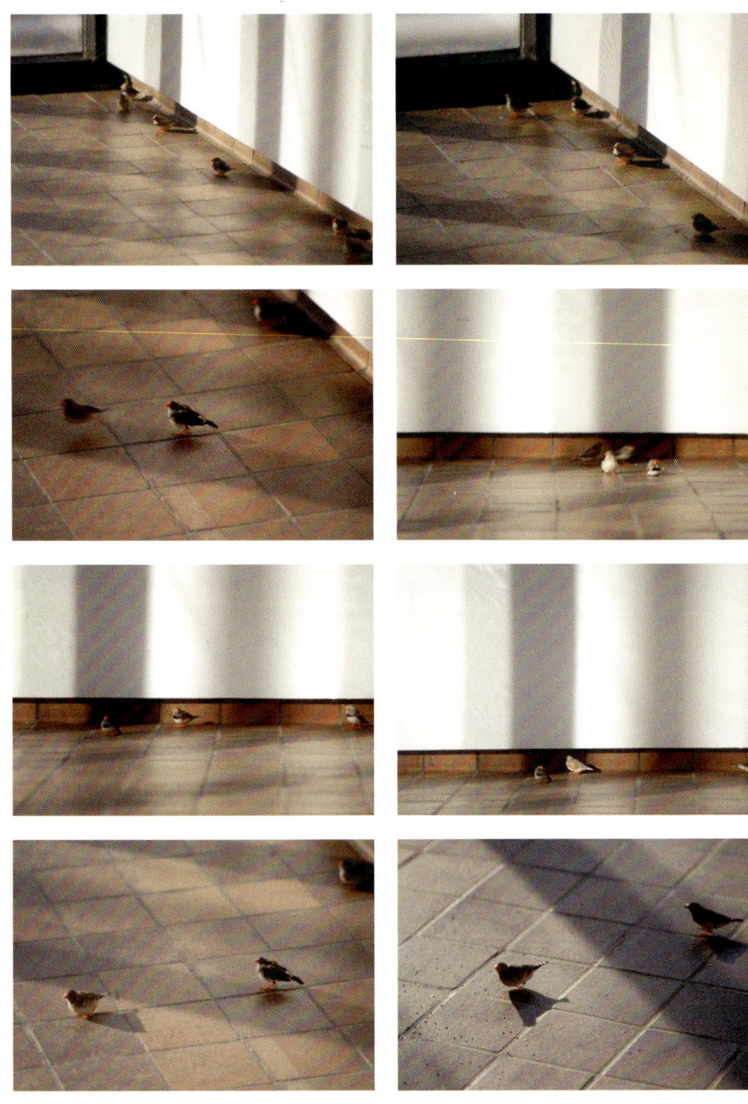

Finches that lived in *Inside Today's Home,* 2005
Photo: Hutch Hutchinson, Courtesy of The Edmonton Art Gallery

Inside Today's Home, 2005 (detail)
Installation view at The Edmonton Art Gallery, Edmonton, Alberta, 2005
IKEA products, video cameras, birds
106.7 x 134.6 x 340.4 cm (42" x 53" x 32") sculpture only
4.27 x 7.62 x 7.0 m (14' x 25' x 23') room enclosure
Photo: Hutch Hutchinson, Courtesy of The Edmonton Art Gallery

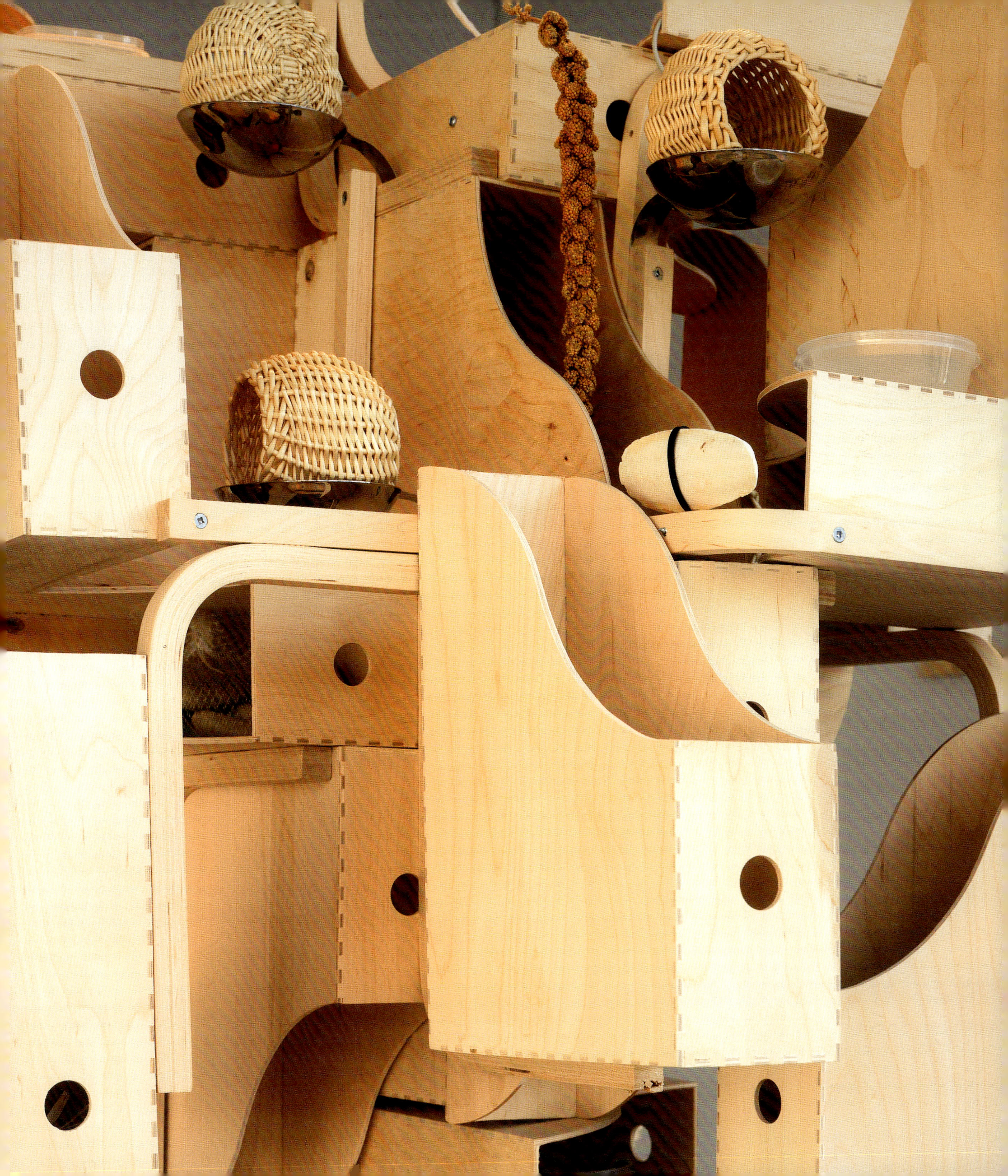

Born in Fort St. John, British Columbia, Canada, 1970
Lives and works in Vancouver, British Columbia

Education

1992

Emily Carr College of Art, Vancouver (Diploma of Visual Art)

Solo Exhibitions

2005

• *Brian Jungen,* organized by Vancouver Art Gallery, touring to New Museum of Contemporary Art, New York (2005); Vancouver Art Gallery, Vancouver (2006), and Musée d'art contemporain de Montréal, Montreal (2006) (catalogue: Daina Augaitis, Cuauhtémoc Medina, Ralph Rugoff, Kitty Scott, Trevor Smith, Simon Starling in conversation with Brian Jungen)

2004

• *Capp Street Project 2004: Brian Jungen,* Wattis Institute for Contemporary Arts, California College of the Arts, San Francisco (brochure: Ralph Rugoff)
• *Brian Jungen,* Triple Candie, New York
• *Habitat 04: Cité radieuse des chats/Cats Radiant City,* Quartier Éphémère/Fonderie Darling, Montreal with Montreal SPCA (brochure: Kitty Scott)

2003

• *Brian Jungen: Cetology,* Henry Art Gallery, Seattle
• *Brian Jungen,* Secession, Vienna (catalogue: Matthew Higgs)

2002

• *Brian Jungen,* Catriona Jeffries Gallery, Vancouver

2001

• *Brian Jungen,* Contemporary Art Gallery, Vancouver (catalogue: Scott Watson, Lindsay Brown)
• *Happy Medium,* Art Gallery of Calgary, Calgary
• *Brian Jungen,* Art Gallery of Windsor, Windsor, Ontario

2000

• *Brian Jungen,* Solo Exhibition Space, Toronto
• *Shapeshifter,* Or Gallery, Vancouver
• *Brian Jungen,* YYZ Artists' Outlet, Toronto
• *Brian Jungen,* Dunlop Art Gallery, Regina

1999

• *Brian Jungen,* Charles H. Scott Gallery, Vancouver (catalogue: Cate Rimmer, Reid Shier)

1997

• *Half Nelson,* Truck, Calgary

Group Exhibitions

2005

- *Re: Building the World—Artists Interpret Architecture,* The Edmonton Art Gallery, Edmonton (catalogue: Catherine Crowston, forthcoming)
- *Material Time/Work Time/Life Time,* Reykjavik Arts Festival, Reykjavik
- *10 Year Anniversary Exhibition,* Casey Kaplan Gallery, New York (forthcoming)
- *Intertidal: Art in Vancouver Now,* Museum voor Hedendaagse Kunst, Antwerp (forthcoming) (catalogue: Dieter Roelstraete, Scott Watson et al., forthcoming)

2004

- *A Question of Place,* Walter Phillips Gallery, The Banff Centre for the Arts, Banff (online essay: Candice Hopkins)
- *Artists' Favourites, Act I,* Institute of Contemporary Arts, London, England (catalogue: Jens Hoffman, Brian Jungen)
- *Noah's Ark,* organized by the National Gallery of Canada at Cité de l'énergie, Shawinigan (catalogue: Pierre Théberge and Mayo Graham, Greg A. Hill)
- *A Grain of Dust, A Drop of Water,* Gwangju Biennale 2004, Gwangju, Korea (catalogue: Brian Jungen, Kit Grauer, Milena Kalinovska et al.)

2003

- *Baja to Vancouver: The West Coast and Contemporary Art,* collaboratively organized by and toured to Museum of Contemporary Art San Diego, San Diego (2004); Vancouver Art Gallery, Vancouver (2004); Wattis Institute for Contemporary Arts, California College of the Arts, San Francisco (2004) and Seattle Art Museum, Seattle (2003) (catalogue: Ralph Rugoff, Daina Augaitis et al.)
- *Newmodulr,* Art Gallery of Calgary, Calgary
- *I Moderni/The Moderns,* Castello di Rivoli–Museo d'Arte Contemporanea, Torino (catalogue: Carolyn Christov-Bakargiev, Anthony Huberman)
- *nation,* Frankfurter Kunstverein, Frankfurt
- *Exhibitions of an Exhibition,* Casey Kaplan Gallery, New York
- *MosaiCanada: Sign and Sound,* Seoul Museum of Art, co-organized by The Power Plant Gallery, Toronto; Seoul Museum of Art, Seoul, and the Canadian Embassy, Seoul (catalogue: Wayne Baerwaldt, Nancy Campbell, Wonil Rhee, Keunhye Lim)

2002

- *watery, domestic,* Renaissance Society, Chicago
- *Think Big/Voir Grand,* Saidye Bronfman Centre of the Arts, Montreal
- *Bounce,* organized by The Power Plant, Toronto (2002), toured to Bellevue Art Museum, Bellevue, Washington (2003) (catalogue: Philip Monk)
- *This Place: Works from the Collection,* Vancouver Art Gallery, Vancouver
- *The Beachcombers,* organized by The Drawing Room, London, England, and toured to England's Gasworks Gallery, London (2002); Middlesbrough Art Gallery, Middlesbrough (2002), and Mead Gallery, University of Warwick, Coventry (2003) (catalogue: Andrew Renton, Katherine Stout)
- *Newmodulr,* Blackwood Gallery, Mississauga, Ontario
- *Hammertown,* The Fruitmarket Gallery, Edinburgh (2002) (organized in association with the Contemporary Art Gallery, Vancouver), toured to Bluecoat Gallery, Liverpool (2003), and Winnipeg Art Gallery, Winnipeg, Manitoba (2004) (catalogue: Reid Shier, Michael Turner)

2001

- *ARS 01,* Kiasma Museum of Contemporary Art, Helsinki (catalogue: Maaretta Jaukkuri, Nikos Papastergiadis, Irit Rogoff, Jeff Derksen)
- *Présent composé,* The Ottawa Art Gallery, Ottawa
- *Museopathy,* Agnes Etherington Art Centre, Queen's University, Kingston, Ontario (catalogue: Jim Drobnick et al.)
- *A Better Place,* MacKenzie Art Gallery, Regina (catalogue: Timothy Long)
- *Long Time: Selections from the Permanent Collection,* Vancouver Art Gallery, Vancouver

2000

- *Message by Eviction: New Art from Vancouver,* Illingworth Kerr Gallery, Calgary
- *Curatorial Mutiny Part 2,* Konstakuten Gallery, Stockholm

1998

- *Here and Now: First Nations Alumni,* Emily Carr Institute of Art + Design, Vancouver

1997

- *Buddy Palace,* Or Gallery, Vancouver

Bibliography

2004

Buhmann, Stephanie. "Brian Jungen," *Brooklyn Rail,* March 2004, 13.

Burnham, Clint. "Aperto Vancouver," *Flash Art* 37, no. 239 (November/December 2004): 57–59.

Cooke, Susan. "Cats in the City," Art, *McGill Tribune,* March 18, 2004, 14.

Cotter, Holland. "Art In Review: Brian Jungen," *New York Times,* March 5, 2004, B33.

Crevier, Lyne. "Refuge au Poil," *Ici,* March 25, 2004.

Gleeson, David. "Seattle Art Museum, Baja to Vancouver: The West Coast and Contemporary Art," *Contemporary* 59 (2004): 72.

Goodbody, Bridget. "Reviews: Brian Jungen," *Time Out New York* 438 (February 19–26, 2004): 60.

Grauer, Kit. "Viewer Participant" in *Gwangju Biennale 2004: A Grain of Dust, A Drop of Water* (catalogue), Pusan: Yeuleumsa Publishing Co., 2004, 262–65.

Hellman, Michel. "Condos pour minou," *Le Devoir,* March 20–21, 2004, E6.

Higgs, Matthew. "Brian Jungen in conversation with Matthew Higgs" in *Brian Jungen* (catalogue). Vienna: Secession, 2004, 18–29. Published in collaboration with Art Metropole, Toronto.

Hopkins, Candice. "A Question of Place." Online curatorial statement from the Walter Phillips Gallery, April 3–May 23, 2004, http://www.banffcentre.ca/wpg/exhibits/2004/2004-04-03_question/default.htm.

Jungen, Brian. "*Birch Bark Bitings* by Pat Bruderer and Bernice Beatty" in *Artists' Favorites Act I* (catalogue). London: Institute of Contemporary Arts, 2004, 11.

Kalinovska, Milena. "Matter of Engagement" in *Gwangju Biennale 2004: A Grain of Dust, A Drop of Water* (catalogue). Pusan: Yeuleumsa Publishing Co., 2004, 19–22.

LaBelle, Charles. "Brian Jungen," *Frieze* 83 (May 2004): 101–02.

LaFortune, Wes. "From anger to hope: Aboriginals Examine Identity and Change," *Fast Forward Weekly* 9, no. 24 (May 20, 2004): 24.

Laurence, Robin. "B2V Finds West Coast Context," *Georgia Straight,* June 3–10, 2004, 55.

McLaughlin, Bryne. "Rewind: Brian Jungen," *Canadian Art* 21, no. 2 (Summer 2004): 78.

——. "Vibrant local scene connects with the community," *Globe and Mail,* May 1, 2004, V6–V7.

Milroy, Sarah. "Artists of the world, unite," *Globe and Mail,* February 7, 2004, R2.

New Yorker, "Galleries Uptown, Brian Jungen," March 1, 2004, 21.

Nichols, Robert Darcy. "Brian Jungen: Quartier Éphémère Fonderie Darling, Montreal, March 12–May 9," *Parachute* 116 (October 2004): 2–3.

Redgrave, Veronica. "SPCA fundraiser showcases 'city' for cats," Social Notes, *Montreal Gazette,* April 4, 2004, B2.

Rugoff, Ralph. "Capp Street Project 2004: Brian Jungen" (poster/brochure). San Francisco: California College of the Arts, 2004.

Schmitz, Edgar. "Ein Fernsehtraum von Lieblingsbissen," *Texte Zur Kunst* 56 (December 2004): 199–200.

Schor, Gabriele. "Hybridity, Eros and Death," *Parkett,* no. 70 (2004): 175–77.

Scott, Kitty. "Dear Brian" in *Habitat 04—Cité radieuse des chats/Cats Radiant City* (brochure). Montreal: Quartier Éphémère/Fonderie Darling, 2004.

Scott, Michael. "Separating West Coast dream from reality," *Vancouver Sun,* June 5, 2004, D1, D5.

Townsend-Gault, Charlotte. "Struggles with Aboriginality/Modernity" in *Bill Reid and Beyond: Expanding on Modern Native Art,* eds. Karen Duffek and Charlotte Townsend-Gault. Vancouver/Seattle: Douglas & McIntyre/University of Washington Press, 2004, 225–50.

Turner, Michael. "Not so quiet on the Western front." Review of *Baja to Vancouver: The West Coast and Contemporary Art, Globe and Mail,* July 14, 2004, R5.

Whyte, Murray. "Finding Art in Sports and Sweatshops," *New York Times,* February 8, 2004, 29.

——. "Vancouver artist links sweatshops, sports," *Vancouver Sun,* February 14, 2004, F1, F5.

Woodley, Matthew. "I tought I taw a Habitat," *Montreal Mirror,* March 18–24, 2004, 39.

2003

Augaitis, Daina. "Brian Jungen" in *Baja to Vancouver: The West Coast and Contemporary Art* (catalogue). San Francisco: CCA Wattis Institute for Contemporary Arts, 2003, 66.

Casciani, Stefano. "Il moderno colpisce ancora?" *Domus,* no. 860 (June 2003): 14–17.

Christov-Bakargiev, Carolyn. "The Moderns" in *I Moderni/The Moderns.* Rivoli-Turin: Castello di Rivoli Museo d'Arte Contemporanea, 2003, 21–27.

Fanelli, Franco. "Dal post-moderno ai neo-moderni," *Vernissage: Il fotogiornale dell'arte,* no. 38 (May 2003): 6–7.

——. "Moderni si, modaioli no: chi sono gli artisti della generazione post–Twin Towers," *Il Giornale dell'arte,* no. 220 (April 2003): 12.

Hoffmann, Jens. "Brian Jungen," *Flash Art* 36, no. 231 (July–September 2003): 86–88.

Jahn, Jeff. "Review: Baja to Vancouver: The West Coast and Contemporary Art," *Modern Painters,* Winter 2003, 130, 132.

Moliterni, Rocco. "Giubbotti e scarpe fatti d'arte: Addio al video, tornano pittura e scultura," *La Stampa,* April 15, 2003.

Muller, Vanessa Joan. "Wat Heet Normal," *Metropolis M,* no. 6 (2003): 93–102.

Pratesi, Ludovico. "Non ci crederete: questi quadri suonano," *Il Venerdi,* April 11, 2003.

Ramade, Bénédicte. "Question de modernité," *L'oeil,* 2003, 112.

Rugoff, Ralph. "Baja to Vancouver: The West Coast and Contemporary Art" in *Baja to Vancouver: The West Coast and Contemporary Art* (catalogue). San Francisco: CCA Wattis Institute for Contemporary Arts, 2003, 13–19.

Tousley, Nancy. "Spotlight: Brian Jungen: Cool Cooler Coolest," *Canadian Art* 20, no. 2 (Summer 2003): 38–44.

Tranberg, Dan. "Reconstruction: Brian Jungen at the Secession," *Angle: a journal of fine arts + culture* 1, no. 10 (December 2003): 12–13.

Turner, Michael. "Wall and Void," *Modern Painters,* Summer 2003, 39–41.

2002

Brown, Lindsay. "Entitlement" in *Brian Jungen* (catalogue). Vancouver: Contemporary Art Gallery, 2002, 24–27.

Falconer, Morgan. "London: Gasworks—The Beachcombers," *Contemporary* 43 (2002): 25.

Hackett, Sophie. "Summer Breeze: Blowing through the jasmine in my mind," *xtra!,* August 8, 2002, 25.

Jordan, Betty Ann. "Art," *Toronto Life,* July 2002, 38.

Jungen, Brian. "Subject: Volvos on cobblestones" in *Facing History: Portraits of Vancouver.* Karen Love, ed. Vancouver: Presentation House Gallery and Arsenal Pulp Press, 2002, 107.

Milroy, Sarah. "Thoroughly Modern Art," *Globe and Mail,* September 25, 2002, R5.

——. "A tale of two art worlds," *Globe and Mail,* June 20, 2002, R3.

Monk, Philip. "bad seed" in *Bounce* (catalogue). Toronto: The Power Plant Contemporary Art Gallery, 2002, 4–17.

Mottram, Jack. "Refreshing hits from the Canadian Club," *Sunday Herald,* October 20, 2002, 10.

Renton, Andrew. "Disappearing, dislodging and logging off in B.C." in *The Beachcombers* (catalogue). London: The Drawing Room, 2002, 11–16.

Richer, Shawna. "A new face among art prizes," *Globe and Mail,* December 9, 2002, R1, R5.

Scott, Michael. "Nike rearrangement adds to Jungen's art world frenzy," *Vancouver Sun,* February 14, 2002, C3.

Shier, Reid. "Hammertown" in *Hammertown* (catalogue). Edinburgh: The Fruitmarket Gallery (in association with the Contemporary Art Gallery, Vancouver), 2002, 80–87.

Stoffman, Judy. "Whale skeleton emerges from lawn chair closet," *Toronto Star,* June 17, 2002, E3.

Stout, Katherine, "Foreword" in *The Beachcombers* (catalogue). London: The Drawing Room, 2002, 3–8.

Tousley, Nancy. "sympathy, empathy, museopathy," *Canadian Art* 19, no. 1 (Spring 2002): 80–83.

Turner, Michael. "This Land is Your Land" in *Hammertown* (catalogue). Edinburgh: The Fruitmarket Gallery (in association with the Contemporary Art Gallery, Vancouver), 2002, 8–23.

Watson, Scott. "Shapeshifter" in *Brian Jungen* (catalogue). Vancouver: Contemporary Art Gallery, 2002, 12–23.

2001

Barton, Adriana. "Fly-by Culture," *Vancouver Magazine,* March 2001, 24–30.

Beausse, Pascal. "Ars 01," trans. L.-S. Torgoff, *Art Press* 274 (December 2001): 71.

Bergman, Marikka. "Brian Jungen: Prototype for a New Understanding, #1, 2, 3, 4, 7," *Anna,* October 16, 2001, 87.

Bjorkman, Nina. "Ars 01 en frammande plats," *Hufvudstadsbladet,* October 26, 2001.

Coupland, Douglas. "Critical Mass," *Globe and Mail,* May 12, 2001, V1–V2.

Culley, Peter. "Out of the Blue: Three Works on Vancouver," *Border Crossings* 78 (May 2001): 64–70.

Dault, Gary Michael. "Cool Artist: Brian Jungen," *Time,* Canadian edition, August 6, 2001, 43.

Derksen, Jeff. "Cultural Props," *C Magazine,* no. 71 (Fall 2001): 11.

——. "Global Shoes, Local Things, Relations of Production Masks, and Architect Enemies," *Tripwire* 4 (Winter 2000/2001): 8.

——. "Von der > universellen Verdinglichung < zur >

universellen Kulturalisierung <," *Springerin,* October–December 2001, 18–23.

——. "Prototypes for New [Spatial and Temporal] Understanding," *Ars 01,* 2001, 100–01.

Garneau, David. "A Better Place: Practical Utopias," *Vie des Arts* 182 (2001): 78.

Kivirinta, Marja-Terttu, "Ars 01 puhuu Baabelin kielilla," *Helsingin Sanomat,* September 30, 2001.

Koivisto, Kaisu. "Ars 01," *Satakunnan Kansa,* 2001, 17.

Lanas Cavada, Silja. "Nakoala Tilaan Kolmanteen," *Suomen Kuvalehti,* no. 39 (2001): 66.

Laurence, Robin. "Constructing a New View of Construction," *Georgia Straight,* September 13–20, 2001, 69.

Long, Timothy. "Beyond utopia: today's search for a better place" in *A Better Place* (catalogue). Regina: MacKenzie Art Gallery, 2001, 8–9, 14–16, 43.

Luoma, Minna. "On maailmassa monta ihmeellista asiaa," *Kansan Uutiset,* 2001, 12.

Maunuksela, Arja. *Lukuuta,* December 5, 2001, 27.

Medina, Cuauhtémoc. "En el lejano norte," *Reforma,* October 10, 2001, 6C.

Milroy, Sarah. "The Best of the Rest," *Globe and Mail,* November 3, 2001, V7.

Nevanlinna, Tuomas. "Identity, culture and 'third space,'" *Frame News,* February 2001, 16.

Oh, Susan. "Soaring beyond the totem poles," *Maclean's,* May 7, 2001, 65.

Pirtola, Erkki. "Kriisiapua Taiteesta," *Kiasma,* November 1, 2001, 58.

Saksa, Perttu. "Jannitetyt Pakarat: Ars 01," *Image,* 2001, 54–69.

Shaw, Christine. "A Better Place," *Fuse* 24, no. 3 (2001): 32.

Tousley, Nancy. "Jungen: Brian Jungen is a fast rising star in a new generation of Canadian artists," *Calgary Herald,* December 1, 2001, ES09.

Tuominen, Maila-Katriina. "Ars 01 mahtuu kannykkaan," *Aamulehti,* September 26, 2001, B22.

Ward, Ossian. "Running Things," *Dazed and Confused,* December 2001, 34.

——. "ARS Bestiae," *Art Review,* November 2001, 25, 27.

Wolin, Joseph, ed. "Brian Jungen," *Review: Latin American Literature and Arts* 63 (Fall 2001): 12–16.

2000

Anderson, Jack. "Nikes as masks tool for debate," *Regina Leader-Post,* July 20, 2000, C1.

Coupland, Douglas. "Best of 2000," *Artforum,* December 2000, 31.

Garneau, David. "Beyond the One-Liner: The Masks of Brian Jungen," *Border Crossings* 76 (November 2000): 91–93.

Manguel, Alberto. "Nike Unmasked," *Geist* 38 (Fall 2000): 30–32.

McKay, Sally. Review of "Brian Jungen: Bush Capsule and Toronto Field Work at YYZ Artists' Outlet," *Lola,* Fall 2000, 87.

McLear, Kyo. "Rewind: Brian Jungen," *Canadian Art* 17, no. 4 (Winter 2000): 74.

Milroy, Sarah. "The art of the double take," *Globe and Mail,* November 4, 2000, V10–9.

"Prototype for a new understanding," *NeWest Review* (Summer 2000): 37–38.

Rimmer, Cate. "Brian Jungen," *Mix* 26, no. 3 (Winter 2000/2001): 22.

Shier, Reid. "Cheap" in *Brian Jungen* (catalogue). Vancouver: Charles H. Scott Gallery, 2000, 3–7.

Turner, Michael. "Prototypes + Petroglyphs + Pop," *Mix* 26, no. 3 (Winter 2000/2001): 30–33.

Wood, William. "Access Codes and Avoided Objects," *Parachute* 99 (July 2000): 12–19.

1999

Gopnik, Blake. "Crossing the Line Between Past, Future," *Globe and Mail,* October 26, 1999, R7.

1998

Derksen, Jeff. "Fun Critique in Ethnographic Fields," *Fuse* 21, no. 3 (August 1998): 47–48.

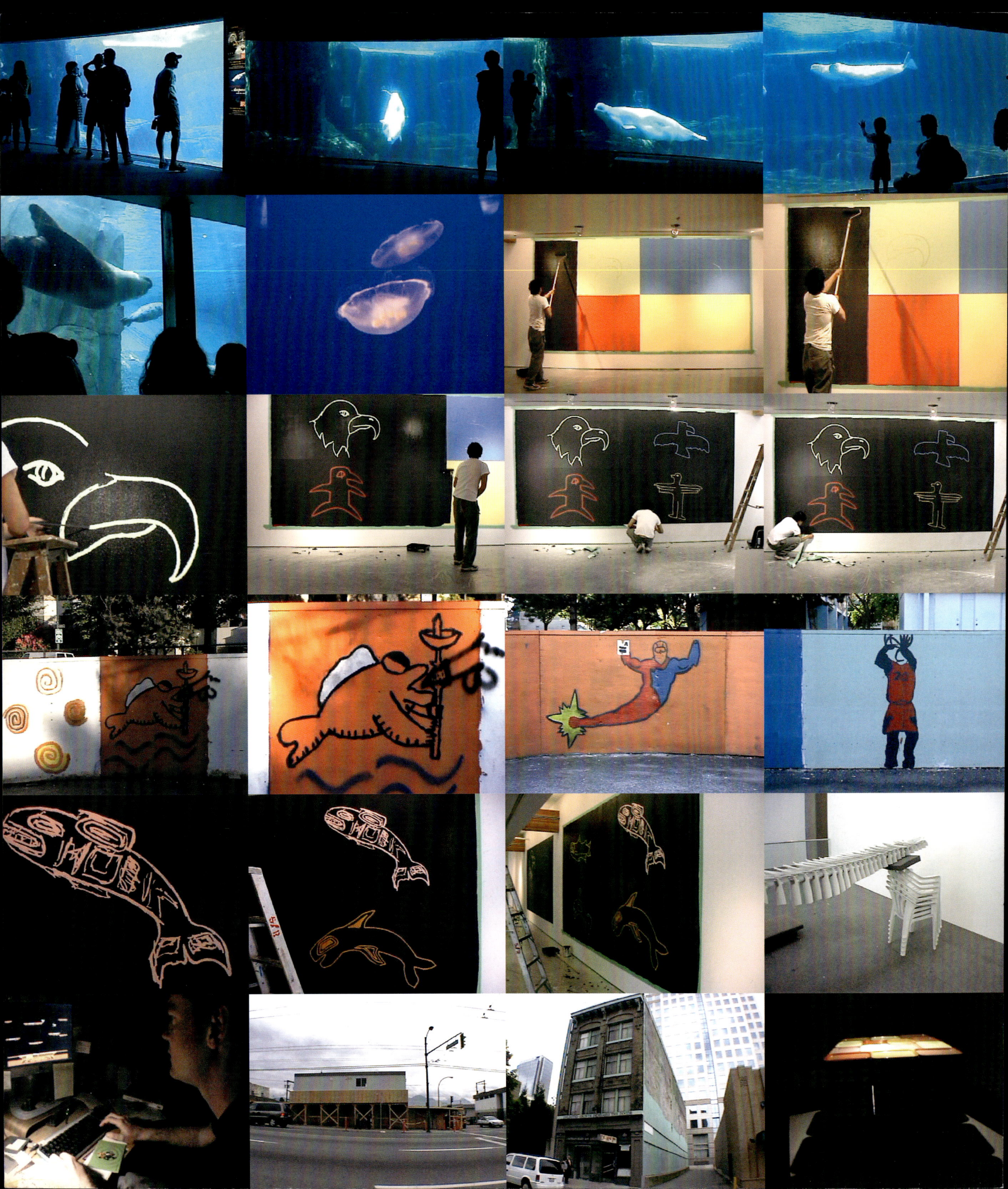

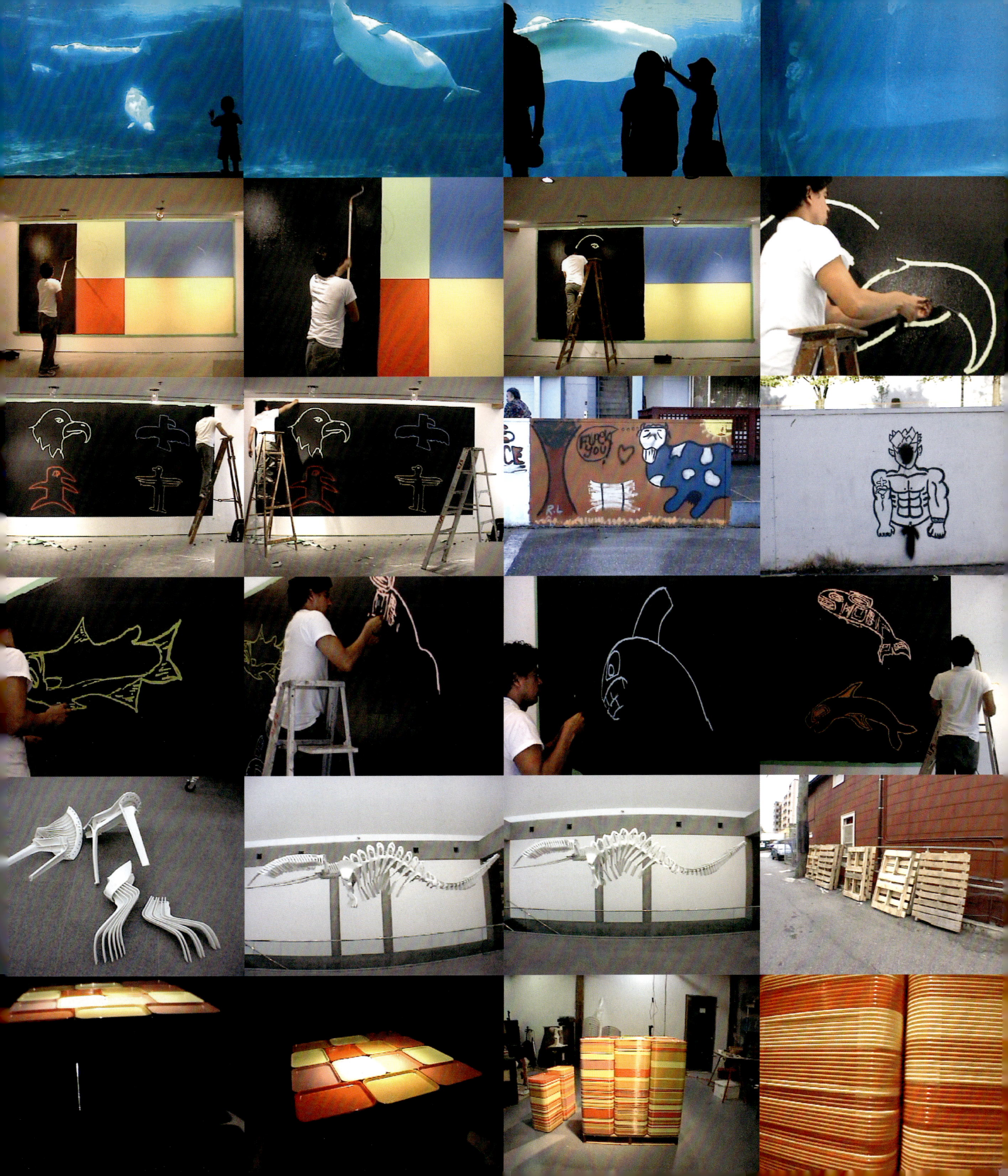

List of Works in the Exhibition

(dimensions listed as height x width x depth)

Dream Sequins, 1993
ink and watercolour on paper
30.6 x 23 cm (12″ x 9″)
Collection of the Morris and Helen Belkin Art Gallery,
Vancouver
Purchased with financial support from the Canada Council
for the Arts Acquisition Assistance Program and the Morris
and Helen Belkin Foundation, 1998

Mountie Bottom, 1993
ink on paper
35.8 x 27.3 cm (14″ x 10 3/4″)
Collection of the Morris and Helen Belkin Art Gallery,
Vancouver
Purchased with financial support from the Canada Council
for the Arts Acquisition Assistance Program and the Morris
and Helen Belkin Foundation, 1998

Untitled [Three Birds], 1997
ink on manila paper
35.8 x 27.3 cm (14″ x 10 3/4″)
Collection of the Morris and Helen Belkin Art Gallery,
Vancouver
Purchased with financial support from the Canada Council
for the Arts Acquisition Assistance Program and the Morris
and Helen Belkin Foundation, 1998

Untitled [First Nation, Second Nature], 1997
ink on manila paper
35.7 x 27.1 cm (14″ x 10 1/2″)
Collection of the Morris and Helen Belkin Art Gallery,
Vancouver
Purchased with financial support from the Canada Council
for the Arts Acquisition Assistance Program and the Morris
and Helen Belkin Foundation, 1998

Untitled [First Person, Third World], 1997
ink on manila paper
35.7 x 27.2 cm (14″ x 10 3/4″)
Collection of the Morris and Helen Belkin Art Gallery,
Vancouver
Purchased with financial support from the Canada Council
for the Arts Acquisition Assistance Program and the Morris
and Helen Belkin Foundation, 1998

Untitled [Two Figures], 1997
ink on manila paper
35.7 x 27.1 cm (14″ x 10 1/2″)
Collection of the Morris and Helen Belkin Art Gallery,
Vancouver
Purchased with financial support from the Canada Council
for the Arts Acquisition Assistance Program and the Morris
and Helen Belkin Foundation, 1998

Vernacular, 1998–2001
graphite, watercolour, ink, wax crayon and watercolour
on paper
73 x 112 cm (28 3/4″ x 44″)
Collection of the National Gallery of Canada, Ottawa,
purchased 2002

Prototype for New Understanding #1, 1998
Nike Air Jordans
17.3 x 37.4 x 34.5 cm (6 3/4″ x 14 3/4″ x 13 3/8″)
Collection of the artist

Prototype for New Understanding #2, 1998
Nike Air Jordans, human hair
48.9 x 21 x 25.5 cm (19 1/4″ x 8 1/4″ x 10″)
Collection of the Vancouver Art Gallery
Purchased with the financial support of the Canada Council
for the Arts Acquisition Assistance Program and the
Vancouver Art Gallery Acquisition Fund, 1999

Prototype for New Understanding #3, 1999
Nike Air Jordans
28 x 13.2 x 23.8 cm (11″ x 5 1/8″ x 9 3/8″)
Collection of the Vancouver Art Gallery
Purchased with the financial support of the Canada Council
for the Arts Acquisition Assistance Program and the
Vancouver Art Gallery Acquisition Fund, 1999

Prototype for New Understanding #4, 1998
Nike Air Jordans, human hair
45.7 x 34 x 17.8 cm (18″ x 13 5/8″ x 7″)
Collection of Claudia Beck and Andrew Gruft, Vancouver

Prototype for New Understanding #5, 1999
Nike Air Jordans, human hair
55.8 x 68.6 x 12.7 cm (22″ x 27″ x 5″)
Collection of Douglas Coupland, Vancouver

Prototype for New Understanding #6, 1999
Nike Air Jordans
43.2 x 30.5 x 15.2 cm (17″ x 12″ x 6″)
Collection of the Art Gallery of Ontario, Toronto
Purchased with the financial support of the Canada Council
for the Arts Acquisition Assistance Program and with the
assistance of the E. Wallace Fund, 2001

Prototype for New Understanding #7, 1999
Nike Air Jordans
27.9 x 35.6 x 55.9 cm (11″ x 14″ x 22″)
Collection of Joe Friday, Ottawa

Prototype for New Understanding #8, 1999
Nike Air Jordans
58.5 x 19 x 38.1 cm (23″ x 7 1/2″ x 15″)
Collection of Colin Griffiths, Vancouver

Prototype for New Understanding #9, 1999
Nike Air Jordans, human hair
60.5 x 25.4 x 12.7 cm (23 3/4″ x 10″ x 5″)
Collection of Greg and Lisa Kerfoot, West
Vancouver/Whistler

Prototype for New Understanding #10, 2001
Nike Air Jordans
27.9 x 35.6 x 58.4 cm (11″ x 14″ x 23″)
Collection of Bob Rennie, Rennie Management Corporation,
Vancouver

Prototype for New Understanding #11, 2002
Nike Air Jordans, human hair
67.3 x 58.4 x 25.4 cm (26 1/2″ x 23″ x 10″)
Collection of Gilles and Julia Ouellette, Toronto

Prototype for New Understanding #12, 2002
Nike Air Jordans
58.4 x 27.9 x 30.5 cm (23″ x 11″ x 12″)
Collection of Ruth and William True, Seattle

Prototype for New Understanding #13, 2003
Nike Air Jordans, human hair
63.5 x 23.8 x 39.3 cm (25″ x 9″ x 15 1/2″)
Private collection, Vancouver

Prototype for New Understanding #14, 2003
Nike Air Jordans, human hair
63.5 x 35.6 x 30.6 cm (25″ x 14″ x 12″)
Collection of Lawrence B. Benenson, New York

Prototype for New Understanding #15, 2003
Nike Air Jordans, shoelaces
63.5 x 48.9 x 48.9 cm (25″ x 19 1/4″ x 19 1/4″)
Private collection, Toronto

Prototype for New Understanding #16, 2004
Nike Air Jordans, human hair
57.3 x 30.5 x 45.7 cm (22 1/2″ x 12″ x 18″)
Collection of Joel Wachs, New York

Prototype for New Understanding #17, 2004
Nike Air Jordans
33 x 48.3 x 25.4 cm (13″ x 19″ x 10″)
Private collection, Vancouver

Prototype for New Understanding #18, 2004
Nike Air Jordans
67.5 x 45.7 x 19.7 cm (26 5/8" x 18" x 7 3/4")
Private collection, West Vancouver

Prototype for New Understanding #19, 2004
Nike Air Jordans
61 x 61 x 20.3 cm (24" x 24" x 8")
Collection of Donald R. Sobey, Stellarton, Nova Scotia

Prototype for New Understanding #20, 2004
Nike Air Jordans
43.2 x 25.4 x 50.8 cm (17" x 10" x 20")
Collection of Alexandre Taillefer and Debbie Zakaib,
St. Lambert, Quebec

Prototype for New Understanding #21, 2005
Nike Air Jordans
50 x 36 x 33 cm (19 3/4" x 14 1/8" x 13")
Private collection, New York
Courtesy of the artist and Casey Kaplan Gallery, New York

Prototype for New Understanding #22, 2005
Nike Air Jordans
49 x 51 x 21 cm (19 1/4" x 20" x 8 1/4")
Collection of Glenn Fuhrman, New York
Courtesy of the artist and Casey Kaplan Gallery, New York

Prototype for New Understanding #23, 2005
Nike Air Jordans
47 x 52 x 15 cm (18 1/2" x 20 1/2" x 5 7/8")
Collection of Debra and Dennis Scholl, Miami Beach, Florida
Courtesy of the artist and Casey Kaplan Gallery, New York

Bush Capsule Study, 2000
graphite and ink on paper
101.6 x 132.1 cm (40" x 52")
Collection of John Cook, Griffiths Rankin Cook Architects,
Ottawa

Shapeshifter, 2000
plastic chairs
144.8 x 152.4 x 660.4 cm (57" x 60" x 260")
Collection of the National Gallery of Canada, Ottawa,
purchased 2001

Mise en scène, 2000
plastic chairs, polyethylene, fluorescent lights
128.3 x 37.5 x 34.3 cm (50 1/2" x 14 3/4" x 13 1/2")
Collection Agnes Etherington Art Centre, Queen's
University, Kingston
Purchase, Canada Council for the Arts Acquisition
Assistance Program and the Chancellor Richardson
Memorial Fund, 2001

Untitled [pallets], 2001
red cedar
116.2 x 119.4 x 101.6 cm (45 3/4" x 47" x 40")
Collection of Bob Rennie, Rennie Management Corporation,
Vancouver

Isolated Depiction of the Passage of Time,
2001
plastic food trays, television monitor, VCR, wood
112.5 x 117.5 x 100 cm (44 1/4" x 46 1/4" x 39 1/4")
Collection of Bob Rennie, Rennie Management Corporation,
Vancouver

Variant I, 2002
Nike athletic footwear
132.1 x 114.3 cm (52" x 45")
Collection of Michael J. Audain and Yoshiko Karasawa,
Vancouver

Beer Cooler, 2002
cooler, beer cans
40.6 x 71.1 x 40.6 cm (16" x 28" x 16")
Collection of the Art Gallery of Nova Scotia, Halifax

Cetology, 2002
plastic chairs
403.9 x 421.6 x 1491 cm (159" x 166" x 587")
Collection of the Vancouver Art Gallery
Purchased with the financial support of the Canada
Council for the Arts Acquisition Assistance Program
and the Vancouver Art Gallery Acquisition Fund, 2003

Vienna, 2003
plastic chairs
125 x 130 x 850 cm (49 1/4" x 51 1/4" x 334 3/4")
Collection of the National Gallery of Canada, Ottawa
Purchased 2004 with the Joy Thompson Fund of the
National Gallery of Canada Foundation

Michael, 2003
screen print on powder-coated aluminum, 10 boxes
86.4 x 117.8 x 83.8 cm (34" x 44" x 33") approximate installation dimension
24.1 x 38.1 x 13.3 cm (9 1/2" x 15" x 5 1/4") each box
Collection of Bob Rennie, Rennie Management Corporation,
Vancouver

Little Habitat I, 2003
Nike Air Jordan boxes
65 x 65 x 30 cm (25 1/2" x 25 1/2" x 11 3/4")
Collection of Secession, Vienna

Little Habitat II, 2004
Nike Air Jordan boxes
65 x 65 x 30 cm (25 1/2" x 25 1/2" x 11 3/4")
Collection of Brett Shaheen, Cleveland

*Arts and Crafts Book Depository/Capp Street
Project 2004,* 2004
Architectural model (scale 1:5 of Greene and Greene's
Gamble House) made of plywood sectioned into four
quadrants, locking casters, built-in bookshelves, two
framed glass cabinets with electrical source and lighting
unit, handmade fabric pillows for seating benches, video
monitor, ongoing accumulation of library inventory of
magazines, journals, books and videos
255.2 x 422.4 x 554.4 cm (108" x 192" x 252") approximate
installation dimensions
255.2 x 185 x 185 cm (108" x 84" x 84") approximate
dimensions for each quadrant
Collection of Pamela and Richard Kramlich, San Francisco

talking stick, 2005
carved baseball bats
83.8 x 7.6 cm diameter (33" x 3" diameter) each bat
Produced with support from the Province of British
Columbia Spirit of BC Arts Fund

**All works are courtesy of the artist and Catriona Jeffries
Gallery, Vancouver, unless otherwise noted.**

**List of works reflects the Vancouver Art Gallery presenta-
tion at time of printing and does not include new work.**

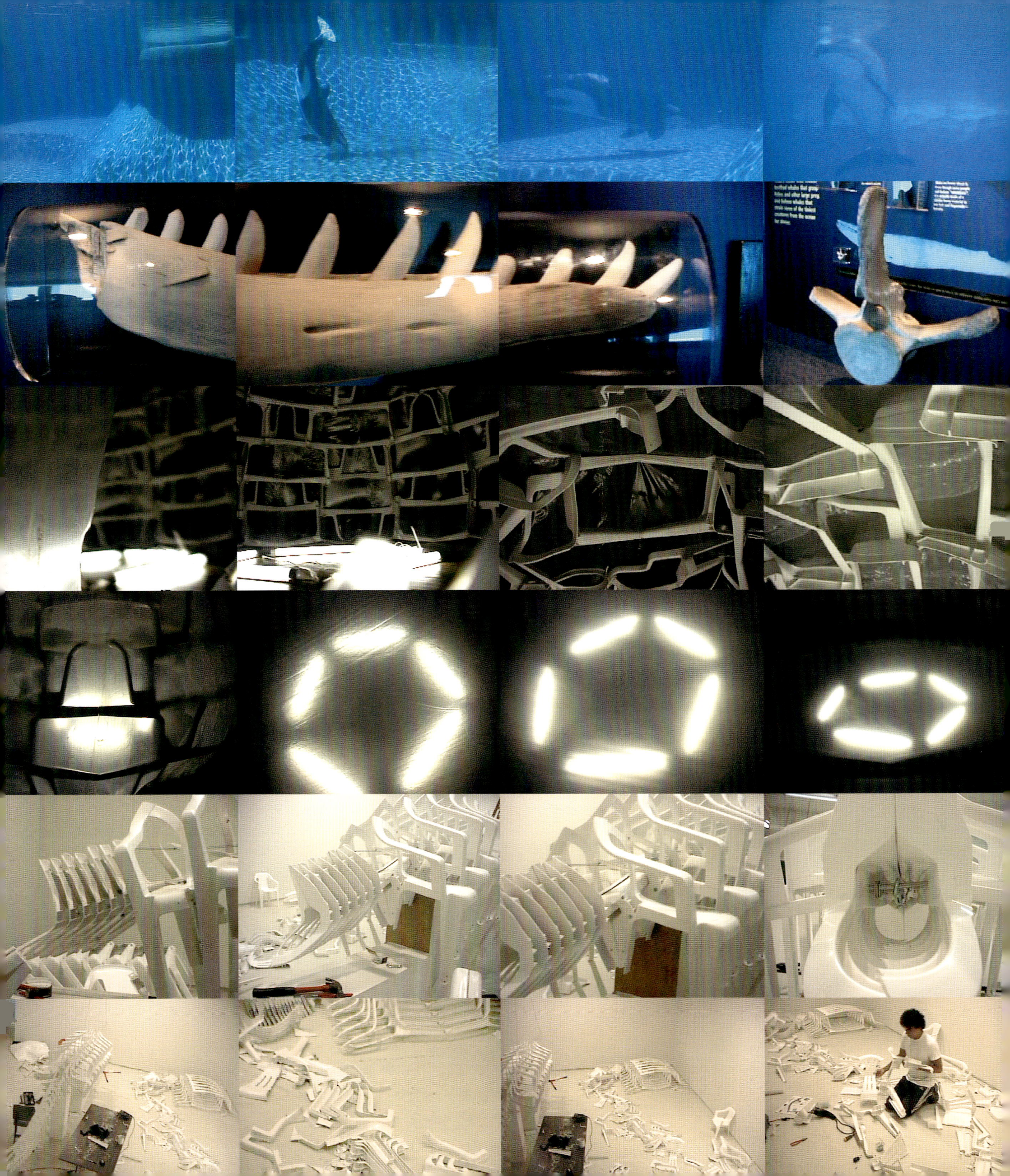

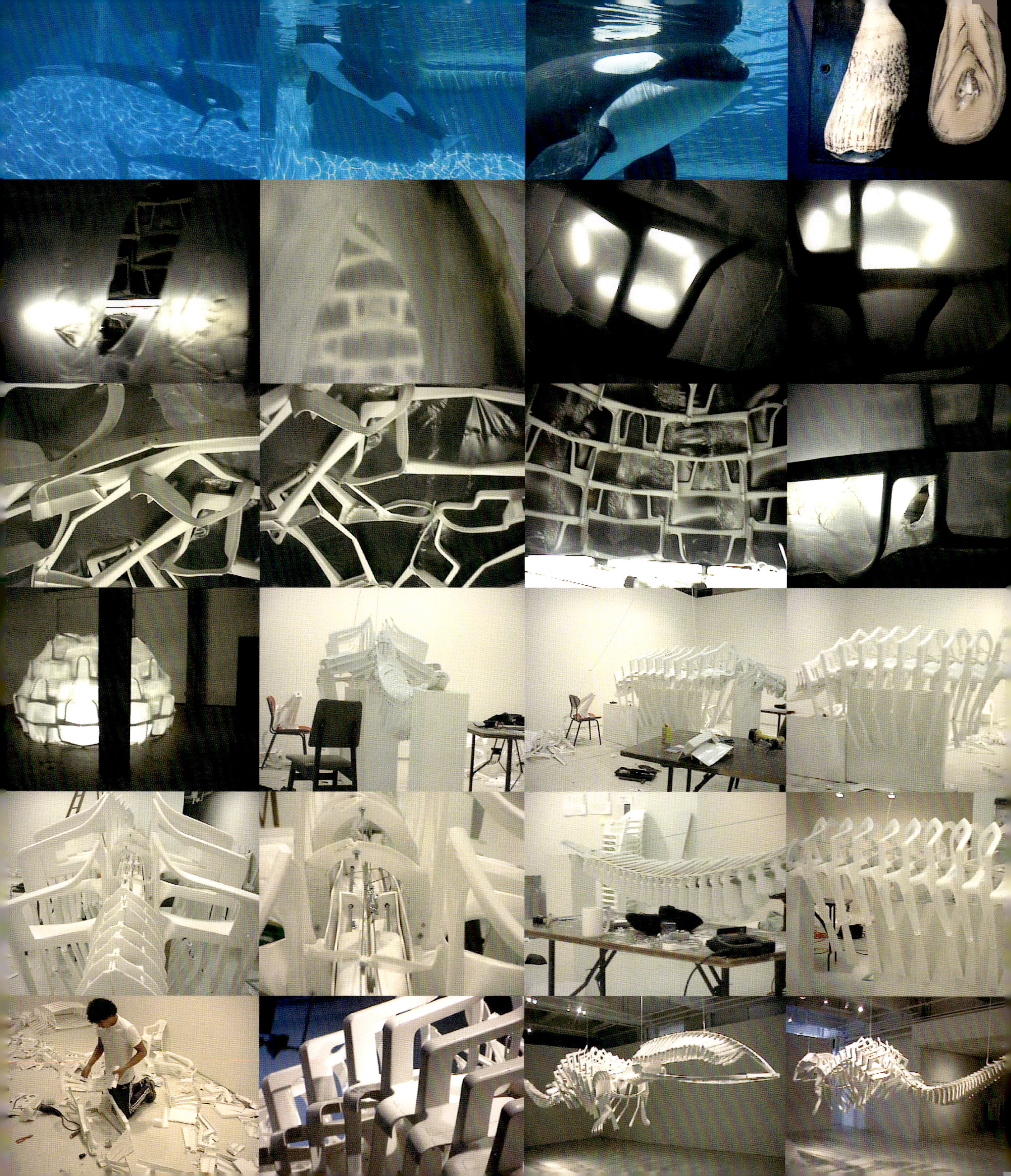

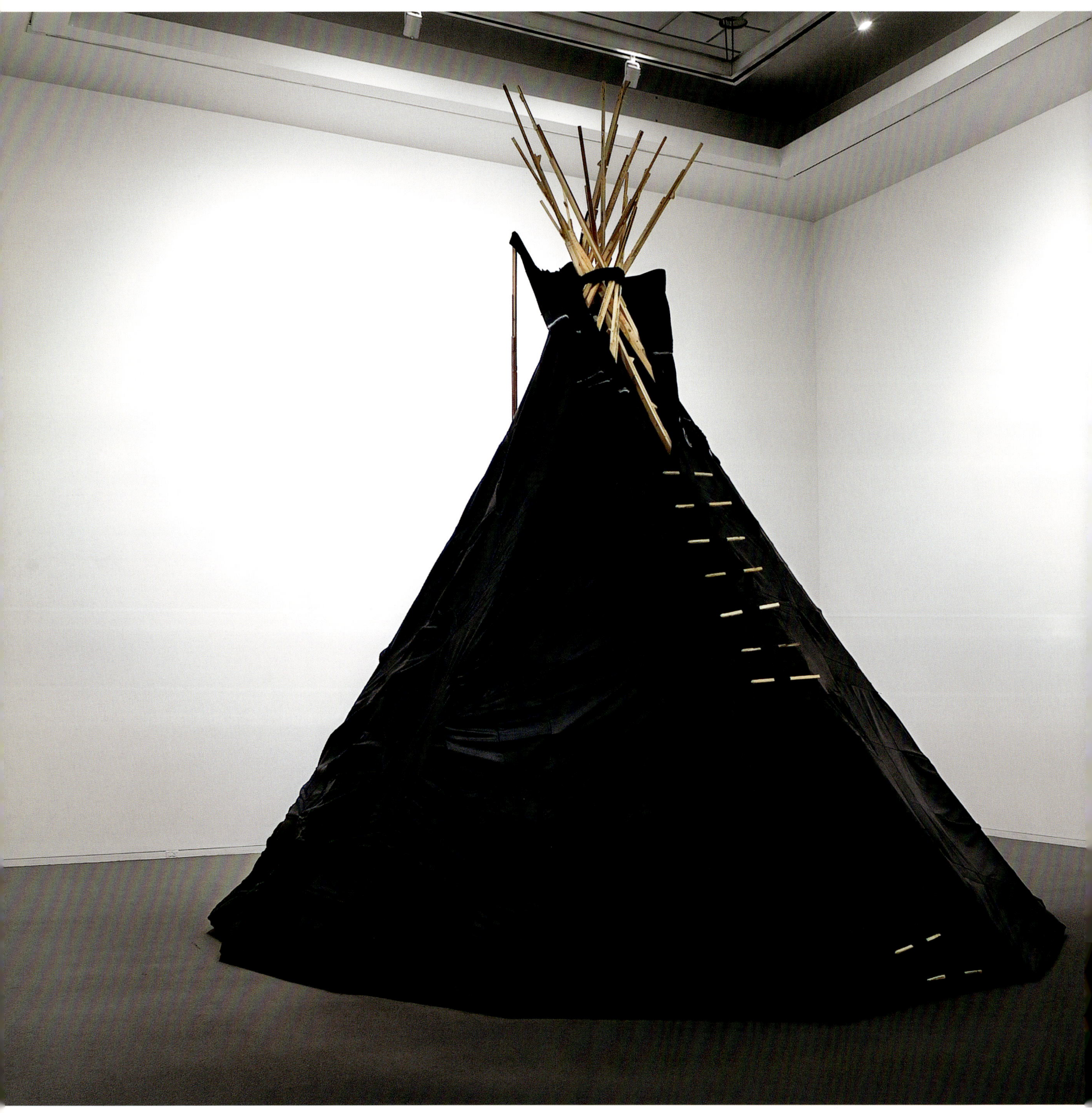

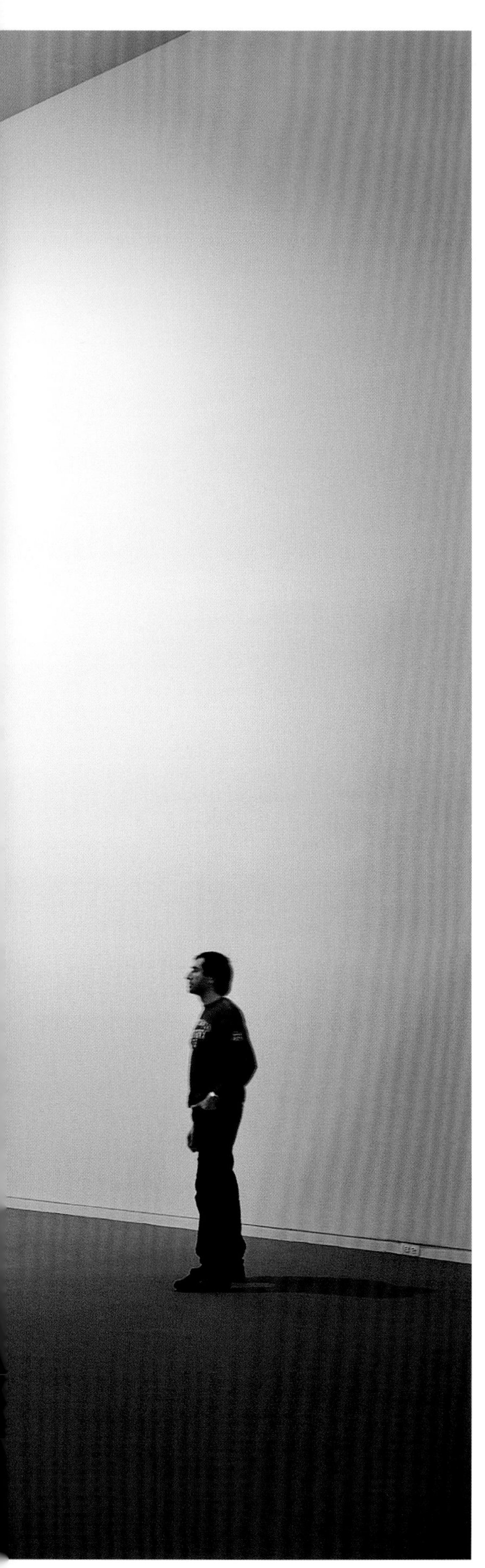

Furniture Sculpture, 2006
11 leather sofas
619.8 x 589.3 x 721.4 cm (244" x 232" x 284")
Collection of the Vancouver Art Gallery, purchased with
significant financial support from the Audain Foundation;
additional contribution from Rick Erickson and the
Vancouver Art Gallery Acquisition Fund
Photo: Tomas Svab, Vancouver Art Gallery

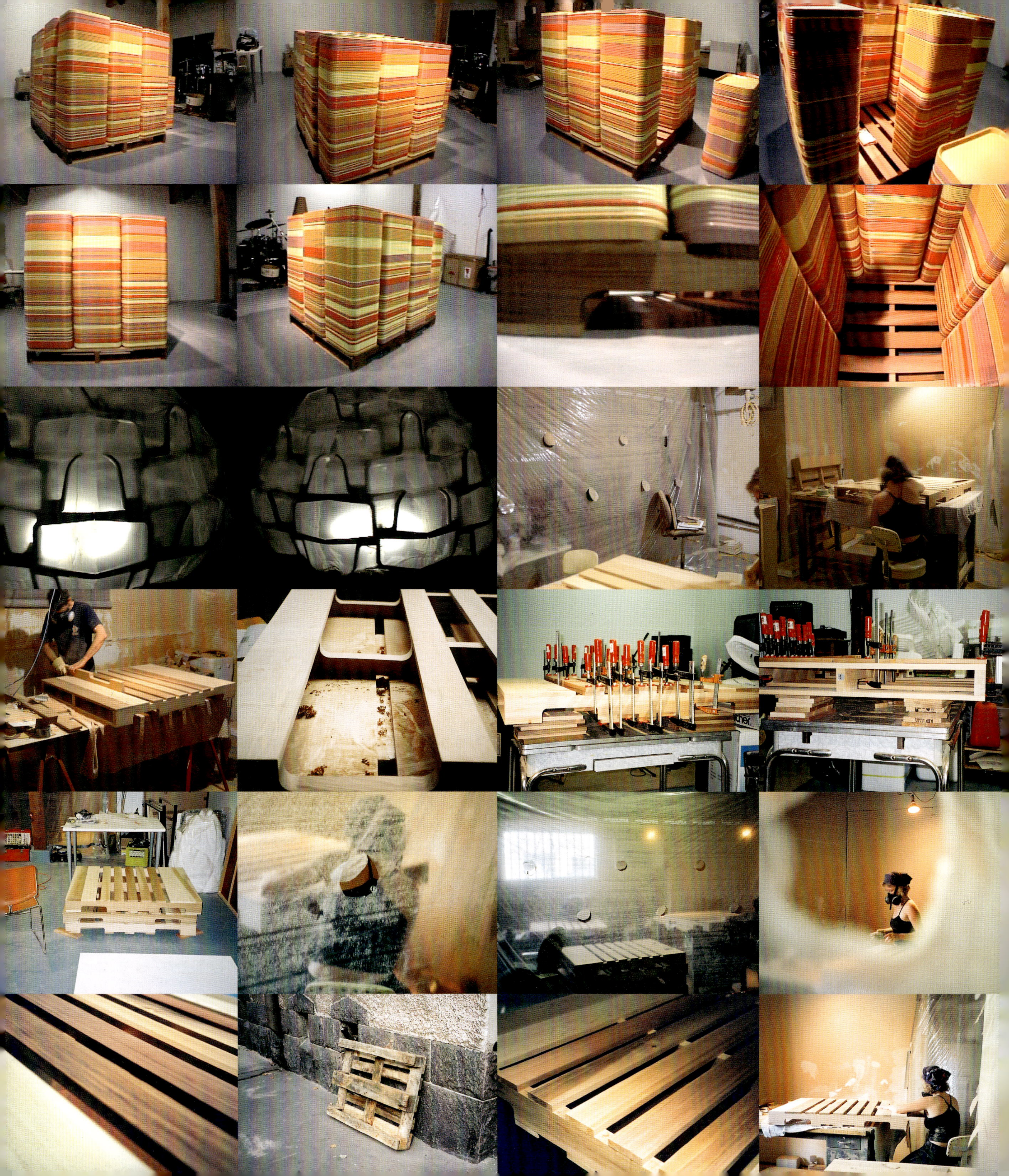

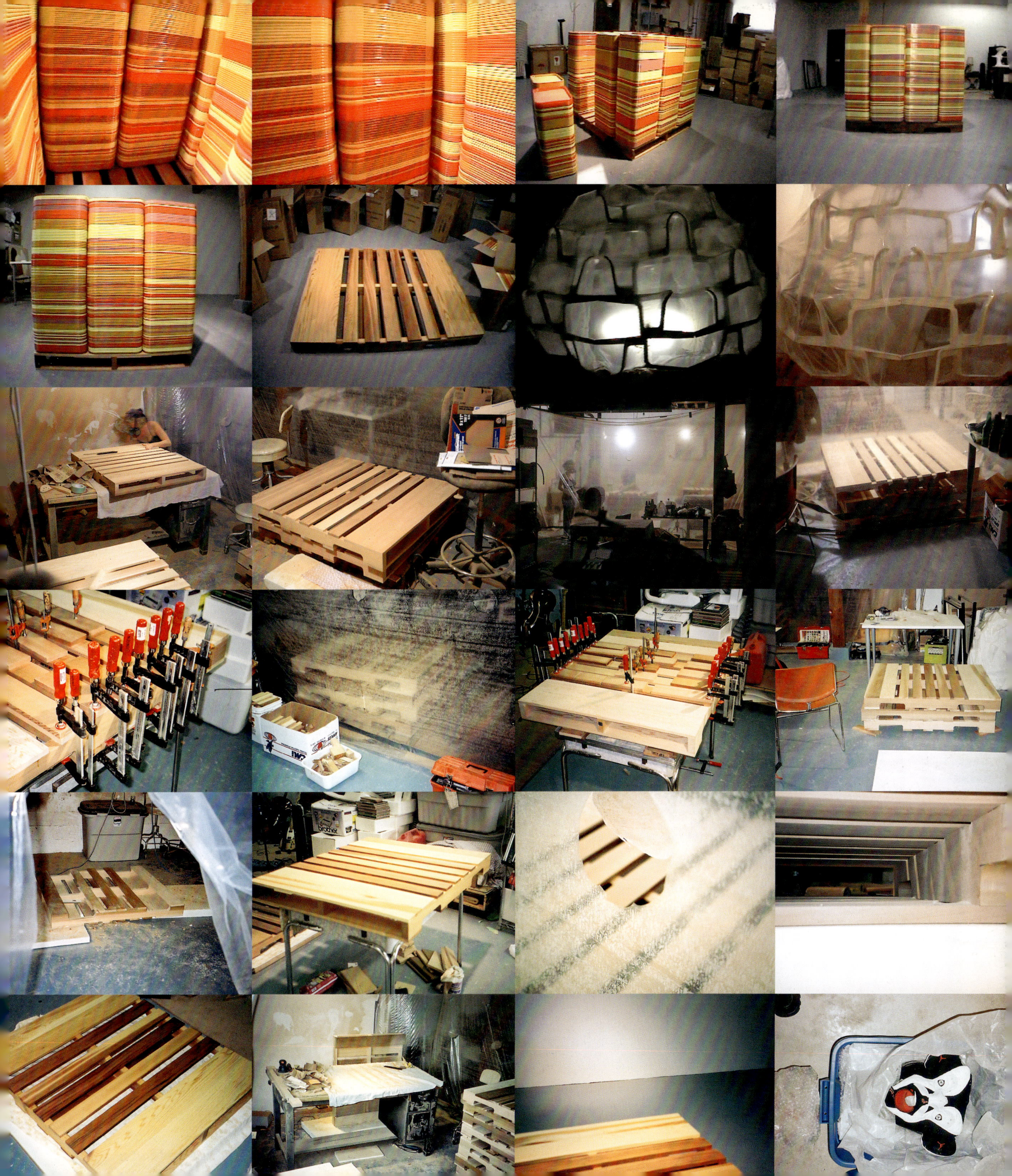

Acknowledgements

Curator's Acknowledgements

The exhibition *Brian Jungen* would not have been possible without the ongoing and steadfast support of many individuals and organizations and I extend my gratitude to all of them. I am grateful to the Audain Foundation, sponsor of the Vancouver presentation of the exhibition, and for early support in a grant from The Andy Warhol Foundation for the Visual Arts. Important financial support was provided by the Jack and Doris Shadbolt Endowment for Research and Publications at the Vancouver Art Gallery, and the Department of Foreign Affairs and International Trade—thank you!

This ambitious project received tremendous support from the lenders to the exhibition and its tour. My heartfelt thanks to all who generously parted with their works.

Special thanks are in order to Catriona Jeffries and Arabella Campbell at Catriona Jeffries Gallery for their support in facilitating loans and for immeasurable assistance offered throughout the months of preparation for this exhibition, tour and book. Casey Kaplan and his gallery staff also provided invaluable assistance for which we are very appreciative.

Linda Chinfen, Brian Jungen's studio assistant, has been an essential part of the team—many thanks for her tremendous skill, loyalty and good humour. A heartfelt thank you to numerous other individuals for their help in securing loans and photographs: Catherine Crowston, Chris Eamon, Carey Fouks, Rike Frank, Eric Fredricksen, Annabel Hansen, Eleanor King, Sue Klabunde, Elisabeth Ross-Wingate and Jane Rhodes, among many others.

The writers, Cuauhtémoc Medina, Ralph Rugoff, Kitty Scott, Trevor Smith and Simon Starling, warrant my deep appreciation for responding enthusiastically and with great insight. Thank you to Michael Worthington for his elegant and distinctive design and to Scott McIntyre, Susan Rana and Lucy Kenward at Douglas & McIntyre, our co-publisher, for their belief in finding new audiences for contemporary art of this region. Photographer Trevor Mills deserves special recognition for his exacting work, often with challenging timelines, in photographing and preparing the majority of the images for this publication.

In planning the tour of this exhibition, I have had the pleasure to work with Trevor Smith, Paulette Gagnon and Réal Lussier and the dedicated staff of the New Museum of Contemporary Art in New York and the Musée d'art contemporain de Montréal.

I extend my sincere gratitude to all my colleagues at the Vancouver Art Gallery who have participated in the excitement and challenges of this project, including those in Administration and Finance, Curatorial, Development, Marketing, Museum Services, Public Programs and Security/Visitor Services. I particularly want to thank Kathleen Bartels, whose enthusiastic leadership was felt all along the way, and especially Monika Szewczyk, Assistant Curator, whose unwavering commitment and spirited energy have contributed immensely to every aspect of this project.

Finally, a very special and big thank you to Brian Jungen for being a pleasure and an inspiration to work with.

Daina Augaitis

Artist's Acknowledgements

Brian Jungen wishes to thank: Alex Morrison, Alice Sharpe, Alix and Alan Brown, Andy Warhol Foundation for the Visual Arts, Anthony Kiendl, Arabella Campbell, Barbara Fischer, Barr Gilmore, Bev Best, Bill Wood, Bob Rennie, Brandon Thiessen, Brian Boulton, Bruce Grenville, Candice Hopkins, Caroline Andrieux, Carolyn Christoph-Bakargiev, Casey Kaplan, Cate Rimmer, Catherine Crowston, Catriona Jeffries, Charlotte Townsend-Gault, Christine Corlett, Christine Goodchild, Christopher Eamon, Claudia Beck and Andrew Gruft, Cuauhtémoc Medina, Daina Augaitis, Damian Moppett, Dave St. Onge, David Carter, Dennis Smolej, Derek Barnett, Don and Terry Parminter, Donald Sobey, Doris Shadbolt, Douglas Coupland, Elaine Jungen, Elizabeth Brown, Elliot Vivian, Fiona Bowie, friends and family of the Doig River First Nation, Garry Oker, Geoffrey Farmer, Grant Arnold, Greg Bellerby, Greg Hill, Gregor Muir, Gregory Elgstrand, Guillermo Calzadilla, Hamza Walker, James Koester, Jan Allen, Jari-Pekka Vanhalla, Jason McLean, Jeff Derksen, Jennifer Allora, Jens Hoffman, Jessica Morgan, Jim Drobnick, Joe Friday, Joe Wallin, Jonathan Wells, Josée St-Louis, Judith Steedman, Judy Radul, Karen Love, Katherine Stout, Kathleen Bartels, Kathryn Walter, Kathy Slade, Keith Higgins, Keith Wallace, Ken Lum, Kirk McLean, Kirsten McGhie, Kitty Scott, Kyla Mallett, Lee-Ann Martin, Leigh Markopolous, Linda Chinfen, Lindsay Brown, Lisa Deanne-Smith, Lisa Prentice, Marina Kalinovska, Matthew Higgs, Matthias Herrmann, Melanie O'Brian, Melinda Mollineaux, Michael Audain, Michael Turner, Michael Worthington, Mike Harskamp, Monika Szewczyk, Nicholas Shafhausen, Pamela Meredith, Patrick Andersson, Paul Tavin, Paul Zingrone, Paulette Gagnon, Peter Nesbett, Philip Monk, Pierre Barnoti, Ralph Rugoff, Réal Lussier, Reid Shier, Rike Frank, Ron Moppett, Russell Baker, Sabine Bitter, Scott Watson, Shelley Bancroft, Simon Starling, Stan Douglas, Sydney Hermant, Sylvie Fortin, Svava Juliusson, Terence Gower, Timothy Long, Trevor Mills, Trevor Smith, Troy Jungen, Una Knox, Wayne Baerwaldt and Zoe Lasham.

Brian Jungen

Lenders to the Exhibition

Individuals:

Michael J. Audain and Yoshiko Karasawa
Claudia Beck and Andrew Gruft
Lawrence B. Benenson
John Cook, Griffiths Rankin Cook Architects
Douglas Coupland
Joe Friday
Glenn Fuhrman
Colin Griffiths
Brian Jungen
Greg and Lisa Kerfoot
Pamela and Richard Kramlich
Gilles and Julia Ouellette
Bob Rennie, Rennie Management Corporation
Debra and Dennis Scholl
Brett Shaheen
Donald R. Sobey
Alexandre Taillefer and Debbie Zakaib
Ruth and William True
Joel Wachs
five anonymous private lenders

Institutions:

Agnes Etherington Art Centre, Kingston
Art Gallery of Nova Scotia, Halifax
Art Gallery of Ontario, Toronto
Morris and Helen Belkin Art Gallery, Vancouver
National Gallery of Canada, Ottawa
Secession, Vienna
Vancouver Art Gallery, Vancouver

Financial Support

Publication:
Jack and Doris Shadbolt Endowment for Research and
Publications at the Vancouver Art Gallery

Exhibition and Tour:
Audain Foundation, Vancouver
The Andy Warhol Foundation for the Visual Arts,
New York
Government of Canada's Department of Foreign Affairs
and International Trade, Ottawa

Published in conjunction with the Brian Jungen exhibition
organized and circulated by the Vancouver Art Gallery

Curated by Daina Augaitis

Exhibition tour:
New Museum of Contemporary Art, New York
September 29–December 31, 2005

Vancouver Art Gallery
January 28–April 30, 2006

Musée d'art contemporain de Montréal
May 25–September 10, 2006

Witte de With, Rotterdam
December 2, 2006–February 11, 2007

Museum Villa Stuck, Munich
March 8–May 20, 2007

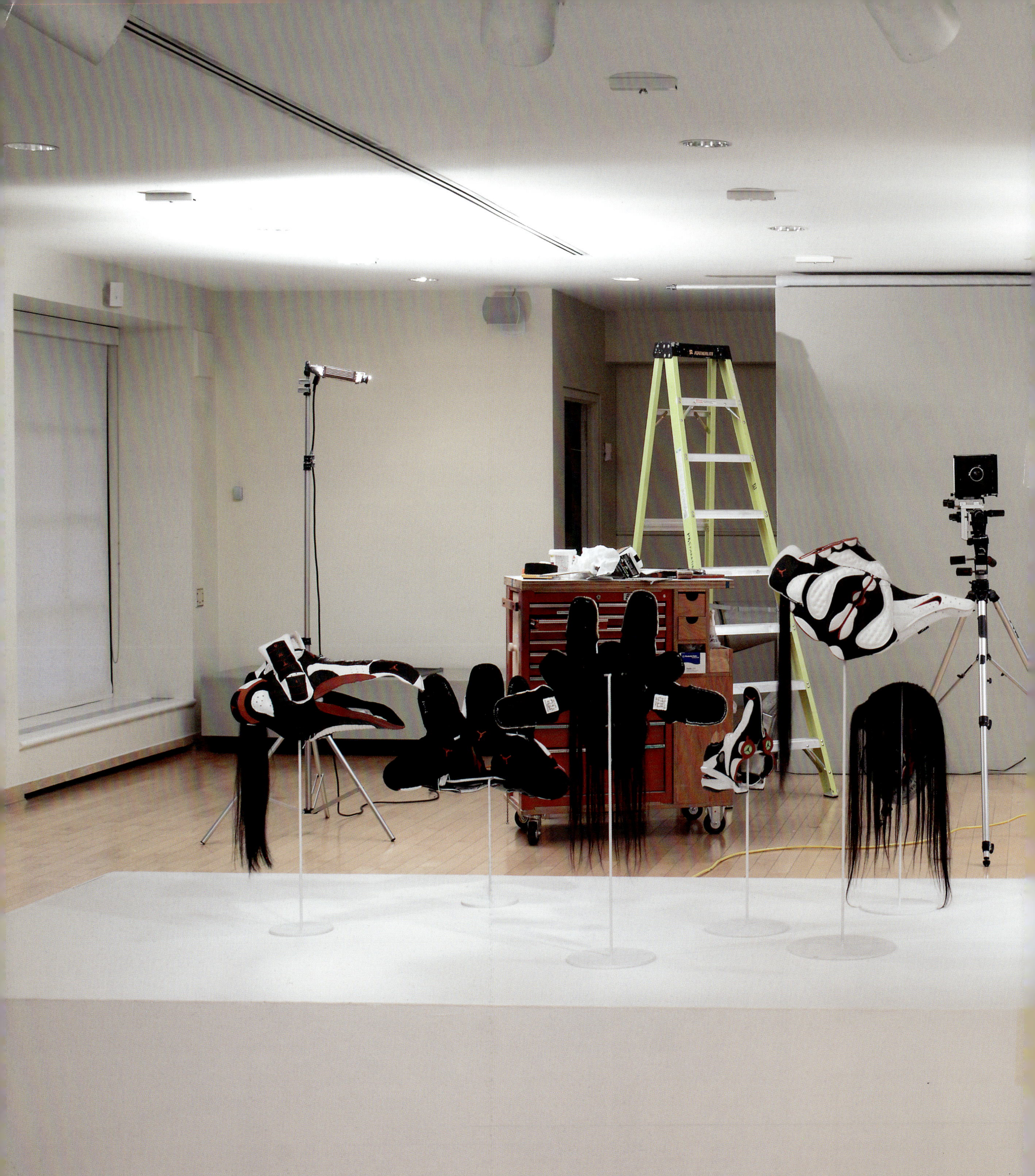